DANCING IN TH

Modern Dance and European ...
of the First World War

EDWARD ROSS DICKINSON

University of California at Davis

CAMBRIDGE
UNIVERSITY PRESS

CAMBRIDGE
UNIVERSITY PRESS

University Printing House, Cambridge CB2 8BS, United Kingdom

One Liberty Plaza, 20th Floor, New York, NY 10006, USA

477 Williamstown Road, Port Melbourne, VIC 3207, Australia

4843/24, 2nd Floor, Ansari Road, Daryaganj, Delhi – 110002, India

79 Anson Road, #06-04/06, Singapore 079906

Cambridge University Press is part of the University of Cambridge.

It furthers the University's mission by disseminating knowledge in the pursuit of education, learning, and research at the highest international levels of excellence.

www.cambridge.org
Information on this title: www.cambridge.org/9781316647219
DOI: 10.1017/9781108164573

© Edward Ross Dickinson 2017

First published 2017

Printed in the United Kingdom by Clays, St Ives plc

A catalogue record for this publication is available from the British Library.

Library of Congress Cataloging-in-Publication Data
Names: Dickinson, Edward Ross, author.
Title: Dancing in the blood: modern dance and European culture on the eve of the first World War / Edward Ross Dickinson, University of California at Davis.
Description: New York, NY: Cambridge University Press, 2017. |
Includes bibliographical references and index.
Identifiers: LCCN 2017003645 | ISBN 9781107196223 (hardback) |
ISBN 9781316647219 (paperback)
Subjects: LCSH: Modern dance – Social aspects – Europe. | Europe – Civilization – 20th century. | Europe – Social life and customs – 20th century. | Modern dance – History – 20th century. | Modern dance – Social aspects. | BISAC: HISTORY / Europe / General.
Classification: LCC GV1643.D53 2017 | DDC 792.8094/0904–dc23
LC record available at https://lccn.loc.gov/2017003645

ISBN 978-1-107-19622-3 Hardback
ISBN 978-1-316-64721-9 Paperback

Contents

Illustrations

Acknowledgments

This study was made possible by grants from the Charles Phelps Taft Memorial Fund at the University of Cincinnati, the German Academic Exchange Service, and the Committee on Research of the Academic Senate at the University of California at Davis.

I am grateful for the assistance of numerous archivists and librarians, including particularly Christel Dreiling and the staff at the Deutsches Tanz-Archiv Köln/SK Stiftung Kultur in Cologne; Hans van Keulen and the staff at the Theatercollectie, Bijzondere Collecties, Universiteit Amsterdam; Ana Triviño-Lopez and the staff at the Museo de les Arts Escèniques (MAE), Institut del Teatre in Barcelona; Kirsten Tanaka at the Museum of Performance and Design in San Francisco; and the staff at the Jerome Robbins Dance Division of the New York Public Library for the Performing Arts at Lincoln Center.

Parts of this book appeared first in "Modern Dance before 1914: Commerce or Religion?," *Dance Chronicle* 36 (2013): 297–325 and " 'Must We Dance Naked?' Art, Beauty, and Politics in Munich and Paris, 1911 and 1913," *Journal of the History of Sexuality* 20 (2011): 95–131. I thank the Taylor and Francis Group and the University of Texas Press for their kind permission to use material from those articles here.

I shared the adventure of writing this book with Shelley Alden Brooks; she has an extraordinary talent for adventure, and made this one – and so many others – fun, rich, and delightful. Her son Alden has been a role model: a kind spirit and a good keen man. My daughter Elizabeth has made the whole world light up for me for the past thirteen years. I can't imagine having gotten this book or anything else done without her.

Abbreviations

DC	*Dance Chronicle*
DRJ	*Dance Research Journal*
DTAK	Deutsches Tanz-Archiv Köln/SK Stiftung Kultur, Cologne
GSAPKB	Geheimes Staatsarchiv preussischer Kulturbesitz, Berlin
JRDD	Jerome Robbins Dance Division, New York Public Library for the Performing Arts, New York City
JRDD-IDC	JRDD, Irma Duncan Collection of Isadora Duncan Materials
LAB	Landesarchiv Berlin
MAE	Museo de les Arts Escèniques, Institut del Teatre, Barcelona
MPDSF	Museum of Performance and Design, San Francisco
STAM	Staatsarchiv München, Munich
TBCUA	Theatercollectie, Bijzondere Collecties, Universiteit Amsterdam

Introduction: Modern Dance and the Birth
of the Twentieth Century

I.1 Modern Dance: Questions and Answers

Upon opening their Sunday morning paper on December 3, 1911, readers of the progressive Berlin newspaper *Berliner Tageblatt* (Berlin Daily News) were confronted with a rather unsettling question: "Must One Dance Naked?" In the article under this headline the prominent ballerina Antonietta dell'Era – whose accomplishments included being the first Sugarplum Fairy in the world premiere of *The Nutcracker* in 1892 – took to task the young French dancer Adorée Villany, who had been arrested in Munich two weeks earlier on a charge of public indecency. Villany had been performing in cities around Central Europe for some years; her standard procedure, which she followed in Munich as well, was to rent a theater, send "personal" invitations to buy tickets to most of the city's artistic and social elite (normally an effective means of getting around decency laws, which did not apply to "private" performances), and present a dance program that included a good deal of exposed skin. By the standards of the day a woman who exposed her legs below the knee and her arms below the shoulder was as good as naked; but Villany's performance included a certain amount of outright nudity, as we would define it today. Dell'Era regarded Villany's act as a travesty, a degradation of the art form. Performances like hers might be "pleasing to the eye," but they had nothing to do with "true dance art." The latter was a matter of the mind. It was the product of "years of difficult, demanding study"; it was intended to "free the body from the coarse law of gravity"; and it "laid the highest value on decency." The standard female dance costume – the tutu – was designed to be like a "light, incorporeal cloud covering the body," effectively "suspending the very concept of clothing" by denying that there was anything merely material there to cover up.[1] Ballet, in short, was art; Villany was an amateur appealing to mere prurient interest.

[1] Antonietta dell'Era, "Muss man nackt tanzen?," *Berliner Tageblatt*, no. 628, December 3, 1911; Ivor Guest, *The Dancer's Heritage: A Short History of Ballet* (London: Dancing Times, 1977), p. 60.

Villany got a chance to reply in the following Sunday's edition, in which she wrote – under the same title – scathingly of the ballet's "ridiculous distortions" of natural movement. Ballet was "soulless" and "mechanical," it valued "military precision" and "drill" over any meaningful expression. Her own dance in contrast replaced the "unnatural, forced movements" of ballet with naturally beautiful, graceful, organic "life-filled lines" (*lebensvolle Linien*) that authentically expressed the artist's "feelings" or "moods." *This* was art – not just physical technique, but real art, with real expressive power, performed not by a windup doll but by a real person. It required nudity because the expressive medium of the dance as an art form is the human body; clothes could only obscure its expressive potentials. This was not mere frilly decoration and empty technique: it expressed the essential, the real. "I shed my shirt," Villany claimed, "in order to bare my soul." Ballet costumes were artfully coquettish, suggestive, hinting at forbidden pleasures where forthright nudity would allow the viewer to develop a pure appreciation for the real beauty and expressive power of the female body – and through it, for the dancer's *soul*.[2]

This debate in the pages of one of Berlin's popular daily newspapers was just one skirmish in a wider battle that radically reshaped the dance in Europe in the years before World War I. Between 1902 and 1914 the culture market of Western and Central Europe was invaded and occupied by a small mercenary army of slender, scantily clad, young female dancers. These women transformed dance as an art form – its aesthetic language, content, organization, and audience. But they also transformed the place of dance in European and ultimately world culture, giving it incomparably wider resonance and prominence. Before 1900, dance in Europe was a peripheral art – often not considered an art at all but a form of entertainment, and almost never a respectable or "high" art, with profound philosophical or spiritual or political implications.[3] For a period of decades between the 1900s and the 1940s, the modern dance explosion made dance one of the most important art forms in Europe – not only aesthetically, but also philosophically and politically. Leading painters, sculptors, and composers took dance seriously as a theme and resource for their own artistic productions. The avant-garde intellectual elite regarded it as an art form with profound spiritual, philosophical, and political implications. Dancers were taken seriously by leading

[2] Adorée-Via Villany, "Muss man nackt tanzen? Eine Antwort," *Berliner Tageblatt*, no. 628, December 10, 1911.
[3] See, particularly, Hanna Järvinen, *Dancing Genius: The Stardom of Vaslav Nijinsky* (New York: Palgrave MacMillan, 2014), p. 41.

political figures of the day – kings, prime ministers, and political party leaders. Even the religious implications and functions of the dance were widely discussed, both by those who thought the new dance sacred and those who thought it sinful. Dancers made significant amounts of money from performances in theaters both "respectable" and popular; they were highly paid entertainers for the social elite; and they played a key role in the emergence of a new form of middle-brow spectacular entertainment – neither popular culture nor "high" culture, but "mass" culture. But they were also ubiquitous in the emerging mass consumer economy of the early twentieth century – for example, in advertising campaigns promoting cosmetics, perfumes, dietary supplements, fitness regimes, and fitness equipment (sometimes of their own devising); in the fashion industry; and in the new and explosively expanding film industry. Dance was a big deal.

A theme that sounds odd to the modern ear was central to the discussion of this dance revolution. Both the modern dancers and those who appreciated and supported them frequently asserted that the aesthetic qualities of modern dance – the qualities that made it exciting and revolutionary – sprang from the "blood" of those who performed it. Some argued straightforwardly that the qualities of a performer's art could be explained by her ethnic background or family heritage – her Greek, Hungarian, Italian, German, African, Celtic, Slavic, German, Gypsy, Indian, or even American "blood." German dancers were soulful; Celtic dancers were romantic; Spanish dancers passionate, and so on. Dancers of mixed parentage could combine these qualities in particularly fruitful and interesting ways. Equally important, however, others argued that modern dance expressed a potential and an aspiration that was universal in all human beings: the aspiration to embody a beauty, grace, and spiritual power beyond the merely human. In fact, the modern dancers from the outset claimed to embody a process of upward progression that was immanent in every human being and indeed in all of nature, in the "blood" of all living things: the process of evolution. Evolution toward greater perfection was, indeed, understood by a great number of people around 1900 to be the aim of nature, of all of creation. It was the purpose of life, and what gave life meaning. Modern dance claimed to give it artistic expression. Specifically, modern dance constantly appealed both to the archaic – to ancient Greek or Middle Eastern art forms, and to the "primitive" archaic aesthetic forms of "less civilized" societies – and to the future, to liberation from the past and its conventions and restrictions. In combining these two apparently contradictory gestures, it enacted the magnificent history of evolution – the connection, through the body of the dancer, between the primitive past and the transcendent future of humanity.

Modern dance, then, performed two themes, both addressed by the language of "blood." On the one hand, modern dance embodied and expressed the diversity of human life, which gave the world its spice and interest and much of its creative potential. On the other hand, it embodied the common purpose of all human life – transcendence, what filled life with meaning and promise.

These themes were appealing at the time for specific historical reasons. The three or four decades before World War I were the first great age of globalization, a period of remarkable global political, economic, and cultural cross-fertilizations. Modern dance, with its celebration of diversity and of crossings and admixtures of "blood," partook of the excitement those processes generated. These were also decades of tremendous scientific, technical, and material progress – as yet not darkened by an immediate experience of the destructive potential of modern technologies. The idea of progress and of evolution was given greater power by the evidence of rapid change and improvement that was all around Western people in these decades. Ultimately these themes proved equally attractive to people in many other parts of the world as well. Modern dance before World War I was, then, an aesthetic language in which to discuss the ultimate implications of central features of the modern condition as it was emerging during the early period of globalization in the decades around 1900.

Beyond being an artistic revolution, then, modern dance was a profound philosophical upheaval as well – an integral part of the revolt of self-conscious modernism against received traditions of knowledge, truth, and authority by those who believed that every aspect of human society must be reformed and reshaped to meet the challenge of the conditions created by rapid technological, social, economic, and cultural change in (at the time) the nineteenth century. In fact, modern dance was part of a much broader cultural "war," a set of interrelated and interlocking struggles in multiple arenas of European life and increasingly of human life globally, between radical modernists and those more inclined to preserve tradition.

Most immediately, the battle over modern dance was part of a much wider struggle over standards of beauty in the arts generally. Antonietta dell'Era, for example, appealed to a definition of beauty that was universally known and acknowledged in European culture at the time: the idea – originating with the eighteenth-century German philosopher Immanuel Kant – that true aesthetic appreciation is purely spiritual, and that real beauty cannot be a function of active desire in the beholder, but only of passive and ideal contemplation.[4] Adorée Villany's response typified that of many artistic modernists: that sensual desire is not egoistic, sinful, and destructive because it is "merely" natural (not spiritual), but vital, life-affirming, and creative because it is wholly natural; and that the appreciation of sensual beauty is therefore morally and aesthetically legitimate. The tendency in the arts to hide the "merely" material (as the tutu did) was a tacit admission that one did not have the maturity to deal with one's natural desires – that one was not so "idealistic" and spiritual after all.

That debate in the arts was very closely related to the broader debate about decency more generally. In this period, some morality activists prevailed on public authorities to glue fig leaves over the offending bits of public statuary; where they failed, some undertook nocturnal raids on public fountains and monuments to chop those bits off. There were major debates, campaigns, and scandals around nudity and sexuality in art, literature, the theater, and advertising. And this debate over decency was in turn closely related to debates over the moral status of sexuality. Was the only morally legitimate sex procreative marital sex? Or was it ethically defensible for people to meet their sexual needs in other ways, as long as they did so responsibly – by using prophylactics, say, or contraceptives, or in the understanding that they were responsible for supporting any children born to nonmarital relationships? There was, for example, a major policy debate across Europe between the 1870s and the 1930s over the regulation of prostitution by the police – a system defended as a public health measure (because the women involved were subject to medical inspections), but condemned for turning the state into a pimp and a procurer.[5]

The struggle over beauty and decency had profound political implications. For the artistic avant-garde, the question was simply this: Does the citizen have the right to set his or her own standards of decency and beauty; or does the state have the right and duty to establish and police those standards for everyone? Is the citizen a morally autonomous and independent personality, with the capacity and right to reason out moral

[4] See Immanuel Kant, *Critik der Urtheilskraft* (London: Routledge, 1994 [1790]), esp. pp. 5, 15, 65.

[5] See Edward Ross Dickinson, *Sex, Freedom and Power in Imperial Germany* (New York: Cambridge University Press, 2014); Steven C. Hause, "Social Control in Late Nineteenth-Century France: Protestant Campaigns for Strict Public Morality," in Christopher E. Forth and Elinor Accampo, eds., *Confronting Modernity in Fin-de-Siècle France* (New York: Palgrave-MacMillan, 2010), pp. 135–150; Deana Heath, *Purifying Empire: Obscenity and the Politics of Moral Regulation in Britain, India and Australia* (New York: Cambridge University Press, 2010).

questions for himself or herself? Or is the individual a morally dependent subject, reliant on obedience to the superior moral judgment and guidance of the political, religious, and social authorities? In the decades before World War I, European societies were in the throes of an intense struggle between the advocates and opponents of political democratization. Modern dance was an important embodiment of that struggle in the arts and entertainment: Attending a modern dance concert – in which artists like Villany appeared nude on stage – was a public performance of the claim to democratic citizenship.

These debates in turn were closely related to another issue of the day: the social role of women. Under the impact of rapid social change, women's roles were being transformed around 1900. Cultural conservatives defended the ideal of the wife and helpmeet who made civilization possible by attending to the home fire, the children, and morality while their husbands fought the hard, competitive battles of productive labor, politics, and artistic creativity. But women were entering public life in growing numbers – as professionals; civil servants; service-sector workers; independent intellectuals, writers, and artists; consumers; even as advocates of women's political, legal, educational, and sexual rights. The "New Woman" of this period was not a frail, shy, retiring, domestic creature; she was strong, independent, and ambitious.

Finally, that debate was just one part of a broader revolution in European conceptions of the self, of what it is to be a person and a member of a particular society. Historians have often referred to this revolution as the revolution of individualism – a profound shift in which people ceased to allow others to govern their lives according to the needs of their families, or the conventions and expectations of their class, or the traditions of their religion and culture (e.g., inherited codes of sexual morality and public decency), and threw themselves into the hard work of answering the question "What do *I* want?" and getting it. But this was also a period in which people were hard at work constructing new collective identities. The ideas of the nation, ethnicity, race, and what it meant to belong to one of them, and how one could tell who belonged to which one, and what that means for us as individuals – all these were burning questions at the time.

Modern dance played a critical role in all these changes. As women using their bodies as their expressive medium and often arguing for – and using – nudity on stage, modern dancers put themselves at the heart of a firestorm of debate over decency. Because the body was thought of as the material counterpart to the spiritual/intellectual ideal, dance posed with particular urgency the question of the function of the ideal and the real in art. The modern dancers epitomized the social revolution in women's roles. Adorée Villany, for example, was an independent artist, not part of a ballet company or dependent on a theater establishment; she was not directed by a male choreographer; and she was not dependent on a male audience because much of the audience for modern dance was female. And dance posed the question of identity not just for women, but for everyone. Race, ethnicity, and nation – again, expressed most frequently using the term *blood* – were understood to be bodily states. Because the medium of dance is the body, dancers confronted the meaning of their "blood" with greater immediacy and urgency than any other artists.

Modern dance, then, was a point of convergence for a whole range of questions raised by social and cultural change around the turn of the twentieth century. But more important for our purposes here, modern dance constituted a powerful response to those questions. In fact, modern dance was a masterful synthesis, a cultural form that developed explosive potential precisely because it could generate synergies between disparate trends and elements in European and indeed world culture at the time.

First, foremost, and as a precondition for its other roles, modern dance was a brilliant marketing strategy – the subject of Chapter 1. In its thematics, styles, and self-consciously multichannel market strategy, it was exquisitely tailored to the emerging "mass" culture market of the modern metropolis – a market that defied and eroded the distinctions between elite and popular culture, between high art and commercial entertainment, between male and female audiences, between distinctive national audiences and tastes. It was above all this success in the culture market that gave dance its remarkable symbolic power. Modern dance did not answer the questions posed by modernism and modernity (i.e., the conditions of life in the modern era) in the abstract; it turned its answers into a practice – a form of entertainment and a business – that was perfectly suited to the changes that were transforming its social environment. Modern dance did not argue that women should be autonomous participants in the public sphere; it *was* autonomous women in the public sphere – demonstratively, even outrageously. It did not argue that honest, open, natural sensuality is in the moral sense chaste and therefore legitimate; it demonstrated that this was so. Modern dancers did not argue that their art expressed something universal about humanity; they proved by their market success that it did – indeed, Chapter 5 will address the fact that, ultimately, many of the stars of modern dance would go on to bring modern dance to the world – to the United States, Latin America, India, Japan, and Australia.

Second, as Chapter 2 will show, modern dance realized with extraordinary force and immediacy the single most important aim of artistic modernism as it emerged in the wake of the Romantic ideal of artistic genius and inspiration: authentic self-expression, the striving to find the individual authorial voice of the artist. Dance was uniquely placed to accomplish that aim because in dance the artist *is* the art. But the modern dancers, unlike most ballet stars or the various exponents of folk or "national" dances in this period, made themselves independent not only of choreographers, but also (so they claimed) of all traditional or inherited movement idiom. Modern dance was the ideal Expressionist (as those most focused on this agenda called it) art form: the artist herself, expressing her "soul" – as Villany put it. The artistic avant-garde not only loved it; repeatedly, they were its most important champions and patrons, undertaking the job of educating the broader public in the meaning and value of the new dance.

Chapter 3 will argue that modern dance developed a rather remarkable answer to the question of individual and of ethnic/racial/national identity. It is an answer that we can trace in other forms of performance (like theatrical acting) as well, but that had particular power and immediacy when it was danced. That answer was a bit surprising: It turned out that being authentically who one is and faking it were the same thing. Building on theories of performance and on philosophical currents that were just being worked out between the 1870s and the 1900s, modern dance developed a highly effective method for producing authentic selfhood. To do that, modern dancers had to reach beyond their own immediate origins, and discover themselves as mongrels – either spiritually or literally, ransacking their family trees for admixtures of exotic blood. Modern dancers were not only experts on identity; they were also alchemists of "blood." By mixing it, they discovered its true properties. Not coincidentally, doing so opened the global culture market to them.

Modern dance was also uniquely powerful because in developing integrated answers to these questions – social change, beauty, truth, art, sexuality, individual identity, belonging – it developed a comprehensive response to the spiritual changes, tensions, and crises of the age. Indeed, modern dance was very often religious – explicitly, self-consciously, and in the eyes not only of performers but of reviewers, commentators, audiences, and critics. Modern dance performance was a revelation and a liturgy for the new religion of evolution – and of freedom, love, joy, and life. This will be the subject of Chapter 4.

Ultimately modern dance was less successful as a religion than as a business; and in the 1920s and 1930s its spiritual element would be largely attenuated. Yet as Chapter 5 will demonstrate, the "revelatory" power of dance before World War I had a lasting impact, in that it gave rise to cultural energies that flowed into and helped to power multiple projects after the war. Most unfortunately, one was radical authoritarian collectivism. Modern dance helped to feed the cultural energies of both communism and fascism. However, modern dance also came to play an important role in various formulations and experiences of democratic culture – in Social Democracy on the continent, in more conservative law-and-civilization democracy in Britain, and in populist and national-chauvinist democracy in the United States. Modern dance in the 1920s also had a formative impact on the culture of celebrity and particularly of the self-destructive complex of sex, drugs, and disorientation. More happily, modern dance played a central role in the development of a whole range of pedagogical and therapeutic methods that are still important today in the fields of mental health, occupational therapy, rehabilitative medicine and physical therapy, and art education. What is more, by the 1920s modern dance as a means of discovering and defining identity was being transferred to multiple other regions around the world, where it made an important contribution to anticolonial nationalism.

In short, in some very important ways, modern dance played a central role in giving birth to the global twentieth century. Whether one must or not is a question; but it is indeed remarkable what can be accomplished by dancing naked.

I.2 Cast of Characters

The chapters that follow will occasionally discuss particular dancers as individuals with particular stories of their own. For the most part, however, they will use stories about individual dancers as examples illustrating broader patterns. It will be useful, therefore, to establish at the outset the cast of characters involved. Doing so is also a way of pointing out two important patterns in modern dance.

The first is that modern dance happened first in Europe, but was not really European. The first wave of modern dancers came primarily from outside Europe. The United States – and particularly California – was exceptionally well-represented. An early cultural bridgehead was established by Loïe Fuller, an American who moved to Europe and eventually established her own dance idiom and her own theater in Paris in

1900, amid an explosion of international dance performance (much of it essentially ethnographic and representative, not modernist and innovative) associated with the Paris World Exposition in that year.[6] The greatest star, advocate, and philosopher of modern dance was Isadora Duncan, who performed and taught in private homes and variety theater in her native San Francisco Bay Area; toured the country with the company of a prominent variety-theater impresario starting in 1895; made a name in New York society circles, performing at private parties, by 1898; moved to London in 1899 and on to Paris in 1900 and was picked up and mentored by Fuller; and became an extraordinary cultural phenomenon in her own right starting with her performances in Munich, Budapest, and Berlin in 1902 and 1903.[7]

Duncan was followed in 1903 by Maud Allan, also from San Francisco. Allan had studied music in Berlin from the middle of the 1890s, but switched to dance. After developing a dance based on the story of Salomé and John the Baptist (Salomé loved John but he spurned her, whereupon she persuaded Herod – by dancing – to decapitate him), she gained some notoriety when Christian conservative morality campaigners managed to have her performance banned in Munich in 1907. She was invited to perform for the King of England while he was on vacation at a spa in Marienbad; on the strength of his approval she moved to London in 1908 and became an enormous success, performing more than 250 times at one of London's leading variety theaters.[8] Shortly after Allan's initial successes, Ruth Dennis (stage name St. Denis), from New Jersey, established herself as a dance phenomenon especially in Germany. St. Denis had worked in

[6] Richard Nelson Current and Marcia Ewing Current, *Loïe Fuller: Goddess of Light* (Boston: Northeastern University Press, 1997); Loïe Fuller, *Fifteen Years of a Dancer's Life* (Boston: Small, Maynard, 1913), p. 221; Gabriele Brandstetter and Brygida Maria Ochaim, *Loïe Fuller: Tanz–Licht–Spiel–Art Nouveau* (Freiburg: Rombach, 1989); Giovani Lista, *Loïe Fuller: Danseuse de la Belle Époque* (Paris: Somogy-Stock, 1995).

[7] The literature on Duncan is enormous; among many other studies, probably the most successful in placing her in broad social and intellectual context are Ann Daly, *Done into Dance: Isadora Duncan in America* (Bloomington: Indiana University Press, 1995); Peter Kurth, *Isadora: A Sensational Life* (Boston: Little, Brown, 2001); Fredrika Blair, *Isadora: Portrait of the Artist as a Woman* (New York: McGraw-Hill, 1986).

[8] On Allan see Felix Cherniavsky, "Maud Allan, Part I: The Early Years, 1873–1903," *DC* 6 (1983): 1–36 (quotation p. 30, Greek vases p. 27); "Maud Allan, Part II: First Steps to a Dancing Career, 1904–1907," *DC* 6 (1983): 189–227; and "Maud Allan, Part III: Two Years of Triumph, 1908–1909," *DC* 7 (1984): 119–158; Amy Koritz, *Gendering Bodies/Performing Art: Dance and Literature in Early Twentieth-Century British Culture* (Ann Arbor: University of Michigan Press, 1995); and "Dancing the Orient for England: Maud Allan's *The Vision of Salomé*," in Jane C. Desmond, ed., *Meaning in Motion: New Cultural Studies of Dance*, (Durham, NC: Duke University Press, 1997); and Judith R. Walkowitz, "The 'Vision of Salomé: Cosmopolitanism and Erotic Dancing in Central London, 1908–1918," *American Historical Review* 108 (2003).

variety theater for some years in the United States, as well as performing at private parties in the homes of the social elite particularly in New York City. In New York she met Indian businessmen, students, and performers, and developed dances and costuming built around Indian themes. In 1906 she went to Europe and became a sensation.[9]

But modern dance in Europe was not just an American phenomenon. The Japanese modernist actor and dancer Sada Yacco performed for some time in Loïe Fuller's theater; she did not take part in the modern dance boom after 1902, but made a tremendous impression on many of its later stars and supporters.[10] Clarissa Campbell, from Australia, played a similar role – her "Spanish" dance act (under the name Saharet) influenced practitioners and supporters of modern dance.[11] Olive Craddock, an Anglo-Indian, performed dances very similar to those of St. Denis around Britain and the Empire after 1911, under the name Roshanara.[12]

European dancers soon developed their own styles and acts. An early and influential example was the Dutch woman Margarethe Zelle, who after a period of living in Indonesia and an ugly divorce made an independent dance career starting in 1905, under the stage name Mata Hari.[13] The Falke sisters from Hamburg, Gertrud and Ursula, launched their own very successful dance careers in 1912. Clotilde von Derp and her husband Alexander Sacharoff became major figures starting in Munich in 1910. Elsa Margarethe Luisa von Carlberg, from Riga, moved to Berlin in 1905 to study art and launched her dance career, also in 1910, under the faux-Egyptian name Sent M'ahesa. Tórtola Valencia performed in variety theater and middle-brow spectaculars in London in 1908, and then launched herself as an independent dancer in 1909. The Danish variety-theater performer Gertrude Bareysen (stage name Barrison) settled in Vienna in 1907 to emerge as a serious modern dancer.[14] And countless other dancers built

---

[9] The single best biography is Sandra Meinzenbach, *"Tanz ist eine Sprache und eine Schrift des Göttlichen": Kunst und Leben der Ruth St. Denis* (Wilhelmshaven: Florian Noetzel, 2013); in English, Suzanne Shelton, *Ruth St. Denis: A Biography of the Divine Dancer* (Austin: University of Texas, 1981).

[10] Shelley C. Berg, "Sada Yacco: The American Tour, 1899–1900," *DC* 16 (1993): 147–196 and "Sada Yacco in London and Paris, 1900: Le Rêve Réalisé," *DC* 18 (1995): 343–404.

[11] Brygida Maria Ochaim, "Miss Saharet," *Tanzdrama* 16 (1991): 34–36.

[12] Iris Garland, "The Eternal Return: Oriental Dance (1900–1914) and Multicultural Dance (1990–2000)," *Dancing in the Millennium: An International Conference: Proceedings* (Washington, DC: n.p., 2000).

[13] Julie Wheelwright, *The Fatal Lover: Mata Hari and the Myth of Women in Espionage* (London: Collins and Brown, 1992).

[14] Gunhild Oberzaucher-Schüller, "Das bislang verschattete Leben der Miss Gertrude," *Tanzdrama* 50 (2000): 6–11 and Nils Jöckel, "Aus dem Moment des Empfindens," *Tanzdrama* 7 (1989): 18–23;

less prominent careers by imitating these stars. Tellingly, for example, one German art journal's discussion of modern dance in 1910 listed not only nine dancers whose names are familiar to most dance historians, but also ten who are virtually unknown in histories of modern dance.[15]

By 1910 modern dance was so successful that it was re-exported to other parts of the world – the British Empire (including India), Latin America, and the United States. It is suggestive of the reach of this still quite new phenomenon, for example, that Russell Meriwether Hughes/"La Meri," living in what was then the very distant and provincial city of Austin, Texas, was able within a five-year period between 1912 and 1917 to see performances by five major international modern dance stars.[16]

The second important pattern, however, is that the full influence of modern dance can by no means be measured by concentrating only on those performers who have conventionally been regarded as "modern" dancers. The success of the major and minor modern dance stars was so enormous that numerous ballet dancers soon developed a hybrid style, including both ballet technique and some of the movement and thematic idioms of what would eventually come to be called "modern" dance. That hybrid style allowed them not only to perform widely in variety theater (which several, particularly in London, already did) but also to revolutionize the ballet. Isadora Duncan's visit to Russia in 1904, for example, profoundly influenced Mikhail Fokine, who in 1908 set up shop in France with a company dubbed "Les Ballets Russes." One of the stars of that company, Ida Rubinstein, established herself in Paris as a not very successful but nevertheless prominent and controversial "modern" dancer.[17] Grete Wiesenthal left the Vienna ballet to launch herself as a very successful modern dancer in 1908, making a hit particularly with her free-form interpretations of waltz music (above all Richard Strauss's "Beautiful Blue Danube"). The Russian ballerina Anna Pavlova established herself as an international star from 1910 forward, with a performance featuring essentially a moderately updated ballet technique.[18] Antonia

---

Maria Pilar Queralt, *Tórtola Valencia* (Barcelona: Lumen, 2005); Iris Garland, *Tórtola Valencia: Modernism and Exoticism in Early Twentieth Century Dance*, ed. Mary Fox (Vancouver, BC: Five/ Cinq, 2013).

[15] Marie Luise Becker, "Die Sezession in der Tanzkunst," *Bühne und Welt* 12 (1910): 27–43.

[16] La Meri (Russell Meriwether Hughes), *Dance Out the Answer* (New York: Marcel Dekker, 1977), pp. 2, 6, 10.

[17] Michael de Cossart, *Ida Rubinstein (1885–1960): A Theatrical Life* (Liverpool, UK: Liverpool University Press, 1987).

[18] Jennifer Fisher, "The Swan Brand: Reframing the Legacy of Anna Pavlova," *DRJ* 44 (2012): 50–67; Fredrika Blair, *Isadora: Portrait of the Artist as a Woman* (New York: McGraw-Hill, 1986), p. 58.

Mercé/"La Argentina" was a similar case: after leaving the Madrid ballet, by 1910 she developed her own dance idiom that more closely followed the conventions of Spanish dance (such as flamenco, fandango, bolero, corrido) than those developed by Duncan and company; but her "synthesis of the two dances, Spanish and modern" (as one enthusiastic critic called it in 1915) was enormous popular (see Figure I.1).[19]

Both modern dancers and modernizing ballet dancers spawned a massive army of lesser imitators, performing in second- and third-tier metropolitan and provincial variety theaters all over Europe and North America. A remarkable case is that of the native San Franciscan Kitty Hayes, who performed in New York under the name Gertrude Hoffmann from 1903 onward. Hoffmann made her national name in 1908 by traveling to London to observe Maud Allan's Salomé dance, and then presenting it at Oscar and William Hammerstein's Paradise Roof Garden Theater in New York four months after Allan opened in London – in a show billed, frankly enough, as "a faithful copy of Maud Allan's 'A Vision of Salomé.'" She later copied Allan's dance to Mendelssohn's "Spring Song"; Ruth St. Denis's dance as the consort of Krishna, "Radha" (again billed as "An Exact, Lifelike Impersonation"); dances by Isadora Duncan and the London ballerina Adeline Genée; and in 1911 she mounted an entire "Saison des Ballets Russes" – six years before the Ballets Russes actually toured the United States.[20] In 1908 a dancer named "Dazié" even opened a school for Salomé dancers in New York. She had copied her own Salomé moves from Bianca Froelich, a Viennese ballerina who performed a Salomé dance in New York vaudeville theaters after the Metropolitan Opera's 1907 production of Strauss's opera *Salomé* (in which she was to perform) was cancelled after one night because it was deemed a threat to public morality. Appropriately enough, Dazié was actually Daisy Peterkin from Detroit, soon to be the world capital of mass production.[21] Nor was New York the only place such things were done. In 1906 Ruth St. Denis arrived in Paris from a series of performances as "Radha" in London to find that a "fake 'Radha'" was already performing there; but St. Denis also offered her own version of the Salomé dance popularized by Maud Allan when

---

[19] Doctor Oscar Quesada (Rocso), in *El Comercio* of Lima, December 12, 1915, clipping in DTAK, Inventory no. 0118, La Argentina, II.2.5.1.

[20] Barbara Naomi Cohen, *The Borrowed Art of Gertrude Hoffman* (New York: Dance Horizons, 1977), pp. 2, 4–7.

[21] See Elizabeth Kendall, *Where She Danced* (New York: Knopf, 1979), pp. 74–76, 84. The Salomé craze was considerably older than modern dance, however; in painting and literature it appears to have started already in the 1870s. See, e.g., Henk van Os et al., *Femmes Fatales, 1860–1910* (Antwerp: Groninger Museum, 2002).

Figure I.1 The Spanish dancer La Argentina/Antonia Mercé

she returned to the United States in 1909.[22] In the 1920s, on her second
visit to Japan in a year, one of the dancers in Ruth St. Denis's company

[22] Ruth St. Denis, *An Unfinished* Life (New York: Harper and Brothers, 1939), pp. 87–88; Helen
Thomas, *Dance, Modernity and Culture: Explorations in the Sociology of Dance* (London: Routledge,
1995), p. 77. The best discussion of the connection between modern dance and vaudeville is

found "Japanese dancing girls performing our numbers with almost the exact steps. And they were wearing duplicates of our costumes."[23]

In what follows, I will focus on those performers conventionally regarded as originators of "modern" dance idiom and forms. But I will draw on examples from the wider universe of performers. This book will, therefore, ultimately resemble a crowd scene, in which the diverse actions of individuals resolve into a broader direction and momentum in the scene as a whole. Modern dance derived its power partly from the fact that this is how it really worked. By 1908 or 1910, the European market was crowded with dancers and dance performances. In Vienna in 1907, for example, at one point Mata Hari, Maud Allan, and Isadora Duncan were all performing simultaneously.[24] In London in March 1908 Maud Allan began her long run of Salomé performances (at the Palace Theater); Tórtola Valencia appeared from late April on (at the Gaiety); Isadora Duncan began her season of performances in July (Duke of York); Loïe Fuller and her students performed in September (Hippodrome); and Ruth St. Denis danced (La Scala) in October and November.[25] The following year Grete Wiesenthal complained of the "dance frenzy" in London, observing that "there are as many theaters in London as stars in the heavens ... and in almost every one of them there's dancing."[26]

In fact, by 1908 it was not uncommon for observers of the culture market to make fun of the plague of modern dance. The *Tatler* in London complained in 1908, for example, that, "at present it seems that any dancer who can paint her toes and wave her arms about does a Salomé act and becomes a 'star.'"[27] In the following year the *New York Times* dance critic Carl van Vechten called Isadora Duncan "the American girl who is directly responsible for a train of barefoot dancers who have spread themselves, like a craze, over two continents in the last five years."[28] By 1912 the German novelist and critic Alfred Döblin declared "We've had enough of bad dancers.... Hopping, gyrating, enraptured doll-like face ... it's getting

Claudia Balk, "Vom Sinnenrausch zur Tanzmoderne," in Brygida Ochaim and Claudia Balk, eds., *Varieté-Tänzerinnen um 1900* (Frankfurt: Stroemfeld/Roter Stern, 1998), esp. pp. 53–57.
[23] Jane Sherman, *Soaring: The Diary and Letters of a Denishawn Dancer in the Far East, 1925–1926* (Middletown, CT: Wesleyan University Press, 1976), p. 43.
[24] Julie Wheelwright, *The Fatal Lover* (London: Collins and Brown, 1992), p. 21
[25] Garland, *Tortola Valencia*, p. 34.
[26] Grete Wiesenthal, "Unsere Tänze," in Leonhard M. Fiedler and Martin Lang, eds., *Grete Wiesenthal* (Salzburg: Residenz, 1985), p. 55.
[27] Quoted in Felix Cherniavsky, "Maud Allan, Part III: Two Years of Triumph, 1908–1909," *DC* 7, no. 2 (1984): 141.
[28] *The Dance Writings of Carl van Vechten*, ed. Paul Padgette (New York: Dance Horizons, 1974), p. 18.

downright tiresome. You can't dance, my dear children, whether academic
or free-form."[29] And a particularly striking case is that of the French dancer
Adorée Villany, whose arrests for indecency on stage in Munich in late
1911 and Paris in early 1913 made the newspapers all around Europe and
even the world – including papers in Budapest, Milan, Madrid, London,
and the *New York Times*.[30] In short, between about 1908 and 1914 modern
dance was an important fact of European cultural life, sufficiently ubiquitous and high profile to spark media firestorms, parliamentary debates,
and exasperated denunciations. Again: Modern dance was a big deal.

I.3 Dance History, Dance Biography, Cultural History

Dance history is a vibrant scholarly field, and there is a very substantial
and rapidly growing literature on the early development of modern dance.
This book is therefore partly a synthesis, drawing on the work of numerous other scholars. The specific characteristics of the scholarship on modern dance make such a synthesis potentially fruitful; for a great deal of
dance history focuses on individual performers, or on three of four key
modern dance pioneers. Most of the extant literature, in other words, is
highly biographical. This emphasis makes sense for dance historians in
particular, who are often primarily concerned with the art form itself –
with the aesthetic qualities of dance performance, the technical innovations of performers, and the motivations and sources of inspiration for
dance artists, specifically as artists.

This book, in contrast, aims to contribute to cultural history more
broadly; and the focus here is accordingly less on the art form than on its
context – the intellectual and cultural currents it drew on or contributed
to; its reception by audiences and critics; the social, political, and business
environment to which it responded; and so on. The aim here will consistently be to examine not the particular qualities of individual dancers'
performance, movement idiom, experience, or inspiration, but rather the
broader patterns common among many dancers, both more and less innovative, more and less famous. The reader attentive to the footnotes and to
attributions in the text will readily discern the debt this book owes to the
work of dance historians. I have drawn here extensively on the research
and interpretive perspectives presented in some dozens of works of dance

---

[29] "Tänzerinnen," in *Alfred Döblin, Kleine Schriften*, Vol. I (Freiburg: Walter, 1985), pp. 128–129.
[30] See clippings in Adorée-Via Villany, *Tanz-Reform und Pseudo-Moral: Kritisch-satyrische Gedanken aus meinem Bühnen- und Privatleben*, trans. Mirjam David (Paris: Villany, 1912); "Dancer Is Acquitted," *New York Times*, March 10, 1912.

history. But this book aims to construct something other than the sum of the parts it assembles from those works – again, not a synthesis of dance history, but a cultural history of modern dance in its early-twentieth-century context.

In more recent years, there have been several other scholarly syntheses of this sort – among others, the works of Gabrielle Brandstetter, Michael Huxley, Ramsay Burt, Kate Elswit, Julia Foulkes, Sabine Huschka, Sandra Meinzenbach, Amelie Soyka, and Helen Thomas. This book differs from those works, however, in that it focuses primarily on the period between 1900 and 1914, rather than on the 1920s. Again, the emphasis on the later period makes sense for dance historians because it was in the interwar years that modern dance became a recognized and established artistic form. It was also in this period that it took on its distinctively "modern" characteristics – for example the concern purely with the expressive potentials of movement, to the exclusion of theatrical props and conventions, narrative line, and sometimes even of music. This was also the period in which the iconic individual performers and teachers of this distinctively "modern dance" tradition (particularly Mary Wigman in Germany and Martha Graham in the United States) emerged, founded their own schools, and developed formative influence on the art form as a whole. Chapter 5 in particular does address this period (and draws heavily on the more recent scholarship). But this book as a whole points out that many of the central concerns and much of the importance and impact of modern dance after 1920 originated in the earlier period, before World War I. Dance historians have used various terms to distinguish the dancers of these years from those of the 1920s – proto-moderns, precursors, pioneers, founders.[31] Whatever we call them, without understanding that period of origins it is impossible fully to appreciate the dynamics and logic of the development of modern dance in the period of greater "maturity" after 1920. In particular, as the final chapter of this study will show, it is impossible to understand why modern dance was able to make its way, and to be influential, in the wider world beyond Western and Central Europe – as it most certainly did and was by the 1930s – without understanding how it defined the relationship between art and identity in the decade before World War I.

[31] Elisa Vaccarino, "Le arti del Novecento e la avanguardie di danza," in Elisa Carandini and Silvia Vaccarino, eds., *La Generazione Danzante: L'Arte del movimento in Europa nel primo Novecento* (Rome: Di Giacomo, 1997), p. 26; Leonetta Bentivoglio, *La danza moderna* (Milan: Longanesi, 1977), p. 39; Jacques Baril, *La danse modern (Isadora Duncan a Twyla Tharp)* (Paris: Vigot, 1977), p. 10.

For this reason, the term *modern dance* as it is used in this book means something somewhat different from what it frequently means in the dance-history scholarship; and several performers will be discussed here whom dance historians might not consider to be "modern" dancers. Here it refers not to any specific aesthetic qualities, but rather to the broadly innovative aspiration and agenda of a wide range of performers, working with various movement idioms and performance styles, between 1900 and 1914 (though, again, Chapter 5 will follow that modern dance revolution into the 1920s and 1930s). This distinction, again, arises from the agenda of the book – not to analyze "modern-ness" in dance, but dance in modernity.

Ultimately the aim of this books is to make a specific point about "modernity" – about the potentials, dynamics, and development of societies (European and non-European) in the twentieth century, and particularly about the aesthetic and intellectual movements ("modernism") that sought to reshape the arts in ways that would make them more relevant to the conditions and needs of those societies. Modernism (as it was embodied in dance), this book will show, was consistently self-contradictory; and precisely that self-contradiction was its greatest strength. The conclusion to this study will argue that this was – and is – true not only of modernism in the arts, but also of modernity more broadly.

Nothing more neatly illustrates the power of modernist self-contradiction than the fact that self-consciously "modern" dance before 1914 was both a rarified art form for the social and intellectual elite and a branch of the emerging commercial entertainment industry that catered successfully to the emerging mass culture market. Chapter 1 will analyze how the modern dance pioneers managed and used this contradiction.

CHAPTER I

Modern Dance and the Business
of Popular Culture

1.1 Dance as "Revolution"

The initial response to modern dance hardly suggested that it would constitute a cultural revolution. After performing in the homes of aristocrats and patricians in New York, London, and Paris, Isadora Duncan was engaged by Loïe Fuller for a tour in Central Europe; she soon went her own way, and in 1902 and 1903 gave public performances in Budapest, Munich, Berlin, and then again back in Paris. The response was mixed. One reviewer in Berlin commented that audiences had been enthusiastic, but "one really has to wonder why" because "Miss Duncan lacks not only shoes and stockings but also a few other things that her colleagues in the ballet have" – namely talent and technical ability. Duncan was clearly "no genius of the dance art." Nor did she display any particular fire or "passion"; her performance was "prim" and suffered from "English sentimentality." Another Berlin reviewer found Duncan's performance "lovely, but academic and boring ... sweetly pretty" rather than powerful. A Dutch newspaper reviewer reported similarly in January 1903 that Duncan "takes things very much in earnest." In March a Vienna paper reported that her dance appealed through its "gentle prettiness" and was a little "pedantic." In June a Paris reviewer reported that her audience, "which is very fond of its ballet tradition," had laughed at her histrionics. Late in the year a German theater journal called her "didactic virtue in motion ... this isn't dance, it's a lesson.... Her choreographic training is mediocre, and her temperament cool." It was all very nice, but her chaste spirit was disquieting. Wasn't the dance supposed to have something sensual at the back of it? By early 1904 another Vienna reviewer remarked that "This Miss Duncan," with her "sweet, childlike demure eyes," her "touchingly pretty face," and her boring "skipping around," was "starting to get on our nerves."[1]

---

[1] Oscar Fischel, "Aus dem Berliner Kunstleben," 1903, unidentified newspaper clipping; Karl Scheffer, "Isadora Duncan," *Die Zukunft* 42 (1903); W., "Miss Isadora Duncan: de veelbesproken hervormste

And yet, by early 1904 the tide was turning. While dance critics were skeptical, most audience response was positive, and in some cases verged on the ecstatic. Duncan recalled in her memoirs that art students in Munich and Berlin were so excited they stormed the stage after numerous encores, or insisted on unharnessing the horses from her carriage and drawing her through the streets; taking her flowers and handkerchiefs and even scraps of her dress and shawl as souvenirs; carrying her off to a pub to dance on the tables; and carrying her back to her hotel in the morning. Her audience "came to my performances with an absolutely religious ecstasy."[2] Most grownups were less euphoric; but newspaper reviews even in the initial months of Duncan's stay in Central Europe were often at least moderately positive. In February 1903, for example, one Vienna paper praised her "well-measured, graceful movement" and her ability "literally to embody classical music" with "artistically refined sensuality"; another German paper reported of a performance in Vienna in March that at first her audience was uneasy with her unfamiliar movement idiom, "but then gradually they found her gentle grace pleasing." Another Vienna paper reported the same process: Duncan's performance was "so completely unexpected" that it took time for the audience to appreciate it; but gradually her "sincerity," her "warmth, roguish charm and serenity," and her "noble and restrained grace" won them over. In January 1904 a reviewer in Munich wrote that Duncan made a "highly charming and aesthetically enjoyable impression"; in March the same paper reported that applause for her dance to Strauss's "Blue Danube" waltz rose to "a paroxysm."[3]

By the middle of 1904 Duncan had developed a growing momentum, and was increasingly perceived – and praised – as powerful and revolutionary, not just sweet and pretty. In June 1904 a Heidelberg paper reported that "yesterday slowly but surely this brave girl conquered her audience," showing them that "dance is a great, chaste art."

van den Dans," *Wereldkroniek* 43 (January 24, 1903); unidentified clipping, June 3, 1903, M. H., "Miss Duncan," unidentified clipping from *Das Theater* 1903/1904, all in DTAK, Inventory no. 69, Duncan-Archiv, II2.6.1.

[2] Duncan, *My Life* (New York: Liveright, 1955 [1927]), pp. 82–83, 179; Lothar Fischer, "Getanzte Körperbefreiung," in *"Wir sind nackt und nennen us Du": Von Lichtfreunden und Sonnenkämpfern – Eine Geschichte der Freikörperkultur* (Giessen: Anabas, 1989), p. 107.

[3] Unidentified clipping, *Wiener Abendpost* (February 13, 1903); "Zwei Tänzerinnen," unidentified clipping (March 22, 1903); "Karl-Theater," *Neue Freie Presse* (March 28, 1903); "Theater und Musik," *Vossische Zeitung* (March 25, 1904); H. v. G., "Isadora Duncan," *Münchener Neueste Nachrichten* (January 19, 1904); "Miss Isadora Duncan," *Münchener Neueste Nachrichten* (March 29, 1904), all clippings in DTAK, Inventory no. 69, Duncan-Archiv, II2.6.1. See also Fredrika Blair, *Isadora: Portrait of the Artist as a Woman* (New York: McGraw-Hill, 1986), p. 58.

By February 1905, a retrospective reflection in a German literary journal on the occasion of Duncan's fiftieth appearance in Berlin reported that "after a spirited campaign of three years duration against critics, roués and wastrels, Isadora Duncan strides victorious and laughing across the battlefield." Duncan was a "revolutionary" who had "brought her cause a decisive triumph."[4]

Duncan had been able to convince audiences that what she was doing was legitimately dance, and legitimately art. In doing so she cleared the way for the whole generation of young women who followed her onto the stage – many of them inspired specifically by her performances. How had Duncan accomplished this feat? She had clearly matured as an artist and performer. But more important, she was also a gifted business-woman. As one Dutch reviewer put it already in January 1903, Duncan was "an American, gifted with a healthy portion of practical insight," and had hit on a number of "outstanding advertising ideas." By 1906, a particularly acute German observer remarked that "Miss Duncan is one of the most innovative phenomena in the world of the arts and business. Two souls reside in her pretty breast – the artist and the master of 'business.'"[5] Whatever her artistic gifts and abilities, her contemporaries understood that Duncan had triumphed also, and perhaps above all, by developing a product and a marketing strategy that were perfectly suited to the specific conditions of her time and place. Those who emulated her would further refine the product and expand the strategy. Ultimately they succeeded in making modern dance not just a powerful emotional or spiritual experience for many in its audience, but also a lucrative performance form and even an important political and philosophical phenomenon.

1.2 Modern Dance, Modern Mass Culture, and Modern Marketing

As an exercise in product design and in marketing, the strategy of modern dance was shaped by a set of profound shifts taking place in the art market in the decades around 1900. Historians often refer to this as the emergence of a "mass" culture market. The term *mass* is used here in a

---

[4] "Isadora Duncan-Abend," *Heidelberger Zeitung* 0(June 13, 1904); Wilhelm Spohr, "Isadora Duncan," *Neue Magazin für Literatur, Kunst und soziales Leben* 74 no. 5/6 (February 15, 1905), clippings in DTAK, Inventory no. 69, Duncan-Archiv, II2.6.1.

[5] W., "Miss Isadora Duncan," *Wereldkroniek* 43 (January 24, 1903); "Isadora Duncans Freitanz-Schule," *Das Theater* 1906, clippings in DTAK, Inventory no. 69, Duncan-Archiv, II2.6.1

very specific sense, indicating not just a quantitative change but also a qualitative change. The modern market as it emerged in this period was a "mass" market specifically in the sense that it was not segmented by class, region, or culture. "Mass" culture is neither the culture of the upper nor of the lower classes, neither "high" culture nor folk culture. It was first developed and remained centered in large cities; but its appeal was by no means limited to urban audiences and its geographic reach was in principle unlimited. Indeed mass culture was pan-regional and cross-cultural. Modern mass culture as it emerged in the late nineteenth century was increasingly global culture – just as mass culture is today. In short, "mass" culture ignores and erodes every form of structuring boundary between potential audiences. The entrepreneurs who organized it deliberately set out to draw large and socially mixed audiences – white- and blue-collar; men and women; urban, suburban, and rural; "respectable" and "advanced"; conformist and avant-garde. In doing so they built a cultural pattern that was structured fundamentally not by the loyalties, traditions, and identities of class, locality, region, religion, or even nationality, but by the market. Mass culture is commercial culture. That makes it protean and adaptive, rather than prescriptive: It measures its success not by its ability to reproduce particularly fine recapitulations of aesthetic tradition, not by its rootedness in a particular local or social setting, but by its innovative and therefore expansive capacity and by its mobility – as measured, ultimately, by sales.

The expansion of the mass culture market in the decades around 1900 was a result of a whole range of processes. Rising average incomes driven by the ongoing industrial-technical revolution raised average per capita incomes in Western and Central Europe by more than half between 1870 and 1910 (and doubled them in the United States), creating armies of consumers with some disposable income to spend on cultural products such as performances, publications, or images.[6] Rising literacy gave a steadily expanding proportion of the population access to the urban culture market. By 1900, every major European city had a kind of dual existence: one the real city, and one the city as portrayed in the mass daily press, which, with circulations in the tens and hundreds of thousands, was a critical source of cultural coherence and the decisive underpinning of the emerging culture market. Indeed, the daily press penetrated well beyond cities, informing – as one German skeptic put it already in 1889 – "almost every family," including "the youth and the servants," even in "the most remote

[6] www.ggdc.net/maddison/maddison-project/data.htm.

corners of our fatherland" of what was going on in the great cities.[7] The growth of the mass labor union movement particularly from the beginning of the 1890s led to gains in working conditions, such as hours of work, giving a growing number of working people some disposable time. The expanding communications and transportation network played a critical role in creating a transnational cultural market, by making travel (particularly by train) incomparably faster, cheaper, and more frequent. But it also helped to homogenize the culture market locally by making it possible to concentrate cultural institutions – theaters, museums, music halls, shopping districts, amusement parks, cinemas – in particular locales, especially in the center of cities. Finally, in some cases particular technologies had a profound impact. The most obvious was moving pictures, which were first introduced in the late 1890s, and by 1914 were the single most popular art form in European societies. Another example was the phonograph, which revolutionized the consumption of music. Advances in lithographic and photographic reproduction transformed the consumption of images – giving rise, for example, to a wave of photographic pornography, the picture postcard, the illustrated newspaper, and the handheld Kodak single-lens reflex camera and mail-in roll-film development.

These changes brought with them profound transformations in patterns of cultural consumption. Commercial entertainment enterprises could now appeal beyond their neighborhoods and even beyond their cities, drawing on a vastly expanded and more socially diverse potential audience. By the 1910s, in many cases even rural people could travel to the nearest town or city to take in a movie or a show or go shopping. The rising importance of this mass audience gave a tremendous impetus to cultural forms that are now entirely familiar to us, but were quite new at the time – the advertising industry, the modern fashion industry, the custom of going shopping. In the latter case the transformation of the social role of women was momentous; the emergence of shopping in central business districts drew women out of their homes and neighborhoods and created what the historian Judith Walkowitz has called "heterosocial spaces" where men and women mingled, anonymously, in public.[8]

---

[7] "Die Tagespresse ...," *Korrespondenzblatt* 3 (1889): 10; "Petition christlicher Frauenvereine, betr. Asschluß der Öffentlichkeit bei Skandalprozessen," *Volkswart* 1 (1908): 45; F. Weigl, "Das gegenwärtige Hervordringen des Nackten in die Öffentlichkeit," *Volkswart* 1 (1908): 19. For a wonderfully evocative study see Peter Fritzsche, *Reading Berlin 1900* (Cambridge, MA: Harvard University Press, 1996).

[8] Judith R. Walkowitz, *City of Dreadful Delight* (Chicago: University of Chicago Press, 1992), p. 68.

This in itself undermined prevailing codes of gendered behavior and the gendered organization of society. In many cities, indeed before World War I, the police had a difficult time distinguishing women who took part in this emerging "heterosocial" world from prostitutes; a series of arrests of women out shopping in German cities in the late 1890s, for example, sparked major protests from German women's organizations. But the mass market for consumer goods and entertainments undermined the traditional markers of class, as well. More conservative upper-class observers were horrified, for example, by the fact that young working-class men dressed up like people "better" than they were to go out on a Sunday afternoon, or by the "tendency toward addiction to fashion, vanity" and desire for "the greatest possible pleasure in life" among young working-class people who bought nice clothes and went out dancing, or to the movies.[9]

Early modern dance was a creation of this new mass culture market. Its pioneering performers drew on a whole range of traditions and innovations to create a hybrid form that appealed across a range of cultural registers, and to a range of audiences – or rather, again, to a "mass" audience. The success of the form derived, in no small part, from the versatility that this synthesis generated. In multiple ways, moreover, modern dance drew quite specifically on the most dynamic *new* developments in the European culture market, turning them into highly effective and prestigious marketing channels that associated it with the cultural cachet of innovation and progress. In that sense, the term *modern* refers not just to the fact that this art form developed in the twentieth century, but also to the fact that it very self-consciously associated itself with the latest trends in politics, philosophy, marketing, and technology.

The modern dance synthesis operated, first, at the level of technique, drawing on and synthesizing three distinct movement traditions to create something that was at once familiar and new. Those traditions were variety-theater and vaudeville dance, a venue and performance form historically closely associated with the urban lower-middle and lower classes; ballet, an established if not terribly respectable part of the "high" culture of the social elite; and a system of movement training developed earlier in the nineteenth century by the French theorist François Delsarte, which was quite widely practiced particularly among the European and North American middle classes.

---

[9] "Auf zur Rettungsarbeit an den Gefallenen!," *Frauenblätter* 17 (1908): 18.

From variety theater modern dance took elements of "skirt dancing," popular in variety theaters and music halls for two or three decades prior to the modern dance boom. Skirt dancing was a high-energy form involving various gymnastic moves such as high-kicks, backbends, splits, and so forth; the "can-can" was the most well-known later offshoot. Most of the early modern dancers had at least brief careers in skirt dancing before launching their own independent productions. Loïe Fuller and Ruth St. Denis, for example, performed for some years in vaudeville; but Isadora Duncan, too, worked first in popular theater.[10] Many of the European dancers, too, started out as variety theater dancers; and most of them continued to perform primarily in variety theaters in London, Berlin, and Paris. The extreme case was Gertrude Bareysen/Barrison, who had a very successful career as part of an off-color variety theater song-and-dance act (with her four sisters, who dressed up in baby clothes and sang suggestive songs) in Europe and the United States before becoming a successful "serious" dancer in Vienna in her twenties.[11]

The emphasis in variety theater dancing was on high energy, acrobatic flexibility, and acting ability; and while modern dance only remotely resembled skirt dancing, all the modern dancers adopted and adapted these elements to one degree or another. This meant that modern dance was founded in part on a movement idiom that had an established appeal among lower-middle and working-class audiences.

Most of the modern dancers also, however, had at least some ballet training. Many of them vigorously denied that; but ballet was one of the dominant dance idioms of the period, and anyone interested in movement was exposed to it. A number of modern dancers incorporated at least some gestures or steps from the classical ballet into their acts. Grete Wiesenthal was unusual in having a first career in the Vienna opera corps de ballet; Ruth St. Denis took lessons from the famous ballerina Marie Bonfanti in New York; Antonia Mercé/"La Argentina" was also trained in classical ballet in Madrid before striking out on her own. In addition, by the 1900s a number of prominent European ballerinas danced both in ballet and opera companies and in variety theaters, particularly in London. In such

---

[10] Jochen Schmidt, *Tanzgeschichte des 20. Jahrhunderts in einem Band* (Berlin: Henschel, 2002), pp. 17, 20, 24.

[11] Suzanne Shelton, *Ruth St. Denis: A Biography of the Divine Dancer* (Austin: University of Texas, 1981), 22–28; Gunhild Oberzaucher-Schüller, "Das bislang verschattete Leben der Miss Gertrude," *Tanzdrama* 50 (2000): 6–11; Elizabeth Kendall, *Where She Danced* (New York: Knopf, 1979), 27–29; Arthur Moeller-Bruck, *Das Variete* (Berlin: Julius Bard, 1942), pp. 171–173; Claudia Balk, "Vom Sinnenrausch zur Tanzmoderne," in Brygida Ochaim and Claudia Balk, eds., *Varieté-Tänzerinnen um 1900* (Frankfurt: Stroemfeld/Roter Stern, 1998), especially 53–57.

venues they seem to have offered hybrid performances that showcased both the technical mastery of ballet and some of the crowd-pleasing energy of vaudeville dance.[12] Critics often observed that the modern dance pioneers had no real technique, and again, the performers prided themselves on that fact (even when it was not entirely true). But many of the modern dancers adopted some of the gestural language of ballet.

This was not the only element that helped to make the modern dance aesthetic accessible and legitimate to middle-class audiences, however. Most of the modern dancers had studied the movement training first created by François Delsarte in the mid-nineteenth century, and developed and propagated later by others, particularly in the United States.[13] By the late nineteenth century Delsarte movement was widespread among women of the upper and middle classes, in part as a form of training in comportment and gracefulness. The early modern dancers drew on Delsarte poses as well as on the rhetoric of "natural" movement and moral improvement that underpinned Delsarte's system.[14] Both Duncan and Ruth St. Denis, for example, had Delsarte training and engaged early in their careers in a noncommercial, living-room performance form derived from it, often called "statue posing." One London newspaper in 1908 even referred to Ruth St. Denis as "the latest exponent of the Delsartian school."[15]

1.3 Familiar Exotics

The modern dance synthesis operated also through dancers' choice of themes – not only how they moved, but also what they portrayed by

[12] See, e.g., Shelton, *Ruth St. Denis*, 83; Ochaim, "Varieté-Tänzerinnen," in Ochaim and Balk, eds., *Varieté-Tänzerinnen*, 132–133; Claude Conyers, "Courtesans in Dance History: Les Belles de la Belle Époque," *DC* 26 (2003): 230; Sibylle Dahms and Stephanie Schroedter, eds., *Der Tanz – Ein Leben: In Memoriam Friderica Derra de Moroda* (Salzburg: Selke Verlag, 1997), 19, 22. For a good discussion see Sandra Meinzenbach, *Neue alte Weiblichkeit: Frauenbilder und Kunstkonzepte im Freien Tanz* (Marburg: Tectum, 2010), p. 27.

[13] See Nancy Chalfa Ruyter, "American Delsartism: Precursor of an American Dance Art," *Educational Theater Journal* 25, no. 4 (1973): 421–435; Gabriele Brandstetter, *Tanz-Lektüren: Körperbilder und Raumfiguren der Avantgarde* (Ph.D. diss., Frankfurt, 1995), pp. 66–69.

[14] See Shelton, *Ruth St. Denis*, 29, 57; Brygida Ochaim, "Die getanzten Bilder der Rita Sacchetto," *Tanzdrama* 14 (1991): 23; Kendall, *Where She Danced*, 23–27; Deborah Jowitt, "The Impact of Greek Art on the Style and Persona of Isadora Duncan," *Proceedings, Tenth Annual Conference of the Society of Dance History Scholars* (Irvine, CA, 1987), 195–197.

[15] See Kendall, *Where She Danced*, 29, 54; Brygida Ochaim and Claudia Balk, eds., *Varieté-Tänzerinnen um 1900* (Frankfurt: Stroemfeld/Roter Stern, 1998), pp. 74–75; Alexandra Carter, "London, 1908: A Synchronic View of Dance History," *DRJ* 23 (2005): 39; and particularly Carrie J. Preston, *Modernism's Mythic Pose* (New York: Oxford University Press, 2011), pp. 58–91, 152–173.

moving. They drew self-consciously on two fashionable aesthetic and cultural references already well established in the arts in Europe. On the one hand, they appealed almost compulsively to the authority of the classical Greek past. On the other, just as frequently they drew on the "seductive" charms of the "Orient" – a rather indeterminate cultural geography that included East and South Asia, the Middle East, and North Africa.

The reliance on classical Greek themes was particularly central in the early years of modern dance; and indeed Isadora Duncan wedded herself to the Greeks with extraordinary enthusiasm and tenacity. In her earliest independent performances in New York in 1899, she included readings from Theocritus (and Ovid) by her brother Raymond; at her first performances in London it was the young classics scholar Jane Ellen Harrison who read from Greek texts while Duncan danced. She returned again and again to this practice and point of reference.[16] She spelled out the connection between ancient Greece and modern dance most clearly in her address in Berlin in March 1903 on "The Dance of the Future," a kind of manifesto of the modern dance movement. In that address Duncan invoked the Greeks as the authors of an art that was perfectly rational and universal, but also perfectly natural and individual. As "the greatest students of the laws of nature," the Greeks understood that in nature "all is the expression of unending ever increasing evolution, wherein are no ends and no stops." Greek depictions of dance – for example in statuary and in figures on vases – therefore suggested fluid, organic, dynamic movement. But the Greeks also understood that "the movements of the human body must correspond to its ... individual form. The dance of no two persons should be alike." Her own dance idiom, derived from these principles, was therefore Greek (see Figure 1.1): "dancing naked upon the earth I naturally fall into Greek positions."[17]

In fact, there was a certain deliberate confusion between dance and statuary in Duncan's description of what she wanted to do. On the one hand, she claimed to have studied Greek art for endless hours – first in the British Museum and then at the Parthenon – in order to absorb and capture the wisdom and grace of ancient Greek movement. On the other hand,

---

[16] Leonetta Bentivoglio, *La danza moderna* (Milan: Longanesi, 1977), p. 39; Preston, *Modernism's Mythic Pose*, p. 173.

[17] Isadora Duncan, *Der Tanz der Zukunft (The Dance of the Future): Eine Vorlesung*, trans. Karl Federn (Leipzig: Diederichs, 1903), pp. 17–18, 25. The literature on Duncan is enormous; among many other studies, probably the most successful in placing her in broad social and intellectual context is Ann Daly, *Done into Dance: Isadora Duncan in America* (Bloomington: Indiana University Press, 1995).

Figure 1.1 Isadora Duncan Dover Street Studios

because Greek statuary captured the essence of that natural movement, her aim was to capture the essence of Greek statuary. "If I could find in my dance a few or even one single position that the sculptor could transfer into marble," she remarked, "my work would not have been in vain."[18] The references to Greek statuary in Duncan's performances were so self-conscious that one critic accused her of offering mere "archaeological show-and-tell for upper-class girls," while another observed that she "has something of the very winning and passionate devotion to beauty of a professor of archaeology."[19] Others were more positive, exclaiming, for example, that she was "the Schliemann of ancient choreography," for just as the archaeologist Heinrich Schliemann had rediscovered ancient Troy and created "restorations of ancient statues and palaces," Duncan "restores, revives the ancient Greek dances."[20]

Other performers constantly drew on the same vocabulary, as did reviewers, promoters, and fans. A decade after Duncan's debut in Central Europe, Tórtola Valencia too claimed to have spent "many hours in the British museum" in preparation for her dance career.[21] Karoline Sofie Marie Wiegmann, who would become one of the most influential exponents of the dance in Germany under the name Mary Wigman, offered a version of modern dance that, like Duncan's, was in part inspired by portrayals of dancers on Greek vases – which she claimed to have seen not in the British Museum but in the Vatican.[22] Alexander Sacharoff, who performed solo in 1910–1913 and then formed a successful dance duo with Clotilde Margarete Anna Edle von der Planitz (Clotilde von Derp), discovered Greek art instead in the museums of Paris. His solo dances were so deliberately modeled on classical sculpture that one critic

[18] Duncan, *Der Tanz*, p. 21; Duncan, "The Parthenon" (1903 or 1904), in Isadora Duncan, *The Art of the Dance* (New York: Theatre Arts, 1928), p. 65. On Duncan and classical art, see particularly Daly, *Done into Dance*, pp. 109–110.

[19] Evelyn Dörr, "'Wie ein Meteor tauchte sie in Europa auf...': Die philosophische Tänzerin Isadora Duncan im Spiegel der deutschen Kritik," in Frank-Manuel Peter, ed., *Isadora & Elizabeth Duncan in Deutschland/in Germany* (Cologne: Wienand, 2000), p. 33; Hugo von Hofmannsthal, "Die unvergleichliche Tänzerin," in *Gesammelte Werke: Prosa*, vol. 2 (Frankfurt: S. Fischer, 1951), p. 263. On the connection between avant-garde art and archaeology, see Jeffrey Schnapp, Michael Shanks, and Matthew Tiews, "Archaeology, Modernism, Modernity," Julian Thomas, "Archaeology's Place in Modernity," and (for a critical comment) Robert Harrison, "Archaeology on Trial," all in *Modernism/Modernity* 11 (2004): 1–36. See also Carrie J. Preston, "The Motor in the Soul: Isadora Duncan and Modernist Performance," *Modernism/Modernity* 12 (2005): 273–289.

[20] Valerian Svetlov, "Duncan," *Birzhevyie Vedomosti* (December 15, 1904), translation in JRDD, Natalia Roslasleva files, folder 4.

[21] "Dancing for Health," *The Morning Leader* (April 20, 1912), clipping in MAE, Fonds Tortola Valencia, L3.

[22] Gabriele Fritsch-Vivié, *Mary Wigman* (Reinbek: Rowohlt, 1999), pp. 12–13.

dismissed them as "museum art."[23] One fan wrote to Maud Allan to praise her "essentially Hellenic spirit," insisting that one was impressed by her "just as one is by a Greek sculpture, only that a living being is vastly more expressive than marble."[24] Of Adorée Villany's dances, one reviewer wrote that they were "based on a genuine archaeological foundation"; another found that she was "a Greek statue brought to life"; a third called her an embodiment, literally, of "the ethical culture of our humanistic education"; a French reviewer called her a "statue de chaire" – a statue made of flesh.[25] Ida Rubinstein was said to offer audiences "the exact equivalent of a gallery of antique statues."[26] Another reviewer praised the "noble, calm beauty of classical Antiquity" that characterized Gertrud Leistikow's dance performances.[27] Tórtola Valencia, according to a particularly enthusiastic reviewer, was "like a marble [statue] animated by the gods, transformed into human flesh by a miracle of music"; another found that she embodied the "serene beauty of Hellenic rhythms" (as well as the "cosmopolitan elegance of the 'music halls' of Europe").[28] Here too there was confusion between the real and the artistic image: One reviewer believed that Valencia had "brought back to her country in feminine flesh the perfect impression of those Oriental dances which, in the centers of the arts, are portrayed in marble sculpture," a "human sculpture ... such as Praxiteles or Fidus [prominent German graphic artists close to the nudist movement] should see in their creative dreams."[29]

This classical Greek theme was important for modern dance for two reasons. First, classical Greece had quite extraordinary cultural cachet at the time, particularly among the upper and middle classes. Ancient Athens

23 Rainer Stamm, "Alexander Sacharoff – Bildende Kunst und Tanz," in Frank-Manuel Peter and Rainer Stamm, eds., *Die Sacharoffs–zwei Tänzer aus dem Umkreis des Blauen Reiters* (Cologne: Wienand, 2002), p. 34.
24 Felix Cherniavsky, "Maud Allan, Part III: Two Years of Triumph, 1908–1909," *DC* 7 (1984): 134; Maud Allan, *My Life and Dancing* (London: Everett, 1908), p. 105.
25 "Die Reformtänzerin Villany," *Prager Tageblatt* 277 (October 8, 1910); "Der Münchener Theaterskandal," *Berliner Tageblatt* 598 (November 24, 1911); clippings in Adorée-Via Villany, *Tanz-Reform und Pseudo-Moral: Kritisch-satyrische Gedanken aus meinem Bühnen- und Privatleben*, trans. Mirjam David (Paris: Villany, 1912), pp. 267, 301, 309; Adorée Villany, *Phryné moderne devant l'Areopage* (Munich: Bruckmann, 1913), p. 19.
26 Michael de Cossart, *Ida Rubinstein (1885–1960): A Theatrical Life* (Liverpool, UK: Liverpool University Press, 1987), pp. 9, 50.
27 Stl., "Tanzabend Gertrud Leistikow," *Danziger Allgemeine Zeitung* (October 8, 1913), clipping in TBCUA, Archief Gertrud Leistikow, Map 4a.
28 Pompeyo Gener, "Tortola Valencia," *Mundial* 2 (1912): 527; Tomas Borrás, "El arte de la danza: Tórtola de Valencia," *España Nueva* (December 14, 1911), clipping in MAE, Fonds Tórtola Valencia, L3.
29 "Del Cartel de Anoche: Romea," *El Mundo* (Madrid) (December 16, 1911), clipping in MAE, Fonds Tórtola Valencia, L3.

was widely understood to be the origin, pinnacle, and embodiment of Western civilization – of aesthetic refinement, political wisdom, and philosophical depth. Attitudes toward warlike Sparta were more ambivalent; but the Spartans were often depicted as the pinnacle of Western moral virtue – a society of disciplined, self-abnegating soldier-citizens unflinchingly devoted to the common weal, even unto death. Mastery of ancient Greek and Latin was still, in most of Europe, a marker of upper-class status – of education and refinement. One study of 1935 even referred in its title to the "tyranny of Greece over Germany"; and while the Germans were perhaps particularly enthusiastic, the myth of Greece as the cradle of Western Civilization was European in scope.[30]

Ancient Greece was also identified as politically progressive, both because Athens was the model of republican civic virtue and because the ancient Greeks were still, in 1900, widely understood to have been rational and skeptical thinkers rather than superstitious religious fanatics. In some parts of Europe, in fact, the classical Greek tradition was portrayed as the antidote to later Europe's own medieval fanaticisms of faith and belief. In appealing to classical antiquity, then, modern dance not only established itself as high culture, but also associated itself with liberal humanism and civic spirit.

Second, however, these associations were all the more important because in European culture at the time the dance was widely seen as not really a respectable art form. Because its medium was the body, dance blurred the line between the ideal and aesthetic, which were coded in European culture at the time as high, pure, good, and disinterested, and the merely corporeal or material, which were coded as low, dirty, sinful, and egoistic. The aesthetic theory codified by Immanuel Kant in the *Critique of Aesthetic Judgment* of 1790 had a powerful purchase on European thinking around 1900. The key distinction in Kant's theory of beauty was between the (aesthetically) beautiful and the (sensually) pleasing. The latter is a perception of the value placed on an object by an observer who, in one way or another, desires it or its qualities; the former is a judgment based on completely disinterested, detached contemplation. The pleasing has "always a relationship to the capacity for desire," whereas the beautiful is perceived by "pure contemplation (observation or reflection)." Whereas desiring a thing produces a state of inward dependence on it (because "all interest posits a need"), the appreciation of beauty is "a disinterested and

---

[30] Eliza Marion Butler, *The Tyranny of Greece over Germany* (Cambridge: Cambridge University Press, 1935).

free pleasure." Appreciation of beauty also implies a claim to universality: Whereas the pleasing is pleasing in relationship to a particular viewer's desires, appreciation of beauty is a pleasure of pure mind, pleasure in the object viewed or contemplated for its own sake.[31]

In this code dance could only ever have a marginal position in the arts. As Friedrich Theodor Vischer put it his massive multivolume *Aesthetics, or the Science of the Beautiful* (1846–1857), dance focused on the "use of the living natural stuff" – that is, the body – "in a system of pleasing movements," and therefore had a tendency to be "seduced" into offering "merely material titillation" rather than ideal values.[32] Vischer did not treat the dance as one of the arts: He merely discussed it briefly in an appendix, on pages 1,152 to 1,158 of his work.

To make matters worse, as a matter of social practice ballet and variety-theater dance were often regarded as, effectively, part of the upper and middle ranges of the sex market. This perception appears to have been rooted in reality, at least in some places: Grete Wiesenthal, for example, reported that while her colleagues in the Vienna Opera corps de ballet were not granted access to respectable bourgeois salons, they were assiduously pursued by "young and old aristocrats," who as "worshippers" or "chivalrous friends" offered gifts and patronage in return for a more or less openly acknowledged sexual arrangement.[33] And the *New York Times* dance critic Carl van Vechten, who went to see variety-theater dance in London in 1907, "was more fascinated by the brilliantly caparisoned ladies of pleasure who strolled back and forth" in the back of the theater "than I was by the action on the stage."[34] In France too, as the dance historian Ilyana Karthas has found, the ballet had become "primarily eroticized entertainment," and public discussion of dance (e.g., in reviews) "catered to the male gaze, male desires, and male expectations by emphasizing dancers' sensuality, personality, and physical appearance."[35] As the dance historian Ramsay Burt has put it, then, "dancing and prostitution had

[31] Immanuel Kant, *Critik der Urtheilskraft* (London: Routledge, 1994), pp. 5, 15.

[32] Friedrich Theodor Vischer, *Aesthetik, oder die Wissenschaft des Schönen*, part 3, section 2 (Stuttgart: Mäcken, 1857), p. 1155.

[33] Grete Wiesenthal, *Der Aufstieg* (Berlin: Rowohlt, 1919), pp. 70, 123–125. For a general discussion see Jörn Runge, *Olga Desmond: Preussens nackte venus* (Friedland/Mecklenburg: Steffen, 2009), pp. 10–11; Lynn Garafola, "The Travesty Dancer in Nineteenth-Century Ballet," *DRJ* 18 (1985): 36–37; Hanna Järvinen, *Dancing Genius: The Stardom of Vaslav Nijinsky* (New York: Palgrave MacMillan, 2014), pp. 30–31.

[34] Carl van Vechten, "Terpsichorean Souvenirs," in Paul Padgette, ed., *The Dance Writings of Carl van Vechten* (New York: Dance Horizons, 1977), p. 5–6.

[35] Ilyana Karthas, *When Ballet Became French: Modern Ballet and the Cultural Politics of France, 1909–1939* (Montreal: McGill-Queen's University Press, 2015), pp. 12–13.

for some time been established as characteristic forms of metropolitan entertainment."[36]

The result was not only that dance was not taken seriously as art, however, but even that anyone associated with it had to deal with a certain moral stigma. As the English sexologist and dance enthusiast Havelock Ellis put it in 1914, by the late nineteenth century "it became scarcely respectable even to admire dancing."[37] Hans Brandenburg, who penned an early study of modern dance in 1912, recalled in his memoirs that "even close friends held my interest in the dance ... for a pointless frivolity," while serious art critics told him he was "on the way to nowhere."[38] When Maud Allan's mother wrote the family lawyer for advice concerning her daughter's intention to go into dance, he advised her that "a dance is a dance, and sooner or later it will be given in the Variety halls," and then the "Church people" would be up in arms.[39] And one early American history of modern dance, published in 1912, recalled that just ten years earlier music pundits had experienced Isadora Duncan's use of music from the European classical canon as "a desecration." High art, like the music of Beethoven, Gluck, Schubert, or Mendelssohn, should not be associated with "so 'primitive' an art as dancing."[40]

As the dance historian Iris Garland argues, then, the scholarly research in museums that the modern dance pioneers claimed to have undertaken and their evocation of classical sculpture was important because it "created an aura of cultivation, refinement and authenticity" for their performances. Deborah Jowitt is more blunt, observing that by "reminding her audiences of Greek statues, Duncan knew she was assuring them of the high moral tone of her dancing."[41] Maud Allan played on this same cultural reference in an interview in 1908: Because her performances

[36] Ramsay Burt, *Alien Bodies: Representations of Modernity, '"Race" and Nation in Early Modern Dance* (New York: Routledge, 1998), p. 22.
[37] Havelock Ellis, "The Philosophy of Dancing," *Atlantic Monthly*, February 1914, p. 204, at https://www.unz.org/Pub/AtlanticMonthly-1914feb-00197.
[38] Hans Brandenburg, *München leuchtete: Jugenderinnerungen* (Munich: Herbert Neuner, 1953), p. 430.
[39] Quoted in Felilx Cherniavsky, "Maud Allan, Part II: First Steps to a Dancing Career, 1904–1907," *DC* 6 (1983): 200.
[40] Caroline and Charles H. Caffin, *Dancing and Dancers of Today* (New York: Dodd, Mead and Company, 1912), p. 46. See Ann Wagner, *Adversaries of Dance: From the Puritans to the Present* (Urbana: University of Illinois Press, 1997); Junius H. Browne, "The Ballet as a Social Evil," *The Northern Review* 2 (1868): 522–538; Carl van Vechten, "Duncan Concerts in New York," in Paul Magriel, ed., *Nijinsky, Pavlova, Duncan: Three Lives in Dance* (New York: Da Capo, 1977), p. 20.
[41] Iris Garland, "The Eternal Return: Oriental Dance (1900–1914) and Multicultural Dance (1990–2000)," *Dancing in the Millennium: An International Conference: Proceedings* (Washington, DC: n.p., 2000), p. 195; Jowitt, "The Impact of Greek Art," p. 197.

were "a serious and reverent attempt" to give expression in movement to the aesthetic qualities of classical sculpture, she claimed, "[m]y dancing is perfectly chaste" (see Figure 1.2).[42] And the German/American dancer Elizabeth Selden stated the case succinctly in 1935: "[T]he prestige of an approved and exalted past" helped to "get the dance rooted in many places that would otherwise reject that flighty art."[43]

The word Allan used – *chaste*, in multiple languages – appeared over and over again in descriptions of modern dance performance; and so did countless variations of the claim that modern dance was not suggestive or sensual, but ideal, decent, respectable, inoffensive. In fact, as we have seen, at the outset many reviewers found the self-conscious "chasteness" of Isadora Duncan's performances mystifying or boring; and some continued to find her annoying precisely because she was prim, proper, and asexual. The German painter Max Liebermann complained, for example, that Duncan was "too chaste for me." Harry Graf Kessler found her sentimental and philistine, and felt that what made her attractive to the less discerning public was that "she is naked and conventional." The English theater critic Max Beerbohm complained of Maud Allen that "I cannot imagine a more ladylike performance," while a colleague called her "the English Miss in art."[44]

Ultimately, however, it became clear that this "chaste" quality was precisely the point. As Duncan put it in her address on "The Dance of the Future," her aim was to achieve "a new nakedness, no longer at war with spirituality and intelligence" – a nakedness that was ideal, pure, and innocent, not gross, material, and sinful.[45] The idea that the (relative) nakedness in modern dance performance was not erotic nudity but authentic, "natural" nakedness – just like in Greek statuary – was absolutely ubiquitous in the discussion of the dance, ultimately becoming an outright cliché.

Already in March 1903, for example, one German reviewer assured readers regarding Isadora Duncan "that the nakedness of her legs, the veil-thin transparency of her dress make a highly respectable, even

[42] "Is It, or Isn't It – Indecent?," *San Francisco Examiner*, July 12, 1908, in Maud Allan clippings files, MPDSF.
[43] Elizabeth Selden, *The Dancer's Quest: Essays on the Aesthetic of the Contemporary Dance* (Berkeley: University of California Press, 1935), pp. 20–21.
[44] Harry Graf Kessler, *Harry Graf Kessler: Das Tagebuch, Dritter Band 1897–1905*, eds. Carina Schäfer and Gabriele Biedermann (Stuttgart: Cotta, 2004), pp. 533 (Liebermann) and 539; Cherniavsky, "Maud Allan, Part III," p. 138; Titterton quoted in J. E. Crawford Flitch, *Modern Dancing and Dancers* (Philadelphia: Lippincott, 1912), p. 115.
[45] Duncan, *Der Tanz*, p. 25.

Figure 1.2 Isadora Duncan's chaste nudity, 1900

a pleasingly healthy impression."[46] In December 1904 a St. Petersburg newspaper reported that "the *nudité* of her legs does not arouse sinful thoughts. It's a sort incorporeal nudity." Another found that the "barefoot girl shocked nobody, and her nudity was pure and imperceptible." A third, in 1906, explained that Duncan was "undressed but not nude."[47] One London newspaper observed of Maud Allan that "none but the most prurient could see the slightest appeal to any sense but that of beauty of motion and pose" in her dance, while another praised "its natural girlishness, its utter absence of sensuous appeal," and a third believed that her "nudity was not intended to have an erotic effect." A Hungarian critic even claimed that "during the dancer's performance, I did not even think about her nakedness," and the *San Francisco Chronicle* told readers in 1910 that "you scarcely stop to consider that she is a woman at all" because her performance was "the art of absolute beauty ... as modest as the sunrise, as chaste as the leaves of the forest and as sweet as the spring."[48] One French reviewer reassured readers that Mata Hari's performance was "very gracious and artistic and not at all pornographic"; another described her as "naked as Eve before she committed the first sin."[49] Tórtola Valencia's performance, "semi-nude, does not evoke the slightest shadow of eroticism."[50] A reviewer of Anna Pavlova wrote in 1910 that in "the presence of art of this stamp, one's pleasure is purely aesthetic. Indeed the sex-element ... counts for very little."[51] One reviewer described Adorée Villany's "absolutely chaste dances" as "completely free of any profane undertones"; another asserted that her "beauty stands far above any sweaty, torrid eroticism"; a third reported that "artistry is so great that when the final veil falls, the nakedness of her body is not

[46] "Zwei Tänzerinnen," unidentified clipping (March 22, 1903) in DTAK, Inventory no. 69, Duncan-Archiv, II2.6.1.
[47] N. Georgievich, "Duncan," in *Peterburgskaya Gazeta* (December 14, 1904); Y. V., "Theatre and Music," *Novoye Vremiya* (December 15, 1904); Valerian Svetlov, "Antique Choreography and Miss Duncan," *Terpsichore* (1906), all translations in JRDD, Natalia Roslasleva files, folders 2, 3, 12.
[48] Quoted in Cherniavsky, "Maud Allan, Part II," pp. 207–208, 222–223 and "Maud Allan, Part III," p. 125; Ralph E. Renaud, "House Goes Wild with Enthusiasm: Most Wonderful of Dancers Exhibits Purest Beauty in Dance Series," *San Francisco Chronicle*, April 6, 1910, in Maud Allan clippings files, MPDSF.
[49] Julie Wheelwright, *The Fatal Lover: Mata Hari and the Myth of Women in Espionage* (London: Collins and Brown, 1992), p. 23; Sam Waagenaar, *The Murder of Mata Hari* (London: Arthur Barker, 1964), p. 55.
[50] Kurro Kastañares, "'Tórtola' triunfante," *España Libre* (December 12, 1911), clipping in MAE, Barcelona, Fonds Tortola Valencia, L3.
[51] Quoted in Keith Money, *Anna Pavlova: Her Life and Art* (London: Collins, 1982), p. 109.

disturbing even for a moment." One Munich newspaper reported before her arrest there that

> Hardly anyone will have been offended by [her performance]. For despite her complete nudity – or perhaps because of it – one did not even for a moment have the sense that this was indecent. One merely delighted in the blossom-like charm and wonderful expressive capacity of this graceful body.... The sight of her had the effect of a refreshing bath after a hot and dusty summer's day.

After her arrest in that city on a charge of public indecency, another reviewer wrote that "the human mind was educated" by her performance "to see in nudity, in the end, something merely aesthetically self-evident" (see Figure 1.3). In a rather odd formulation, he concluded that "nudity was conquered by nakedness" (using the same word, *Nacktheit*, twice in one sentence).[52]

But while reference to the "ideal" art of classical Greece was central to the appeal of modern dance in its early years, again, this was not the only theme on which the modern dance pioneers drew. Isadora Duncan continued to focus her marketing message very explicitly on Greece; and most later modern dancers based some of their dances on Greek themes. But within a very short time a second set of archaeological and ethnographic references came to play an even more important role in modern dance: references to "Oriental" art. By 1906, Ruth St. Denis would build her tremendous success particularly in Germany almost exclusively on Indian themes, inspiring a raft of lesser imitators (see Figure 1.4). By 1907 Maud Allan was building a highly lucrative career primarily in England on her Salomé dance, that is on an ancient Hebrew (hence, at the time, "Oriental") theme. Mata Hari's career, mostly in France, was built on a mish-mash of Indian, Egyptian, and Javanese references. Elsa von Carlberg/Sent M'ahesa performed primarily "ancient Egyptian" dances (which she claimed to have derived from her study of Egyptian art in Berlin's museums)(see Figure 1.5). Gertrud Leistikow performed what she termed Greek, Moorish, Japanese, Indian, and Egyptian dances, as well as "Women's Lives and Loves in the Orient" and a dance of harem guards.[53] A special case was that of "Spanish" dance, as performed, for example, by Saharet/Clarissa

[52] R. B., "Mlle. Villany," *Münchner Zeitung* #268 (November 17, 1911); F. Kl., "Tanz-Matinee Mlle Adorée Via Villany," *Münchner Post* #269 (November 20, 1911).
[53] Jacobien de Boer, *Dans voluit, dat is leven: Gertrud Leistikow (1885–1948)* (Wezep: Uitgeverij de Kunst, 2014), pp. 40–53.

Figure 1.3 Adorée Villany portrays grief, 1913

Figure 1.4 Ruth St. Denis, Indian dancer, 1908

Campbell, Antonia Mercé/La Argentina, or Tórtola Valencia. Because of the Moorish past, Spain was considered by many Europeans to be an outpost of "the Orient."

The use of Oriental themes built in particular on a distinctly less "chaste" and respectable tradition in European culture, appealing in particular to the taste for the spectacular, the exotic, and the suggestive. The

Figure 1.5 Sent M'ahesa, ancient Egyptian, ca. 1910

Orient, as Europeans understood it, served that purpose well. Around 1900 Europeans commonly associated the Orient with opulence and luxury – probably an echo of the greater wealth and power of Middle Eastern and South and East Asian societies in the early modern era, and of the immense fortunes made by some Europeans in trade with Asia. The Orient was also associated with sensuality, sexual license, pleasure, and perversity; this was presumably an echo of earlier Christian prejudice against Islam, Hinduism, and other "Eastern" religions as immoral and lascivious. The Orient was further associated with mysticism and religion (a theme addressed in Chapter 4); but there was often a close connection in European minds between eroticism and the mystical and ecstatic, particularly in stereotypes of "Eastern" religion.

By the early nineteenth century, in any case, the "Orient" was no longer frightening or unsettling, having been domesticated by European economic dominance and the imperial experience. The conquest of a large portion of the Orient in the late nineteenth century – including Algeria and much of India already by the 1860s, and Egypt, Burma/Myanmar, and Vietnam in the 1880s – contributed to a widening awareness of the cultures of those regions in European culture.

In fact, in the last two decades of the nineteenth century a growing number of performers from various parts of "the Orient" showed up in the West, performing in variety theaters and also at the world's fairs. The Paris fair in 1900 in particular appears to have been an important moment for modern dance: It was, as one observer put it, "nothing but one huge agglomeration of dancing," including Turkish, Egyptian, Cambodian, Japanese, and other non-Western performers, among them Sada Yacco, who influenced many of the modern dance pioneers.[54] For the most part such performances were primarily of ethnographic interest. But Europeans soon developed their own dance acts that combined costumes and some of the movement and gestural vocabulary of "Oriental" dance with more familiar elements. A good example is Cléo de Mérode, a Paris opera ballerina, who made a hit at the World Exposition of 1900 with a "Cambodian" dance copied from a bona fide visiting Cambodian dance troupe; another is the dancer and courtesan Liane de Pougy, who appeared as a "Hindu priestess" in variety theaters in 1901.[55]

[54] Quoted in Shelton, *Ruth St. Denis*, 42.
[55] Conyers, "Courtesans in Dance History," p. 230; Brygida Ochaim, "Varieté-Tänzerinnen um 1900," in Brygida Ochaim and Claudia Balk, eds., *Varieté-Tänzerinnen um 1900* (Frankfurt: Stroemfeld/ Roter Stern, 1998), p. 89. A number of performers –e.g., Duncan, St. Denis, Allan – appear to have been influenced by the Japanese actress Sada Yacco, who performed in the United States and Europe in 1899/1900, including at Loïe Fuller's theater in Paris during the world's fair there in 1900. See Duncan, *My Life*, p. 94; Ruth St. Denis, *An Unfinished Life* (New York: Harper and Brothers, 1939),

By 1900, in other words, modified forms of Oriental dance idiom were only nominally "exotic"; in practice, they were very familiar. The (allegedly) Indian elements in St. Denis's dance, the "Egyptian" ones in Sent M'ahesa's, or the "Moorish" ones in Tórtola Valencia's were not innovations; they played on the well-established craze for all things Oriental in this period. Already by the early nineteenth century, Oriental themes had been important in European ballet, opera, vaudeville, and variety-theater entertainments; they became more so with the onset of the New Imperialism from the 1880s until World War I.

Modern dancers drew on "Oriental" themes in effect as a counterpoint to "classical" themes, establishing a productive, dynamic tension. They used Greek references to communicate the Apollonian – the rational, harmonious, balanced, and ideal. As Duncan put it, "In no country is the soul made so sensible of Beauty and of Wisdom as in Greece," and "The true dance" – Greek dance – "is an expression of serenity."[56] The Orient they used instead to communicate the Dionysian – wild, emotional, sensual, sexy beauty, not wisdom but passion, not measure but appetite.

A particularly good example is that of Adorée Villany. Villany did perform in "Greek" mode; but a number of her dances were themed around particular intense and often negative emotions – grief, despair, melancholy, rage, jealousy, fear. In these more emotionally expressive dances, she often cast herself as an "Oriental" – an ancient Egyptian, Assyrian, Persian, or, in her own version of the Salomé act (including a recitation from Oscar Wilde's play, in the French original), an ancient Hebrew. These figures permitted her, according to contemporary cultural stereotypes, to embody the passionate and the sensual. Reviewers reported, for example, that her performance of Wilde's piece effectively portrayed "raving eroticism" or "the character of a wild-cat, the perverse woman's combination of lust and cruelty"; that her portrayal of passionate, uncontrolled eroticism was a "significant histrionic achievement"; or that she portrayed "the inner feelings of the passionate Oriental woman."[57]

Villany was, then, able to use references to ancient cultures to combine in her performances, as one reviewer put it, "wonderfully soulful gracefulness" with "passionate expressive capacity" – the best of both

p. 81; Gabriele Brandstetter and Brygida Maria Ochaim, *Loïe Fuller: Tanz–Licht–Spiel–Art Nouveau* (Freiburg: Rombach, 1989), pp. 45–50; Shelley C. Berg, "Sada Yacco: The American Tour, 1899–1900," *DC* 16 (1993): 147–196 and "Sada Yacco in London and Paris, 1900: Le Rêve Réalisé," *DC* 18 (1995): 343–404.
[56] Duncan, *Art of the Dance*, pp. 66, 99.
[57] Villany, *Tanz-Reform*, pp. 266, 269, 271.

worlds.[58] She was both a wild, out-of-control, active, perverse Oriental and a poised, balanced, static Greek, both unadorned ideal nakedness and (semi-)costumed Oriental exotic. Villany sought – apparently with some success – to embody what Kenneth Clark, in his classic study of *The Nude* in Western art, saw as the two divergent versions of the nude: the Celestial Venus, symbolizing divine, universal, ideal beauty; and the Earthly Venus, symbolizing carnal, individual, and sensual beauty.[59]

Villany was anything but exceptional in this respect; other dancers in the period adopted precisely the same strategy. The low point was surely an advertisement for Maud Allan's early London performances that billed her as "a delicious embodiment of lust" and described her "satin smooth skin" with its "tracery of delicate veins that lace the ivory of her round bosom," her mouth "ripe as pomegranate fruit, and as passionate as the ardent curves of Venus herself," and "the desire that flames from eyes and bursts in hot flames from her scarlet mouth" – and yet also billed her as "the breathing impersonation of refined thought and dei-fied womanhood." Reviewers responded by praising not only her "utter absence of sensuous appeal" but also her "nudity expressive, vaunting and triumphant"; or her ability to exert a "fascination ... animal-like and carnal ... hot, barbaric, lawless" but the next moment be "pure as the hilltop air."[60] Mata Hari, too, was described as displaying both "wild voluptuous grace" and "true antique beauty"; in Tórtola Valencia's case it was "wild abandon" and "stateliness."[61] One of only two male dancers who inspired similar enthusiasm in this period, Vaslav Nijinsky, was not exempt; he too could be both "a Greek god" and "the embodi-ment of lust."[62]

Ruth St. Denis played on this dualism perhaps most furiously of all. In her signature dance she impersonated Radha, the consort of Krishna, awakened from motionless contemplation to enjoy each of the five senses in turn (hence the alternative title, "Dance of the Five Senses") in a devotional dance that ended in an almost openly orgasmic paroxysm of

[58] Ibid., p. 267.

[59] I am following here Lynda Nead, *The Female Nude: Art, Obscenity and Sexuality* (New York: Routledge, 1992), p. 19.

[60] Quoted in Cherniavsky, "Maud Allen, Part III," p. 122, 127–128.

[61] Wheelwright, *The Fatal Lover*, p. 16; Iris Garland, "Early Modern Dance in Spain: Tórtola Valencia, Dancer of the Historical Intuition," *DRJ* 29 (1997): 3.

[62] Jörg Schuster, ed., *Harry Graf Kessler: Das Tagebuch, Vierter Band 1906–1914* (Stuttgart: Cotta, 2004), pp. 574, 685, 689, 737. On the "Orientalization" of Nijinsky and the Ballets Russes, see Hanna Järvinen, "The Russian Dancing – Vaslav Nijinsky in Western Imagination," *Conference Proceedings, Congress on Research in Dance, October 26–28, 2001* (New York: New York University, 2001), 165–166.

sensuality, before returning to devotional immobility. As one early history of the dance reported it, during the dance she wreathed herself with flowers,

> drawing them luxuriously around her, crushing them against her shimmering flesh ... satin-petalled lotus, laid in turn to her cheek, her arm, her lips; while the smooth ripples of muscles under her glossy skin respond with shivers of sensitive sympathy to the caressing pressure of her foot upon the ground. Every nerve is sensitive and in turn conveys the message.[63]

Yet St. Denis set this suggestive and sensual dance in the context of a religious rite in a temple. As the Austrian poet, playwright, and critic Hugo von Hofmannsthal put it, St. Denis's dance "goes right up to the borders of lust, but is chaste"; Harry Graf (Count) Kessler admired St. Denis's ability to combine "animal beauty and mysticism," both "sexless divinity and merely-sexual woman," both the "sexlessness" of the American woman and the "almost animal sexual feeling of the Oriental woman" – as well as remarking, of course, that she appeared "as if climbed down from a Greek vase."[64]

At the turn of the century "animal" sensuality was widely associated in the European social elite not only with the Orient but also with the lower classes – so much so, for example, that some early scientists of sex just after 1900 assumed that sexual perversions were particularly common among Muslims, "primitive" peoples, and the working classes.[65] Not surprisingly, therefore, "Oriental" modern dance was often seen as appropriate for the variety-theater audience, while "Greek" modern dance was more tasteful. To some extent dancers conformed to this prejudice: The "Greek" Isadora Duncan, for example, very demonstratively refused to perform in variety theaters, while the "Orientals" Ruth St. Denis and Maud Allan performed primarily in them. Adorée Villany is, again, a particularly striking case: After being tried for indecency in Paris in early 1913 for performances in a rented theater, she moved to the Folies-Bergères, the leading variety theater in Paris, and danced on unmolested – still, as one wag put it, "almost nude" but "very chaste." As one German language newspaper in Paris commented, it appeared that the Philistines of Paris were happy to tolerate immorality in popular entertainment, as long as it didn't claim to be art for the elite.[66]

[63] Caffin and Caffin, *Dancing and Dancers of Today*, p. 85.
[64] Hofmannsthal, "Die unvergleichliche Tänzerin," p. 262; Schuster, *Harry Graf Kessler*, p. 192; Hugo von Hofmannsthal, *Hugo von Hofmannsthal/Harry Graf Kessler: Briefwechsel 1898–1929*, ed. Hilde Burger (Frankfurt: Insel, 1968), p. 130.
[65] Iwan Bloch, *Beiträge zur Aetiologie der Psychopathia sexualis* (Dresden: Dohrn, 1902), pp. 11–12, 26, 34, 58, 63.
[66] Duncan, *My Life*, p. 84; Villany, *Phryné*, pp. 22, 38, 65.

And yet, the interest in things Oriental was at least as common among the middle and upper classes as among the working classes, and no less in high art than in mass entertainment. Oriental themes were common in European painting, theater, literature, opera, architecture, and ballet from the early nineteenth century onward. St. Denis's "Radha" dance, for example, was performed to music from Leo Delibes's "Oriental" opera *Lakmé* of 1883.[67] And collecting Oriental art was among the fashionable pastimes of the wealthy throughout the century. A striking case example of the convergence of modern dance and upper-class interest in the "Orient" is Mata Hari's debut in Paris in 1905, which took place in the private Musée Guimet. Émile Guimet was an industrialist who had traveled to Asia and the Middle East in 1876, at the behest of the Ministry of Public Instruction, to study Eastern religions and buy up Asian and Islamic art.[68]

As St. Denis's use of opera music for her "Indian" dance suggests, an important strategy for rendering Oriental themes more respectable and hence appropriate for middle-class audiences was the use of European music as accompaniment not only for Greek dance but also for dances that played on Oriental themes. That reassured audiences that such performances were serious art, not frivolous (and morally questionable) entertainment. In some few cases where they wanted something more audibly "Oriental," these performers commissioned music or even hired bona fide "Oriental" musicians. Both Ruth St. Denis and Mata Hari, for example, hired the Indian musician Inayat Khan and his ensemble to play for some performances.[69] For the most part, however, the modern dance pioneers simply ransacked the canon of great European composers for music. In particular, they appear to have relied heavily on the romantics and on the more lush of contemporary composers. Both Greek and Oriental dances were performed to the music of Beethoven, Mendelssohn, Schumann, Schubert, Liszt, Chopin, Wagner, Strauss, Delibes, Bizet, Debussy, and Brahms; less common choices were Sibelius, Tchaikovsky, Grieg, Satie, Milhaud, and Mussorgsky. Classical and baroque composers (Gluck, Händel, Bach, Scarlatti, Couperin) came a distant second; and non-Western music was the exception.[70]

[67] See Kendall, *Where She Danced*, p. 29, 54.
[68] Anne Décoret-Ahiha, *Les danses exotiques en France, 1880–1940* (Paris: Centre Nationale de la Danse, 2004), p. 130; www.guimet.fr/fr/musee-guimet/histoire-du-musee-guimet.
[69] Julia Keay, *The Spy Who Never Was: The Life and Loves of Mata Hari* (London: Joseph, 1987), p. 41; Inayat Khan, *Biography of Pir-o-Murshid Inayat Khan* (London: East-West, 1979), p. 124; Waagenaar, *The Murder of Mata Hari*, p. 104.
[70] See, e.g., the lists in Claudia Jeschke and Gabi Vettermann, "Isadora Duncan, Berlin and Munich in 1906: Just an Ordinary Year in a Dancer's Career," *DC* 18 (1995): 228; Felix Cherniavsky, "Maud

Itisworthrememberingthattherewereplentyofoptionsatthetime–tango, folk tunes, jazz, music-hall tunes, or authentic African, Near Eastern, East Asian, or South Asian music. But the overwhelming impression given both by reviews and performers' own accounts is that dancing to the European romantics and moderns was effectively self-evident. Part of the appeal of early modern dance appears to have been that these performers sought to "embody" the romantic musical tradition – which we might see as a striking example of the translation of a nineteenth-century "high" cultural form for twentieth-century "mass" audiences.

The agenda of the modern dancers dovetailed neatly here with that of the variety theaters they performed in. Variety theater was widely under-stood to have originated as lower-class entertainment, and to be less than fully respectable. In London in particular there had been a major effort by morality campaigners to shut down variety theaters as dens of vice. In response to such campaigns and to the evolution of the more integrated, cross-class "mass" audience for commercial entertainments, metropoli-tan variety theaters were by the turn of the century deliberately moving away from their lower-class origins and catering to a "family" – that is, respectable – audience, including both men and women and members of the middle class, and to more established artists as well as the bohe-mian avant-garde. Variety theater in Germany and France passed through a similar development in the same years.[71] Modern dance performers were clearly part of this development: In place of the suggestive skirt-dance rou-tines of the 1880s and 1890s, in the new millennium they offered a dance form that was identifiably "artistic." Maud Allan's extraordinarily success-ful engagement at the Palace Theater in London, for example, was a delib-erate response to the middle-class moralists' success in forcing the theater to abandon nude "statue posing" acts; after her the theater recruited the great ballerina Anna Pavlova for the same purpose.[72]

Both the technique and the thematic content of early modern dance, then, were tailored to meet the needs of a culture market undergoing rapid

Allan, Part I: The Early Years, 1873–1903," *DC* 6 (1983): 29; Nils Jockel and Patricia Stöckemann, *"Flugkraft in goldene Ferne": Bühnentanz in Hamburg seit 1900* (Hamburg: Museum für Kunst und Gewerbe, 1989), p. 23; de Boer, *Dans voluit*, p. 73.

[71] See, e.g., Helen Thomas, *Dance, Modernity and Culture* (New York: Routledge, 1995), pp. 58–59; Ruth Freydank, ed., *Theater als Geschäft: Berlin und seine Privattheater um die Jahrhundertwende* (Berlin: Hentrich, 1995); Claudia Balk, "Vom Sinnenrausch zur Tanzmoderne," in Ochaim and Balk, eds., *Varieté-Tänzerinnen*, pp. 31–32; Peter Jelavich, *Berlin Cabaret* (Cambridge, MA: Harvard University Press, 1993), pp. 21–23; Karthas, *When Ballet Became French*, p. 23.

[72] Judith R. Walkowitz, *Nights Out: Life in Cosmopolitan London* (New Haven, CT: Yale University Press, 2012), p. 82.

transformation around the turn of the century. Where ballet had been coded as "high" culture for the middle and upper classes, and skirt-dancing or various forms of nude posing as "low" culture for the popular variety theater, modern dance was built to appeal to a "mass" audience in which such distinctions were increasingly irrelevant.

A special case of this kind of appeal was the participation of some of the modern dancers in a new kind of spectacular middle-brow entertainment that combined dance, music, and theater for giant "shows" with high production values and wide audience appeal, under the direction of well-known impresarios. In Europe, the most remarkable case was that of Max Reinhardt, who mounted major productions in – among other cities – Berlin, London, Paris, and Munich. Grete Wiesenthal took part in major Reinhardt productions in 1909, 1910, and 1912; Tórtola Valencia performed in multiple Reinhardt productions in London, Paris, and Munich between 1908 and 1912; Clotilde von Derp was in Reinhardt shows in Munich in 1909 and in London in 1911.[73] In the United States, the productions of David Belasco played a similar role; among others, Ruth St. Denis appeared in some of his productions early in her career.[74] Such programs achieved a broad middle- and lower-middle-class audience. They were an important vehicle to audience acceptance and stardom for many of the modern dance pioneers.

The modern dance pioneers were sufficiently successful in making their art "respectable" that a number of them also were able to vault themselves directly into the realm of "high" art, and to appear, for example, in some of Europe's leading opera houses. Isadora Duncan choreographed dance scenes for the 1904 production of *Tannhäuser* in Bayreuth. Ruth St. Denis performed a number of her dance compositions during intermissions of some productions at the Comic Opera in Berlin in 1906, and Mata Hari danced in opera productions in Milan and Monte Carlo.[75] A number of dance stars adopted, too, another marketing strategy that allowed them to gain access to respectable theater audiences: renting legitimate theaters for solo appearances for periods of a few days or a week, and inviting "select" audiences – often the local arts community – to "private" performances. Such performances were not always uncontroversial; Maud Allan, for

[73] Schmidt, *Tanzgeschichte*, p. 28; Garland, "Early Modern Dance in Spain," p. 7; Thomas Betz, "Der Russe und die Münchnerin," *Tanz-Journal* 1, no. 1 (2003): 37; Leonhard M. Fiedler, "'nicht Wort – aber mehr als Wort …': Zwischen Sprache und Tanz – Grete Wiesenthal und Hugo von Hofmannsthal," in Gabriele Brandstetter and Gunhild Oberzaucher-Schüller, eds., *Mundart der Wiener Moderne: Der Tanz der Grete Wiesenthal* (Munich: Kieser, 2009), p. 134.
[74] Kendall, *Where She Danced*, pp. 44, 46.
[75] Theresa Cameron, "The Tannhäuser Bacchanale in Bayreuth," in Gunhild Oberzaucher-Schüller, Alfred Oberzaucher, and Thomas Steiert, eds., *Ausdruckstanz* (Wilhelmshaven: Florian

example, was prevented from performing in theaters in Munich, Vienna, and Manchester, and Adorée Villany was tried in Munich and Paris, obliged to wear a bodysuit in Vienna, and prevented from performing in Prague.[76] But the modern dancers were clearly successful in eroding the fairly rigid boundaries of the "respectable."

1.4 Beyond Dance

In all these respects, then, the modern dance pioneers were able to achieve a synthesis that appealed to audiences across the whole spectrum of theater venues – from opera down to variety theater. Beyond that, however, many of them were able to move from theater into entirely new forms of performance, and new marketing channels, that were rapidly becoming characteristic of the twentieth-century mass consumer market.

The single most important of these was the cinema. The movies were largely understood to be primarily a lower-class entertainment form, a kind of poor-man's theater. In fact film played a role in variety theater, where the short clips typical of the early film industry fit into the program well. But the market for the movies was soon clearly a "mass" market, crossing class boundaries; and that made it an ideal vehicle for the modern dance stars. The association of dance with cinema can be traced back to the beginning of both, when Thomas Edison made a two-minute film of Ruth St. Denis in 1894, or when an early French film company filmed Cléo de Mérode in 1900. But virtually every major and many minor dance stars appeared in film, with participation rising particularly after 1912 – including Grete Wiesenthal, Friderica Derra de Moroda, Rita Sacchetto, Gertrude Leistikow, Stacia Napierkowska, Saharet, and Olga Desmond.[77] There was a clear thematic connection between early film and modern dance, in that filmmakers too often played on the same themes that modern dance did, and for the same reasons. Some early German titles included, for example, "Sculpture Works," "The Rape of the Sabines," and, of course, "The Dance of Salomé"; and in 1913 Grete Wiesenthal

Noetzel, 1986), pp. 280–283; Shelton, *Ruth St. Denis*, 75; Christine Lüders, *Apropos Mata Hari* (Frankfurt: Verlag Neue Kritik, 1997), pp. 24, 26.

[76] Cherniavsky, "Maud Allan, Part II," pp. 212, 215–216 and "Maud Allan, Part III," p. 134; Villany, *Tanz-Reform*, pp. 264, 344–345; "All London Is Agog over Maud Allan's Barefoot Dance," *San Francisco Examiner*, July 12, 1908, in Maud Allan clippings files, MPDSF.

[77] Karin Ehrich, "Im Sauseschritt," *Tanzdrama* 58 (2001): 8 (Gertrud Leistikow); Brygida Ochaim, "Die getanzten Bilder der Rita Sacchetto," *Tanzdrama* 14 (1991): 25 (Sacchetto); Kendall, *Where She Danced*, p. 39 (St. Denis); Leonhard M. Fiedler and Martin Lang, eds., *Grete Wiesenthal: Die*

starred in a film that offered "intimate scenes from the harem, which otherwise remain veiled from Europeans eyes."[78] But even aside from such connections, of course, the alliance between dance and film was an obvious one: Dance was the art of movement, and the moving pictures were the logical means for dance artists to extend their reach beyond the theater audience.

There was, then, an important "comarketing" arrangement between the movies and modern dance. Film offered the dance stars another income stream; using dancers helped to give the movies a certain aura of raciness, by presenting moving images of beautiful, partially clad young women. But it also helped to give cinema a certain cultural cachet as the only medium that could fully capture and preserve a new, exciting art form.

The modern dancer's use of still photography played on precisely this same ambiguity. Most of the early modern dance stars marketed still photographs of themselves. In some cases these were sold as cheap picture postcards; in others they were sold as relatively high-priced "artist's studies." In either case they were part of a new genre generated by the falling price of photographic reproduction, one that occupied a place midway between what we would today consider soft-core porn and a serious resource for artists, for whom the cost of paying models could be considerable. Isadora Duncan took a relatively restrained and high-brow approach, having her photo taken by the progressive and feminist Elvira photo atelier in Munich. Adorée Villany, in contrast, marketed large numbers of photographic images of herself in various states of undress, from fully wrapped up in black cloth (Chopin's "Funeral March") to completely naked (Mendelssohn's "Spring Song"). These images were sold at her performances, at ticket outlets, and in other outlets in cities where she was performing. The Italian-German dancer Rita Sacchetto, Gertrud Leistikow, and Maud Allan used a similar marketing strategy, though their photographs were less daring.[79]

Schönheit der Sprache des Körpers in Bewegung (Salzburg: Residenz, 1985), pp. 39–41, 155 (Wiesenthal); Brygida Ochaim, "Varieté-Tänzerinnen" and "Biographien," in Ochaim and Balk, *Varieté-Tänzerinnen*, pp. 76, 133, 135–138 (Sacchetto, Napierkowska, Olga Desmond, Anita Berber, Polaire, Saharet); de Boer, *Dans voluit*, p. 45; Cléo de Mérode, *Le ballet de ma vie* (Paris: Horay, 1985 [1955]), p. 227; Runge, *Olga Desmond*, p. 76.

78 Jeanpaul Georgen, "Der pikante Film: Ein vergessenes Genre der Kaiserzeit," in Thomas Elsaesser and Michael Wedel, eds., *Kino der Kaiserzeit: Zwischen Tradition und Moderne* (Munich: text + kritik, 2002), p. 47; Fiedler and Lane, *Grete Wiesenthal*, esp. pp. 39–40 (quotation).

79 See the illustrations in *Tanz-Reform*, passim; de Boer, *Dans voluit*, p. 53; Gisela Barche and Claudia Jeschke, "Bewegungsrausch und Formbestreben," in Gunhild Oberzaucher-Schüller, Alfred Oberzaucher, and Thomas Steiert, eds., *Ausdruckstanz* (Wilhelmshaven: Florian Noetzel, 1986), pp. 318–320, 325; Fiona Macintosh, "Dancing Maenads in Early 20th-Century Britain," in

Critics of the form regarded the sale of such images as clear evidence of merely prurient interest. In fact the development of the picture-postcard industry (and related forms of image marketing, such as collectible images sold in packs of cigarettes) had given rise to considerable debate about the artistic merits of mass-reproduced artworks. Some argued that even great artistic nudes or scenes from mythology in this form constituted pornography, not art; others argued that this was a way of bringing art to the masses. But whether the one or the other, for some performers such as Villany they were apparently a not-insignificant source of income. We can see this, too, as a form of comarketing arrangement with a rapidly expanding new cultural industry.

While modern dancers' participation in the film and photographic industry appealed primarily to a lower-class audience, their participation in the burgeoning fashion industry placed them squarely in the context of middle-class culture. The modern dancers played an important role in the establishment and propagation of a new conception of female beauty, and of the clothing built around it. One of the odder aspects of the modern dance revolution was the importance of skinniness to reviewers, audiences, and even performers. In early reviews, for example, Duncan was a "maiden" or "girl," or a "pale slender American girl."[80] Mata Hari was slender and "snake-like" or "serpentine."[81] Grete Wiesenthal was described by one critic as "a little maiden, skinny, even haggard."[82] Anna Pavlova was "thin as a skeleton and her ugliness is off-putting"; or, in a slightly more charitable key, "neither beautiful nor specially well-built, but thin."[83] Ruth St. Denis attributed part of her success in Germany in 1907 and 1908 to the "amazement of the German mind at seeing so slender a body." One critic called her "exquisitely slender."[84] Maud Allan was "slender" or "slender and lissome" or a "slender deer."[85] Other dancers were described as "youthfully slender," "sapling-slender," slender like a birch-tree, or an eel (see Figure 1.6)[86]

The Ancient Dancer in the Modern World: Responses to Greek and Roman Dance, ed. Fiona Macintosh (Oxford: Oxford University Press, 2010), p. 196; Patrizia Veroli, *Baccante e dive dell'aria: Donne danza e società in Italia, 1900–1945* (Castello: Edimond, 2001), p. 113.

[80] Quoted in Peter Kurth, *Isadora: A Sensational Life* (New York: Little, Brown, 2001), p. 100.

[81] Quoted in Wheelwright, *The Fatal Lover*, pp. 13, 15, 20; Enrique Gomez-Carillo, *El misterio de la vida y de la muerte de Mata Hari* (Madrid: Renaciemento, 1923), p. 41.

[82] Quoted in Schmidt, *Tanzgeschichte des 20*, p. 28.

[83] Oleg Kerensky, *Anna Pavlova* (London: Hamilton, 1973), p. 32.

[84] St. Denis, *An Unfinished Life*, pp. 92, 96; Flitch, *Modern Dancing and Dancers*, p. 192.

[85] Quoted in Cherniavsky, "Maud Allan, Part I," pp. 30–31, Cherniavsky, "Maud Allan, Part II," pp. 196, 203; Shaemas O'Sheel, "To Maud Allan," *Maud Allan and Her Art* (London: n.p., n.d.), p. 9.

[86] Quoted in Charles S. Mayer, "Ida Rubinstein: A Twentieth-Century Cleopatra," *DRJ* 20 (1988): 34; Kessler, in *Tagebuch*, vol. 4, p. 574; Karl Ettlinger, in a review of 1910, reprinted in *Tanzdrama* 14

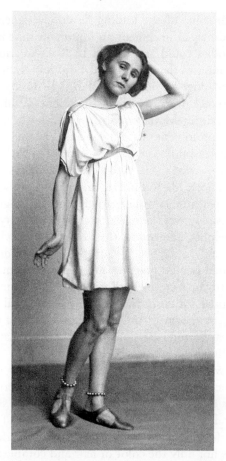

Figure 1.6 The slender young Grete Wiesenthal, 1908

The endless repetition of such terms seems a little obsessive and creepy to the modern mind; but to the attentive reader it reveals the almost subconscious impact and importance of the way in which the modern dancers were rethinking femaleness – from the foundation up, from a reimagining of female physicality.

We will return to this issue in Chapter 2; for now what is important is that the modern dancers formed another and very important comarketing

(1991): 32; Dahms and Schroedter, eds., *Der Tanz – Ein Leben*, p. 19; Frank-Manuel Peter, "Die 'neie Minchener Derpsichore': Clotilde von Derp – die früheste Vertreterin des Ausdruckstanzes?," in Frank-Manuel Peter and Rainer Stamm, eds., *Die Sacharoffs–zwei Tänzer aus dem Umkreis des Blauen Reiters* (Cologne: Wienand, 2002), p. 98; Program of the Kleines Theater, undated, in STAM, Pol. Dir. 3806/4.

arrangement with some of the leading fashion designers of the period, who built on and helped to cement an important shift in perceptions of what women's bodies could and should be like. America was the original home of the ideal of slenderness; but European fashion played a crucial role in articulating the new ideal of female beauty after 1900.[87] Of particular importance were the French designer Paul Poiret and the Spanish/Italian designer Mariano Fortuny; and both had close working relationships with prominent modern dancers. Isadora Duncan and Poiret were close friends, and threw extravagant parties in each other's honor in Paris once Duncan settled there. Poiret designed dresses for her, as well as for the Russian dancers Ida Rubinstein and Anna Pavlova. Duncan and a number of other performers wore Mariano Fortuny's signature garments, which not surprisingly were modeled on Greek statuary and "Oriental" designs. His "Delphos" dress and the "Knossos" shawl were particular favorites of the modern dancers.[88] Ruth St. Denis modeled the latter at a kind of combined fashion opening and dance performance at the great Wertheim department store in Berlin in 1907; and some version of the "Delphos" was used variously by Duncan, Wiesenthal, St. Denis, and others. In the 1920s the great American dancer Martha Graham, among others, would wear Fortuny creations. Rita Sacchetto played a similar role for Poiret, modeling his clothes in Paris.[89]

This alliance with fashion designers was a brilliant marketing move for modern dance because it helped to make modern dancers models not only for clothes, but also for an entire new style or mode of feminine physicality. As the designer Erté remarked of the very skinny Russian dancer Ida Rubinstein's influence on Paris fashions in 1913, fashion "dictates not only the color of hair and complexion but also the shape of the body."[90] Becoming co-arbiters of that new code of beauty

[87] See Ulrike Thoms, "Dünn und dick, schön und hässlich: Schönheitsideal und Körpersilhouette in der Werbung 1850–1950," in Peter Borscheid, ed., Bilderwelt des Alltags: Werbung in der Konsumgesellschaft des 19. und 20. Jahrhunderts, (Stuttgart: Steiner, 1995), pp. 242–281. See also Arthur Marwick, IT: A History of Human Beauty (London: Hambledon Press, 2004); Peter N. Stearns, Fat History: Bodies and Beauty in the Modern West (New York: New York University Press, 2002), especially 12–13 and 159–167.

[88] See Peter Wollen, "Fashion/Orientalism/The Body," New Formations 1 (1987): 10, 12; Kurth, Isadora, p. 245; Judith R. Walkowitz, "The 'Vision of Salomé: Cosmopolitanism and Erotic Dancing in Central London, 1908–1918," American Historical Review 108, no. 2 (2003): 342; Paul Poiret, My First Fifty Years, trans. Stephen Haden Guest (London: Gollancz, 1931), pp. 177, 201–206; Gabrielle Brandtstetter, "Tanzreform und Reformkleid: Zur Textilkunst von Mariano Fortuny," Tanzdrama 14 (1991): 4–7 and Tanz-Lektüren, p. 136; Paolo Peri, "La trama della sua vita," in Leonardo Fumi, ed., Fortuny nella belle époque (Milan: Electa, 1984), pp. 62–64.

[89] See Shelton, Ruth St. Denis, p. 82; Ochaim, "Die getanzten Bilder der Rita Sacchetto," p. 24; Peri, "La trama," 64; Brandtstetter, Tanz-Lektüren, pp. 129, 130–136, 138.

[90] De Cossart, Ida Rubinstein, p. 57; see also Järvinen, Dancing Genius, p. 71.

gave the modern dancers a claim to be vehicles of a profound kind of cultural authority.

It is, of course, hard work creating the kind of body that the modern dancers "demonstrated" – trim, strong, graceful, and well cared for. It should not be surprising, therefore, that some also launched themselves into the self-care industry – into cosmetics and the fitness and diet market. An extraordinary case is that of Olga Desmond (real name Sellin), a Polish-German performer who made a major splash in London in 1906 by taking part in a statue-posing act, and then in Berlin with a dance routine presented at "beauty evenings" in Berlin (see Figure 1.7). Desmond's performances were highly controversial, and in fact in early 1909 were even debated in the Prussian state parliament.[91] But that notoriety was outstanding advertising. Over the following few years, Desmond sold photographs and postcards of herself performing her nude dances; made a short film; opened a dance school and attempted to open an Academy of Beauty and Physical Culture; performed in variety theaters around Germany and in St. Petersburg and Vienna; and marketed a massage apparatus, a soap, a beauty cream, a breast-enhancement cream, a cream to prevent freckles, and a book of beauty tips. During and after World War I she wrote an autobiography, published a system of dance notation, got into the movies, published a how-to manual on healthy living and fitness titled "The Secrets of Beauty," and marketed a fitness apparatus involving large rubber bands attached to the feet and waist (the "Auto-Gymnast").[92]

Desmond was an extreme case of multichannel marketing, but by no means unique. Tórtola Valencia, for example, was for a time the advertising face for a number of products of the French cosmetics company Myurgia (particularly the perfume "Maja," but also bath salts and other self-care products). Her image was also used by the Louis Roederer champagne company; a British hat manufacturer (see Figure 1.8); "Mr. Seymour Churchill, the Greatest Authority on Feminine Beauty in the World" and merchant of beauty tips; and, perhaps ironically, a corset manufacturer. She also choreographed for other dancers; made and sold oil paintings of herself; sold photographs and postcards; and starred in films (*A Woman's Heart* in 1913, *The Struggle for Life* in 1914).[93]

[91] *Stenographische Berichte über die Verhandlungen des preussischen Hauses der Abgeordneten*, 13. session, January 13, 1909, columns 937–968.

[92] Runge, *Olga Desmond*, pp. 23–76.

[93] María Pilar Queralt, *Tórtola Valencia* (Barcelona: Lumen, 2005), pp. 47–48; Carlos Murias Vila, "La magicienne aux yeux d'abîme," *Danser* 103 (1992): 27; Michelle Clayton, "Touring History: Tórtola Valencia between Europe and the Americas," *DRJ* 44 (2012), pp. 34–45; advertisements in *The Sketch* (April 8, 1908) and *The Daily Mirror* (April 1, 1908), unidentified advertisement for Sandow's Corset (1911?), clippings in MAE, Fonds Tortola Valencia, L2.

Figure 1.7 Olga Desmond's "Beauty Evening," 1909

A LEWIS HAT

BEAUTIFUL

SPRING

MODELS.

MISS TORTOLA VALENCIA

Photo. Adart, Ltd.

MAISON LEWIS
210, REGENT STREET. W.
AND AT
PARIS, MONTE CARLO, BIARRITZ, AND OSTEND.

Figure 1.8 Tórtola Valencia in an advertisement for fashionable hats, ca. 1910

Clotilde von Derp modeled for fashion designers, photographers in Munich and Paris, the school where she studied dance, and a German designer of dance clothes; her photograph was used in advertising for the dietary supplement Lebertran in Japan and for the Fiat automobile company in Europe.[94] Anna Pavlova endorsed a cold cream and a mouthwash, and a brand of silk stockings named after her.[95]

In all these ways, the modern dancers were tapping into the new mass market for consumer goods, and into the new mass media. A very important part of the mass-market appeal of modern dance, however, was its association as well with the social elite – the aristocracy and the business and financial elite. And here too, modern dance achieved a remarkable degree of success. Among the European and American social elite, the modern dancers were in demand as performers at private salons and parties, as embodiments and proofs of the sophistication and "advanced" ideas of the wealthy, and in some cases as sexual partners. Among their other accomplishments, in short, the modern dancers also established themselves as a luxury commodity.

This connection was established very early. An early handwritten biographical sketch of Isadora Duncan reported that even in her early teens she had taught dance to "all the wealthiest children of San Francisco" at the home of the "wealthiest woman" in the city. She danced at private parties for some of the cream of New York society – including Astors, Vanderbilts, and Palmers – before leaving for Europe; before her departure, her name appeared most often in newspaper accounts of private parties at the summer homes of the New York plutocracy.[96] In London she gave similar performances at prominent citizens' houses. Various French aristocrats helped to launch her in Paris, including the novelist, poet, and leading salon host the Countess de Noailles; the Countess de Greffulhe; and the influential music patron Winaretta Singer, Princess (by marriage) de Polignac and heir to the Singer sewing-machine fortune. At their parties, she met luminaries such as the composer Gustave Fauré, the lawyer and future president of the French Republic Georges Clemenceau, and the sculptor Auguste Rodin. When she opened a school of dance in Berlin in 1906, she appealed to wealthy patrons through a benefit concert

---

[94] Thomas Betz, "Die Duncan dichtet, die Sacchetto malt," *Tanz-Journal* 1, no. 5 (2003): 30; Betz, "Der Russe und die Münchnerin," p. 36; DTAK, Inventory no. 56, Clotilde und Alexander Sacharoff, II.2.18.11.

[95] Jennifer Fisher, "The Swan Brand: Reframing the Legacy of Anna Pavlova," *DRJ* 44 (2012): 54.

[96] Linda J. Tomko, *Dancing Class: Gender, Ethnicity, and Social Divides in American Dance, 1890–1920* (Bloomington: Indiana University Press, 1999), pp. 58–70.

selling tickets to members of the Imperial Court, the high nobility, and residents of Berlin's central high-rent Tiergarten district (home to various villas and embassies) for up to 1,000 Marks, which was about a year's salary for an industrial worker. One theater journal reported that "in fact a number of ladies from these circles have laid a thousand Mark note on the altar of Greek dance art."[97] When Duncan's sister Elizabeth reopened the school in Darmstadt in 1911, under the patronage of the Grand Duke of Hessen, there was one gift of 40,000 Marks and eight of more than 5,000, and a consortium of three wealthy donors guaranteed a loan of 200,000. In the meantime, plans launched by the Duchess of Manchester to help Isadora start a school in Britain, or perhaps in Scarsdale, New York, fell through. Short of money for her many projects, Duncan repeatedly remarked that "I must find a millionaire!" The millionaire duly appeared in the form of Paris Singer, brother of the Princess de Polignac and co-heir to the Singer sewing machine fortune, who saw her perform in 1909 and was immediately smitten.[98] In short, Duncan's multifarious and varied – and carefully cultivated – connections with the American, European, and ex-patriate American social elite played a critical role in her entire early career.

The patronage of the social elite was almost equally important for Ruth St. Denis. The architect and art patron Stanford White played a role in St. Denis's career in New York. So too did a number of prominent society matrons (including a sister and a daughter of J. Pierpont Morgan), who at one early juncture even rented a theater for her; as she recalled in her memoirs the "names of the patronesses meant attention in the newspapers. I was interviewed tirelessly." The Duchess of Manchester was an important early advisor and patron to St. Denis in London, as was the extraordinarily wealthy Duchess of Thurn und Taxis in Vienna. The poet, critic, and wealthy aristocrat Hugo von Hofmannsthal figured prominently in St. Denis's early European success, as did Harry Graf (count) Kessler, a patrician art critic, museum director, and son of a banker from Hamburg. In Berlin she started her performances with a special appearance for

---

[97] Kurth, *Isadora*, p. 76; "Isadora Duncans Freitanz-Schule," *Das Theater* 1906, clipping in DTAK, Inventory no. 69, Duncan-Archiv, 2.9.2; Blair, *Isadora*, pp. 40–41.

[98] DTAK Inventory no. 69, Duncan-Archiv, 1.2 (this document appears to have been written by Duncan's lover Gordon Craig, in German handwriting, but is identified as having been written by Duncan); Duncan, *My Life*, p. 80; "Verein zur Förderung und Erhaltung der Elizabeth Duncan-Schule, Darmstadt, e.V.," in DTAK Inventory no. 69, Duncan-Archiv, II.1.1.6; Kay Bardsley, "Isadora Duncan's First School," Dance Research College, *Dance Research Annual* 10 (1979): 219–249; Sylvia Kahan, *Music's Modern Muse: A Life of Winaretta Singer, Princesse de Polignac* (Rochester, NY: University of Rochester Press, 2003), pp. 117, 157; Duncan, *My Life*, pp. 215, 229.

the press and "everyone of importance in Berlin ... and the papers the next morning established my success." She adopted the same strategy in London, where a "committee" of prominent friends and fans arranged a special performance for the artistic and social elite, including princes, dukes, duchesses, and a maharajah as well as painters, sculptors, and playwrights. The "evening had the desired effect. The audience increased ... everyone but the King and Queen came ... and picture postcards of my dances began to appear on the streets."[99]

None of this was untypical. Early on in her dance career Maud Allan was supported by a circle of prominent American expatriates living in Brussels, including the American ambassador and his wife. Later, she gave a private performance for the King of England and Emperor of Germany at the elite spa Marienbad in 1907, met the Queen after performing at a party given by the Earl and Countess of Dudley, and formed a close social and personal connection with Margot Asquith, wife of the Prime Minister of England.[100] She earned the very substantial sum of £200 per night performing at private parties of the social and financial elite. Less happily, she reported that her patrons in Brussels had to protect her from the amorous advances of the King of Belgium, and that she had to speak sharply to the son of the Emperor of Germany before he would leave her alone during a journey by ship to India; but she recorded with evident pride her command performances for kings and emperors, counts and rajahs.[101] Margarethe Zelle/Mata Hari performed in a number of Paris salons, including those of the American heiress Natalie Clifford Barney and the extremely wealthy doctor, entrepreneur, and patron of the arts and sciences Henri de Rothschild; she went on to be the mistress of a series of wealthy men – bankers, aristocrats, and military officers.[102] Regina Woody/Nila Devi performed for wealthy patrons in both London and Paris, as well as in variety theater.[103] Allan and St. Denis gave private performances for royalty in Britain and Germany, as did Friderica Derra de Moroda in Russia, and both Mata Hari and Cléo de Mérode in Berlin; Tórtola Valencia may have had a relationship with Duke Franz Josef of Bavaria; Isadora Duncan danced for the Prince of Wales (shortly to become King of England); long

[99] St. Denis, *An Unfinished Life*, pp. 68, 90, 117; Tomko, *Dancing Class*, pp. 47–58.

[100] Allan, *My Life*, pp. 82, 97; Philip Hoare, *Wilde's Last Stand* (London: Duckworth, 1997), pp. 80–81.

[101] Cherniavsky, "Maud Allan, Part II," p. 140; Maud Allan, "How I Startled the World," *San Francisco Call and Post*, December 8 and 16, 1921, in Maud Allan clippings files, MPDSF.

[102] Waagenaar, *The Murder of Mata Hari*, pp. 45–46 and passim.

[103] Regina Woody, *Dancing for Joy* (New York: Dutton, 1959), pp. 154–155, 168, 198.

sections of Loïe Fuller's autobiography might have been titled "European Royalty I Have Known."[104]

In some cases, relationships like these ended in marriages into the European aristocracy. Olga Sellin/Desmond was briefly married to a Hungarian aristocrat; Rita Sacchetto married a Polish count; Liane de Pougy married a Rumanian prince.[105] But the tone of such relationships and of the milieu in which they thrived is perhaps better revealed by a letter home to his parents penned by Harry Graf Kessler in 1900, reporting that a friend "has a very cute and funny lover, an Australian who dances here in the Folies-Bergères. She's named Miss Saharet and has the most charming way of dancing on a dinner table or on a piano."[106] Saharet's lover was Alfred Heymel, a wealthy wastrel and minor poet who was a fixture in Munich's bohemian arts community.[107] Mata Hari was partially financially dependent on a series of wealthy (and mostly married) lovers. And a number of dancers on the margins of the early stages of the modern dance revolution had made their way partly or primarily as courtesans – Liane de Pougy, Cleo de Merode, or "La Belle Otero" (Caroline Otero).[108]

The appeal of modern dance was, however, by no means limited to men; modern dancers' connections with women of the upper class appear to have been at least as important. Wealthy women, not men, more often hired the modern dancers to perform at parties. "Society" women played a crucial role in launching modern dance by hiring Duncan and St. Denis to perform at parties in New York or at their summer homes in Rhode Island. Prominent American expatriate women played a crucial role as early patrons of the American dancers who launched the modern dance revolution in Europe. They included Winaretta Singer; another American heiress in Paris, Natalie Barney; in Britain the Duchess of Manchester, who was of Cuban parentage but raised in New Orleans; Madame Rienzini, an early patron of Regina Woody (and married to an Italian

[104] Cherniavsky, "Maud Allan, Part II," pp. 219–223; St. Denis, *An Unfinished Life*, pp. 77–78; Duncan, *My Life*, p. 80; Dahms and Schroedter, eds., *Der Tanz*, p. 16; Queralt, *Tórtola*, p. 31; Kurth, *Isadora*, p. 64; Loïe Fuller, *Fifteen Years of a Dancer's Life* (Boston: Small, Maynard, 1913), passim and particularly later chapters; Ochaim, "Varieté-Tänzerinnen um 1900," in Balk and Ochaim, eds., *Varieté-Tänzerinnen um 1900*, pp. 91, 131–132.

[105] Brygida Ochaim, "Die Barfusstänzerin Olga Desmond," *Tanzdrama* 39 (1997): 19–21; Brygida Ochaim, "Die getanzten Bilder der Rita Sacchetto," *Tanzdrama* 14 (1991): 22–25; Ochaim, "Varieté-Tänzerinnen um 1900," in Balk and Ochaim, eds., *Varieté-Tänzerinnen um 1900*, p. 90.

[106] See Hugo von Hofmannsthal, *Hugo von Hofmannsthal, Briefwechsel mit Alfred Walter Heymel*, ed. Werner Vole (Freiburg: Rombach, 1998), p. 10, n. 3.

[107] On Heymel see Hermann Wilhelm, *Die Münchener Bohème* (Munich: Buchendorfer, 1993), pp. 130–131.

[108] La Belle Otero/Caroline Otero, *My Story* (London: Philpot, 1927); de Mérode, *la Ballet de ma vie*.

banker in London); and Maud Allan's patron in Brussels, the American ambassador's wife Natalie Townsend.[109]

In part, this relationship can be explained by the role of aristocratic women as patrons of salons – more or less regular but informal social gatherings for influential figures from the arts, literature, politics, and sometimes finance. The thematic content of modern dance "worked" in this setting as well: "Oriental" themes appealed to the craze for Buddhism, New Thought, Theosophy, and "Eastern" décor in this social milieu around the turn of the twentieth century, while "Greek" models were familiar to them as well as part of European high culture.[110] Modern dance was, then, an appropriate adornment for private parties – like a string quartet, or a poetry reading.

In some cases these relationships with elite women may have been sexual. Here too, the thematics worked; for in addition to being the cradle of Western Civilization, ancient Greece was also widely understood to be the original home of homosexuality – including "Sapphic" love, particularly after the rediscovery of much of Sappho's poetry in the early 1890s.[111] In fact it appears that the modern dance revolution played a not insignificant role in the establishment of the modern subculture of lesbianism. Loïe Fuller was more or less openly homosexual, and surrounded herself with adoring young female dancers – a role Duncan claimed, in her autobiography, to have found off-putting and incomprehensible.[112] But Duncan may have played deliberately on her sensual appeal to women, including the Princess de Polignac and Natalie Barney. In later years she appears at least to have penned rather explicit amorous poetry to women friends ("My kisses like a swarm of bees/Would find their way/Between thy knees").[113] It may not be coincidental, too, that one of the more influential series of early photographs of Duncan was produced by the photo-atelier Elvira, which was operated by a radical feminist couple, Anita Augspurg and Sophia Goudstikker.[114] Tórtola Valencia appears to

---

[109] Tomko, *Dancing Class*, pp. 41–64; Shelton, *Ruth St. Denis*, p. 71; Woody, *Dancing*, pp. 154–157; Allan, *My Life*, p. 82; on the Duchess of Manchester see Ruth Brandon, *The Dollar Princesses: Sagas of Upward Nobility, 1870–1914* (New York: Alfred A. Knopf, 1980), pp. 30–31.

[110] On Delsartean "salon performers" and upper-class Orientalism, see Thomas, *Dance*, pp. 63, 78–79.

[111] Samuel N. Dorf, "Dancing Greek Antiquity in Private and Public: Isadora Duncan's Early Patronage in Paris," *DRJ* 44 (2012): 8, 14.

[112] Duncan, *My Life*, p. 93.

[113] Susan Manning, "Isadora Duncan, Martha Graham und die lesbische Rezeption," *Tanzdrama* 44/45 (1999), pp. 19–21 (quotation); Suzanne Rodriguez, *Wild Heart* (New York: HarperCollins, 2002), p. 113; Dorf, "Dancing Greek Antiquity," pp. 7–11.

[114] Wilhelm, *Münchener Bohème*, pp. 116–121; on early modern dance and photography, see Sabine Huschka, "Bildgebungen tanzender Körper: Choreographierte Blickfänge 1880 bis 1920," *Fotogeschichte* 101 (2006): 41–50.

have had long-term relationships with at least two adopted "daughters." The name of one was sometimes given as Rosita Corma, and sometimes as Rosa Carne Centellas – which might be roughly translated as Sparkly Pink Meat. Valencia was buried with her. Some newspapers made carefully veiled references to her preferences – for example referring to her as a "much-discussed Sappho" or hinting at a lover's quarrel between Valencia and her English companion "Miss Nella" in a railway-car sleeping compartment.[115] Maud Allan was eventually – during World War I – at the center of a libel trial involving allegations of her homosexual relationship with Margot Asquith, or perhaps a romantic triangle involving both her and her husband; and she does appear to have had intimate relationships with other women later.[116]

Whether with men or with women, over time such relationships were of declining importance, as modern dance established itself as a widely accepted performance genre with a reliable commercial market. Performances at private parties of the social elite continued to be an important source of revenue; but by 1910 the market was sufficiently robust that this was one of many income streams, and probably important primarily because it helped to keep the dancers in the media. This too was a marketing strategy – a whiff of polymorphic sexual adventurism, the cachet of "advanced" and/or decadent ideas and aristocratic admirers, a note of newsworthy scandal. A decade before marrying her Rumanian prince in 1910, for example, Liane de Pougy published in novel form a thinly veiled blow-by-blow account of her torrid affair with Natalie Barney.[117] This was a way of gaining media attention and marketing pull – one of those forms of "eccentricity" that prominent women cultivated to sustain media interest.[118]

1.5 Modernity, America, Business

Collectively, then, the early modern dance stars adopted an extraordinarily effective multichannel marketing strategy, exquisitely suited

[115] Iris Garland, *Tortola Valencia: Modernism and Exoticism in Early Twentieth Century Dance*, ed. Mary Fox (Vancouver: Five/Cinq Limited, 2013), p. 58; "Del Cartel de Anoche," *El Mundo* (Madrid), December 16, 1912 and Periquin, "Tórtola Valencia," *El Liberal* (Barcelona), January 20, 1912, "Tórtola Valencia – Riña en el treno," *El Noticiero Universal* (February 17, 1912), clippings in MAE, Fonds Tortola Valencia, L3.

[116] Hoare, *Wilde's Last Stand*, p. 85.

[117] Rodriguez, *Wild Heart*, p. 91.

[118] See, e.g., Mary Louise Roberts, "Rethinking Female Celebrity: The Eccentric Star of Nineteenth-Century France," in Edward Berenson and Eva Giloi, eds., *Constructing Charisma* (New York: Berghahn, 2010), pp. 103–116.

to the emerging mass cultural market – for art, for entertainment, for fashion, for soft-core pornography, and ultimately also for a "modern" image of female selfhood. None of this was entirely new. Nineteenth-century ballet dancers too were required to be slender, ethereal creatures; as Deborah Jowitt pointed out, they too were "supple" and snakelike; they too embodied both "female sensuality and female chastity." And a sizable proportion of the ballet repertoire, too, had been built around "Oriental" themes.[119] Nor was the cult of the female dancer as celebrity a novelty: The modern dancers of the turn of the century were clearly running down paths first laid down the great ballerinas of the romantic ballet, such as Carlotta Grisi, Marie Taglioni, or Fanny Elssler, who were also sometimes received with wild enthusiasm, as early as the 1830s and 1840s.[120] Even the classical references were not entirely new: the poet and critic Théophile Gautier, for example, had described Taglioni as having the same "rounded and polished forms" as a "divine marble [statue] from the times of Pericles," and Fanny Elssler as resembling "figures from Herculaneum or Pompei" – already half a century before Isadora Duncan appeared.[121]

Modern dance, then, "modernized" an existing role, and a degree of familiarity may have contributed to its success. Nevertheless, something new was happening in modern dance after 1900. Most obviously, in many cases the modern dancers were combining some of these older elements with a very astute mobilization of the potentials of new technologies and new markets – photography, moving pictures, fashion and beauty, the new "respectable" variety theater, the burgeoning advertising industry. This broadened strategy could be extremely lucrative. During one particularly prosperous period in 1909 and 1910, Olga Desmond earned between 6,000 and 15,000 German Marks monthly – six to fifteen times an industrial worker's annual wages. During the same period, Maud Allan earned £250 per week for her variety-theater performances alone. Four years later the director of the theater she performed at reported that she had amassed at least £25,000 – not the wealth of the aristocracy or industrial barons, but a comfortable fortune.[122]

[119] Deborah Jowitt, *Time and the Dancing Image* (New York: Morrow, 1988), pp. 60–61 and passim.
[120] See Conyers, "Courtesans"; Jennifer Homans, *Apollo's Angels: A History of Ballet* (New York: Random House, 2010).
[121] Quoted in Jean-Pierre Pastori, *A corps perdu: La dance nue au XXe siècle* (Lausanne: Favre, 1983), p. 25; Théophile Gautier, "Fanny Elssler in 'La Tempête,'" in Roger Copeland and Marshall Cohen, eds., *What Is Dance?: Readings in Theory and Criticism* (Oxford: Oxford University Press, 1983), pp. 431, 433.
[122] Runge, *Olga Desmond*, p. 58; Cherniavsky, "Maud Allan, Part II," p. 139.

As a marketing phenomenon, then, modern dance was an extraordinary achievement, and a remarkably well-timed one. Tapping into some of the most profound social, cultural, and technological transformations of their time, the pioneers of modern dance were able to build an audience that crossed class lines. Founding their success on what was originally a working-class form, they were nevertheless able to speak the language of middle-class cultural respectability, while also mobilizing the social and cultural cachet (and money) of the European social elite. In short, the modern dance pioneers translated their grasp of *Zeitgeist* into a remarkable marketing coup.

It is not coincidental that American performers played a central role in pioneering this marketing strategy in Europe, nor that American patrons played an important role in first establishing modern dance in Europe. Their role is just one instance of a broader pattern, paralleled in the cinema, pulp fiction, fashion, managerial and production techniques, and advertising. The social and cultural changes to which these forms responded took hold earliest and most thoroughly in the United States, the most technologically advanced and structurally fluid society of the period. Culture was also much more exclusively subject to market pressures in the United States than in most of Europe – where the aristocracy and the state, including official institutions (like art academies, opera houses, and ballet companies) played a much more important role in shaping the arts. The techniques of marketing to a modern mass consumer audience were pioneered in the United States.

In this sense, it is not really paradoxical that one reviewer for a Madrid newspaper observed in 1919 that he admired Tórtola Valencia's "North American-style journalistic talent, more than everything else, her stupendous intuition for exorbitant publicity and scandal," and reflected that if she retired from the stage he "would like to join her as partners in a formidable ... publicity business."[123] And Maud Allan clearly reveled in her role as pragmatic American in a defense of her art published at the height of her success in 1910:

> Unpleasant comment has been made on the size of my audiences, leading to the charge that I dance for money. I do. I have found, unromantic as it may seem, that neither art nor artists can exist without it.[124]

David Belasco – a successful arts entrepreneur – remarked of Ruth St. Denis that "the energy and ambition of this girl had no limit.... I never

---

[123] Quoted in Garland, "Early Modern Dance," p. 17.
[124] Unidentified clipping of April 1910, "Maud Allan Makes Answer to Critics," in Maud Allan clippings files, MPDSF.

saw a girl with such a keen desire to succeed." St. Denis was ambivalent about money, and not particularly good at keeping it; she told her students they "should *think* of dance as Art although you may have to *do* it as business."[125] One could see the modern dance revolution, then, as one of many successful trans-Atlantic commercial and cultural ventures. It combined American business know-how with the cachet of European culture – for Europe was still regarded, probably even by most Americans, as the heartland of tradition, refinement, and sophistication.

This synthesis worked on two further and extremely important levels, however. First, modern dancers understood themselves not to be the heirs of European artistic tradition, but as rebels against it. At the same time, they sought to present themselves as legitimate and respectable artists, not as businesspeople and entertainers. An important part of their marketing strategy, therefore, was to align themselves not with European artistic tradition, but with the European artistic avant-garde. This they did with extraordinary success. Second, the United States was at the turn of the century not only the great home of capitalist enterprise but also the greatest center of feminist activism in the world, and a society in which gender roles were being reconfigured more radically and rapidly than anywhere else – specifically in the direction of autonomy and independent agency for women. Modern dance brought these two elements together in a powerful and, for the time, radical synthesis. That connection is the subject of Chapter 2.

[125] David Belasco, *The Theatre through Its Stage Door* (New York: Harper and Brothers, 1919), p. 7; Jane Sherman, *Soaring: The Diary and Letters of a Denishawn Dancer in the Far East, 1925–1926* (Middletown, CT: Wesleyan University Press, 1976), p. 23.

CHAPTER 2

Art, Women, Liberation

2.1 Soul Movement: Dance and Self-Expression

The debate between Antonietta dell'Era and Adorée Villany in the *Berliner Tageblatt* in 1911 exactly recapitulated a broader debate between the champions of European aesthetic traditions and the modernist spokesmen of a radical revision of aesthetic standards. A central tenet of the theory of modernism in the arts was that each individual has a distinctive, idiosyncratic creative urge, an individual aesthetic sense; and to create authentic, meaningful art they had to be guided by that individual drive. In this, modern dance like all the modernist aesthetic idioms was self-consciously a revolt against academic art – that is, against the techniques, themes, practices, theories, and marketing strategies that were championed by the royal or national art academies. The modernists around 1900 criticized academic art for being formulaic, stifled by conventions and rules, decorative but spiritually barren – pure mechanical technique, taught in a manner that crushed individual creativity. Art historians often refer to modernism around the turn of the twentieth century as "neo-Romanticism," for this reason. One branch of modernism that had particularly close ties to modern dance was called "Expressionism"; but the aim of modernism generally was to express the artist's authentic, unique individuality and feeling. Modernists or Expressionists criticized the system of official exhibitions, public commissions of artworks for museums or public buildings, and government subsidies for establishing a system of privilege that enforced conventional, conservative, purely academic styles.

In the field of dance this critique was leveled at the ballet, which was cultivated in part in royal ballet companies and was regarded by modernist critics as rigidly rule-bound, mechanical, and soulless. This characterization of the ballet appeared again and again in the words and publications of performers, reviewers, and theorists of modern dance. Isadora Duncan thought ballet was "a false and preposterous art, in fact, outside the pale of all art ... an enemy to Nature and to Art."[1] An article in the *London Times* in July 1910 lamented the fact that ballet, "when it is not a mere display of clothes or the lack of them, is apt to be simple acrobatics."[2] Adorée Villany poked fun at the "stereotypical tricks" and "fancy footwork" of ballet; she argued that it "represses any subjective understanding of the dancer" and all intellectual content in favor of "monotonous, marionette-like" movement; it was "conventional," "artful," "routinized," and empty.[3] One Paris newspaper, reporting on Villany's trial for indecency there, argued in 1913 that ballet as it was taught in the academies was "an unexpressive art," or better yet not an art at all but a particularly "demanding trade" that fetishized technical mastery and had "lost track of the aim of ... art, which is to communicate feelings and ideas."[4] The *San Francisco Chronicle*, in a rave review of Maud Allan in 1910, called ballet "a piece of soulless technique" that expressed "few or none of our thoughts." And the German dance critic and historian Ernst Schur lamented in the same year that the ballet was "ugly, even ridiculous and repulsive" because it stifled "every natural movement," it was stiff, routinized, and "without soul."[5]

This critique of ballet as mere technique was part of a broader rhetorical assault on the mechanization and soul-less-ness of industrial civilization as a whole – what the dance historian Laure Guilbert has called "romantic anticapitalism," or perhaps better anti-industrialism.[6] This was another theme central to aesthetic modernism; and sometimes it peeked through in the writing of dancers and dance critics, as well. Ruth St. Denis, for example, mused that perhaps the dance renaissance came when it did "as a counterbalance to the growing concern with a mechanized world."[7] One visitor to Isadora Duncan's dance school in Berlin in 1906 reported standing, after two "dreamlike" hours in the school, "in the midst of the bustle of the street, in the midst of hurrying, sweating, burdened and striving humanity" and wondering "what's the big idea? What is this piece of ancient Greece to modern machine-people in an age of the shrillest disharmonies" – but then concluding "that even without any particular practical use, it is very charming if ... here and there a few [such] protected

---

[1] Duncan, *My Life*, pp. 164, 166.

[2] "Dancing," *London Times*, July 20, 1910.

[3] Villany, "Muss Man nackt tanzen – Eine Antwort," *Berliner Tageblatt* no. 628, December 10, 1911.

[4] Villany, *Phryné moderne devant l'Areopage*, pp. 58, 7–8.

[5] Ralph E. Renaud, "Maud Allan's Performances Breathe Beauty in Motion," *San Francisco Chronicle*, March 27, 1910, in Maud Allan clippings files, MPDSF; Ernst Schur, *Der moderne Tanz* (Munich: Gustav Lammers, 1910), p. 23.

[6] Laure Guilbert, *Danser avec le IIIe Reich* (Paris: Editions Complexe, 2000), p. 24.

[7] St. Denis, *An Unfinished Life*, p. 91.

gardens, with beautiful blossoms" were preserved.[8] And Arthur Moeller-Bruck, in a 1902 study of variety-theater dance, saw its "passionate and unthinking wild high spirits" as a welcome respite from the "suffocating heat of machinery-rooms of our lives" in industrial society.[9]

In place of what they portrayed as the mechanical quality of the techniques and conventions of the ballet, modern dance advocates offered a tightly inter-woven collection of themes and key terms, a language or vocabulary of concepts. These included, particularly, feeling, truth (or honesty), nature, life, soul, and joy. The meanings of these terms were rarely spelled out explicitly; instead, they were used in a highly evocative manner. They were repeated over and over again, so that they constituted clichés or stereotypes; and they were almost always used in combination, with at least two or three terms used in any given context. And they were often used virtually interchangeably, as part of a kind of rich stew of emotionally loaded words and ideas.

An essential starting point for the theory of modern dance, in fact, was the idea of feeling, of emotion. Modern dance, its advocates argued, was simply the richness and the power of human feeling expressed in move-ment. Thus Ernst Schur praised what he called the "documentation of [the dancer's] inner, spiritual experience" in modern dance performance.[10] The dancer Friderica Derra de Moroda, also in 1910, informed a newspa-per reporter that "I cannot learn to dance what the people want ... I must dance what I feel."[11] Maud Allan claimed that it was because the "dancing of the ancients was evidently so emotional that I am trying to revive it"; ancient Greek dance was "the outcome as well as the expression of the primal emotions of human life; it was saturated in emotion, and therefore it was full of spontaneity, purity of thought, depth and meaning."[12] Others believed that pretending to be Indians, Egyptians, or Hebrews allowed dancers to give reign to "the oriental violence of emotional expression."[13] Grete Wiesenthal reported that her dances with her sister were "free expressions of our feelings," liberated from the "un-freedom" of their ballet training.[14] Isadora Duncan told students at her dance school that

---

[8] Victor Ottmann, "Im Hause der Isadora Duncan," *Der Tag*, August 17, 1906, clipping in DTAK, Inventory no. 69, Duncan-Archiv, I.2.9.2.

[9] Moeller-Bruck, *Das Variete*, p. 189.

[10] Schur, *Der moderne Tanz*, p. 33.

[11] Dahms and Schroedter, eds., *Der Tanz*, p. 18.

[12] Maud Allan, "My Aims and Ideals," in *Maud Allan and Her Art* (London: n.p., n.d.), pp. 2–3.

[13] Kineton Parkes, "Dancing the Emotions: The Art of Sent M'ahesa," undated *Dancing Times* clip-ping in JRDD, Sent M'ahesa Clippings, p. 142.

[14] Grete Wiesenthal, "Unsere Tänze," in Leonhard M. Fiedler and Martin Lang, eds., *Grete Wiesenthal* (Salzburg: Residenz, 1985), p. 56.

mere gracefulness was not enough, their dancing must arise from "inner emotion."[15] A reviewer of Sent M'ahesa's first performance in Munich in December 1910 believed that her dance was "simply the expression of her most personal feelings and conceptions," of her "spiritual experience" (as well as being the product of "serious study of Egyptology").[16] In fact, it was precisely the range of emotions modern dance portrayed that often impressed observers. One Russian critic in 1904, for example, was astonished when Isadora Duncan acted out "fears, tears, horror ... grief," but then "suddenly flew like a bird and soared carefree, joyfully," then embodied "autumnal beauty and sadness"; another saw her enact "naiveté" and "joy in the plenitude of existence," then be "imperious and strong," then again dance her "submission to fate."[17]

This authentic expression of feeling made modern dance – so its advocates argued – more real, more honest, more *truthful* than ballet. A central claim of modern dance was that it was not in the strictest sense art, or artistry; it did not seek to create an illusion, but was rather simply true dancing. Thus one appreciative critic of Maud Allan wrote that she danced with "natural simplicity and artless purity," while Allan insisted that "[a]bsolute spontaneity is the first principle of my technique." At her first encounter with the ballet she "pondered over the *truthfulness* of such dancing," and was filled with "longing and sadness" over its brainless artifice.[18] One reviewer of Adorée Villany in 1908 asserted that there was "no artifice" in her dance; the following year another praised her "un-artificial charm."[19] A German arts journal found that Olga Desmond's "naiveté is convincing and honest."[20] An enthusiastic review of one of Gertrud Falke's early appearances in Hamburg claimed that her performance had an "overmastering purity! Here is no artifice, nothing that aims at mere dancerly effect" – that is, nothing that was intended to show technical mastery as opposed to genuine expression. Another review praised her for dancing "the inner experiences of her impulsive heart."[21] And an English

[15] Duncan, *My Life*, p. 3; Margherita Duncan, "Isadora," in Sheldon Cheney, ed., *The Art of the Dance* (New York: Theatre Arts, 1928), p. 22.
[16] Oberzaucher-Schüller, "Das bislang verschattete Leben," p. 9; Eugène Carrière quoted in Balk, "Vom Sinnenrausch," p. 57; Ettlinger, "Sent M'ahesa," pp. 33–34.
[17] N. Georgievich, "Duncan," *Peterburgskaya Gazeta*, December 14, 1904; A. G. Hornfeld, excerpt from "Books and People" (1908), translations in JRDD, Natalia Roslasleva files, folders 2, 10.
[18] *Otago Times*, April 5, 1914, reprinted in Allan, *Maud Allan and Her Art*, p. 21; Allan, "My Aims and Ideals," p. 2; *My Life and Dancing*, pp. 46, 47.
[19] Villany, *Tanz-Reform*, pp. 270.
[20] Quoted in Olga Desmond, *Mein Weg zur Schönheit* (Berlin: Bücherzentrale, n.d.), p. 6.
[21] "Gertrude Falke," *Hamburger Fremdenblatt*; "Gertrude Falke als Tänzerin," *Weserzeitung*, clippings in DTAK, Inventory no. 10, Gertrud und Ursula Falke, II.2.2.

reviewer wrote of Isadora Duncan's dance that "[t]he beauty of it rests in its essential truthfulness."[22]

This was why it was so important in the world of modern dance to deny that one had any dance training – or at least to report that one couldn't stomach ballet training. Tórtola Valencia, for example, claimed to have studied singing, cooking, fashion, literature, and languages, and that "the only thing I have never studied is the dance." She had "had no teachers"; all her dances were the product of pure "inspiration."[23] Isadora Duncan took some ballet lessons, but couldn't tolerate the discipline – which she characterized as being like the "torture" visited on heretics by the medieval Inquisition.[24] Olga Desmond claimed that "I follow no system and am not influenced by any particular school of dance" but rather let herself be guided by "feelings and instincts."[25] And Loïe Fuller reduced this idea to a principle: "Let us try to forget educational processes in so far as dancing is concerned," she wrote in her memoirs in 1908; movement should be "the expression of a feeling"; it should be the "natural outcome of the motives which first impelled men to dance ... instinctive passion ... without special preparation. This is the true dance."[26]

In short, as the dance historian Claudia Balk has remarked, the "constant insistence that they had no dance training" underpinned the modern dancers' claim of "freedom from tradition and rules" and the myth of the "genesis of the new dance out of the 'spirit of un-deformed Nature.'"[27] Indeed, even dancers who started in ballet later disavowed that background. Grete Wiesenthal could hardly deny having any training because she had been a professional ballerina; but her brother-in-law assured readers of his account of the Wiesenthal sisters' careers (there were initially three of them) that they had "completely outgrown the ballet; nothing in their movement, nothing in their conception could permit one to think that they came from that school."[28] La Argentina claimed to have started dancing at age five, and merely to have passed through ballet on her way to a more spontaneous interpretation of Spanish popular dance tradition.[29]

[22] Quoted in Bardsley, "Isadora Duncan's First School," p. 241.
[23] Quoted in Carlos Murias Vila, "La magicienne aux yeux d'abîme," *Danser* 103 (1992): 24; Frederico García Sanchiz, "Tórtola ... de Triana," *España Libre*, December 6, 1911, clipping in MAE, Fonds Tortola Valencia, L3.
[24] Duncan, *My Life*, p. 166.
[25] Runge, *Olga Desmond*, p. 29.
[26] Fuller, *Fifteen Years*, pp. 68–69; Schmidt, *Tanzgeschichte*, p. 18.
[27] Balk, "Vom Sinnenrausch," p. 48.
[28] Rudolf Huber-Wiesenthal, *Die Schwestern Wiesenthal: Ein Buch eigenen Erlebens* (Vienna: Saturn, 1934), p. 83.
[29] Antonia Mercé, "Mes premiers essais," in DTAK, Inventory no. 0118, Antonia Mercé.

The modern dancers and their supporters in fact argued over and over again that their dance idiom was derived directly from nature itself. Isadora Duncan played on this theme consistently, arguing that "the movement of all nature runs also through us, is transmitted to us from the dancer"; that "the Greeks were the greatest students of the laws of nature" and "evolved their movements from the movement of nature"; that "Woman is not a thing apart and separate from all other life.... She is but a link in the chain, and her movement must be one with the great movement that runs through the universe ... the movements of Nature."[30] The German feminist art critic Margarete Zepler – among countless others – certified that Duncan's art represented a "return to original naturalness," was "simple and natural," and that therefore she "appeared like the ancient Hellenes resurrected."[31] But this image was ubiquitous in the discussion of modern dance. Newspaper reviews reported that Olga Desmond's dance gave the audience "a purely aesthetic pleasure" because it put on display "the incomparable artistic talent of Nature"; that she "danced with unabashed naturalness, without artifice"; or that she displayed "delightful naiveté, charm, and naturalness."[32] Tórtola Valencia claimed that "My art is born from within me and I limit myself to observing nature" in developing her dances.[33] Ernst Schur felt that when Grete Wiesenthal danced, "One feels that one breathes the perfume of fresh meadows, one hears springs murmuring, one feels the sun. It is as if happy nature were smiling at us through this person."[34] Maud Allan got the word twice into one sentence, claiming that "I am trying to give a natural form of expression to all that I feel concerning music and all the world of nature around me."[35]

The term *life* was closely related to nature in this vocabulary. Modern dance, its advocates argued, was an expression of the natural rhythms and urges of life. Their usage of the term often implied life in the biological sense, the energies and rhythms of the body; but more frequently it seems to have been intended in a more philosophical sense – "life" as shorthand for authenticity, energy, freedom, creativity, motion, warmth, vitality. Life was understood as the opposite of mechanical or artificial

---

[30] Duncan, *Der Tanz*, pp. 17–18; Duncan, "The Dancer and Nature," in *The Art of the Dance*, ed. Sheldon Cheney (New York: Theater Arts, 1928), p. 68.

[31] Margarete Zepler, "Der Tanz und seine neueste Priesterin Isadora Duncan," *Frauen-Rundschau* I (1902): 189–190.

[32] Desmond, *Mein Weg zur Schönheit*, p. 6; Runge, *Olga Desmond*, pp. 30, 33.

[33] Quoted in Carlos Murias Vila, "La magicienne," p. 27.

[34] Schur, *Der moderne Tanz*, p. 108.

[35] Allan, *My Life*, p. 3.

rules, conventions, laws, discipline. Life was organic, natural energies in revolt – if need be – against all constraint. Thus the *London Times* declared in 1910 that the "born dancer ... seems to express the essence of life free from all the irrelevances of the world," while Havelock Ellis wrote in 1914 that dance was "an art which has been so intimately mixed with all the finest and deepest springs of life"; it was "no mere translation or abstraction from life; it is life itself."[36] His compatriot Arthur Symons wrote that the "dance is life, animal life, having its own way passionately ... it is more than a beautiful reflection, it has in it life itself."[37] The literary critic and reform activist Karl Federn, who translated Isadora Duncan's address on "The Dance of the Future" into German, saw in her dance "the struggle of nature against mechanical routine, a struggle for the direct expression of real life as opposed to convention and tradition." The early dance historian Marie Luise Becker argued in 1910 that dance "is vital life," the embodiment of "harmony and naturalness ... the expression of temperament and mood" rather than technical "bravura" or "feats of strength."[38] The Americans Caroline and Charles Caffin, in a history of modern dance published in 1912, saw the modern dance revolution as "life ... truly making itself felt," people responding to "the throb and call of life."[39] And one Russian reviewer held that by "rejecting the dead formalism of the ... ballet" Isadora Duncan was able to create a dance "not severed from nature and life, but flowing from life."[40]

But the motor of life is, of course, the soul; and this was perhaps the most important key term in the language of modern dance. Isadora Duncan made it central to her speech on "The Dance of the Future" in 1903: "The dancer of the future," she held, "will be one whose body and soul have grown so harmoniously together that the natural language of the soul will have become the movement of the body"; her movement would be "so pure, so strong, that people would say: it is a soul we see moving."[41] Others once again took their cue from her. Tórtola Valencia argued that "natural dance surges forth, it is born, it is not invented" or taught, it was "a product neither of science nor of reflection, but of inspiration, defying

---

[36] Ellis, "The Philosophy of Dancing," p. 207, at https://www.unz.org/Pub/AtlanticMonthly-1914feb-00197.

[37] Arthur Symons, *Studies in the Seven Arts* (London: Archibald Constable, 1906), pp. 387–388.

[38] Karl Federn, "Einleitung," in Isadora Duncan, *Der Tanz der Zukunft* (Leipzig: Eugen Diederichs, 1903), p. 7; Marie Luise Becker, "Die Sezession in der Tanzkunst," *Bühne und Welt* 12 (1910): 27.

[39] Caffin and Caffin, *Dancing*, pp. 248–249.

[40] Quoted in Francis Steegmuller, *Your Isadora: The Love Story of Isadora Duncan & Gordon Craig* (New York: Random House, 1974), p. 46.

[41] Duncan, *Der Tanz*, pp. 24–25, 15; Kurth, *Isadora*, p. 30.

all rules and conventions" to express "the most inward impressions of the soul."[42] Gertrude Barrison believed that her "dance comes from within, from the soul."[43] Having denounced ballet for having "very little soul" or even being "soulless," Ernst Schur praised Isadora Duncan in contrast as a "glowing young soul."[44] Clotilde von Derp, too, was praised for expressing "the sensitivity of the human soul" in her dance debut.[45] And one Hamburg newspaper gave its review of a Gertrud Falke performance the title "Triumph of the Soul."[46]

This was the vocabulary of modern dance: spontaneity, feeling or emotion, truth, nature, life, soul – all in revolt against routine, convention, tradition, mechanism, constraint, discipline. These terms appeared with extraordinary frequency in dance discourse – at least some of them, in one combination or another, in virtually every favorable description of dance performance and theory. At bottom, the idea was that modern dance was not really "art," or performance; it simply translated the truth of the dancer's essence, her soul, her self, into movement. Grete Wiesenthal summed it up neatly: The aim of modern dance was to "express our feelings in dance, that is, to dance ourselves."[47] Ernst Schur found Isadora Duncan convincing because "she dances herself," and Ruth St. Denis because "her personality is the point of departure" in her performance.[48] One observer, looking back from 1918, argued that the essence of modern dance generally was that "the personality of the dancer is the center, is simultaneously the beginning point, the means, and the aim of the new art, its beginning and its end." Modern dance, in short, was essentially a "cult" of the dancer's own individuality.[49]

In some cases, performers, audiences, and reviewers alike arrived at a very odd conclusion on the basis of this vocabulary, this set of assumptions, values, or postulates: That the modern dancer really did not care about her audience – or was not even aware of them. One English reviewer of Isadora Duncan wrote, for example, that in her performance the "joy and the dance are as innocent, as free from self-consciousness,

[42] Tórtola Valencia, "Mis danzas," *Nuevo Mundo*, January 16, 1913.

[43] Oberzaucher-Schüller, "Das bislang verschattete Leben der Miss Gertrude," p. 9.

[44] Schur, *Der moderne Tanz*, pp. 33, 36.

[45] Quoted in Horst Koegeler, "A Single Being in a Single Soul with Two Bodies," *DC* 26, no. 2 (2003): 256; Rudolf von Delius, "Clotilde von Derp (1910)," in Frank-Manuel Peter and Rainer Stamm, eds., *Die Sacharoffs* (Cologne: Wienand, 2000), p. 137.

[46] "Der Triumph der Seele," *Neue Hamburgische Zeitung*, November 14, 1913, clipping in DTAK, Inventory no. 10, Gertrud und Ursula Falke, II.2.4.

[47] Wiesenthal, *Der Aufstieg*, p. 174.

[48] Schur, *Der moderne Tanz*, pp. 38, 78, 86.

[49] Alphons Török, *Tanzabende: Kritische Monographien* (Vienna: Merker, 1918), p. 4.

as though there were no one to see."[50] Grete Wiesenthal reported that after her debut in Vienna, when most of the audience was gone, she danced on "not caring about those who watched."[51] Friderica Derra de Moroda remarked that "in most of my dances I am so carried away by the music, and perhaps you would also say by my temperament, that I forget everything around me."[52] The French author and variety-theater actress Colette Willy declared in 1906 that she would "dance naked or clothed for the sheer pleasure of dancing, of suiting my gestures to the rhythm of the music and spinning around ablaze with light," regardless of moral standards or audience expectations.[53] In short, the modern dancers appear often to have given the impression that they danced because they felt like it, and however they felt like, without regard to their audience.

Modern dance, then, enacted the liberation of the individual. The modern dancer freed herself to express her essential nature through movement, free of any technique, aesthetic standard, or social convention. Isadora Duncan argued that to dance we must "get down to the depths, to lose ourselves in an inner self" – not the socially constructed self-conscious artificial self, but the true, inner, authentic, natural, unconstrained self.[54] Tórtola Valencia offered dance instruction in which there were "no fixed rules" at all because "individuality and self-expression is what I aim at ... [I] ask my pupil to dance as she feels, regardless of me." One dance critic reported of Olga Desmond's school that "since Olga Desmond's teacher is nature ... her instruction has the effect of allowing people to move freely and without constraint."[55] A Munich newspaper described Clotilde von Derp as "a personality freed from all constraint," while the *Berliner Tageblatt* described St. Denis as dancing "with complete naturalness and freedom ... as if for the first time."[56] The Caffins summed it up neatly by calling Isadora Duncan "freedom personified."[57]

[50] Quoted in Mary Simonson, *Body Knowledge* (New York: Oxford University Press, 2013), p. 85.
[51] Wiesenthal, *Der Aufstieg*, p. 212.
[52] Quoted in Dahms and Schroedter, eds., *Der Tanz*, pp. 26–27.
[53] Quoted in Toni Bentley, *Sisters of Salome* (New Haven, CT: Yale University Press, 2002), p. 187.
[54] Isadora Duncan, "Depth," in Sheldon Cheney, ed., *The Art of the Dance* (New York: Theater Arts, 1928), p. 100.
[55] "Dancing for Health," *The Morning Leader*, April 20, 1912, clipping in MAE, Fonds Tortola Valencia, L3; Runge, *Olga Desmond*, p. 88.
[56] "Tanzabend Clotilde von Derp," *Münchener Neueste Nachrichten*, April 27, 1910, clipping in DTAK Inventory no. 56, Sacharoff, II.2.7; quotation in Jeschke and Vettermenn, "Isadora Duncan, Berlin and Munich in 1906," p. 225.
[57] Caffin and Caffin, *Dancing and Dancers of Today*, p. 65. There is a fine discussion of this theme in Brandstetter, *Tanz-Lektüren*, pp. 246–252.

This was one reason that relative nudity was an essential part of the message of modern dance – because it communicated the undeniable corporeality of individuality, and because it flaunted social convention. Its aim was to demonstrate that the dancer would not be governed by conventional standards of decency – any more than by anything else.

The argument of modern dance was that happiness would result from this freeing of the individual from all constraint. The modern dancers often did dance negative emotions – rage, fear, grief, jealousy, and so on. The best example is, of course, the ubiquitous Salomé dance, in which a woman's rage at rejection leads to murder and (in most versions) remorse. But another favorite musical choice was Chopin's *Funeral March*, for dances featuring physical expression of unbearable grief. Nevertheless, again and again reviewers and critics played on the idea that modern dance expressed above all simple *joie de vivre*.

An extraordinary case was Max Osborn's account of Grete Wiesenthal's performance at a private party at the home of Max Reinhardt. Wiesenthal, he recalled, danced through the night and into the morning "as if enchanted by the command of the magician in an Oriental tale, as if she must and could only let the overwhelming feeling of her happy being, and her ability to make others happy, pour forth to the point of stunned, exalted exhaustion. Morning came, it grew light – she danced on, beautiful, possessed, until tears of emotion rolled down her smiling little face."[58] But in less extreme form this image of the happy dancer was ubiquitous. Another contemporary thought Weisenthal's performance was "not dance. It's a shout of jubilation [*Aufjauchzen*]" (see Figure 2.1)[59] The Caffins praised Isadora Duncan for expressing in movement "the epitome of all the pure natural joy that belongs to the beginning of life.... So joyous is it, so unpremeditated, that it seems like the play of a child to whom sorrow is unknown and unbelievable." The Austrian feminist Marie Lang, too, reported that Duncan's performance was "the sweetest play of joy ... she is bathed in blessed joy."[60] Frank Harris was charmed by Maud Allan's "pure joy, the happy gaiety of a child, tripping, bouncing hither and thither, out of sheer lightheartedness."[61]

[58] Max Osborn, "Grete Wiesenthal," in Leonhard M. Fiedler and Martin Lang, eds., *Grete Wiesenthal: Die Schönheit der Sprache des Körpers in Bewegung* (Salzburg: Residenz, 1985), p. 74.
[59] Quoted in Gabriele Brandstetter, "Grete Wiesenthals Walzer," in Gabriele Brandstetter and Gunhild Oberzaucher-Schüller, eds., *Mundart der Wiener Moderne: Der Tanz der Grete Wiesenthal* (Munich: Kieser, 2009), p. 16.
[60] Caffin and Caffin, *Dancing*, p. 55; Marie Lang, "Offenbarung," *Dokumente der Frauen* 6 (1902): 637.
[61] Allan, *Maud Allan and Her Art*, p. 8.

GRETE WIESENTHAL IM DONAUWALZER.

Figure 2.1 Grete Wiesenthal's joyful "Beautiful Blue Danube"

Gertrud Falke danced with "bubbling happiness"; Regina Woody titled her autobiography *Dancing for Joy*; and Marie Luise Becker saw Grete Wiesenthal as "the embodiment of youth and joie de vivre."[62] Mata Hari "danced ... with all the gladness of her sunny nature."[63] Gertrud Leistikow danced with "humor ... laughing affirmation of life," in a "whirl of happiness."[64] Arthur Symons was thrilled by "all these young bodies ... full of the sense of joy in motion."[65] The free person, in short, is a happy person, a person free of cares; this too was at the core of the modern dance revolution.

The modern dancer was, then, youthful, graceful, passionately alive, unconstrained, slender (not weighed down), natural and without artifice, intelligent but not calculating, free, and joyful. No wonder dancers were in demand among advertising executives. Who would not want to be that person, or at least buy something that would make them more like that person?

[62] *Neue Hamburger Zeitung*, clipping in DTAK, Inventory no. 10, Gertrud und Ursula Falke, II.2.4; Woody, *Dancing*; Becker, "Die Sezession in der Tanzkunst," p. 40.
[63] Quoted in Waagenaar, *The Murder of Mata Hari*, p. 51.
[64] Oe., "Tanzabend Gertrud Leistikow," *Münchener Neueste Nachrichten*, October 27, 1913, clipping in TBCUA, Archief Gertrud Leistikow, Map 4a.
[65] Symons, *Studies*, p. 389.

2.2 The Modernist Arts Community as Marketing Channel

In virtually every respect, again, the language of modern dance echoed or rather was an integral part of that of aesthetic modernism more broadly – in painting, sculpture, composition, and literature. The central aim of modernism was to liberate the aesthetic instinct or urge of the individual artist to give completely free rein to creativity. The German painter Max Liebermann laid out the Expressionist agenda shortly after the turn of the century: Art should seek not "an academic ideal of beauty, but the power with which the artist expressed that which to *him* seemed beautiful"; works should be judged "not by imposing traditional academic patterns, but according to the individuality expressed in them"; it would "ruin art if we tried to create something new by studying existing masterpieces"; the artist excels not by "slavishly copying nature" but by conveying "the impression nature made on him."[66] Or we could take the composer Anton Schönberg's definition in a letter to the painter Vassily Kandinsky: "Art belongs to the subconscious! One must express oneself! Unmediatedly! Not one's taste or one's upbringing, or one's intelligence, knowledge or skill. Not all these acquired characteristics, but that which is inborn, instinctive." Kandinsky argued that art should be governed by "the principle of inward necessity" – that the artist should express what he or she "had to" express.[67] And Edward Gordon Craig, a stage designer and director who fathered Isadora Duncan's first child, declared in 1913 that "[i]n Art ... the soul must speak ... it is the Soul which moves."[68]

Modern dance embodied this program, and the modern dancers were often explicitly understood to be representatives of modernism more broadly, in fact of the same impulse of innovation and revolt that had led to the various "Secessions" of artists from the official art academies. One German commentator in 1910 referred to modern dance generally as "The Secession in Dance." Another remarked in the same year that Clotilde von Derp had translated the painterly style of the secessions to the stage, and was herself "a genuine Secession." In 1914 one reviewer found that Gertrud Falke – like Isadora Duncan, Rita Sacchetto, or Grete

---

[66] Quoted in Peter Paret, *The Berlin Secession* (Cambridge, MA: Harvard University Press, 1980), pp. 166–167.
[67] Quoted in Christopher Butler, *Early Modernism: Literature, Music, and Painting ion Europe, 1900–1916* (Oxford: Oxford University Press, 1994), p. 25; Fritsch-Vivié, *Mary Wigman*, p. 35.
[68] Arnold Rood, ed., *Gordon Craig on Movement and Dance* (New York: Dance Horizons, 1977), p. 94.

Wiesenthal – danced "in Secessionist style."[69] And some observers explicitly saw dance as a part of a much broader aesthetic revolution going on in all the arts. Thus one reviewer in 1916 compared Tórtola Valencia to a whole pantheon of modernists in other fields of art, including the poets Rubén Darió and Gabriele D'Annunzio, the playwrights George Bernard Shaw and Hendrik Ibsen, the sculptor Auguste Rodin, and so forth. The German dance critic Hans Brandenburg, looking back from 1921, saw the modern dance pioneers as just one expression of a much broader cultural "expansion" that underlay and drove the revolution in the arts – including, for example, the "flaming social-critical literature of the most recent years" and the "purification" of architecture and the industrial arts and design under the influence of ideas about the relationship between form, materials, and function.[70]

Such comments were justified not only by similarities at the level of theory and rhetoric, but also by numerous concrete connections between modern dance and Expressionist or Secessionist art. These connections were particularly active in Vienna. The Austrian poet Hugo von Hofmannsthal, for example, was an important patron for both Ruth St. Denis and Grete Wiesenthal, for whom he wrote two pantomime plays in 1911 (which were filmed in 1913).[71] The painter Gustav Klimt helped to develop the sets and costumes for Grete Wiesenthal's debut as a modern dancer; he helped arrange for Isadora Duncan's Vienna debut in the headquarters of the Vienna Secession in 1902; together with Koloman Moser he developed the sets for Rita Sacchetto's Vienna debut in 1906. Grete Wiesenthal gave her first performance in the "Bat" (Fledermaus) cabaret in Vienna, in which Klimt, Oskar Kokoschka, Koloman Moser, and the writer Peter Altenberg, among other Expressionist leading lights, were involved.[72] Mata Hari, too, had her Vienna debut in the headquarters

---

[69] Becker, "Die Sezession in der Tanzkunst," pp. 27–43; F. M. in *Münchener Neueste Nachrichten*, November 19, 1910, clipping in DTAK, Inventory no. 56, II.2.7; "Aus Kunst und Leben," *Wiesbadener Tageblatt*, April 28, 1914, clipping in DTAK, Inventory no. 10, II.2.4.

[70] Review cited in Garland, *Tórtola Valencia*, p. 53; Hans Brandenburg, *Der moderne Tanz*, (Munich: Georg Müller, 1921), p. 25.

[71] *Grete Wiesenthal in Amor und Psyche und Das Fremde Mädchen: Szenen von Hugo von Hofmannsthal* (Berlin: S. Fischer, 1911); Hermann and Marianne Aubel, *Der künstlerische Tanz unserer Zeit* (Köngstein/Ts: Langewiesche, 1930), p. 46. On this relationship see Leonhard M. Fiedler, "'nicht Wort – aber mehr als Wort …': Zwischen Sprache und Tanz – Grete Wiesenthal und Hugo von Hofmannsthal," in Gabriele Brandstetter and Gunhild Oberzaucher-Schüller, eds., *Mundart der Wiener Moderne: Der Tanz der Grete Wiesenthal* (Munich: Kieser, 2009), pp. 127–150.

[72] Wiesenthal, *Der Aufstieg*, pp. 207, 209; Alfred and Gunhild Oberzaucher, "Wer waren die Lehrer von Gertrud Bodenwieser," *Tanzdrama* 33 (1996): 16; Brygida Maria Ochaim, "Die getanzten Bilder der Rita Sacchetto," *Tanzdrama* 14 (1991): 22; Hermann and Marianne Aubel, *Der künstlerische Tanz unserer Zeit* (Köngstein/Ts: Langewiesche, 1930), p. 45. On Wiesenthal and the Vienna Secession community see Brandstetter, *Mundart der Wiener Moderne*.

of the Secession; Peter Altenberg was among her fans, declaring that her body was "ideal," "in accord with God's aesthetic designs," and "fills the artistic person with reverence."[73] Altenberg later appeared in joint dance/poetry-reading performances in modernist cabarets with Gertrude Barrison – the latter, on at least one occasion, in a costume designed by Koloman Moser.[74] Friderica Derra de Moroda was yet another dancer who performed first in public at the Vienna Secession headquarters, in 1912.[75] And one 1926 history of modern dance recalled that "Saharet became the slogan of the rising generation of artists, their program and battle-cry."[76]

Munich was an even more important nexus between modern dance and modernist art. Clotilde von Derp and Alexander Sacharoff were closely associated with the Munich secession and the Russian artists' colony in that city, including the painters Vassily Kandinsky, Marianne Werefkin, and Victor Jawlensky.[77] Saharet's lover Alfred Heymel was a major fixture in Munich's bohemian arts community.[78] The modernist poet and arts journalist Hans Brandenburg (whose aim was to preach the "gospel of youth" and of "life") declared Munich the capital of the new dance.[79] But the less aesthetically radical Munich painters Franz von Lenbach, Franz von Stuck, and Friedrich von Kaulbach, too, were up to their necks in dancers. All three knew Clotilde von Derp personally (their children went to the same dance school) and urged her to make a career in dance. Lenbach and Kaulbach painted numerous dancers, including Cléo de Mérode, Saharet, and Duncan – in some cases with great popular success.[80]

Such connections were legion across the whole spectrum of modern dance. Loïe Fuller was lionized by Stéphane Mallarmé and other French Symbolist poets and painters; the French author (and Nobel laureate) Anatole France wrote the forward to her memoirs; she was friends with the Irish poet William Butler Yeats (another Nobel Prize winner) and

[73] Lüders, *Apropos Mata Hari*, pp. 82, 91.
[74] Oberzaucher-Schüller, "Das bislang verschattete Leben der Miss Gertrude," pp. 8–9.
[75] Dahms and Schroedter, eds., *Der Tanz*, p. 14.
[76] John Schikowski, *Geschichte des Tanzes* (Berlin: Büchergilde Gutenberg, 1926), p. 129.
[77] Patrizia Veroli, "Auf der Suche nach der Ekstase," *Tanzdrama* 20 (1992): 22; Frank-Manuel Peter and Rainer Stamm, eds. *Die Sacharoffs – zwei Tänzer aus dem Umkreis des Blauen Reiters* (Cologne: Wienand, 2002), passim; Koegeler, "A Single Being and a Single Soul with Two Bodies," pp. 253–259.
[78] On Heymel see Wilhelm, *Die Münchener Bohème*, pp. 130–131.
[79] Thomas Betz, "Dichten und Trachten: Hans Brandenburg und der Tanz," *Tanzdrama* 55 (2000): 7, 9.
[80] Clotilde von Derp, "La vie que nous avons dansée," in DTAK, Inventory no. 56, I.1.1, p. 12; Betz, "Die Duncan dichtet, die Sacchetto malt," p. 27; Mérode, *La Ballet de ma vie*, p. 253.

the French sculptor Auguste Rodin – who also asked Ruth St. Denis and Isadora Duncan to model for him.[81] St. Denis's and Wiesenthal's patron Harry Graf Kessler was a patrician arts promoter who lost his job as director of a small public museum in central Germany in 1906 because he was overly interested in collecting the French and moderns.[82] Even in Britain – hardly a hotbed of modernism in the arts, excepting literature – Isadora Duncan first performed at the New Gallery in London, a center for artists who had seceded from the Royal Academy in 1877. With sponsorship, support, and guidance from prominent figures such as the philosopher and novelist Henry James, the painter Sir Lawrence Alma-Tadema, and the music critic of the *London Times* J. Fuller-Maitland, Duncan was able to establish her reputation as a serious and radical artist.[83] Alma-Tadema, the Duchess of Manchester, Edward VII, the Duke of Lonsdale, the American ambassador Whitelaw Reid, and the Maharaja of Kapurthala were all patrons of Ruth St. Denis on her arrival in Britain in 1906.[84] Gertrude Falke and her sister Ursula were supported by a coteries of prominent Hamburg artists, including the founder and director of Hamburg's leading art museum Alfred Lichtwark, the prominent author and playwright Detlev von Liliencron, and the poet Richard Dehmel.[85] Ida Rubinstein collaborated with the Italian poet, playwright, and later war hero and would-be "Duce" Gabriele D'Annunzio.[86] The modern dancers also modeled for a wide range of modernist artists – from the French sculptors Auguste Rodin and Aristide Maillol to the German painters Ernst Kirchner and Emil Nolde.[87] And it is worth noting that the

[81] Schmidt, *Tanzgeschichte*, p. 18; Volker Drehsen, "Körper Religion: Ausdruckstanz um 1900," in Volker Drehsen, Wilhelm Gräb, and Dietrich Korsch, eds., *Protestantismus und Ästhetik* (Gütersloh: Chr. Kaiser, 2001), p. 233; St. Denis, *An Unfinished Life*, p. 86.

[82] Peter Paret, "The Tschudi Affair," *Journal of Modern History* 53 (1981): 589–618; Theodor Fiedler, "Weimar contra Berlin: Harry Graf Kessler and the Politics of Modernism," in Françoise Forster-Hahn, ed., *Imagining Modern German Culture: 1889–1910* (Hanover: National Gallery of Art, Washington, 1996), pp. 119–120.

[83] Deborah Jowitt, "Isadora Duncan: The Search for Motion," *DRJ* 17 (1985): 25; Kurth, *Isadora*, pp. 61–62; Blair, *Isadora*, pp. 34–36.

[84] Sandra Meinzenbach, *"Tanz ist eine Sprache und eine Schrift des Göttlichen": Kunst und Leben der Ruth St. Denis* (Wilhelmshaven: Florian Noetzel, 2013), pp. 52, 68.

[85] Nils Jöckel, "Aus dem Moment des Empfindens," *Tanzdrama* 7 (1989): 18.

[86] Charles R. Batson, *Dance, Desire and Anxiety in Early Twentieth-Century French Theater: Playing Identities* (Aldershot, UK: Ashgate, 2005), pp. 8–50.

[87] See particularly the collection Karin Adelsbach and Andrea Firmenich, eds., *Tanz in der Moderne. Von Matisse bis Schlemmer* (Cologne: Wienand, 1996); Barche and Jeschke, "Bewegungsrausch und Formbestreben," p. 317; Runge, *Olga Desmond*, p. 11; Susan Laikin Funkenstein, "There's Something About Mary Wigman: The Woman Dancer as Subject in German Expressionist Art," *Gender and History* 17, no. 3 (2005): 826–859; and Jill Lloyd, *German Expressionism: Primitivism and Modernity* (New Haven, CT: Yale University Press, 1991), especially pp. 87–96.

Salomé theme, which played an important part in the career particularly of Maud Allan, was one that had obsessed some aesthetic modernists since the period of Decadence and aestheticism in the second half of the nineteenth century.[88]

In short, there were in effect many comarketing arrangements between modernist artists and modern dancers. In some cases, such connections were of critical importance to the modern dancers – and were used quite deliberately to crack open more conservative audiences. The most telling case is that of Tórtola Valencia. After appearing in London and other North European cities between 1908 and 1910, in 1911 Valencia ventured to Madrid, until then relatively untouched by modern dance and known for its moral and aesthetic conservatism. Her early performances were greeted with incomprehension and lewd comments; but she was soon picked up and lionized by a circle of Spanish modernist intellectuals, and Latin American intellectuals living in Spain – including the prominent painters Ignacio Zuloaga and Anselmo Nieto; the Nicaraguan poet Rubén Darió; the playwrights Pompeyo Gener and Ramon del Valle-Inclan; the composers Manuel Falla and Enrique Granados. They arranged special performances for her, sponsored by various artists' associations in Madrid; elected her to the Madrid Atheneum, an exclusive arts association; painted her portrait; and encouraged her to switch from "Indian" and "ancient" dance to dances inspired by Spanish dance traditions. Thereafter, Valencia adopted the cultivation of leading figures in the artistic and intellectual avant-garde as a successful marketing strategy in other countries as well, particularly in Latin America.[89]

But in this Valencia was following a strategy already deployed by Isadora Duncan in her "conquest" of Central Europe – and other dancers did the same. One Dutch reviewer, for example, pointed out that Duncan had first performed before a "select audience of art experts" and "men of position" before going on the public stage.[90] She also quite strategically cultivated the friendship and approval of influential critics and producers, intellectuals, and theorists, tailoring her message to suit the intellectual and artistic currents of the day. As the influential editor and art critic Max Osborn saw it, in both Vienna and Berlin Duncan first

---

[88] See Maurice Samuels, "France," in Pericles Lewis, ed., *The Cambridge Companion to European Modernism* (New York: Cambridge, 2011), pp. 19–20.

[89] Queralt, *Tórtola Valencia*, p. 41; Garland, *Tórtola Valencia*, pp. 38–39; Odelotte Solrac, *Tórtola Valencia and Her Legacy* (New York: Vintage, 1982), pp. 54–55.

[90] W, "Miss Isadora Duncan: De veelbsproken hervormster van den Dans," *Wereldkroniek* 43 (January 24, 1903), clipping in DTAK, Inventory no. 69, Duncan-Archiv, II.2.6.1.

"secured the interest and protection of serious artistic authorities," in private performances and conversations, and only then presented herself to a broader public. Or take Osborn's account of Grete Wiesenthal's arrival in Berlin: After she and her sisters had given a few performances at an avant-garde cabaret in Vienna, Hugo von Hofmannsthal unveiled her at a surprise performance for a gathering of the modernist elite at the private villa of Max Reinhardt.[91] Rita Sacchetto, too, invited a select audience of journalists, intellectuals, and artists to her hotel the day before her debut in Rome in 1911 to explain that her dance was serious art, the outward expression of deep emotion.[92] Maud Allan danced for an invited audience of artists, writers, journalists, and even members of Parliament some days before her first public performance in London.[93] Gertrud Leistikow, like Tórtola Valencia, learned this approach the hard way: Her first performances in Holland were marred by less than appreciative audiences, who laughed at her serious dances and sat seriously through her comic ones. She then invited an audience of painters, musicians, architects, and the editors of art magazines to a special performance and reception, and rescued her public image in Holland, eventually becoming a cultural icon there – much as Valencia did in Spain.[94]

Obviously, this was a mutually beneficial relationship. The producers, painters, sculptors, and mavens who mentored or gushed over the modern dance stars were engaging in their own form of marketing by associating themselves with attractive and demonstratively free-spirited young women. They had good reason to do so because the ability of modern dance to appeal across class lines, and to reshape widely held conceptions of physical beauty, realized one of the central aspirations of modernism – to achieve broad social relevance and reshape aesthetic norms even at the level of daily life.[95] But these associations and connections, and the testimonials of prominent artists in other, more respected artistic disciplines or media, also helped to give modern dance the imprimatur of Art.

---

[91] Max Osborn, *Der bunte Spiegel; Erinnerungen aus dem Kunst-, Kultur-, und Geistesleben der Jahre 1890 bis 1933* (New York: F. Krause, 1945), pp. 171–172.

[92] Veroli, *Baccanti e dive dell'aria*, p. 112.

[93] Catherine Hindson, *Female Performance Practice on the Fin-de-Siècle Popular Stages of London and Paris* (Manchester, UK: Manchester University Press, 2007), p. 45.

[94] De Boer, *Dans voluit, dat is leven*, pp. 69–70.

[95] There is a lucid summary in James Shedel, "Aesthetics and Modernity: Art and the Amelioration of Change in *Fin de Siècle* Austria," *Austrian History Yearbook* 19, no. 1 (1983): 135–142.

2.3 Dance by, of, and for Women?

There was, however, one very important difference between the modernist artistic avant-garde and the modern dancers. The former were overwhelmingly male; the latter were overwhelmingly female. It is tempting to see in this predominance of women evidence that modern dance was playing on very well-established associations between sexuality and women's bodies. Perhaps modern dance was simply part of a broader objectification of women's bodies in the new mass commercial culture? And some of the relationships between dancers and male artists or patrons seem to suggest that modern dance was also playing on a more traditional form of sexploitation – essentially replicating the role of the ballet as a source of charming companions for wealthy men. Saharet's relationship with Alfred Heymel might be seen in that light; or Isadora Duncan's early relationship with the German critic and art professor Henry Thode; or Anna Pavlova's with a member of the St. Petersburg city council.[96]

What we know about the audiences for modern dance, however, does not match this more cynical perspective on modern dance. As we have seen in Chapter 1, the modern dancers cultivated friendly, and possibly also romantic, relationships more often with women of the social elite than with its men. But it appears that a good portion of the audience for modern dancers' public performances, too, was female. While some more skeptical commentators (and some of the scholarly literature on modern dance) asserted that variety-theater audiences for modern dance were primarily male and drawn by the prospect of bare female skin, actually they appear more likely to have been disproportionately female. As Suzanne Shelton points out in the case of Ruth St. Denis, the modern dancers often performed in matinees, where audiences were predominantly female; and they sometimes approached evening performances, where more men would be in the audience, with some trepidation.[97] One reviewer commented that audiences for Maud Allan's Salomé matinees were "almost entirely feminine."[98] But even in some evening performances, women may well have predominated. One London newspaper, for example, remarked of Maud Allan's performances that "ladies have formed the bulk of the audience night after night"; another estimated that 90 percent of the

---

[96] Oleg Kerensky, *Anna Pavlova* (London: Hamilton, 1973), p. 29.
[97] Kendall, *Where She Danced*, pp. 77, 80–81; Alexandra Kolb, *Performing Femininity: Dance and Literature in German Modernism* (New York: Peter Lang, 2009), p. 122.
[98] Hindson, *Female Performance*, p. 52.

audience were women, and remarked that "it might have been a suffragist meeting"; an early dance historian remarked that her performances were attended "particularly [by] feminine devotees."[99] According to the dance historian Ann Daly, during a tour of the United States after her initial European successes Isadora Duncan's audiences were "predominantly female."[100] After Adorée Villany's arrest in Munich in 1911, the fact that respectable upper-class women were prominent in the audience was even used in court as evidence that her dancing could not have been immoral.[101] In short, modern dance played primarily *to* women, as well as being performed primarily *by* women.

What is more, in some cases not only wealthy female patrons but also women's organizations played an important direct role in launching the dance stars. As the dance historian Linda Tomko has pointed out, for example, after performing for a dozen years in variety theater, Ruth St. Denis launched her career as an independent dancer with appearances at wealthy women's salon parties, and had her public debut in 1906 at a ladies' matinee organized by some of them. Dancing at upper-class women's clubs, culture and arts groups, charity performances, and private parties continued to be crucial to her career in the United States and in Europe. She was introduced to Harry Graf Kessler by the Englishwoman Constance Smedley, who was founder of an international network of women's clubs. In March 1914, she danced at a birthday party for Anna Howard Shaw, leader of the American Women's Suffrage Association.[102] None of this was atypical. Loïe Fuller began her career as a temperance lecturer, before moving into variety theater for a decade and then establishing herself as an independent artist in Paris.[103] Gertrude Falke first appeared in public at the Hamburg Women's Club, in 1912.[104] Isadora Duncan's earliest public performances in Europe were praised in the influential Austrian

---

[99] Shelton, *Ruth*, p. 84; Cherniavsky, "Maud Allan, Part II," p. 150; Walkowitz, *Nights Out*, p. 80; Mark Edward Perugini, *A Pageant of the Dance and Ballet* (London: Jarrolds, 1935), p. 262. For evidence to the contrary, however, see Villany, *Phryné moderne*, p. 43, or Karl Storck's review of Isadora Duncan's performance in Berlin in January 1903, "Ganz ohne Cancan," reprinted in *Tanzdrama* 1 (1987): 24.

[100] Ann Daly, *Done into Dance*, p. 107.

[101] Villany, *Tanz-Reform*, p. 354.

[102] Tomko, *Dancing Class*, pp. 47–58; Hofmannsthal, *Hugo von Hofmannsthal/Harry Graf Kessler*, p. 132; Meinzenbach, *"Tanz ist eine Sprache und eine Schrift des Göttlichen,"* p. 39.

[103] Tomko, *Dancing Class*, pp. 41–47.

[104] "Frauenklub Hamburg," *Hamburger Fremdenblatt*, October 28, 1912, clipping in DTAK, Inventory no. 10, Gertrud und Ursula Falke, II.2.4; Nils Jöckel and Patricia Stöckemann, *"Flugkraft in goldene Ferne"*: *Bühnentanz in Hamburg seit 1900* (Hamburg: Museum für Kunst und Gewerbe, 1989), p. 17.

feminist journal *Dokumente der Frauen* as "a revelation" in 1902.[105] Grete Wiesenthal married the son of the woman who wrote those words – Marie Lang, prominent Austrian feminist, social reformer, and editor of the *Dokumente der Frauen*.[106]

This was part of a broader pattern; for there were close connections between feminist movements and organizations promoting healthy physicality, fitness, and exercise among women. In Britain, for example, the Feminine League for Physical Culture was founded by militant suffragists, who believed that a slimmer body would give women greater physical grace and a more "decisive demeanor," as one historian has put it.[107] One German dance critic observed that it made sense that the pioneers of modern dance were Americans because the women's sports movement in the Anglo-Saxon world "has trained women's bodies for more than a generation" and allowed those with a gift for dance to move "in more free and original manner" than continental women, and because women in Britain and America "have been more independent than women of other nations for over a generation, and thinking women can decide to go into artistic dance more easily" there.[108] There were connections, too, between dress reform, the fashion industry, feminism, and dance – specifically in the rejection of the "hour-glass" shape literally pressed upon women by the corset. Isadora Duncan, for example, was probably consciously referring to this trend when she spoke of the "deformation" of women's bodies by the clothing code of classical ballet.[109] Ruth St. Denis's mother campaigned against the corset in the 1890s, before Ruth began her stage career.[110] And dress reform also influenced the fashion designers Duncan and other dancers helped to popularize, such as Poiret and Fortuny.

In some cases, finally, the connection between dance and women's liberation was quite explicit in the modern dancers' self-presentation. The most obvious example was Isadora Duncan, who reported in her memoirs of 1927 deciding, in early youth, to "fight against marriage and for the

---

[105] Lang, "Offenbarung," pp. 636–638.

[106] Aubel and Aubel, *Der künstlerische Tanz unserer Zeit*, p. 42.

[107] Mary Lynn Stewart, *For Health and Beauty: Physical Culture for Frenchwomen, 1880s–1930s* (Baltimore: Johns Hopkins University Press, 2001), p. 154.

[108] Becker, "Die Sezession," p. 32.

[109] Duncan, *Der Tanz*, pp. 14, 25; Ann Daly, "Isadora Duncan's Dance Theory," *DRJ* 26 (1994): 26–27; Barche and Jeschke, "Bewegungsrausch und Formbestreben," pp. 325, 331; Susan Manning, "The Female Dancer and the Male Gaze: Feminist Critiques of Early Modern Dance," in Desmond, ed., *Meaning in Motion*, p. 162; Kendall, *Where She Danced*, p. 60.

[110] Walter Terry, *Miss Ruth: The "More Living Life" of Ruth St. Denis* (New York: Dodd, Mead, 1969), p. 23.

emancipation of women," never married her various lovers or the fathers of her children, and praised the Soviet government for abolishing marriage. She also believed that the dancer of the future "shall dance the freedom of woman" and that woman "must *live* this beauty, and her body must be the living exponent of it."[111] Rita Sacchetto was author of a "dance symphony" called "The Intellectual Awakening of Woman," which took Walt Whitman's "Woman of the Future" ("She has no reason to fear and she does not fear ... she is strong/She too is a law of nature – there is no law stronger than she is") as its text and traced woman's rise from "materialism, sex slavery, and convention" toward "the awakening ... of the world."[112]

Such stances were not absolutely universal in the world of modern dance. Maud Allan, for example, explicitly rejected women's suffrage in her "memoirs" of 1908.[113] Yet like all the modern dancers, she lived in a manner that spoke volumes about women's roles and potentials. Diana Cooper's mother, a woman of advanced ideas "untrammeled by convention," sent her once a week to "watch and learn" from performances in which Allan demanded and got John the Baptist's head.[114] One commentator remarked that Isadora Duncan was "an educated and independent woman"; but more than that, she was an educated and independent woman who was making headlines.[115] Olga Desmond declared after divorcing her Hungarian husband that she was "glad that I followed the urging of my heart" and left him so that she could "belong once again to my art."[116] The role of these dancers as independent artists, hobnobbing with respected figures in the arts and intellectual life, for the most part unmarried, and some of them making a very good living, was an object lesson. All of this stood traditional assumptions about women's proper, domestic, and subordinate social and cultural roles on their heads.

Some men found the subliminal message of the new dance exciting. Peter Altenberg wrote admiringly, for example, that whereas other women were "cowardly" and governed their actions to please "whoever they are emotionally or financially dependent upon," Grete Wiesenthal "follows her own moods, doesn't want to captivate anyone, not even the

---

[111] Duncan, *My Life*, p. 17; Duncan, *Der Tanz der Zukunft*, p. 25; "The Dancer and Nature" (1905), in *The Art of the Dance*, p. 67.

[112] Caffin and Caffin, *Dancing and Dancers of Today*, pp. 225–226. The quotation is from Whitman's *Chants Democratic*, No. 2.

[113] Allan, *My Life*, pp. 116–117.

[114] Diana Cooper, *The Rainbow Comes and Goes* (Boston: Houghton Mifflin, 1958), p. 82.

[115] Gustav Möckel, "Isadora Duncan," *Kraft und Schönheit* 1 (1902/1903): 138.

[116] Desmond, *Mein Weg zur Schönheit*, p. 14.

audience."[117] But others expressed either a mild disquiet or even resentment. Thus, for example, one critical reviewer of Isadora Duncan believed she "acted out the emancipation of woman from man," that she "danced in every sense alone" and "drunk on herself."[118] Looking back from 1925 in an appreciation of Mary Wigman, Rudolf von Delius, a minor poet and close friend of a number of dancers, satirized this male discomfort with the new dance: "[S]ome men take this amiss ... Mary Wigman, they say, is not a real woman, there must be some pathology there, the erotic element is missing ... I think the poor dears are disappointed."[119] In short, some men were disturbed by one possible implication both of the dancers' behavior and of the composition of dance audiences: That as men, they weren't very important to the modern dancers.

2.4 Beauty Lite: A New Ideal Body

The obsession of reviewers with the slenderness of the modern dancers, oddly enough, actually reflects this role of modern dance as entertainment specifically for "modern" women, or "New Women" as they were called at the time. The prevailing ideal of female beauty at the end of the nineteenth century was what might be called reproductive beauty – big hips and big breasts, or what one recent study called a "luxurious hourglass figure."[120] Around the turn of the century, the new style or code of female beauty was gaining ground against this older ideal – the smooth, unbroken line, the lissome, slender, or girlish figure that would prevail through the 1920s. The message of this code had less to do with fecundity or nurture than with energy, competence, and activity; it was appropriate to an age in which social and physical restrictions on women were being rapidly eroded. Women were increasingly not only participating in the work force, associations, and even politics, but also literally moving around more, physically – whether they were going shopping, cycling, or on their way to and from work. Codes of physical beauty reflected this shift from constraint to activity. Images from the 1890s suggest that female beauty

[117] Peter Altenberg, *Das grosse Peter Altenberg Buch*, ed. Werner J. Schweiger (Vienna: Paul Zsolnay, 1977), pp. 335–336.
[118] Quoted in Roland Kischke, "'Die Berauschendste Verkettung von Gebärden': Faszination des Tanzes um 1900," in Gernot Frankhäuser, Roland Krischke, and Sigrun Paas, eds., *Tänzerinnen um Slevogt* (Munich: Deutscher Kunstverlag, 2007), p. 26.
[119] Rudolf von Delius, "Clotilde von Derp (1910)," p. 14; Rudolf von Delius, *Mary Wigman* (Dresden: Carl Reissner, 1925), pp. 32–33.
[120] Conyers, "Courtesans in Dance History," p. 222. See also Katja Schneider, "Schlank, biegsam, grazil: Das Körperbild im klassischen Tanz des 20. Jahrhunderts," *Tanzdrama* 36 (1997): 11–15.

at that time was defined primarily by a kind of blissful passive stateliness. There is still a very good measure of that posture in photographs of Isadora Duncan, Loïe Fuller, and Maud Allan. Photographs of later performers (Villany, the Wiesenthals, Clotilde von Derp, Sent M'ahesa) suggest in contrast an intermediate stage on the way to the outright athleticism of women dancers in the 1920s – which, in the eyes of some conservative critics, produced "muscular freaks" performing "grotesque and unesthetic contortions," or, in the view of a more sympathetic American critic, "a body stripped to muscle and sinew, plastic and controlled, instantly responsive to the will within."[121]

Men at the time clearly understood the meaning of this shift. For the nineteenth century, again, passive and serene fecundity was "sexy"; and many men could not see the new style of feminine beauty as sexually attractive. Adorée Villany is a striking case. Well more than half of the available reviews of her performances between 1905 and 1912 explicitly remark on her skinniness, often in mildly pejorative terms or with the implicit suggestion that she was lovely, but not sexy. Thus German reviewers called her not only slender but also "overly slender," "exceedingly slender," or even "almost too slender." French reviewers concurred, calling her figure "virginal," "slight and slender," "strangely supple and slender," "fragile and supple," and so forth. One German review even called her body "almost unremarkable" (*fast unauffällig*), implying one would not necessarily notice her, or that she would not attract notice – which is a rather remarkable thing to say about a woman dancing naked on stage before an audience.[122] One Spanish report found that "her body, without hips, has something dry about it, something anti-pagan."[123] After her arrest, a Berlin newspaper made a joke of this notion, observing in verse that some people feared her impact on public morals even "though her skinniness mitigated/What her nakedness dared."[124] And Villany, at her second trial in Paris in 1913, gave in evidence a report that an older male member of the audience had commented after the show that it was "a pity she's so skinny."[125]

---

[121] Quoted in John Martin, "The Dance: On Bringing Back Yesterday's Beauty," *New York Times*, February 19, 1933, p. X2; Henry Taylor Parker, "The Dancer in this Day without Peer" (1931), in *Motion Arrested: Dance Reviews of H. T. Parker*, ed. Olive Holmes (Middletown, CT: Wesleyan University Press, 1982), p. 186.

[122] F. Kl., "Tanz-Matinee Mlle Adorée Via Villany," *Münchner Post*, November 20, 1911; Villany, *Tanz-Reform*, pp. 263, 265, 267 273; Villany, *Phryné*, pp. 24, 27–28, 36, 38.

[123] Gomez-Carrillo, "El teatro en Paris," *Mundial* 3 (1913): 475.

[124] " Reprinted in Villany, *Tanz-Reform*, p. 326.

[125] Villany, *Phryné*, p. 25.

In this respect, Villany was typical; the idea that the modern dancers were too skinny to be sexy was quite common. As the great ballerina Tamara Karsavina remarked, at the turn of the century "meagerness" was "considered an enemy of good looks."[126] One Russian reviewer reported in 1904 that Isadora Duncan was "not at all beautiful," though she did have an "exotic" face; another reported that her "face, her figure, her manner – all this, judged very indulgently, will get a three-minus" (presumably on a beauty scale of ten).[127] The playwright and critic Max Halbe found her repulsively "masculinized," and complained about the "troupe of narrow-hipped, boyish girls" who studied and toured with her.[128] Grete Wiesenthal was described by one critic as "a little maiden, skinny, even haggard."[129] Maud Allan was "not pretty but she is thin."[130] Ida Rubinstein had a "very narrow boyish body," and Gabriele d'Annunzio even described her as "incorporeal"; a less appreciative observer found that "her body was unwomanly, therefore not beautiful."[131] One Munich reviewer held that Gertrud Leistikow's "overly slender and wiry figure is, in and of itself, not exactly attractive" unless it was moving to music; other reviewers found her "boyish," "no flower of maidenly beauty," mannish, or even that her appearance reminded one of the "Hellenic ideal of hermaphrodism."[132] Clotilde von Derp was "overly slender and fragile"; one south-German newspaper remarked in 1912 that she had an "austere, almost boyish form," and was an example of the fact that the modern dancers, as a group, no longer had "specifically feminine charms."[133]

[126] Quoted in A. H. Franks, "A Biographical Sketch," in *Pavlova: A Biography*, ed. Franks (New York: Da Capo, 1979), p. 15.

[127] N. Georgievich, "Duncan," *Peterburgskaya Gazeta*, December 14, 1904; G., "Isadora Duncan," *Slovo*, December 18, 1904, translations in JRDD, Natalia Roslasleva files, folders 2, 6.

[128] Max Halbe, *Jahrhundertwende: Geschichte meines Lebens 1893–1914* (Danzig: Kasemann, 1935), pp. 165, 164.

[129] Quoted in Schmidt, *Tanzgeschichte*, p. 28.

[130] O'Sheel, "To Maud Allan," p. 9.

[131] Quoted in Mayer, "Ida Rubinstein," p. 34; Kessler, in *Tagebuch*, vol. 4, p. 574; quoted in de Cossart, *Ida Rubinstein*, pp. 17, 10, 42, 56.

[132] Program of the Kleines Theater, undated, in STAM, Pol. Dir. 3806/4; H. W. F., "Gertrud Leistikow: Tanzabend im Hamburgerhof," *Neue Rheinische Zeitung*, October 31, 1913; "Der Tanzabend Gertrud Leistikow," *Elbinger Zeitung*, October 10, 1913; Dr. Lassbiegeln, "Gertrud Leistikow," *Braunschweiger Neueste Nachrichten*, October 30, 1913; Fr. S., "Gertrud Leistikow," *Frankfurter Nachrichten*, January 21, 1914, all clippings in TBCUA, Archief Gertrud Leistikow, Map 4a.

[133] Ettlinger, in a review of 1910, reprinted in *Tanzdrama* 14 (1991): 32; Dahms and Schroedter, eds., *Der Tanz*, p. 19; Frank-Manuel Peter, "Die 'neie Minchener Derpsichore: Clotilde von Derp – die früheste Vertreterin des Ausdruckstanzes?," in Peter and Stamm, *Die Sacharoffs*, p. 98; "Tanzabend Clotilde von Derp," *Schwäbischer Merkur*, March 19, 1912, clipping in DTAK, Inventory no. 56, Sacharoff, II.2.7.

This is not to say that men viewed modern dance performances without interest; many did appreciate the youthful vigor of slender bodies. At times, in fact, the terms in which male reviewers described modern dancers suggested a kind of pederastic prurience. A particularly bizarre case is that of Rudolf von Delius, who with his wife more or less adopted Clotilde von Derp. By the time von Derp was sixteen, Delius was clearly in love with her. She believed his love to be "not amorous, it was something more profound, reserved and pure." But ultimately he seems to have completely lost his composure: On the occasion of a visit by von Derp to his house in the country, he pulled out a revolver and apparently threatened to shoot himself unless she bent to his desires. She went to get his wife to help calm him down, and fled back to Munich the next day. After that Delius no longer wrote enthusiastic reviews about the "gracile charm" of her "awkward young limbs" and "budding" body – a physique he obviously found delectable, but which von Derp described as "weak and skinny."[134]

Delius's attraction to von Derp was not the only such case. Gertrud Falke's own father described her, at her dance debut, as "almost a child, of untouched purity." Writing in 1912, the early dance historian J. E. Crawford Flitch observed of Ruth St. Denis that, "[w]hile her beauty has much of the allure of sex," it had also a "childish character." One critic described Grete Wiesenthal in terms that were explicit to the point of creepiness: She had a "childish slender body"; she "wants to give herself, yet forbids herself"; she "cowers away from the unfamiliar man, shaking with shame; she overcomes this shame hesitantly, shyly, not knowing what is blossoming in her; she frees herself ever more joyfully in the rhythm of her body," expressing the "mixing of maidenhood and womanliness ... austerity and sensual joy."[135]

It was not, then, that the modern dancers were not sexy. But they were sexy in a different way. The feminine promise that modern dance communicated was not the robust, opulent promise of fecundity and passive self-sacrifice but the mobile grace of "girlish" activity, energy, joy. The modern dancers' bodies were symbolic of their liberation from enforced passivity, from social roles that, at the time, were coded as specifically feminine.

---

[134] "Les Sakharoff: La vie que nous avons dansée," ms. in DTAK, Inventory no. 56, Clotilde und Alexander Sacharoff, 1.1.1; Delius, *Mary Wigman*, p. 15; Clotilde Sacharoff, "La vie que nous avons dansée," in Frank-Manuel Peter and Rainer Stamm, eds., *Die Sacharoffs* (Cologne: Wienand, 2002), p. 158.

[135] Gustav Falke, "Tanzphantasie: Meiner Tochter Gertrud gewidmet," clipping in DTAK, Inventory no. 10, Gertrud und Ursula Falke, personalia; Flitch, *Modern Dancing*, p. 192.

Specifically *as women*, they acted out the bursting of bonds and constraints. As the Italian philosopher Benedetto Croce remarked in a treatise on "Aesthetics as the Science of Expression" just before the turn of the century, "activity always has a liberating effect, because it overcomes passivity."[136] Or, as Ernst Schur put it in 1910, "dance is liberated energy."[137]

2.5 Wild Movements: Dance and Codes of Comportment

This new style of feminine beauty corresponded to a new style of female movement, also exemplified by the modern dancers. In fact it is difficult to understand the full emotional force of modern dance, particularly for middle-class audiences, without a knowledge of the extraordinarily strict code of etiquette that governed physical self-expression in European societies around 1900 – and especially for women. One particularly influential German etiquette book told young people, for example, that one should sit straight enough, but not too straight, and avoid being "unquiet" or "noisy" when sitting; "rocking back and forth on one's chair is just as inappropriate as jumping up suddenly and running about." One should rise and be seated "as silently as possible." One should avoid strong facial expressions, grimacing, squinting, and the like; and "one should master one's glance, as one masters one's passions." Frowning, nervous ticks, looking around too often, or staring were "evil habits." "Sad thoughts" should be "mastered" as well, so that one did not present a "dark, ill-humored aspect"; people with heavy sorrows "should probably stay home alone with them." If that was impossible, one should cultivate "that composure or resignation of which an educated and pious person is capable" so as not to disturb others. Neither should one yawn, sneeze, sigh, or whistle in public; one's hands should remain at one's sides, not on one's hips; and one should not bend or turn when laughing. For men "a robust, hearty laugh is permissible" – but not for women. While "a certain decisiveness" was appealing in a man, he should also not cultivate a "so-called 'doughty'" or abrupt manner. The requirements for women's gait were more restrictive: They should "not walk glidingly or heavily, not with pathos or with a so-called theatrical gait, and avoid too forward a manner."[138] In short, one should not be "remarkable," in the literal sense,

---

[136] Benedetto Croce, *Aesthetik als Wissenschaft des Ausdrucks und allgemeine Linguistik*, trans. Karl Federn (Leipzig: E. A. Seemann, 1905), p. 21.

[137] Schur, *Der moderne Tanz*, p. 33.

[138] Clara Ernst, *Der feine Ton im gesellschaftlichen und öffentlichen Leben* (Mülheim: Bagel, 1885), pp. 25–31; also published later as *Was sich schickt—Was sich nicht schickt* (Mülheim, Bagel, 1900).

especially if one were female. In particular, one should not give physical expression to one's feelings.

Germans and especially German women were regarded in this period as particularly stiff in their movements; but etiquette books across the European world offered similar advice. In France, one observer wrote that French people could not dance because "we are too civilized, too polished, too prone to self-effacement. We have lost the knowledge of our ability to express feeling with our whole bodies; why, we are almost afraid to let it transpire in our features, or in the words we utter.... Our very gestures have become impoverished, restricted, tight.... We all live in our heads. Our bodies, so speak, have been abandoned."[139] An American manual of manners suggested that for women "volubility is to be avoided ... the words should be gently spoken"; that one's "way of looking ... must be regulated.... The audacious stare is odious; the sly, oblique, impenetrable look is unsatisfactory. Softly and kindly should the eyes be raised to those of the speaker." One's "private vexations" should not be allowed to affect one's manner; if a young lady were "unfit for society, let her refrain from entering it" until she was in command of her feelings again.[140] As late as 1937 another American manual suggested that girls should aim for a "smooth progress achieved by walking on one line, instead of running on two like a street-car." A "woman of grace and distinction will not step at all when she turns – she merely turns on the balls of her feet." When one took a seat, "the movement should be a smooth and continuous one – a flowing movement, all in the same tempo." All in all, "If we really move well, other people do not even see how we do it." And, of course, movement should be minimized: For example, foot tapping or twiddling one's feet were "seldom seen" in good company, and one should never "spoil your effect by making little jabbing motions at anything. Always take that little extra instant to be smooth."[141]

One might have excused a young woman around 1900 for concluding that the best thing she could do would be to turn herself into a statue – perhaps mounted on wheels. In the 1930s the French anthropologist Marcel Mauss offered a trenchant analysis of the social

[139] Quoted in Serge Lifar, *Serge Diaghilev: His Life, His Work, His Legend* (New York: Putnam, 1940), p. 163.

[140] *The Habits of Good Society: A Handbook for Ladies and Gentlemen* (New York: Carleton, 1872), pp. 233–234.

[141] Margery Wilson, *The New Etiquette: The Modern Code of Social* Behavior (New York: Frederick Stokes, 1937), pp. 54–56, 71.

function of the extraordinary degree of bodily discipline common up until then: "[E]ducation in composure" was a means of asserting the "domination of the conscious over emotion and unconsciousness."[142]

People accustomed to this kind of code of good manners found it difficult to come to grips with almost any physical activity, particularly for women. As the cultural historian Cas Wouters has argued in a study of etiquette books, strict physical self-control and self-discipline had come in the course of the previous century or two to be associated with moral worth, the capacity for orderly and reliable social relations, and social status; rigid control of "impulses and emotions" were signs that one was capable of subordinating oneself to "social controls" and an "authoritative conscience" and hence controlling one's animalistic, egoistic desires and instincts. "Negligence in these matters indicated an inclination toward dissoluteness" and antisocial behavior.[143] The body must be subordinate at all times to the mind; it should not attract attention because it was, after all, really completely peripheral to what makes us human beings, with a spiritual life and social responsibilities – indeed it was potentially a dangerous distraction from these truly human parts of us.[144] This taboo was so strong, in fact, that even painted depictions of emotionally intense body language could excite anxiety. Some viewers took exception, for example, to the leading Secessionist painter Max Liebermann's controversial 1879 image of *Jesus in the Temple* because it depicted Jesus underlining his arguments with decisive gestures of the hands – which made him look like an "impertinent Jewish boy" rather than our sovereign and serene Lord – and the scribes reacting with grimaces and other signs of emotion.[145]

More conservative people believed in particular that athletic or strenuous movement was a threat to women's "womanliness," and hence ultimately to the moral welfare of society – which rested on woman's ability to embody and defend the moral code that underpinned the Christian family order. Hedwig Dransfeld, chair of the Catholic Women's League in Germany, wrote in 1914, for example, that while she supported physical exercise for girls and women for health purposes, "it is quite certain

---

[142] Excerpted in "Marcel Mauss: Techniques of the Body," in Mariam Fraser and Monica Greco, eds., *The Body: A Reader* (London: Routledge, 2005), pp. 76–77.
[143] Cas Wouters, *Informalization: Manners and Emotions Since 1890* (Los Angeles: SAGE, 2007), p. 31. See also Järvinen, *Dancing Genius*, p. 46.
[144] Edward Ross Dickinson, "Citizenship, Reaction, and Technical Education: Vocational Schooling and the Prussian 'Youth Cultivation' Decree of 1911," *European History Quarterly* 29 (1999): 138–139.
[145] Paret, *The Berlin Secession*, p. 45.

that not every sport is appropriate for girls and women. Woman's nature demands more proportion and reserve, in this case too."[146]

This understanding of the necessary restrictions on women's movement closely paralleled a particular understanding of the function and nature of beauty in the arts. Conservative aesthetic theory was centered around the Kantian notion that beauty was necessarily and by nature serene, dignified, and contemplative. It must appeal to man's higher, more organized nature, not to his disorderly and protean instincts and desires. This tradition was particularly strong in Germany. Thus in 1900 the German jurist and later prominent conservative politician Dietrich von Oertzen argued that the function of art was to "raise people up, to transport them into the kingdom of the beautiful, the great, the noble and the elevated," and not simply to portray life as it really was, with all its "meanness and baseness" and misery.[147] The following year the Emperor of Germany told his subjects that art must not portray the real world in all its ugliness, but devote itself to "the cultivation of ideals."[148] In 1912, the great Catholic moral theologian Joseph Mausbach observed in a speech to the annual conference of German Catholics that "art can and must always be a teacher of higher morality, in that it always tries ... to bring form and order into the chaos of feelings in the human breast."[149] And the Heidelberg art history professor (and friend of Isadora Duncan) Heinrich Thode, in one of his lectures pillorying modernist painting as alien to the German spirit and degrading to women, argued that true art was characterized above all by "calm unity," as opposed to "unquiet."[150]

As we have seen, Isadora Duncan in particular was very careful, at the outset of her European career, not to offend such sensibilities, maintaining a sweet, serene, decorous demeanor. And girlish untroubled *joie de vivre* remained an important arrow in the quiver of many of the modern dancers. Yet even Duncan moved in ways that contemporaries found strikingly free (or sometimes libertine). As one Russian reviewer remarked, with Duncan "everything dances – waist, arms, neck, head, and, I daresay, also

[146] Hedwig Dransfeld, "Die Teilnahme des katholischen Frrauenbundes an der Bekämpfung gefährlicher und unsittlicher Bestrebungen," *Die christliche Frau* 12 (1914): 186.

[147] Dietrich von Oertzen, "Sittlichkeit und Standesehre," *Verhandlungen der Halle'schen Konferenz der deutschen Sittlichkeits-Vereine vom 8. und 9. Mai 1890* (Berlin: Berliner Stadtmission, 1890), p. 89.

[148] Wilhelm II, "Die Wahre Kunst. 18. Dezember 1901," in Johannes Penzler, ed., *Die Reden Kaiser Wilhelms II* (Leipzig: Philipp Reclam, 1913), p. 61.

[149] Joseph Mausbach, "Der Kampf gegen die moderne Sittenlosigkeit–eine Kulturaufgabe des deutschen Volkes," *Volkswart* 5 (1912): 134. Mausbach was quoting the painter Hans Thoma.

[150] Quoted in Paret, *Berlin Secession*, p. 176.

legs" and even her "pale, thin feet. They are not beautiful at all ... but
sometimes even they are expressive."[151] And again, rather quickly modern dance moved on from joyful "Greek" or Apollonian serenity to more
intense and often negative "Oriental" or Dionysian emotions, and to a
movement idiom that included not only the harmonious and happy but
also the wild, passionate, and even ugly. The portrayal of intense and sometimes very negative emotional states through "wild" movement was soon
understood to be an important part of the power and appeal of modern
dance. That may be, as the historian Cas Wouters argues, because the
"social and psychic tensions" created by the extremely strict cult of self-
control generated a "longing to defy these tensions in spontaneous, relaxed,
and informal conduct" – that is, "natural" and "expressive" behavior and
movement.[152]

In fact modern dance often sought not to give order to feelings nor
even really to "portray" them, but simply to give vent to them – to explore
them as legitimate potentials and expressions of the human soul. Ernst
Schur applauded Ruth St. Denis's ability to embody "unchained passion,"
to "dance the dance of raging lust awakened" in which "the limbs seem
to be thrown about by a whirlwind," to express the "intoxicating feeling of love."[153] Hugo von Hofmannsthal praised her "fabulous intensity,
severity, sensuality, and tempo."[154] One reviewer praised Tórtola Valencia's
performances because "within an area of a few square yards almost every
expressive movement of which the body is capable is made. The changes
of position are taken with incredible rapidity.... All the while expression
blazes from brow, eyes, lips and from sensitive nostrils."[155] Sent M'ahesa, as
one critic remarked in 1910, "does not even seek to be 'beautiful' or to have
'suggestive' effect. Feelings like fear, horror, greed, despair simply cannot
be expressed in 'pleasing' fashion"; so she used angular, geometric, awkward, "almost unnatural broken lines" to portray them.[156] Many dancers
adopted a "cooler" emotional register; but part of the excitement of modern dance was precisely the intensity of dances that expressed darker emotional potentials, through a less harmonious movement vocabulary. By the
1920s, some dancers would focus their performance personas around the

[151] N. Georgievich, "Duncan," in *Peterburgskaya Gazeta*, December 14, 1904, translation in JRDD,
    Natalia Roslasleva files, folder 2.
[152] Wouters, *Informalization*, p. 32.
[153] Schur, *Der moderne Tanz*, pp. 86, 84.
[154] Hofmannsthal, *Hugo von Hofmannsthal/Harry Graf Kessler Briefwechsel*, p. 174.
[155] Quoted in Garland, "Early Modern Dance," p. 3.
[156] Ettlinger, "Sent M'ahesa," pp. 33–34.

potentials of the intense, elemental, grotesque, and shocking; but that was a development already under way by 1914.

Metropolitan audiences soon became more accustomed to such dancing: After all, Maud Allan danced lust and horror more than 250 times, as Salomé, in London alone. But as late as 1917 one reviewer in Warsaw found himself "surprised, alienated, even frightened by the wild lawless anarchy that seems to spring out at him from these new dances" as performed by Olga Desmond.[157] And even in the Western European heartland of modern dance, accomplished performers could still achieve intense emotional impact with "wild" movement in the years just before the war. The fashion designer Paul Poiret, for example, wrote of Isadora Duncan's performance at a private party at his house in 1912 that Duncan "danced magnificently, marvelously, divinely … accelerating her movements from minute to minute, she precipitated the rhythm of her incantation to the point of exhaustion in wild whirlings, and finally fell to the ground as if in final overthrow. How many times had I, elsewhere, seen this spectacle …?" But Duncan "did it with a greatness of feeling that won to her everyone who saw her." Later, with a dance "disordered, pathetic, rending, and most human," she moved Poiret to tears.[158]

2.6 Good Dance, Bad Dance I: Gender

In short, the modern dancers were – as the dance historian Susan Funkenstein writes of Mary Wigman – "the embodiment of the liberating possibilities of physical expression for women" and understood by many to be the "quintessence of women's emancipation."[159] Susan Manning, too, has remarked that early modern dance served as "a metaphor for women's heightened social mobility and sense of possibility" after 1900.[160] Iris Garland, a biographer of Tórtola Valencia, saw the modern dancers' initiative in becoming "creators of their own dances" independent of male

[157] Runge, *Olga Desmond*, p. 91.

[158] Poiret, *My First Fifty Years*, pp. 200–203.

[159] Funkenstein, "There's Something," p. 829. For similar readings of Wigman see Susan Manning, "Feminism, Utopianism, and the Incompleted Dialogue of Modernism," in Gunhild Oberzaucher-Schüller, Alfred Oberzaucher, and Thomas Steiert, eds., *Ausdruckstanz* (Wilhelmshaven: Florian Noetzel, 1986), pp. 105–106; Dee Reynolds, "Dancing as a Woman: Mary Wigman and 'Absolute Dance,'" *Forum for Modern Language Studies* 35 (1999): 297–310.

[160] Duncan, *Der Tanz*, pp. 14, 25; Ann Daly, "Isadora Duncan's Dance Theory," *DRJ* 26 (1994): 26–27; Barche and Jeschke, "Bewegungsrausch und Formbestreben," pp. 325, 331; on "Elvira," Wilhelm, *Münchener Bohème*, pp. 116–121; Manning, "The Female Dancer and the Male Gaze," p. 162. On early modern dance and photography, see Huschka, "Bildgebungen tanzender Körper," pp. 41–50.

choreographers, taking "control of the creative process," as "a 'New Woman' strategy" that undermined the objectification and eroticization of women's bodies.[161] Gustav Frank and Katja Schneider contrast the "role of the ballet dancer as a mechanical puppet merely executing" the dance created by the male choreographer with the "new dance as original art" created by a female author.[162] Catherine G. Bellver, in a study of Spanish modernism, found that the new dance undermined men's tendency to create "dehumanized, defaced, eroticized" fantasy women because in it "women became soloists, innovators, and successful entrepreneurs of dance."[163] Annie Suquet saw Mata Hari as breaking down "the taboo on female sexuality"; she "represented, for the female public and for the dancers ..., new bodily and sexual liberties."[164] And Elizabeth Kendall suggested that "women filled the matinées" of the modern dancers because the "astonishing physicality" of women dressed in "light draperies or strings of jewels" was "an impelling sight, a prophecy" to women "securely laced into corsets that amplified their fronts, swelled their hips, and diminished them drastically in the middle."[165] As one earlier study put it, the modern dancers were "feminists avant la lettre."[166] And one might point to instances in which the strength of these women's personalities was evident – as when Isadora Duncan, hissed by an audience in Moscow for (as they saw it) dishonoring Beethoven by dancing to his music, stopped the show to reprimand her detractors, telling them (in French): "This is impolite and unamiable! This offends me, as a woman. Those who don't like [my dances] may leave."[167]

And yet, this positive view of modern dance – we might call it the "Good Dance" perspective – is not completely convincing. After all, the association of women with feeling, wildness, and passion, with at least the more emotive varieties of spirituality, with nature, organic "life," sexuality, self-absorption and the cultivation (or cult) of one's own beauty, and indeed with the past – the eternal and unchanging – was a central element in patriarchal ideology. It was the counterpart to the association of men

[161] Garland, *Tórtola Valencia*, p. 16.
[162] Gustav Frank and Katja Schneider, "Tanz und Tanzdebatte der Moderne," *Tanzdrama* 63 (2002): 4.
[163] Catherine G. Bellver, *Bodies in Motion* (Lewisburg, PA: Bucknell University Press, 2010), p. 90.
[164] Annie Suquet, *L'Eveil des modernités: Une histoire culturelle de la danse (1870–1945)* (Paris: Pantin/ Centre national de la danse, 2012), p. 270.
[165] Kendall, *Where She Danced*, pp. 80–81.
[166] Bentivoglio, *La danza moderna*, p. 34.
[167] "Isadora Duncan's Address to the Public," *Birzhevyie Vedomosti*, February 24, 1905, translation in JRDD, Natalia Roslasleva files, folder 22.

with reason, system, self-control, society, and the future. The language of modern dance was inflected by very powerful stereotypes about women. It is hard not to see in Hugo von Hofmannsthal's fascination with Ruth St. Denis's ability to embody "both poles: animal beauty and mysticism ..., sexless divinity and merely sexual woman" precisely those very old and very limiting stereotypes of femininity: the Madonna and the whore.[168] One report on Tórtola Valencia put the point differently: She was "a classic duchess, and a Carmen" at the same time.[169]

Partly for this reason, the few male dancers who achieved some fame in this period faced a terrible uphill battle against the prejudice that dance was essentially a feminine art. Clotilde von Derp's performance partner (and eventually husband) Alexander Sacharoff in particular was subject to vicious critiques that characterized him as unnatural and hermaphroditic. One Munich newspaper, for example, delighted in 1910 in Clotilde von Derp's "natural feeling ... grace and temperament" and found her "highly gifted"; but it found Alexander Sacharoff "in a certain sense tragic" because his dance "inspires a revulsion for [his] softness and demasculinization, paired with a bit of pity, and it inspires fear – fear for us, that this kind of thing might gain supporters at a time when mawkish *Weltschmerz*, effeminate emotion and sexual perversity threaten to undermine masculinity at the same time that femininity is rising up stronger and more self-assured."[170]

Many dance historians, therefore, have been ambivalent about the message of modern dance. Catherine Bellver, for example, admitted that the male avant-garde often saw women's bodies even in the new dance as "totally carnal ..., tending to objectify woman and focusing on her exclusively as erotic fantasy."[171] Jane Desmond saw Ruth St. Denis's fame and independence as "emblematic of the social changes in the women's sphere at the turn of the century," but believed that "her work remains conservative in its assertion of spirituality as the realm of woman and also in its presentation of woman's body as sexualized."[172] Iris Garland, who saw Tórtola Valencia as "part of a vanguard that liberated expression of the feminine body from Victorian standards," agreed that "what has been

---

[168] Hofmannsthal, *Hugo von Hofmannsthal/Harry Graf Kessler Briefwechsel 1898–1929*, p. 131.

[169] Frederico García Sanchiz, "Tórtola ... de Triana," *España Libre*, December 6, 1911, clipping in MAE, Fonds Tortola Valencia, L3.

[170] F. M., "Theater und Musik: Tanzabend Alexander Sacharoff," *Münchner Neueste Nachrichten*, June 4, 1910, clipping in DTAK, Inventory no. 56, Clotilde und Alexander Sacharoff, II.2.7.

[171] Bellver, *Bodies*, pp. 48, 82.

[172] Jane Desmond, "Dancing Out the Difference: Cultural Imperialism and Ruth St. Denis's 'Radha' of 1906," *Signs* 17 (1991): 48.

termed the 'male gaze' was a significant factor in Tórtola's success" because she not only "epitomized the 'New Woman,' a self-sufficient, independent career woman" but also "simultaneously embodied and indulged patriarchal fantasies of the archetypal 'eternal feminine.' "[173] Ulrike Wohler is particularly critical, arguing that the modern dancers' insistence that their art was "chaste" merely reproduced conventional bourgeois notions of the innate morality of women; the "ideology of naturalness" was "rigid, that is strict and puritanical" and asexual, and robbed nude dance of its revolutionary potential. "The apparent 'liberation of the body' turned out to be merely a transition from older to newer forms of dependence."[174]

Much of this more critical perspective on modern dance is directed specifically at the "Oriental" mode cultivated by, for example, Ruth St. Denis or Maud Allan. But the "Greek" mode too could easily be interpreted as fitting what was, by 1900, a very well-established Western tradition of portraying the female nude. Lynda Nead has given an insightful analysis of the ideological function of this tradition. Women's bodies, she suggests, are coded in Western culture as the symbolic embodiment of "unformed, undifferentiated matter." The centrality of the female nude in the Western artistic tradition is a product of the desire to impose masculine control – reason, structure, boundaries, universality, law – on this threatening, wild, chaotic materiality. Transformed into art, the female nude is "contained by convention, form and technique; she poses no threat to patriarchal systems of order."[175] This transmutation was essential to Isadora Duncan's very influential argument for "nude" dance: Because she was a statue, she was chaste.

It is tempting to engage in calculations that might enable us to choose between these two interpretations – modern dance as feminist self-assertion or modern dance as adoption of sexist stereotypes affirming masculine superiority and control. Does the importance of male patrons like Hugo von Hofmannsthal or Stanford White suggest the latter interpretation? Does the role of female patrons like the Duchess of Manchester or the Princess de Polignac, or the independence of the dance stars, suggest the former? Were nude dance and wild movement claims to bodily liberation for women, or were they simply playing on male desires and stereotypes?

[173] Garland, *Tórtola Valencia*, p. 49.
[174] Ulrike Wohler, "Tanz zwischen Avantgarde und klassischer Moderne: Anita Berber und Mary Wigman," in Lutz Hieber and Stephan Moebius, eds., *Avantgarden und Politik: Künstlerischer Aktivismus von Dada bis zur Postmoderne* (Bielefeld: transcript, 2009), p. 208.
[175] Nead, *The Female Nude*, pp. 4, 7.

The dance historian Susan Manning offers a formulation that allows us to avoid this kind of sleuthing, which is predictably fruitless. Manning argues that we should "give equal weight to the resistive and recuperative dimensions" of modern dance; for it was "precisely the double move of subverting the voyeuristic gaze while projecting essentialized notions of identity that defined the practice of early modern dance." This was, she concluded, "the paradoxical social function of the form, its ability to contest and to conform at the same time."[176] As Hugo von Hofmannsthal wrote of Ruth St. Denis's dance, "[I]t is wild, and it is governed by eternal laws." Max Osborn, too, wrote of Grete Wiesenthal that from her "smile the magnetic current of sensual seduction flows out, but is completely chaste and innocent and yet retains its attraction."[177] In fact, we should see this essential ambiguity as yet one more aspect of the extraordinarily effective, protean marketing strategy of modern dance. Modern dance could appeal both to men psychologically committed to the Madonna/whore dichotomy *and* to women committed to dissolving it. It could play to, with, and across the tension between incitement and disavowal of desire.[178] As Lynda Nead points out, Western art has been obsessed with the female nude for a good two hundred years precisely because the distinction between the wild, disorderly naked and the contained, controlled nude is not a stable boundary, but "a frontier that is itself endlessly policed, invoked, transgressed and replaced."[179] Modern dance turned that process – not any one outcome of it – into a highly marketable commodity. It did not resolve the threat implicit in the polarity between chaste and sexual, wild and civilized, reason and passion. Instead, it generated it over and over, fed on it, used it, and drew energy from it.

The Salomé dance that so many of the modern dancers performed epitomizes this technique. Amy Koritz is probably right that part of the appeal of the Salomé dance – one reason it generated what some historians call the "Salomania" of the period – was that it made murderous sexual passion safe.[180] But it surely appealed just as much because it pointed out how powerful and dangerous sexual passion was. One reviewer of Maud Allan put the point in particularly odd but suggestive terms in 1910: Her

---

[176] Manning, "The Female Dancer," pp. 154, 163.

[177] Hofmannsthal, "Die unvergleichliche Tänzerin," p. 262; Osborn, *Der bunte Spiegel*, p. 174.

[178] I have borrowed this formulation from Dagmar Herzog, "Hubris and Hypocrisy, Incitement and Disavowal: Sexuality and German Fascism," in Dagmar Herzog, ed., *Sexuality and German Fascism* (New York: Berghahn Books, 2005), pp. 3–21.

[179] Nead, *The Female Nude*, p. 9.

[180] Amy Koritz, "Dancing the Orient for England: Maud Allan's 'The Vision of Salomé,'" *Theatre Journal* 46 (1994): 65, 69–70.

"performance struck me as indecent but handled in a way to make it appear perfectly modest." Half the audience was there, he thought, "because they think it is the most improper act ever put upon the stage"; the other half was there "because they regard the performance as the highest expression in motion of the pure and chaste" (see Figure 2.2).[181]

Such performances were deliberately mixed; they drew their power precisely from ambiguity, from what the theater historian Heather Marcovitch calls the "tension between sexual desire and lofty spirit," or "asexual sexuality."[182] The chasteness of modern dance made its performers all the more sexy because they were not low, vulgar, primitive, savage, uncultured, decadent, degenerate – the audience knew this because they looked like Greek statues and danced to Chopin. But their sexiness made them all the more chaste – for what could be more chaste than a performer who was able to achieve the miracle of rendering nakedness innocent, who could prance about naked on stage without being sexually suggestive? The German sex-radical Johannes Guttzeit made this lesson explicit in 1908: "When [Isadora] Duncan appears in a little red dress that leaves her knees free ... and nevertheless makes a pure and noble impression, that is all the more evidence of the moral force that she can exert."[183] And one San Francisco reviewer wrote in 1910 that "[a]rt has never performed a greater miracle" than in Maud Allan's performance, where nudity was rendered chaste – literally, a "chaste exhibition."[184] Indeed, even the skeptics were impressed: One Russian reviewer who warned that Isadora Duncan's "nude legs and bare feet ... create an enormous danger – that of reducing art to coarse sensuality" also observed that "what we are dealing with here is merely a stunt: that of how to be decent in an almost nude state."[185]

2.7 "Brothel Art" versus Moral Citizenship

Some contemporary men understood the essentially feminist message of modern dance, and deplored it. The German playwright and critic Max

---

[181] "Maud Allan's Dance at Close Range," in Maud Allan clippings files, MPDSF.
[182] Heather Marcovitch, "Dance, Ritual, and Arthur Symons's London Nights," *English Literature in Transition, 1880–1920* 56 (2013): 466.
[183] Johannes Guttzeit, *Schamgefühl, Sittlichkeit und Anstand* (Dresden: Berthold Sturm, 1908), p. 278. See also Steegmuller, *Your Isadora*, p. 44: reviewers mentioned Duncan's "nude" legs and feet "almost as though her greatest triumph were to have distracted the concentration of public attention from them."
[184] Allan, *Maud Allan and Her Art*, p. 20.
[185] G., "Isadora Duncan," *Slovo*, December 18, 1904, translation in JRDD, Natalia Roslasleva files, folder 7.

Figure 2.2 Maud Allan as Salomé with the head of John the Baptist, 1908

Halbe, for example, decried what he saw as the intellectualism, unnatural instincts, and emancipation of the "masculinized American female ideal" represented by Isadora Duncan as "one of the consequences of women's emancipation." Halbe also objected to what he saw as Duncan's lack of passion, of sensuality.[186] But in this Halbe was very distinctly in the minority (and he would later become an impassioned supporter of modern dance). By far the more common objection to modern dance was that it was indecent and a threat to morality. The early history of modern dance was peppered with scandals generated by the efforts of moral conservatives to prevent women from appearing on stage in a state of undress. In some cases, they succeeded. Maud Allan, for example, was prevented from performing her Salomé dance in Munich and Nuremberg in 1907 and in Manchester in 1908. Methodist ministers in St. Louis adopted a resolution condemning Isadora Duncan's performance there in 1909. Adorée Villany was charged with indecency in Munich in late 1911 and in Paris in early 1913, while she was prevented from performing in Prague and had to wear a bodysuit in Vienna. Tórtola Valencia faced censorship attempts in various cities in Spain, and later in Latin America – including in Colombia, where a "mystical mafia" of conservative Catholics, as one secular progressive put it, attempted a "detortolization" of the country.[187]

Those who favored such measures, obviously, simply did not accept that looking like a statue made one chaste. In fact, some reversed the meaning of references to ancient art, by arguing that modern dance was replicating the kind of decadence that had led – as they saw it – to the decline and collapse of Greece and Rome. Modern dance, they argued, was flat suggestive. Thus one critic of Maud Allan wrote in 1908 that she

> writhes and postures before us.... Her flesh gleams with dusky light under her gleaming jewels ... her hot bursting lips suck out our soul. She moves in the dance; slow and sensual, with calculating provocative gestures; faster and faster – passionate – all thought lost in the clutch of her whirling lust.... The horrible mad music curls around us in throbbing

[186] Halbe, *Jahrhundertwende*, pp. 164, 163. Admittedly Halbe was writing in 1935, and may have had reasons to want to endear himself to the Nazi authorities in Germany.

[187] Allan, *My Life*, p. 84; Cherniavsky, "Maud Allan, Part II," p. 216 and "Maud Allan, Part III," p. 133; "Denounce Classic Dance," *New York Times*, November 2, 1909, p. 9; Edward Ross Dickinson, "'Must We Dance Naked?': Art, Beauty and Politics in Munich and Paris, 1911 and 1913," *Journal of the History of Sexuality* 20 (2011): 95–131; Villany, *Tanz-Reform*, pp. 264, 344–345; Garland, "Early Modern Dance," p. 19; Irene Peypach, *Tórtola Valencia* (Barcelona: Edicions de Nou Art Thor, no year), pp. 9–10; newspaper clippings in MAE, Fonds Tórtola Valencia, L14, fols. 233, 235, 245, 292; quotation fol. 236, Maciantonio Peraza, "Detórtolación," *Antioquia Liberal*, September 22, 1924.

sweeps. Broken light and shadow play liquidly over the flood of her flesh ..., over the great rush of her breasts, over the naked mad magic of her quivering belly.... I cannot imagine anything more immoral and less artistic.[188]

A London newspaper complained that "London has never seen such a glorification of the flesh!" Allan's nudity was "expressive, vaunting, triumphant," a thing from the "Eastern tropical swamps," exerting the "fascination" of the "animal-like and carnal."[189] Tórtola Valencia, too, was accused, in Spain, of offering "lascivious dances that nauseate decent persons."[190] Adorée Villany, according to one critic in Munich in 1911, was "an outgrowth of the most disgusting brothel-art." A leading Catholic newspaper in Cologne wrote of "disgusting pornographic displays" and "un-costumed swinishness," asking "what sort of makeup does an 'artiste' have who surrenders herself up to making her body an object of ... lust in a public display?"[191] And in Moscow one reviewer found that Isadora Duncan had not even the mediocre talent of a cabaret dancer, observing that for her performances were merely "a source of income, and here we are taking them seriously? ... Greece? No – a disgrace – nothing else! ... The crowd numbering in thousands stared at the beautiful young body and seared it with their eyes. Is that art?" Another told readers that Duncan's alleged art amounted to nothing more than "vulgar, purely American tricks" and "obvious publicity-seeking."[192]

Moral conservatives objected to such public indecency on two grounds. One was that it objectified and implicitly denigrated women, by reducing them to merely carnal beings. This was the position, for example, advanced in a public manifesto put out by fifteen Catholic women's organizations in Munich after Adorée Villany's arrest there in late 1911. They fully supported the action of the police, arguing that all women had an interest in seeing to it "that their sex is not degraded by public exposure and insults to modesty," which were "deeply insulting to women, mothers and families."[193] These conservative Christian women were objecting to the advancing sexualization and commercialization of women's bodies – what Gail

[188] Quoted in Cherniavsky, "Maud Allan, Part III," pp. 135, 137.
[189] Ibid., p. 127.
[190] Quoted in Murias Vila, "La magicienne aux yeux d'abîme," p. 27.
[191] Villany, *Tanz-Reform*, p. 284; "Schmutz," *Kölnische Volkszeitung*, December 1, 1911; "München," *Kölnische Volkszeitung*, November 25, 1911.
[192] Dubov-diez, "Miss Duncan," *Slovo*, December 15, 1904; Lord Kurbalstone, "The School of New and Free Dance," *Teatralnaya Rossia*, February 5, 1905, translations in JRDD, Natalia Roslasleva files, folders 5, 20.
[193] Reprinted in Villany, *Tanz-Reform*, pp. 351–352.

Finney has called the "cultural construction" of woman as "spectacle and commodity."[194]

The second focus for conservative critiques was more overtly political. The state, they argued, had to protect its citizens from indecent images, publications, and entertainments because otherwise they would be "enslaved" to their carnal lusts. As the German moral philosopher Friedrich Wilhelm Foerster put it in 1907, they would become "helpless slaves of their erotic urges," subject to the "absolute dictatorship of Eros."[195] And the Minister of the Interior of Prussia remarked – quoting Kant directly – during a parliamentary debate in January 1909 over Olga Desmond's "beauty evenings" in Berlin that true art "seeks to idealize, seeks to raise us up and free us from the slag of earthly imperfection," whereas Desmond's dances "draw the audience down to the actual model" in her merely material corporeality, encouraging mere carnality.[196] Conservative Christians argued that such "enslavement" would so weaken the moral fiber of the citizen that he or she would become incapable of living in an ordered society, of obeying a higher law than that of their own carnal and greedy desires. A society made up of such people would be a mere chaos, in which the strong would exploit the weak to gratify their appetites. It would degenerate into a war of all against all, in which tyrants would ultimately prevail by appealing to the selfish violent passions of the mob or the selfish material interests of the powerful. The defense of public decency was therefore a defense of order, law, individual rights, and ultimately of political liberty. As one German pamphlet on modern dance put it, "the authorities, who are ... responsible for the intellectual and moral uplift of the people" had a clear duty to suppress nudity on stage.[197] This was not only a matter of moral principle, but also a function of internal security. Thus, for example, William Alexander Coote, head of the National Vigilance Association in Britain, decried nude statue-posing (of the kind marketed by Olga Desmond, among others) as both "obviously subversive of the best interests of the growing generation" (i.e., immoral) and as "opposed to the ideals of true citizenship."[198] Some even argued

[194] Gail Finney, *Women in Modern Drama* (Ithaca, NY: Cornell University Press, 1989), p. 82.
[195] Friedrich Wilhelm Foerster, *Sexualethik und Sexualpädagogik* (Kempten: Josef Kösel, 1907), pp. 24, 6, 27.
[196] Interior Minister von Moltke, *Stenographische Berichte über die Verhandlungen des preussischen Hauses der Abgeordneten*, 13. session, 13 January 1909, column 953.
[197] Ernst Lennartz, *Duncan – She – Desmond: Beiträge zur Beurteilung und Geschichte der Nackt-Kultur* (Cologne: Benziger, 1908), p. 12.
[198] William Alexander Coote, ed., *A Romance of Philanthropy* (London: National Vigilance Association, 1916), p. 42.

that nude dance was part of a deliberate revolutionary policy of moral subversion – "a systematically advancing, very serious moral-revolutionary movement that is conquering ever more terrain" in (in this case) German society.[199]

Moral conservatives did not see police intervention against modern dance as an assault on artistic freedom because they were convinced that nudity on stage had nothing to do with art. It was, as the Prussian Minister of the Interior put it, simply "business greed for profit, speculating on low sensuality"; and it had "not the least thing to do with art" but was merely an expression "partly of extravagant hysteria and lewdness, partly of extraordinary business acumen." In this, conservative politicians were sometimes supported by the official academies of art – as when the Prussian Academy concluded that Olga Desmond's performances were "devoid of any higher artistic value." A common assertion, in fact, was that nudity on stage could in principle never have artistic value because "the naked body is not art, but nature."[200]

Liberal opinion saw in such arguments an insulting and insidious abrogation of the moral autonomy of the citizen. In Munich, for example, one critic of the arrest of Adorée Villany suggested that "it's shameful to be a German as long as the police can with impunity proceed against the faculty of the Academy of Arts and the mature art world as it would against a pack of pimps and prostitutes." Another held that "it would take a dirty imagination to see anything objectionable in" Villany's performance. A sculptor published an open letter to the city's chief of police, calling his agency the "Bavaro-Russian" police – a reference to political conditions in the most backward and autocratic state in Europe.[201] A Munich art professor identified the central political issue at stake in an open letter to Villany's theater director: Munich's arts community was in danger of being deprived, by "inquisitorial" busybodies, of "the best we have: spiritual freedom and self-determination."[202] Another supporter, in Berlin, made the stakes still more explicit: "[T]he purification and refinement of moral conceptions," he wrote, "is not the function of the authorities, but of the self-cultivation of every individual, and of the citizenry at large."[203]

[199] Otto von Erlbach, "Bühne und Moral," *Allgemeine Rundschau*, June 6, 1908, p. 372, clipping in STAM, Polizei-Direktion no. 4342/1.
[200] *Stenographische Berichte*, columns 952, 961, 966, 942, 946.
[201] "Der Sieg der Sittlichkeit," *Münchner Zeitung*, November 20, 1911; Villany, *Tanz-Reform*, pp. 325, 319, 315; "Ein Theaterskandal," *Münchner Neueste Nachrichten*, November 20, 1911.
[202] Quoted in "Kinderhändlerinnen und Nackttänzerinnen," *Germania*, November 24, 1911.
[203] Erich Felder, "Münchner Keuschheitsgelüste," *Der Turm* 1, no. 1 (December 1911): 19.

The defense of modern dance, indeed even attending modern dance performances, was thus an implicit – and at certain moments an explicit – claim to political rights and liberties. That claim rested, most crucially, on the underlying assertion of moral maturity, indeed moral superiority. The point was precisely that those who enjoyed Villany's performance did not have a "dirty imagination" – and those who objected did. As the same supporter put it, her performance was "so lovely, so accomplished,that even a piglet could recognize the aesthetic principles" in it. The term he used was *Ferkel*, which can also be translated as "dirty little mind."[204] A St. Petersburg reviewer had made the same argument about Isadora Duncan in 1904: "[O]nly a thoroughly corrupted member of our present bourgeois society will see this nudity of the revived classical statue as a violation of the laws of decency or morality."[205] Here again, modern dance "worked" precisely by invoking *and* denying the sensual. People for whom watching a naked woman dance on stage did not constitute an incitement to lustful sensuality, this argument implied, were *really* morally mature; they were truly in charge of their sensual, egoistic urges. One could trust them with political freedom. The modern dance audience was demonstratively *not* enslaved by sensuality; it was made up of moral grown-ups, ready for responsible citizenship.

This claim was of greater or lesser importance in different parts of Europe. In Republican France, or in liberal Britain, the issue was not terribly urgent; and there the press responded to prohibitions or arrests with satire – and in Paris, in 1913, with a petition circulated among artists in defense of Villany's right to dance naked. In Germany the boundaries of citizenship were still quite restrictive, and the Villany case in particular sparked a national scandal and debate. But in both Munich and Paris, liberal circles also used Villany's problems with the police to demonstrate their power to govern their own lives. Three weeks after her arrest, the student union at Munich's Academy of the Arts invited Villany to give a "private" performance for an audience made up strictly of students and faculty in the same theater where she had been arrested. In late December Villany appeared in yet another private performance, again at the same venue, this time organized by the Munich Artists' Cooperative.[206] At Villany's trial in Munich, both the director of the Munich Academy and the president of

[204] Ibid., p. 18.
[205] Quoted in Steegmuller, *Your Isadora*, p. 45.
[206] "Die Polizei bekehrt sich," *Berliner Tageblatt*, December 20, 1911; "Die Tänzerin Villany," *Münchner Neueste Nachrichten*, December 20, 1911; "Die Tänzerin Villany," *Münchner Neueste Nachrichten*, December 29, 1911.

the Munich Secession from that same academy testified that her performance was wholly artistic.[207] In Paris, Villany gave at least four private performances for invited members of the arts community after she had been charged, again in the same theater; and she gave more informal and intimate performances for painters, sculptors, and at least one member of the French Chamber of Deputies.[208]

Some observers who were more open to the argument that sensual desire was not automatically a bad thing were driven to distraction by this whole debate. The Austrian writer Karl Kraus, for example, lost his composure in an essay on the reception of Mata Hari in Vienna in 1906. He declared that both those who held that Mata Hari should be allowed to continue performing because her act was "purely artistic" and did not "incite sensuality" *and* those who argued that she should be stopped because it did were, in spiritual terms, mere "policemen" – essentially in agreement that sensuality should be prohibited. "God forbid," he ranted, "that an artistic production – much less a variety-theater number – should 'incite sensuality'!… As if 'sensuality' were the worst thing that could be 'incited' in people living in Austria today!"[209] Others pointed out that those who attacked modern dance as indecent were, as one Berlin newspaper observed in 1911, merely creating "excellent publicity" for the dancers – it made them newsworthy, and it advertised the fact that they might offer a sensual thrill.[210] And some commented, finally, on the hypocrisy of those who wanted to ban nudity from the "serious" stage, while tolerating it in "popular" theater. Some commentators in Paris in 1913, for example, observed that Villany's performance was nothing compared with what one called the "abject obscenity" of many variety-theater shows.[211]

In politics and in commerce, however, victory often goes to the one who can keep a straight face the longest. Whatever forms of hypocrisy may have been involved, it made good sense – a good story – that artists in revolt against the aesthetic theory of the official art academies would also be in revolt against the political establishments that supported them. It made sense, too, that an art form obsessively focused on individual expression and autonomy should also be committed to political democracy. As we

[207] "Ein Theaterskandal in München," *Berliner Tageblatt* no. 592(November 20, 1911); "Dancer Is Acquitted," *New York Times*, March 10, 1912; "Prozess Robert-Villany," *Münchner Neueste Nachrichten*, March 8, 1912.

[208] Villany, *Phryné*, pp. 17, 21.

[209] Karl Kraus, "Der Schmock und die Bajadere," in Christine Lüders, ed., *Apropos Mata Hari* (Frankfurt: Neue Kritik, 1997), pp. 85–86, 89.

[210] "Das Ende eines Theaterskandals," *Berliner Tageblatt* 32, January 18, 1912.

[211] Reprinted in Villany, *Phryné*, pp. 35, 14.

will see in Chapter 5, later developments would show that this connection was tenuous and contingent. For the prewar period, however, part of the appeal of modern dance was precisely that conservatives so vehemently rejected it. Modern dance *looked* "progressive," enlightened, democratic, freedom loving. Getting oneself arrested, censored, or debated in parliament was a fabulous marketing strategy. It got the performer's name in the newspapers; it made her appear to be important; and it made her appear to be a martyr for moral and political progress.

2.8 Dancers and Their Mothers (and Fathers)

The reasoning of conservative critics of modern dance was, obviously, intensely paternalistic, even patriarchal. Papa State, they held, had a paternal right and duty to protect his children from their own moral immaturity and poor judgment. One critic of the arrest of Adorée Villany in Munich even bemoaned the fact that the police could send her audience, composed of artists and respectable and well-to-do citizens, "home like schoolboys."[212] It is somewhat curious, therefore, that the conservative critics did not argue that the modern dancers suffered from a psychological problem – the inability to accept the legitimate authority of a father. In a sense this is understandable because moral conservatives were often unwilling to entertain psychological explanations for behaviors they preferred to interpret as the consequence of moral or spiritual failings. And yet, there is plenty of evidence that many of the modern dancers had absent or weak fathers, domineering mothers, and what are commonly called "daddy issues."[213]

Isadora Duncan is a prime example. Her father was a rather unsteady character who was in and out of her life, and whom she was taught to believe had "horns and a tail." He made a fortune in banking in San Francisco, but became embroiled in a financial crash and scandal; made another fortune in real estate in Los Angeles (after a divorce from Isadora's mother occasioned by his womanizing) but went bust again; and at one point gave his ex-wife the use of "a beautiful house which had large dancing rooms, a tennis court, a barn and a windmill" – until he lost it again. "All my childhood," she reported in her autobiography, "seemed to be under

[212] Reprinted in Villany, *Tanz-Reform*, p. 290.
[213] This is not a new insight; see, e.g., Rayner Heppenstall, excerpt from *Apology for Dancing* (1936), in Roger Copeland and Marshall Cohen, eds., *What Is Dance?* (Oxford: Oxford University Press, 1983), esp. pp. 270–271; Kendall, *Where She Danced*, p. 39; Jack Anderson, *Art without Boundaries* (Iowa City: University of Iowa Press, 1997), p. 34.

the black shadow of this mysterious father of whom no one would speak." Her mother in contrast, had a "beautiful and restless spirit" and taught her children "a fine scorn and contempt" for possessions and accompanied Duncan almost everywhere during her first years in Europe.[214] In her professional life, Duncan consistently cultivated an enthusiastic, histrionic, possibly slightly hysterical style, peppered with pronouncements like (in Budapest) "one Hungarian gypsy musician is worth all the gramophones in the world"; or (at the Parthenon in Athens) "I realized that I must find a dance whose effort was to be worthy of this Temple – or never dance again"; or (in Berlin) the "seduction of Nietzsche's philosophy ravished my being."[215] This was no doubt partly a deliberate strategy to portray herself as a creative genius driven by elemental emotion and extreme aesthetic sensitivity. But her private life was entirely in keeping with this professional persona. Duncan stumbled from one sudden, obsessive, rapturous, disastrous romantic entanglement to another for more than two decades, always with men who were frightfully self-absorbed.

The pattern was set by a first sexual experience, with a Hungarian actor more interested in having an audience than a friend. Their physical relationship was "at first sheer torture" and then showed her "Heaven on earth" and convinced her that "God ... has made this one moment to be worth more, and more desirable, than all else in the Universe." Duncan was quite aware this sort of love was a "defeat of the intelligence ... that often leads to the gravest disasters"; but she seems to have been unable to resist it.[216] When the Hungarian moved on, she "spent several weeks in utter prostration and horrible suffering" in a clinic in Vienna and then "languid and sad" at a spa in northwest Bohemia – the first of a number of such episodes. After that, swept away by the "fantastic sensuality and ecstasy" and "irresistible torrent" of "terrible desires," she fell hard for the art professor Heinrich Thode – a man she readily perceived to be "intoxicated with the divine essence of his supreme intelligence." Gazing into his eyes, she "was uplifted and, with him, traversed heavenly spheres or paths of shining light. Such exquisite ecstasy of love ... transformed my being, which became all luminous.... He so completely possessed my soul that it seemed it was only possible to gaze into his eyes and long for death" – a nice unconscious (?) pun because "Thode" is an archaic spelling of the German word *Tod*, or death. But Thode was twenty years older and

[214] Duncan, *My Life*, pp. 16–17, 22. See Kurth, *Isadora*, pp. 12–14 and Blair, *Isadora*, pp. 9–13.
[215] Duncan, *My Life*, pp. 99, 141 and *The Art of the Dance*, p. 65.
[216] Duncan, *My Life*, pp. 103, 105.

married – lucky man – to a "kindly woman … quite incapable of the high exaltation in which Heinrich lived"; and apparently he never did have sex with Duncan. She ended up unable to sleep or eat, and had to pack it in and depart for a triumphal short tour in Russia, in December 1904.[217]

Two years later she fell again, just as instantaneously, into a mad ecstatic obsessive love, this time for Edward Gordon Craig – a stage designer, director, and misanthrope who had also grown up without a father. Craig was another one who was (as Duncan put it) "in a state of exaltation from morning till night," either "in the throes of highest delight" or "in those moods which suddenly followed after, when the whole sky seemed to turn black, and sudden apprehension filled the air." Engaged to be married when he met Duncan, he already had seven children by various women and another on the way, none of whom he would ever consistently support, any more than he did his daughter by Duncan. He followed her home for dinner one night after her performance, "in a wild state of excitement. He wanted to explain all his ideas about his art, his ambitions" and eventually came to the conclusion that "I was the one who invented you. You belong to my scenery." Duncan was "hypnotized … flew into his arms," and even "felt that in our love was some criminal incestuousness." The sex was apparently so wonderful "that earthly passion became a heavenly embrace of white, fiery flame." Duncan hid in his apartment for two weeks, skipping performances and failing to tell her mother where she was.[218] After the birth of their child, Craig apparently decided that "Isadora is impossible" (so Duncan surmised) and moved on to other women, which drove Duncan to a "frenzied state … fits of alternate fury and despair," from which she was distracted by a chap who, when she asked what he did in life, replied that he had "a lovely collection of eighteenth century snuff boxes."[219]

And so it went, essentially, for the next twenty years – though for much of that time she also made herself miserable over Craig, whom she loved despite the fact that he was clearly just no good. In her memoirs Duncan explained her endless, compulsive round of impulsive affairs in various ways. In one passage, it was a product of "pagan innocence" and the discovery that "Love might be a pastime as well as a tragedy." In another, she claimed that "each time a new love came to me … I believed that this

[217] Duncan, *My Life*, pp. 107, 144, 150, 149, 158; Steegmuller, *Your Isadora*, p. 203.
[218] Duncan, *My Life*, pp. 180–184. Craig took issue with the account in Duncan's memoirs; but she seems to have captured the essence of the man. See Steegmuller, *Your Isadora*, pp. 20–21, 31, 101, 105–108; Blair, *Isadora*, pp. 94–101.
[219] Ibid., pp. 208–209.

was the only one for whom I had waited so long, that this love would be the final resurrection of my life." She also admitted that "they all ended badly." It all appears to have been exhausting, and quite possibly essentially empty.[220]

Clotilde von Derp's autobiography is no less disturbing, though the ultimate outcome was happier. Von Derp's father was a gambler with "a carefree and light-hearted nature"; when he lost everything, her "dominating and energetic" mother went to stay with friends in England, leaving Clotilde and a sister for two years in the care of an uncle in the Death's Head Hussars, in a household "devoid of love, strict, precise and imbued with the military spirit." Eventually her mother returned and they settled in Munich, where Clotilde was (she recalled) alone all the time, often cried herself to sleep, and saw her father once a year. She was taken in by Rudolf von Delius, who read the celebrated literary love letters of the English poets Elizabeth and Robert Browning out loud to her and took her to museums to see ancient Greek art. When her uncle Sepp sneaked a kiss, she "felt that I had become all of a sudden important"; but her mother interpreted the incident as a moral failing in her, and "wrapped herself, toward me, in a cold and haughty silence. I was left alone with my pain." Ultimately von Derp was rescued by her husband Alexander Sacharoff, a gay man who took her into his circle of artistic and literary friends, and adored her fresh, innocent, childlike spirit – "a woman like the springtime ... almost supernatural ... like the concept of a young girl, not the young girl herself ... she seemed to live in a dream, she was not wholly there, she was something out of a fairy-tale."[221] Their relationship was not particularly warm, and they spent long periods living in different cities; but it does seem to have been a stable and fundamentally happy marriage.

Similar patterns can be found in many other dancers' lives. Ruth St. Denis's alcoholic father played little role in her life, while her mother, a woman of pronounced feminist and spiritual views, was a dominant influence. Gertrud Leistikow grew up, according to one biographer, in a household that was "disciplined, orderly, very conventional and loveless. Young Gertrud experienced it above all as charged with fear." She was more or

[220] Ibid., pp. 254, 348.
[221] "La vie que nous avons dansée," typescript in DTAK, Inventory no. 56, Clotilde und Alexander Sacharoff, I.1.1.1, pp. 1, 3, 6, 14, 16; Frank-Manuel Peter, "Die 'neie Minchener Derpsichore: Clotilde von Derp – die früheste Vertreterin des Ausdruckstanzes?," and Alexander Sacharoff, "Clotilde," both in Frank-Manuel Peter and Rainer Stamm, eds., *Die Sacharoffs: Zwei Tänzer aus dem Umkreis des Blauen Reiters* (Cologne: Wienand, 2005), pp. 79, 153–154.

less adopted by the dance critic Hans Brandenburg, who took her to the Bohemian nudist arts colony at Monte Veritá near Locarno in Switzerland in the summer of 1914.[222] Olga Desmond's childhood was similar: She had thirteen brothers and sisters, whom her mother "ruled with a stern hand"; her children called her "the sergeant" or "Old Fritz" (Frederick the Great's nickname), and – a biographer records – "had to obey unquestioningly, and often there were blows." By age fifteen Olga escaped to join a variety-theater act in London, posing nude (in white paint) in re-creations of classical statuary.[223] Maud Allan's mother, according to one biographer, was "a domineering, practical, insightful, clever, and desperately lonely woman," and Maud "determined to satisfy her mother's exceedingly high expectations." At the beginning of her musical studies in Berlin in 1895 she wrote in her diary "Give me strength, dear God, to carry out the desires of my dear mother." She too endured a tortured and long drawn-out love affair, and never married.[224] Cléo de Mérode's mother was unmarried, her father not involved in her life until she met him while performing in Vienna as a young adult.[225] Friderica Derra de Moroda's father died when she was five.[226] Mary Wigman's father died when she was nine, and she was sent to boarding schools in England and Switzerland.[227] Ida Rubinstein was orphaned when she was two.[228] We know nothing of Tórtola Valencia's parents, but it may be significant that she claimed in an interview in 1926 that "I believe I am the daughter of no-one. My heart and my soul are Indian ... no one understands me."[229] One biographer of Anna Pavlova believed that she "sought ... a surrogate father," her own having died when she was two; a biographer of Mary Wigman writes of her "longing for a father."[230] Many of these women (including, for example, St. Denis, Duncan, von Derp, and Allan) toured Europe for years in the company of their mothers – a fact that may relativize the notion that they were independent artists. As Ted Shawn remarked in his autobiography, Ruth

[222] Ehrich, "Im Sauseschritt," p. 8.
[223] Runge, *Olga Desmond*, p. 7, 11.
[224] Cherniavsky, "Maud Allan, Part I," pp. 7–8, 11; Cherniavsky, "Maud Allan, Part II," p. 202.
[225] Conyers, "Courtesans in Dance History," p. 229; Mérode, *Le ballet*, p. 272.
[226] Dahms, *Der Tanz – ein Leben*, p. 12.
[227] Susan A. Manning, *Ecstasy and the Demon: Feminism and Nationalism in the Dances of Mary Wigman* (Berkeley: University of California Press, 1993), pp. 49–50.
[228] Vicki Woolf, *Dancing in the Vortex: The Story of Ida Rubinstein* (Amsterdam, The Netherlands: Harwood, 2000), p. 3.
[229] "La sacerdota de la danza," *La Voz de Guipuzcoa*, July 4, 1926, clipping in MAE, Fonds Tortola Valencia, L15.
[230] Money, *Anna Pavlova*, p. 7; A. H. Franks, "A Biographical Sketch," in *Pavlova: A Biography*, ed. Franks (New York: Da Capo, 1979), p. 12; Fritsch-Vivié, *Mary Wigman*, p. 10.

Denis's mother traveled with her "throughout Ruth's professional life ... as the duenna, companion, counselor, and protector"; her most recent biographer observes that during her years in Europe she was "hardly even trying to assert her role as an independent young woman" in the face of her mother's authority.[231]

There are, of course, two ways to interpret this pattern. One would be that the modern dancers were starved of paternal love, dominated by unhappy ambitious mothers, desperate for attention, and often driven to seek out relationships with men who did not love them. The other would be that they had the good fortune to have escaped the pervasive patriarchal culture of the period, and to have had – in many cases – exceptionally strong and capable mothers. That allowed them (and their audiences) to question the instinctual patriarchal authoritarianism of political and religious life in the period, and made their art part of a broader democratization of European culture. It allowed them to develop an art form that appears to have appealed disproportionately to women. Perhaps a childhood relatively free of paternal dominance was at that time, for women, a precondition for the self-confidence necessary for artistic creation. These two perspectives are not mutually incompatible, of course. Given the options available to women at the time, the sadness of having an absent or hostile father may have been the price of the joy of artistic autonomy for women, and a domineering mother the most likely road to professional success.

That kind of upbringing also, however, made it very difficult for them to construct viable relationships with heterosexual men, whose assumption was often that women were there to serve them, and who not infrequently moved on to greener pastures when strong women refused to give up their own independent personalities (and artistic ambitious) and do so. It is telling, for example, that the dénouement of Maud Allan's unhappy affair with the only man she ever wanted to marry, a musician with whom she imagined marriage as an intensification and continuation of their artistic collaboration, came when he told her that "my wife will not be on the stage but at home, having babies."[232] Tórtola Valencia claimed she had never married because "men are so egotistical, every one of them wants me to abandon the theater. I won't leave my art, which has always been

[231] Ted Shawn, *One Thousand and One Night Stands* (New York: Da Capo, 1960), p. 37; Meinzenbach, *"Tanz ist eine Sprache,"* p. 61, 131.
[232] Letter of March 11, 1914, excerpted in letter of Felix Cherniavsky to Russell Hartley, May 15, 1983, Maud Allan clippings files, MPDSF.

true to me …, for a man, who never would be!"[233] Jane Sherman asked early in her career: "Why won't men believe you when you say you want a life and work of your own?"[234] Ruth St. Denis did marry; her husband Ted Shawn was a bisexual man thirteen years younger than herself, a great admirer of her work and for years her artistic and professional collaborator. But she did not take the conventional marital vow to obey him, and did not wear a wedding band. Even so, the marriage was not particularly happy, and eventually foundered in part over issues of artistic direction, and partly over Shawn's growing commitment to male companions and collaborators.[235]

Gertrud Valeska Samosch/Valeska Gert, an influential German dancer and film star of the 1920s and 1930s, is a telling example of the broad pattern. Her father was (she wrote in her autobiography) "kindhearted" but also frustrated in his career, angry, unhappy, and hypercritical; he frequently raged at her mother so bitterly that Valeska "thought I would die of pain," and she was "relieved when he finally died." Her mother was "funny, stubborn, self-righteous, and pleasure-loving," and good at everything except housekeeping, cooking, and child-rearing. Valeska grew up fearful, shy, domineering among her peers, and unhappy. She "learned to laugh properly for the first time in my life" when she was directed to do so while playing a part in a Shakespeare play. She engaged in numerous brief affairs ("adventures"); found love frightening and was disgusted to discover that it compromised her commitment to her art; and fell into a paralyzing, weeks-long depression when an important relationship collapsed.[236]

Gert was also, however, a creative dynamo, who was consistently at the center of the artistic avant-garde and consistently linked her artistic efforts with Left political commitments. She developed a truly original, outrageous, grotesque dance style, and was very highly regarded as a dance innovator. She also explicitly made the connection between modern dance and social criticism. She early discovered that "scandal was my natural element"; because she "didn't like the bourgeoisie," she "danced those they despised – whores, procurers, burn-outs and the downwardly mobile." A gifted actor, she appeared in plays by leading avant-garde authors, including Oskar Kokoschka, Ernst Toller, and Frank Wedekind. She had an extraordinary career as an actor in very highly regarded, often socially

[233] Conrado E. Eggers Lecours, "Tres Suicidos y la implantación de la melena en Alemania," *La Novela Semanal* (Motevideo), October 9, 1928, clipping in MAE, Fonds Tortola Valencia, L15.
[234] Sherman, *Soaring*, pp. 77, 194.
[235] Meinzenbach, *"Tanz ist eine Sprache,"* pp. 93, 96, 111, 133–139, 178, 191.
[236] Valeska Gert, *Mein Weg* (Leipzig: A. F. Devrient, 1931), pp. 3, 4, 22, 39, 51, 53.

critical films, often focused on the darker potentials of the intersection of class and sexuality – particularly those directed by the great Weimar director G. W. Pabst, but also Jean Renoir and Carl Junghanss. Banned from the stage and film by the Nazis because she was Jewish, she married an English actor ("I asked Jack, 'Will you marry me?' 'Naturally,' he replied, for he loved me and my art") and went into exile in London and eventually New York. There she opened her own cabaret and employed, among others, the painter Jackson Pollock and the playwright Tennessee Williams. She returned to Germany immediately after World War II, and among other activities took roles in films by the prominent directors Federico Fellini, Rainer Werner Fassbinder, and Volker Schlöndorf, remaining active until her death at age eighty-six.[237]

Reading between the lines of her autobiography, one can see that Gert was grossly egoistic, terribly self-isolating, entirely ungovernable, and frequently miserable. Her family of origin was undoubtedly a school for loneliness; and she died alone in her apartment and was only found days later. But she was also an unstoppably strong and creative woman, fiercely committed to justice and democracy, and uncompromising in pursuit of her own vision and values. The facts of her life may well justify a diagnosis of some sort of pathology. But by any moderately democratic and feminist standard it was the society in which she grew up and lived most of her life that was pathological.

Within broad parameters, this is the pattern we can see in the lives and personalities of the modern dancers. Their early lives steered them toward painful but productive rebellion against a pathological social order. If we recall the kinds of restrictions "good manners" imposed on women, we might put it this way: They didn't fit into their society very well, but they refused to disappear. There were clear exceptions. The Wiesenthal sisters seem to have had a happy family; and Gertrud and Ursula Falke's father, a prominent lyric poet in Hamburg, accompanied them on the piano at their first performances and wrote poems about them.[238] A high proportion of the modern dancers, however, had very good reason to be hungry for attention, and to craft personas that would get it. A remark Ruth St. Denis made in 1925 is particularly poignant in this respect: "One of the bitterest disappointments of my career," she confessed, "is that I had to be

---

[237] Gert, *Mein Weg*, pp. 26, 39; Valeska Gert, *Ich bin eine Hexe: Kaleidoskop meines Lebens* (Munich: Schneekluth, 1968), p. 85; Frank-Manuel Peter, *Valeska Gert: Tänzerin, Schauspielerin, Kabarettistin* (Berlin: Frölich and Kaufmann, 1985), passim.

[238] "Frauenklub Hamburg," *Hamburgische Fremdenblatt*, October 28, 1912, in DTAK, Inventory no. 10, Gertrud und Ursula Falke, II.2.4.

an Indian – a Japanese – a statue – something or somebody else – before
the public would give me what I craved.... My whole art life has been a
slow tragedy."[239]

There is, of course, something jarring about such a statement coming
from a leading exponent of an art form that claimed to express the soul
of the performer – to allow and require her to dance herself. In fact, the
modern dancers combined the claim to be authentically and uncompro-
misingly themselves with a remarkably acute sense for the theatricality of
selfhood. Authenticity, genuineness, sincerity, truthfulness, naturalness,
and lack of artifice were central to the conceptual world of modern dance.
But so was the understanding that the self is an act. While it may sound
odd, acting talent was one of the key prerequisites for being oneself; and
one of the most common ways for dancers to express themselves was by
pretending to be someone else. Chapter 3 will explore this paradox.

[239] Shelton, *Ruth St. Denis*, p. 99.

CHAPTER 3

Blood and Make-Believe: Race, Identity, and Performance

3.1 Dancing in the Blood: Race and Aesthetics

Obviously, a concern with individuality and individual identity was central to the aesthetic program of modernism, including in modern dance around 1900. But the same broad social transformations that made individual identity a delicate issue also made *collective* identities seem terribly important. The elaboration of those collective identities took the form of a complex of steadily ramifying discussions regarding terms like *race*, *nation*, and *ethnicity*. In the world of dance, an important feature of this period was the "rediscovery" or invention of folk dances all across Europe. "Spanish" dance as practiced by Saharet, La Argentina, and a small army of variety-theater dancers was one example; but there were more localized versions of the phenomenon all over Europe.

The main stream of modern dance was too self-consciously individualistic and modernizing to do more than adopt some of the movement vocabulary of folk dance, which was understood to be both traditional and communal. Instead, the modern dancers, reviewers, and dance theorists opted to establish connections between modern dance and perceived ethnic, national, and racial communities or identities using the term *blood*. In the conceptual vocabulary of the period, communities of descent were very widely understood also to be spiritual communities. Biological, cultural, and historical collectivities were rarely clearly distinguished in European thought; they were assumed to be largely overlapping and identical entities. It was therefore widely assumed that many fundamental psychological characteristics and capacities of the individual were determined by his or her "blood," by her ancestry.

This was widely assumed to be true at every geographic level. Europeans commonly believed that there were very large racial groupings (Germanic, Latin, Slavic) that encompassed many different nations but shared

117

important psychological characteristics across national boundaries. They also assumed that the members of particular nations shared such characteristics; that subnational and even local groupings did as well (in Great Britain: Scots, Welsh, and English; in Germany: Bavarians, Prussians, or Swabians; in France: Bretons, Parisians, or Gascons); and that lineage groups right down to the individual family did too. Musicality, melancholy, or martial spirit, for example, were believed to be inherited, whether in families, nations, or in races. At all these levels "blood" was believed to play a diffuse but decisive role in defining any individual's particular aptitudes, inclinations, emotional tone, sense of humor or of tragedy, acumen in business or love, and so on. People are the way they are because of their blood; individual identity and racial/national/ethnic identity were overlapping quantities.

Because modern dance claimed to express what was in the dancer's soul, therefore, blood and related terms were ubiquitous in the world of modern dance. Individual performers were believed to dance the way they did because of their blood. As Tórtola Valencia put it, "[T]he soul of each nation informs its dancing." Adorée Villany concurred, arguing in her response to Antonietta dell'Era in 1911 that "the different peoples must have quite different dance styles" – another respect in which the ballet was rigid, mechanical, and ignored organic, natural life.[1]

In some cases, the racial and ethnic stereotypes deployed in dance criticism were extremely negative. This was particularly true of critiques of Russian dancers. The Ballets Russes, for example, were lambasted by some English critics who held that the Russians were "excellent workers," "sly," "clever," and "hollow," and that their art was therefore "essentially commonplace"; that they were a big hit in Paris because the French were "impressionable"; that Nijinsky was a drunken sentimental disorderly Pole who was "carrying on in a way calculated to appall some, ravish others"; that just as art was "the creation of a very few individuals on earth and that all the others are more or less imitators" so too "certain nations" – like the Russians – "are purely imitative and never produce creative artists."[2] Alexander Sacharoff in particular, as a homosexual Jewish Russian, faced a barrage of racial stereotypes. Critics found him to be an "effeminate Slav" with an "unmanly nature," overly "soft" and tending toward "over-refined intellectual masturbation," and admired only by "Slavic-Jewish disciples

---

[1] Valencia quoted in Garland, *Tórtola Valencia*, p. 32; Villany, "Muss man nackt tanzen?"
[2] Quotations in Gordon Craig, *Gordon Craig on Movement and Dance*, ed. Arnold Rood (New York: Dancing Horizons, 1977), pp. 80, 84, 100, 191, 106, 194.

of art, of exaggerated and irresponsible extremist gullibility."³ And some critics denounced the Ballets Russes as "Jewish ballets" – and therefore, as the dance historian Ilyana Karthas notes, "lustful, excessive, shrewd, duplicitous, and sensual."⁴

For the most part, however, the vocabulary of "blood" (or race, or nation) was used in a much more positive manner, to explain the aesthetic virtues of artists' different performance styles. Not infrequently, commentators or practitioners sought to associate modern racial or national characteristics with – of course – those of the Greeks. One critic, for example, wrote that Sacharoff had a "handsome profile" with "sharp oriental features" and (therefore?) resembled "an image from a Greek vase." Rudolf von Delius praised his "nervous, delicate sensitivity," his ability as a "wholly modern sensitive person" to "put on foreign cultures like makeup" – for example that of the Greeks, whom he "knows extremely well."⁵ More broadly, the English critic Ethel Urlin believed that the "Slavonic peoples alone now appear to possess the secret" of the "joy and abandon of the dance, as it must have existed among the Greeks."⁶ One review remarked simply that "Gertrud Leistikow is a Pole. So she has a gift for dancing."⁷

However, German commentators in particular believed that their own "race" too was blessed with unique aesthetic and/or spiritual gifts. Rudolf von Delius attributed the raw, powerful quality of Mary Wigman's performance to her Germanic heritage, her "wild Germanic unity of feeling," explaining that "no Germanic artist from Shakespeare to Annette von Droste has ever feared this form of 'ugliness.'"⁸ One reviewer of Olga Desmond claimed that she embodied both the "sensual joyfulness of ancient Hellas ... and the depth of feeling of Germandom."⁹ In the 1920s one critic would attribute the "merciless rigor," "ethical will," and

³ "Tanzabend von Clotilde von Derp und Alexander Sacharoff," *Leipziger neueste Nachrichten*, November 13, 1913, clipping in DTAK, Inventory no. 56, Clotilde und Alexander Sacharoff, II.2.6; Hans Brandenburg, *Der moderne Tanz* (Munich: Georg Müller, 1921), pp. 144, 146; quoted in Patrizia Veroli, "Der Spiegel und die Hieroglyphe: Alexander Sacharoff und die Moderne im Tanz," in Frank-Manuel Peter and Rainer Stamm, eds., *Die Sacharoffs* (Cologne: Wienand, 2002), p. 181.
⁴ Karthas, *When Ballet Became French*, p. 86.
⁵ Quoted in Koegler, "A Single Being and a Single Soul with Two Bodies," p. 254.
⁶ Ethel Urlin, *Dancing Ancient and Modern* (London: Simkin, Marshall, Hamilton, Kent and Co., 1912), p. 159.
⁷ Fr. S., "Gertrud Leistikow, *Frankfurter Nachrichten*, January 21, 1914, clipping in TBCUA, Archief Gertrud Leistikow, Map 4a. Leistikow did not speak Polish – see de Boer, *Dans voluit*, p. 17.
⁸ Quoted in Fritsch-Vivié, *Mary Wigman*, p. 46.
⁹ Quoted in Desmond, *Mein Weg zur Schönheit*, p. 5.

"proud, stringent grandeur" of Edith von Schrenck's performances to her aristocratic Baltic-German "blood."[10]

There were other contenders: Hans Brandenburg thought that it was the "enormously vital race taking shape in America" that was responsible for igniting the modern dance revolution; the French author Anatole France surmised that perhaps the sacral quality of Loïe Fuller's dancing was due to the religious character of the "Anglo-Saxon race"; and the Spanish playwright Pompeyo Gener praised Tórtola Valencia as representative of the "Andalusian race." Others praised Valencia's "southern temperament" or "the fire of her temperament and her southern liveliness"; saw in her "all the individuality and grace of the Southern artist" or the "Spanish type in its most noble form"; claimed that she "dances as only a daughter of Castile can"; or thought she was Algerian and hence "Moorish," or "Spanish by birth" and "English by custom" but "Jewish by origin" – and hence, presumably, authentically Oriental (see Figure 3.1).[11]

What is most striking about the use of the vocabulary of blood and race, however, is that in a great proportion of cases commentators explicitly attributed the valuable aesthetic qualities of modern dance to the *mixing* of blood in the veins of its exponents. The implicit argument was that the great expressive range of modern dance was explained by the fact that the modern dancers combined the qualities of more than one "blood" or ethnic/national/racial community. Most obviously, this principle was invoked to explain the central paradox of modern dance – how it could combine fiery sensual passion with mystic ascetic chasteness. One promoter advertised Maud Allan, for example, as a Canadian and therefore from a "land where the fires of the French temperament glow ardently through the icy purity of the People of the Snow" (by which he apparently meant either Anglo-Canadians or Scots-Irish). The Caffins similarly argued that Ruth St. Denis was both chaste and sensual because "[i]n her the strain of the Celt is mingled with that of the Puritan," her "visionary" ascetic tendency "warmed and humanized by the Celtic

[10] Brochure *Tanzschule Edith von Schrenck, Berlin* (no place, date, or publisher), DTAK, Inventory no. 161 Edith von Schrenck, II.2.1.

[11] Hans Brandenburg, *Der moderne Tanz*, p. 24; Fuller, *Fifteen Years*, p. viii; Gener, "Tórtola Valencia," p. 527; "Theater und Kunst," *Wiener Mittags-Zeitung*, August 19, 1908, "Etablissment Ronacher, Tórtola Valencia," *Das interessante Blatt*, August 20, 1908; "New Dancer at the Palace," *Morning Leader*, December 2, 1908; "In the Public Eye," *The Weekly Budget*, February 26, 1910; "A New Moorish Dancer," *The Morning Leader*, December 1, 1908, clippings in MAE, Fonds Tortola Valencia, L2; "Periquin, "Tórtola Valencia," *El Liberal* (Barcelona), January 20, 1912, in ibid., L3.

Figure 3.1 Tórtola Valencia, "Oriental" dancer, 1911

imagination."[12] One English critic believed that the dance style of Sent M'Ahesa/Elsa von Carlberg "belies her Scandinavian descent" because "she has Russian blood in her veins and is therefore naturally emotional, with the control which a Northern temperament provides.... Of all

[12] Quoted in Cherniavsky, "Maud Allan, Part II," p. 122; Caffin and Caffin, *Dancing*, pp. 88–89.

European peoples the Slav is nearest to the East, and it is in her Slav blood that the fire, which is necessary to great dancing, runs."[13]

Other apparently contradictory qualities of modern dance performance were explained in similar fashion. Rudolf von Delius praised Mary Wigman to the skies as the most German of dancers; but he also found that her "narrow, solid bourgeois" north-German nature was "opened" by a "drop of artistic blood, probably Asiatic." Echoing a widespread conviction that Jews were essentially "Oriental," Delius implied that this was why she was so attracted to the "Orient" when she visited Amsterdam's Jewish quarter as a young woman.[14] Hans Brandenburg believed that Gertrud Leistikow was such a wonderful dancer in part because she had some "Polish blood," which presumably tempered her German discipline and emotional depth with Slavic passion and imagination. Grete Wiesenthal was a wonderful dancer because she came from Vienna, "the city where German emotional culture was refined by Celtic and Jewish admixtures."[15] Both the Caffins and Ernst Schur thought that Rita Sacchetto combined Austrian musicality (from her mother) with Italian vivacity (from her father).[16] Tórtola Valencia claimed a special relationship with the Orient because "We Spaniards have much Moorish blood in us and the Spanish Gypsies are really Eastern." She was "Spanish, I carry Gypsy blood in my veins and I feel all the passion and all the yearning of my race."[17] Max Osborn thought Anna Pavlova's genius derived from the "mysterious mixture of eastern racial elements and general European characteristics."[18] One French reviewer explained that La Argentina was "a Spaniard of pure race, issue of an Andalusian mother and a Castilian father" – the latter giving her presumably pride and martial spirit and a mystic religious turn, the former passion and fiery energy and a touch of the Orient.[19] The French author and dancer Colette Willy claimed to have African blood.[20] This kind of thinking persisted well into the twentieth century; in 1933, for example, the British "Greek" dancer Ruby Ginner

[13] Kineton Parkes, "Dancing the Emotions: The Art of Sent M'ahesa," undated *Dancing Times* clipping in JRDD, Sent M'ahesa Clippings, p. 141–142.

[14] Delius, *Mary Wigman*, p. 35.

[15] Brandenburg, *Der moderne Tanz*, pp. 172, 43.

[16] Caffin and Caffin, *Dancing*, pp. 225–226; Schur, *Der moderne Tanz*, p. 64.

[17] Quoted in Garland, "Early Modern Dance," p. 7; Almoral, "Hablando con Tórtola Valencia," *La Cronica* (Zaragosa), March 7, 1913, clipping in MAE, Fonds Tortola Valencia, L3.

[18] Osborn, *Der bunte Spiegel*, pp. 176–178.

[19] "Mme Argentina," *L'Echo des Champs Elysées* 1923, clipping in DTAK, Inventory no. 0118, Antonia Mercé/La Argentina.

[20] Claude Francis and Fernande Gontier, *Creating Colette*, vol. 1, *From Ingenue to Libertine, 1873–1913* (South Royalton, VT: Steerforth Press, 1998), p. 259.

argued that Greek dance was so wonderful because the ancient Greeks were the product of mixing between a "passionate, superstitious, imaginative and artistic" southern "race" and a blond, blue-eyed, warlike, "brave, chaste, self-controlled, and law-abiding" northern one.[21]

Some commentators, particularly in Central Europe, raised this idea of the aesthetic benefit of race or blood mixing to a general principle. For Hans Brandenburg, for example, Germany was the great homeland of the new dance form precisely because it was here that all the international streams that went into its making came together: "[I]n the new dance America and Australia, English, French, Spanish, German, Swiss, Austrian, Jewish, Gypsy, Russian an Polish blood all participate. Truly, a vision of the peoples, united on German soil" in an "ideal marriage of the races."[22] In her memoirs, published in 1919, Grete Wiesenthal credited her accomplishments partly to the fact that she was descended from Czechs, Hungarians, and Italians as well as Germans – "a proper Austrian mixture," as she proudly saw it. Her brother-in-law agreed in his memoirs of 1934, observing that "blood mixing" was typical of the "most notable Austrians."[23] Hugo von Hofmannsthal speculated that Ruth St. Denis's talent might be derived from a whole rainbow of "bloods." "It is possible," he wrote, "that she is a Canadian, in whom French blood is mixed with Anglo-Saxon and also with a drop of even more foreign blood, a grandmother of Indian [Native American] blood.... Or maybe she's Australian, like Saharet."[24] No matter – the point was that her expressive range was such that there *must* be some mixed blood in there, from somewhere. Such ideas about dance were part of a much broader understanding of the creative potentials unleashed by blood mixing; in 1925, for example, Fritz Giese argued that "Germany has always been a crossroads," and that "the whole modern rise of the industrial state is unthinkable without the Slavs, without the Latin influence, in other words without Berlin and the Rhineland."[25]

In short, both dancers and critics explained the success of modern dance as an example of the power of cultural hybridity, of cultural cross-fertilization. In the period, this was understood to involve literally what

[21] Ruby Ginner, *The Revived Greek Dance: Its Art and Technique* (London: Methuen, 1933), pp. 1, 3.
[22] Brandenburg, *Der moderne Tanz*, pp. 25–26.
[23] Wiesenthal, *Der Aufstieg*, p. 31; Huber-Wiesenthal, *Die Schwestern Wiesenthal*, p. 87.
[24] Hofmannsthal, "Die unvergleichliche Tänzerin," p. 256.
[25] Fritz Giese, *Girlkultur: Vergleiche zwischen amerikanischem und europäischem Rythmus und Lebensgefühl* (Munich: Delphin, 1925), pp. 63–64.

critics of modernity deplored as "mongrelization" or "miscegenation" – the mixing of "blood," of races.

There is, of course, a strange tension at work in such claims. On the one hand, modern dance claimed to be absolutely individual, and hence also universal. In this respect the modern dancers were, again, very much in agreement with their modernist/Expressionist colleagues in many other disciplines. On the other hand, they were convinced that individual character – the individual soul – was shaped by a broader ethnic, national, or racial soul. In this, they shared something with those cultural nationalists who, in the same period, were arguing for the preservation of distinctive national aesthetic traditions against the importation of "alien" styles and foreign influences as not compatible with the local (German, English, French, etc.) national/racial "soul." Such opponents of modern mongrelization included, for example, some of those who were assiduously cultivating and/or inventing folk-dance traditions, fairy tales, traditional costumes and customs, songs and sayings, funding local historical societies, studying regional dialects, and so on.[26]

The modern dancers were, then, what we might call "cosmopolitan nationalists." Like the pioneers of nationalist thought in the late eighteenth (Herder) or early nineteenth centuries (Mazzini), they assumed that people of different nations were fundamentally different, but that each of these fundamentally different forms of humanity was part of the larger project of humanity as a whole, an expression of some particular aspect or blend of its varied potentials. To the modern observer, this use of the language of "blood" is a bit jarring. Because of the later history of Europe, particularly the catastrophe of Nazi Germany, we tend to think of the language of blood as exclusive. In this period, however, the language of blood was most often used to express a very positive appreciation of the creative potentials of cultural cross-fertilization. This is probably best understood as a reflection of the fact that culture and biology had not yet been as radically separated as they would become later in the twentieth century. "Blood" did not mean the same as our modern category "genetics"; it was a reference to lineage, heritage, and a diffuse sense of the psychological and spiritual implications of belonging to a particular human community.[27]

[26] See, e.g., the essays in Michelle Facos and Sharon L. Hirsch, eds., *Art, Culture, and Identity in Fin-de-Siecle Europe* (New York: Cambridge University Press, 2003).
[27] One race and aesthetics see George L. Mosse, *Toward the Final Solution: A History of European Racism* (New York: Fertig, 1978), e.g., pp. 2, 7, 11, 16, 21, 23, 37, 44; Kurt Bayertz, "Biology and Beauty: Science and Aesthetics in *Fin-de-siècle* Germany," in Mikulas Teich and Roy Porter,

3.2 Fraud, Pretense, or Make-Believe?

A further paradox is, however, harder to resolve. In many cases, the modern dancers were claiming to express *someone else's* "soul," the essence of someone else's deep authentic racial/ethnic selfhood. There were certainly dancers who, in some or most of their performances, did not adopt ethnic or historical themes; and this was increasingly the case as modern dance established itself. The second wave of German dancers in particular – Grete Wiesenthal, Gertrud Leistikow, the Falke sisters, Mary Wigman – for the most part did without the Greek or Oriental folderol. By 1917, the English dancer Margaret Morris, who had been deeply influenced by Isadora Duncan's brother Raymond and his obsession with the Greeks (having met him already in 1901), could confess that "I do not claim to be reviving Greek dancing" but rather to be developing a movement idiom that "allows of unlimited development in the future. It is really immaterial to me if it was used by the Greeks or Egyptians or any other ancient nation."[28] In the early years, however, most dancers, in most performances, claimed to be presenting ancient Greek, Egyptian, or Hebrew dances, or "timeless" dances from various "Oriental" traditions – Indian, Spanish, Cambodian, Thai, Javanese, and so on.

Some of the modern dancers explicitly eschewed any claim to be ancient or exotic; their claim was instead that they were recovering or reconstructing the spirit or soul of ancient or Oriental dance. Isadora Duncan, for example, for all that she claimed to "fall into Greek positions" when dancing or to be reviving dance forms that had been "dormant" for two millennia, denied that her "intention is to return to the dances of the old Greeks" because "[w]e are not Greeks and cannot therefore dance Greek dances." Her dance was Greek only in the sense that it was sacral, natural, individual, and universal.[29] Loïe Fuller explained the theory behind this position in her memoirs in 1913. She did not claim to be performing ancient Egyptian or Hindu dance; instead, she argued that "it should be easy, if one put oneself into the state of mind that prompted the dances in times past, to reproduce them to-day with similar action and

---

eds., *Fin de Siecle and Its Legacy* (Cambridge: Cambridge University Press, 1991); Edward Ross Dickinson, "Altitude and Whiteness: Germanizing the Alps and Alpinizing the Germans, 1875–1935," *German Studies Review* 33 (2010): 577–599.

[28] Quoted in Anderson, *Art without Boundaries*, p. 27. See Jim Hastie, "Margaret Morris (1891–1980)," in Jean-Yves Pidoux, ed., *La danse: Art du XXe siècle?* (Lausanne: Editions Payot, 1990), p. 167.

[29] Duncan, *Der Tanz*, p. 24; Isadora Duncan, *Isadora Speaks*, ed. Franklin Rosemont (San Francisco: City Lights, 1981), p. 37.

movement."[30] Because dance expressed an emotional or spiritual state, if one could feel Greek one could dance Greek. This was, of course, the crucial reason many of the modern dancers claimed to have studied ancient and exotic art in museums – they were not trying to reconstruct dance from still figures but rather absorbing the spirit of a culture distant in time or geography, soaking in its ethos, learning to feel it.

In some cases, performers and critics explicitly claimed that the modern dancers were cultural go-betweens translating exotic and alien art forms into forms more accessible to the Western public. The Caffins wrote that Ruth St. Denis's function was to "saturate herself with the spirit and mystery of the Orient and translate them with faithfulness to our Occidental imagination." Due to her "temperament" (perhaps her Celtic blood?), it was "no effort to her to put aside her Caucasian point of view and absorb with all reverence that of the Orient" – which she then turned into "dances which express in a manner not too exotic for our grasp, the passionless rhapsody of a mystical sensuousness."[31] Years later, after actually touring the "Orient" in 1926, St. Denis described her own job in similar terms: "I do hope that we can translate into our Western terms some of this elusive beauty of the East. Can we gather these visions, these sights and sounds and smells into some comprehensible scenes for our American public at home?"[32]

In other cases, modern dancers were less sophisticated, sometimes resorting to outright lies. Tórtola Valencia, one biographer concludes, was a "consummate liar, prevaricator, and self-inventor extraordinaire" who deliberately "shrouded her background in mystery," "continually re-inventing her origins" until no one had any idea who she really was. At various times, she was the orphaned daughter of Spanish parents who left her in the care of British friends when they went off to Mexico and promptly died; the daughter of a Spanish aristocrat and a Gypsy dancer, shunted out of the way to England to avoid scandal; or perhaps the daughter of an Anglo-Indian museum curator and an Indian woman. She was born in Seville, or Barcelona, or Calcutta, or London, or Algeria.[33] Mata Hari, too, was tirelessly mendacious, spinning tales of having "Hindu blood in her veins"; or about her childhood as the orphaned daughter of a Brahmin family in Malabar, rescued from the life of a lowly temple dancer

[30] Fuller, *Fifteen Years*, pp. 156–157.
[31] Caffin and Caffin, *Dancing*, pp. 86–87.
[32] St. Denis, *An Unfinished Life*, p. 301.
[33] Garland, "Early Modern Dance," p. 4; Garland, *Tortola Valencia*, pp. 9–10; Solrac, *Tortola Valencia*, p. 22.

by an English officer; or as (in the words of a London society magazine in 1905) a "woman from the Far East, a native of Java" (and hence "a burst of fresh, free life, of Nature in all its strength untrammeled by civilization"); or as heiress to the vast fortune of an Indonesian prince-regent, come to bring Europeans "the arts of her homeland."[34] Ruth St. Denis, too, was rumored in 1906 to be the child of an English officer and a Brahmin woman, rescued from a career as temple dancer by a French officer; she paraded about Paris in a sari and gave the press a fake biography rather similar to the story of the Delibes opera *Lakmé*. Interestingly, this appears to have been part of a campaign to eclipse an imitator who had arrived in Paris before she did, performing a dance based on her "Radha." St. Denis, in effect, was trying to establish that she was the *real* fake.[35]

In some cases, all this became quite confusing for commentators. The German dance enthusiast Ernst Schur wrote in 1910 that "Gertrude Barrison is culture, Vienna and English culture" – though she was in fact a Dane. Ruth St. Denis, he believed, had the "admirable tact, the spiritual culture" to express the "most delicate magic of this [Indian] foreign culture almost completely unaltered" and was "completely un-European"; but on the next page her "refined culture" was "European and not Indian" again.[36] Friderica Derra de Moroda was variously rumored to be Greek, Hungarian, Russian, Belgian, French, or "A Modern Product of Ancient Greece."[37] Adorée Villany was French, Hungarian, or a Jewish German named Erna Reich.[38] A bizarre case was that of the Anglo-Indian Olive Craddock/Roshanara; the *Times of India* reported in 1915 that "[s]o thoroughly does [she] enter into the spirit of her subject that it is difficult to realize that she is not herself a native" of India, though, of course, technically (at least in modern parlance) she was.[39]

All these stories were very rarely actually deliberately fraudulent. They created a performance persona; they were meant to make a good story, not falsify a truth; and they were often recounted with a broad wink. Margarethe Zelle, for example, called herself both "Mata Hari" and "Lady McLeod" (her ex-husband's name, though he was not a nobleman), and

[34] Lüders, *Apropos Mata Hari*, pp. 21, 82–83; Wheelwright, *The Fatal Lover*, p. 14; Keay, *The Spy Who Never Was*, p. 72; Waagenaar, *The Murder of Mata Hari*, pp. 60, 74.
[35] Shelton, *Ruth St. Denis*, p. 74; Décoret-Ahiha, *Les danses exotiques en France*, p. 139; St. Denis, *An Unfinished Life*, pp. 82, 84.
[36] Schur, *Der moderne Tanz*, pp. 108, 88–90.
[37] Dahms and Schroedter, eds., *Der Tanz*, pp. 22–23.
[38] "Aus dem Gerichtssaale," *Augsburger Abendzeitung*, July 9, 1912, clipping in STAM, Polizei-Direktion, no. 1010/4.
[39] Garland, "The Eternal Return," p. 196.

everyone knew she was Dutch. Ruth St. Denis made up stories about herself for the press, but everyone knew she was an American; she just had, as the dance historian Elizabeth Kendall put it, "a striking commitment to the Pretend."[40] It was never any secret that "Sent M'ahesa" was an ethnic Swede from the Russian Empire, or that "Nila Devi" was a Regina Woody from Boston. Adorée Villany used various first names (Viola, Adorée-Via, Adorée) but never bothered to claim she was Oriental or Greek or Spanish. A comment by one Paris reviewer of Cléo de Mérode's "Cambodian" dance performance at the World's Fair in Paris in 1900 sums up the dominant attitude of the media: "[I]t's not at all Cambodian, but it is delicious."[41]

Tórtola Valencia is an extreme and yet emblematic case. Beginning with deliberately false advertising, over the course of two decades she transformed herself into a recognized scalawag and merchant of tall tales, valued by journalists who could sell her to the reading public as a "colorful" character. At the start of her career in London she was billed as "one of the most toasted beauties and one of the most admired dancers of Spain" who had "just completed a very successful tour of the world," and as "a special favorite of the Court of Madrid" who was "known in all the capitals" and "has danced before King Alfonso" – though she had not been to Spain yet (at least not as an adult), spoke no Spanish, and had never been on tour anywhere (see Figure 3.2).[42]

When she arrived in Spain as a faux-Indian dancer in 1911 she claimed that she had been to India to study dance there. By 1913, she had transformed herself into a Spanish dancer, and admitted that she had never been to India – instead, she explained (with equal truthfulness) that she had spent a summer living with and learning from Spanish Gypsies.[43] By the 1920s her "act" was increasingly outrageous. In one interview in 1926 she claimed to have lost count of the number of men who had killed themselves over her, starting with an Indian prince in London. At first, these incidents had been painful for her; but "later, many more killed themselves, and I got used to it."[44] She told tales of bronze Buddha statues that brought her bad luck; she was rumored to be able to "cure" pearls

[40] Kendall, *Where She Danced*, p. 40.
[41] Suquet, *L'Éveil des modernités*, p. 269.
[42] Clippings from *The Sketch*, February 5, 1908, *London Sketches*, February 15, 1908, and *the Bystander*, February 26, 1908, all in MAE, Fonds Tortola Valencia, L2.
[43] Garland, *Tortola Valencia*, p. 26.
[44] Magda Donato, "Hablando con Tórtola Valencia," *El Liberal*, April 5, 1926, clipping in MAE, Fonds Tortola Valencia, L15.

Figure 3.2 Tórtola Valencia, "Spanish" dancer, 1908

that had lost their luster, and to do so under armed secret service guard for the Louvre or for the Emperor of Russia; she gave an impromptu dance performance for photographers on a beach at Ostend; she filled her house with exotic knickknacks from her world travels; she was rumored to have romantic alliances with the Duke of Leinster, Prince Philip of Coburg, and the Marques de Vinent, an openly gay anarchist decadent writer and critic; she was rumored to have gone mad and died in Havana – a story she was pleased to have circulating because it constituted "admirable advertising ... [;] what would cause me anxiety in life would be silence" in the press.[45] In an interview in 1926 she admitted that "the loveliest thing is lying. But I won't lie to you.... My father was Castilian.... I am Indian! Viva mi raza! ... I am Indian in my heart and my soul. I am the child of no-one. I believe in the reincarnation of spirits."[46] By 1929 she claimed to have been a "queen of the Orient" thousands of years ago, and to have been recognized by street dancers when she went to India – where she had for many years announced she was just about to go, without ever actually doing so.[47]

Journalists got it. In 1923 one Mexican reviewer reported that "[s]he is modest and she is arrogant. When she is modest, she is lying; when she is arrogant, she is also lying. But her lies are magnificent." In 1927 another wrote of "her absurdities and arbitrariness," but praised her as the "dancer of emotion *par excellence.*" A third called her "the eccentric and exotic dancer" Tórtola Valencia.[48] Asked in 1924 whether her own life conformed to her theory that "an artist's life should be no more than a reflection of her art," she replied, "Completely, because I consider it merely as a continuation of my work." Her life, in short, was a fiction – one that made

[45] Pilar Millan Astroy, "El Buda Fatidico: Una Visita a la Encantada Mansión de la Inquietante Tórtola Valencia," *La Nación*, undated, early 1927; "Jewel Doctor! To Be Mother of Sick Pearls at the Louvre?," *The Sketch*, November 8, 1911; "Guarded by Spies She Wears the Czar's Pearls," *New York American*, March 21, 1912; "A Sequel to Our 'Plage Patrol'? The Bather's Dance," *The Sketch*, September 20, 1911, clippings in MAE, Fonds Tortola Valencia, L3; "The Romance [Very Much Interrupted] of the Duke and the Dancer," *New York Sunday American*, June 27, 1909; "In the Public Eye," *The Weekly Budget*, February 26, 1910, clippings in ibid., L2; Joserre, "Tórtola Valencia, Future Marquesa," *La Voz de Aragon*, December 14, 1927, clipping in ibid., L15; Bradomin, "La Danzarina Tragica," *Heraldo de Cuba*, March 12, 1923, clipping in ibid., L14.
[46] "La sacerdota de la danza," *La Voz de Guipuzcoa*, July 4, 1926, clipping in MAE, Fonds Tortola Valencia, L15.
[47] *Los Tiempos Teatral y Cinematografico*, August 6, 1920, unidentified clipping in MAE, Fonds Tortola Valencia, L15.
[48] "Tórtola Valencia y su cortejo inevitable," *El Universal Ilustrada* (Mexico), April 12, 1923, clipping in MAE, Fonds Tortola Valencia, L14, fol. 20; Jose D. Bonavides, "Un rato de charla con Tórtola Valencia," *Selecciones*, September 25, 1927 and "El Debut de esta Noche," *El Diario* (Montevideo), undated, 1928, clippings in ibid., L15.

her sufficiently well-loved that she could declare herself a monarchist before the creation of the Spanish Republic, and a Republican before Franco's victory in the Civil War, and live on unscathed in Barcelona until her death in 1955.[49]

But avant-garde and bohemian poets wanted in on the act as well. Spanish-language poets all over Europe and Latin America vied with each other in producing odes to her cruel and fatal beauty that are often so awful that they can only have been intended as part of a collaborative tongue-in-cheek performance of Valencia as femme fatale. R. Buendia Manzano wrote, for example, that her eyes flashed with "the light of a knife buried in a chest," and exercised the "subtle fascination of a serpent" bearing the "mortal venom of your shamelessness." Antonio Aristoy wrote of her "panther's smile" and the "tragic whiteness of your teeth." José M. Romeo y Martinez wrote of her "incendiary" eyes, of "mouths burning with passion, flesh in lascivious contortions." Casto Pinto wrote of her "body of rare perfection, nude before my eyes," his "nerves distended in crazy convulsions, tensed in a fever of burning eroticism." Martínez Paybe sang of her "Eyes of mystery and eyes of madness/Profound abysses of passion and death/Eyes deeper than the deep dark forest/Where the wolf raises its rough face/And howls against an evil fate." And so forth.[50]

One particularly bizarre strategy adopted by some modern dancers to negotiate the tension between make-believe and reality speaks to the peculiar mix of honesty and fraud that characterized their claims to embody the soul of various exotic or ancient cultures. Some claimed that they were, or might be, or felt themselves to be reincarnated. Maud Allan was an extreme case: In her memoirs, published in 1908, she reflected that perhaps she had in a former life been a Greek dancer in Sicily in the year 210 B.C.

> I think I can see the boats from Argolis, seven hundred years before Christ.... I can skip five hundred years, and stand there in the theater at Taormina.... And then the Carthaginian wars ..., the Roman Triumph.... The Sicily of Theocritus was crushed, its groves were hushed and dead,

[49] El Diablo Cajuelo, "Un Momento de Charla con Tórtola Valencia," *La Republica* (Bogotá), July 3, 1924; Angel Lazaro, "A Grandes Rasgos," *Diario Español*, March 15, 1923, clippings in MAE, Fonds Tortola Valencia, L14, fols. 203, 9.

[50] R. Buendia Manzano, "Los ojos de Tórtola Valencia," ms. in MAE, Fonds Tortola Valencia, L3; Antonio Aristoy, "Tórtola Valencia," José M. Romeo y Martinez, "La Danza des las Pasiones," Casto Pinto, "Tórtola Valencia," all in *Andalucia: Revista Literaria Quincenal, suplemente*, undated (1912), in ibid.; Martínez Payba, "Las danzas de Tórtola Valencia," *Diario del Salvador* (San Salvador), October 6, 1923, ibid., L14, fol. 103.

and I – I think they laid me in a little niche beside a stream ... and
I waited – waited!

She waited until 1908, when she performed her "Dream of Salomé" at the
Palace Variety Theater in London and became famous.

Of course, the essential irrelevance of her claim to be Greek was obvious, because Salomé was a Hebrew, not a Greek. And in the next paragraph, Allan conceded that it was all "a wild fancy." And yet, she went on,

> I do sometimes think that I was one with those ancient dancers, whose
> duty in life was to express in motion the hopes, fears, passions, regrets,
> which rose in men's and women's hearts and found expression in move-
> ment when the world was younger, simpler, and more accustomed to what
> Carlyle has called "all sorts of sudden sincerities."

In the next paragraph, she once again conceded that the whole idea might
be nonsense: "How much I remember, how much I have read – and forgotten – how much I have dreamed of those earliest dancers, I hardly
know." But then a dozen pages later she wrote of how "we danced in the
shady groves and sunlight meadows of Argolis" in ancient Greece, "or by
the murmuring seas of the Sicily of Theocritus."[51] Allan was, in short, playing with the tension between truth and fiction. She was not the only one
to do so. Tórtola Valencia, too, announced – during her "Indian" phase –
that "I thoroughly believe in reincarnation and I am quite convinced that
in a previous existence I was an Oriental dancer. All my soul and my sympathies are with the East, and ... my features are quite Egyptian" (though
she also claimed that "my mother was a Gypsy ... and it's from her that
I inherit my love of dancing").[52]

Some found all this make-believe and arch pretense cutesy, silly, annoying, and/or fraudulent. One English critic, for example, poked fun on the
occasion of Adorée Villany's arrest in Munich in 1911 at the "solemnity
about these undressings. Gods are evoked, masters of music, paintings
and sculpture are dragged in to perform the parts of the high priest, and
then the victim sacrifices herself in all the solemnity of the café chantant"
or nightclub. The London *Daily Mail* expressed outrage at "these traveling performers who traffic in nudity under the guise of it being Fine
Art." They and the professors of art who defended them, it insisted, were
just "out to make money."[53] One London society journal published a

[51] Allan, *My Life and Dancing*, pp. 11, 23.
[52] "Dancing for Health," *The Morning Leader*, April 20, 1912, clipping in MAE, Fonds Tortola
Valencia, L3.
[53] Craig, *Gordon Craig on Movement*, pp. 222, 227, 224.

photograph of St. Denis in costume, with the sardonic caption "Piling on the Atmosphere."[54] The *New York World* wrote knowingly of Gertrude Hoffmann's version of "Radha" that it was "an imitation of something Miss St. Denis imagined was characteristically Burmese or Hindustanee, or, at any rate, mystic." Another newspaper referred to the audience for such dances as the "Society of Esoteric Highbrows." Of St. Denis, another paper wrote that her dances had "aroma, settings and no steps" and suggested that "Miss St. Denis could really dance if she wouldn't be so awfully Hindoo."[55] The German painter Max Beckmann was more serious; he complained in 1912 of the "dependence on ancient primitive styles which in their own time grew organically out of a common religion and mystic awareness"; this "ethnography-museum art" was merely evidence of the incapacity to create a genuine style of one's own.[56]

As the modern dance craze spread commentators became increasingly acerbic. Already by 1908 there were so many Salomé dances on offer that critics started calling it "Salomania," or the "Salomé pestilence" or the "Salomé epidemic."[57] And the French author, actress, and dancer Colette, annoyed by Mata Hari's early successes, characterized her dance as "of no better quality than the ordinary claptrap" of the many "Indian numbers" then on Paris stages.[58]

Even more annoying than the sheer number of dancers, however, was the fact that few of them were very original. Again, there were many dancers who deliberately mimicked the dance stars – Gertrude Hofmann's impersonation of Maud Allan, for example; or the fake Radha Ruth St. Denis found already performing in Paris when she arrived; or Daisy Peterkin's army of trained Salomés.[59] More strikingly, it was quite common even for the leading stars of modern dance to copy each other. The Salomé routine is the most obvious – it was pioneered by Loïe Fuller in 1893 (and reprised in 1907), and performed by Maud Allan, Adorée Villany, Tórtola Valencia, Mata Hari, Ida Rubinstein, and numerous lesser lights.[60] Many of the modern dancers performed a dance to Strauss's waltz

[54] Carter, "London, 1908," p. 40.
[55] Barbara Naomi Cohen, *The Borrowed Art of Gertrude Hoffmann* (New York: Dance Horizons, 1977), p. 7; Jowitt, *Time*, p. 133.
[56] Quoted in Lloyd, *German Expressionism*, p. 85.
[57] Cherniavsky, "Maud Allan, Part IV," p. 4.
[58] Quoted in Wheelwright, *Fatal Lover*, p. 20.
[59] See, e.g.,Becker, "Die Sezession in der Tanzkunst," p. 41, or in Décoret-Ahiha, *Les danses exotiques*, passim.
[60] Frank Kermode, "Poet and Dancer before Diaghilev," in Roger Copeland and Marshall Cohen, eds., *What Is Dance? Readings in Theory and Criticism* (Oxford: Oxford University Press, 1983), p. 151; Wheelwright, *Fatal Lover*, p. 17; Richard Nelson Current and Marcia Ewing Current, *Loïe*

"On the Beautiful Blue Danube."[61] The "serpentine" dance was pioneered by Loïe Fuller in the 1890s, and then performed by almost every modern dancer after, with Ruth St. Denis only the most successful. Numerous dancers copied St. Denis's "Cobra" dance, as well as her "Incense" – in some cases rather exactly. One New York critic, for example, declared Tórtola Valencia's "Incense" to be "infinitely more strange and mysterious" than St. Denis's; and she performed a "cobra" dance clearly derived from St. Denis's, as well.[62] In fact so many performed some version of St. Denis's "Indian" dances that the dance historian Anne Décoret-Ahiha calls them simply "the Hindu number."[63] As the dance historian Michelle Clayton has remarked, then, as the modern dance revolution matured it developed into "a specific repertory of dances, producing a circuit of borrowings and remakes that made it inordinately difficult to escape the circle of imitation."[64]

By around 1910, it was all too much for some critics – particularly in Germany, which was by then the epicenter of modern dance. Ernst Schur remarked in that year that young women were "jumping and hopping all over the place; and Greece is supposed to justify this well-meaning hopping."[65] Rudolf von Delius felt by 1914 that "everyone wanted to dance; every handsome girl practiced physical culture assiduously, rented a hall, and put on a performance ... I was somewhat tired and disappointed by all the dilettantism."[66] The German novelist and critic Alfred Döblin was more blunt in late 1912: "We've had enough of bad dancers.... Hopping, twisting, enraptured doll-like face ... it's getting downright old."[67] One review of Gertrud Leistikow in late 1913 found that there was "ebbing interest among the public" for dance, because dance productions were "shooting up all over the place like weeds," none of them had anything new to offer, and it was "beginning to get boring."[68] But it was not only

Fuller: *Goddess of Light* (Boston: Northeastern University Press, 1997) and Fuller, *Fifteen Years*, p. 221; Schmidt, *Tanzgeschichte*, pp. 17–19; Brandstetter and Ochaim, *Loïe Fuller*; Giovani Lista, *Loïe Fuller: Danseuse de la Belle Époque* (Paris: Somogy-Stock, 1995).

61 "Miss Isadora Duncan," *Münchner Neueste Nachrichten*, March 29, 1904, clipping in DTAK, Inventory no. 69, Duncan-Archive, II.2.6.1; *Der Tanz – Ein Leben*, eds. Sibylle Dahms and Stephanie Schroedter (Salzburg: Selke, 1997), p. 15.

62 Garland, "The Eternal Return," p. 195.

63 Décoret-Ahiha, *Les dances*, p. 137.

64 Clayton, "Touring History," p. 30.

65 Schur, *Der moderne Tanz*, p. 44.

66 Rudolf Delius, *Mary Wigman* (Dresden: Reissner, 1925), p. 5.

67 Alfred Döblin, "Tänzerinnen (Oktober 1912)," in *Alfred Döblin: Kleine Schriften*, vol. 1 (Olten: Walter, 1985), p. 128.

68 K., "Tanzabend Gertrud Leistikow," *Düsseldorfer Zeitung*, November 8, 1913, clipping in TBCUA, Archief Gertrud Leistikow, Map 4a.

Germans who were tired of it. By 1913 the Paris theater correspondent of a Madrid arts magazine observed that in music halls everywhere girls with the same figure, the same smile, and the same gestures were dancing the same dances, as if a Greek sculptor had created a frieze "with a single figure, repeated indefinitely."[69] An English reviewer of Tórtola Valencia in March 1912 found that most dance performances were "wonderfully wanting in originality"; another reported that her performance was "replete with the exaggerated gestures, gyrations, and prostrations to which Oriental dancers have accustomed us."[70]

And yet, most commentators understood that some make-believe was part of the modern dancer's "act" – and in particular part of the function of variety theater. Already in 1902, the German author and historian Arthur Moeller-Bruck praised variety theater precisely because it "does not want to live, because it is life itself" in its "conscious, admitted simulation of another, unreal reality – in short, illusion." That was what made it entertainment. The parallel to the relationship between dance and statues is obvious: Variety-theater performance was real life because it was genuinely striving to create a fake.[71] Everyone knew "Mata Hari" was Dutch, that "Sent M'ahesa" was Swedish, that Ruth St. Denis was not Indian; everyone knew that most of these dancers were variety-theater entertainers as well as artists; everyone knew they were sexy despite being – and because they were – chaste.

The historian James W. Cook has offered a pithy characterization of what was going on in modern dance (though he was writing of the circus). "Artful deception," as he called it, "was never a hard and fast choice" between truthfulness and fraud; instead it "involved a calculated intermixing of the genuine and the fake, enchantment and disenchantment … no producers of such entertainment who wanted to stay in business for long simply fooled their viewers without also drawing attention to the act of fooling." They engaged in what W. J. T. Mitchell called "illusionism" rather than "illusion": The latter is just straight fraud, the former occupies "the boundary between fact and fiction." As the American circus entrepreneur P. T. Barnum put it, "The public appears disposed to be amused even when they are conscious of being deceived."[72] Michelle Clayton, too, writes

[69] E. Gomez-Carrillo, "El teatro en Paris," *Mundial* 3 (1913): 474–475.
[70] "The Palace Theatre," *Morning Post*, March 19, 1912, and "Palace," *Globe*, March 9, 1912, clippings in MAE, Fonds Tortola Valencia, L3.
[71] Moeller-Bruck, *Das Varieté*, pp. 169–170.
[72] James W. Cook, *The Arts of Deception: Playing with Fraud in the Age of Barnum* (Cambridge, MA: Harvard University Press, 2001), pp. 16–17.

of a "fictive contract" between performer and audience – an agreement to pretend, for the sake of entertainment, or art, or edification.[73] And Michael Saler is even more explicit: Modern mass entertainment, he writes, involved a "self-conscious strategy of embracing illusions while acknowledging their artificial status"; they "are understood to be explicitly fictional" but also "taken to be real," through a "willing activation of pretense."[74] Again, the variety theater appears to have played a pioneering role in developing this pattern – what the historian Barry Faulk calls "a new, self-conscious spectatorship."[75]

3.3 Acting – Really

In fact, a central criterion for the evaluation of modern dancers was specifically their *acting* ability – the term used was usually "mimic" talent. Given the emphasis on the expression of emotion, this is hardly surprising, even if to the modern ear the extent of reviewers' focus on dancers' acting talent seems odd. Isadora Duncan, for example, was praised in her early European performances for her "soulful acting," or for the "soulful play of her facial expression ...," which is supported in the most expressive way by the charming language of her arms"; others again praised her ability to use facial expression to depict "consternation ... fear, tears, horror."[76] And indeed the *New York Times* dance critic Carl van Vechten even wrote that "[p]art of her effect is gained by gesture, part by the massing of her body, but the greater part by facial expression"; and in the early 1920s one Russian actor called her "not only a dancer but a tragic actress."[77] Reports on Maud Allan's performances were similar. In 1907 one Russian theater journal wrote that Allan "amazes not with the virtuosity of her dances but with her startling mimic expressions, which convey a deep impression ... she is particularly successful in the dramatic effects, in the places that express complex human passion." Another Russian reviewer

[73] Clayton, "Touring History," p. 33.
[74] Michael Saler, *As If: Modern Enchantment and the Literary Prehistory of Virtual Reality* (Oxford: Oxford University Press, 2013), pp. 13, 28.
[75] Barry J. Faulk, *Music Hall and Modernity: The Late-Victorian Discovery of Popular Culture* (Athens: Ohio University Press, 2004), p. 25.
[76] "Carl-Theater," *Neue Freie Presse* of Vienna, March 28, 1903, clipping in DTAK, Inventory no. 69, Duncan-Archiv, II.2.6.1; Möckel, "Isadora Duncan," p. 137; quoted in Steegmuller, *Your Isadora*, p. 43.
[77] Carl van Vechten, "The New Isadora," in Paul Padgette, ed., *The Dance Writings of Carl van Vechten* (New York: Dance Horizons, 1977), p. 25; Vladimir Sokoloff on Isadora Duncan, in JRD-IDC, folder 170.

derided her, in contrast, for dancing "all too theatrically." A reviewer in San Francisco found that "her face is marvelously expressive," while "her body, swaying in motion, expresses more than we are accustomed to trace in the facial changes of the most subtle actors." Allan reported that she tried to "augment" her "movements by facial expression ... perhaps the most delicate thing I attempt."[78]

Such passages continued to be typical of appreciations – and critiques – of modern dance right through to 1914 and beyond. In 1910 Ernst Schur praised Ruth St. Denis's "*Mimik, Dramatik*, and symbolic portrayal."[79] A Berlin newspaper in 1911 called Gertrud Leistikow a "finely trained actress"; a Munich reviewer praised her "astonishing mimic power of expression."[80] Adorée Villany had "exceptional mimic talent" and was a "gifted actress" of "strong emotions" (1909); "her face is capable of an extraordinarily rich *Mimik*" (1906); she was praised for the "expressive" "lively play of her expressions," "always appropriate to the situation"; one Paris newspaper observed in 1913 that it was actually her mimic talent that made her interesting – though her movements and poses were "not without merit," too.[81] In 1913 one German reviewer praised Friderica Derra de Moroda as "not only an artistic dancer but also a great actress."[82] Anna Pavlova was "an actress of genuine power, as well as a dancer."[83] Such passages could be piled up endlessly; this was one of the many clichés in the reception of modern dance.

We should not be surprised that the names of two great late-nineteenth-century actresses came up frequently in the writings of both modern dancers and critics: Sarah Bernhardt and Eleanora Duse. Ruth St. Denis, for example, recorded in her memoirs that she and a friend went to see Bernhardt perform in New York, and that she was convinced that Bernhardt was dancing on stage. "I feel that my picturesque posings on stage" early in her career, she recalled, "stem from watching this performance of Bernhardt."[84] Maud Allan, too, claimed to have seen Bernhardt perform in San Francisco, and that "the turning point in my career came

---

[78] Felix Cherniavsky, "Maud Allan, Part IV: The Years of Touring, 1910–1915," *DC* 8 (1985): 1–2; Ralph E. Renaud, "House Goes Wild with Enthusiasm: Most Wonderful of Dancers Exhibits Purest Beauty in Dance Series," *San Francisco Chronicle*, April 6, 1910, in Maud Allan clippings files, MPDSF; Allan, "My Aims and Ideals," p. 2.

[79] Schur, *Der moderne Tanz*, p. 90.

[80] Kleines Theater program, December 16–26, 1911, in STAM, Polizei-Direktion, 3806/4.

[81] Villany, *Tanz-Reform*, pp. 263, 264, 266, 268, 269, 270; Villany, *Phryné*, p. 22.

[82] Dahms and Schroedter, eds., *Der Tanz – Ein Leben*, p. 16.

[83] Money, *Anna Pavlova*, p. 122.

[84] St. Denis, *An Unfinished Life*, p. 58.

from my first sight of that great woman."[85] Isadora Duncan wrote ecstatically of Eleanora Duse's performance, which she first saw in 1899: "I remember that I went home dazed with the wonder of it," thinking that if she could "stand as still as Eleonora Duse did tonight, and, at the same time, create that tremendous force of dynamic movement, then I shall be the greatest dancer in the world."[86] In fact, Sarah Bernhardt in particular had pioneered a very great deal of the conceptual vocabulary of modern dance two decades earlier. She too had built her success on the stage on what a recent biographer has called her ability to combine "sensuality and virtue"; she too made a career of "the pathos of externalizing the inner emotions" in "histrionic style"; she too was praised for her "serpentine grace"; she packed tremendous passion into a "frail" body; she struck "sculptural poses."[87]

Modern dance, then, developed its power not just through its medium (bodies in motion), but through the "activation of pretense" central to theater. And yet we should not conclude from this connection that modern dance was simply fiction; for that is not actually what people at the time understood acting to be doing. According to the dominant theories of acting at the time, acting created a *true* fiction; it was considered an important path to truth. The actor did not make things up; he or she expressed genuine and universal human feelings. A crucial element of modern European acting theory was the "psychological realism" advocated by leading Russian dramatists. Psychological realism insisted that the actor must portray a believable character, acting in ways that made sense in the fictional circumstances in which that character was living – "feelings that seem true in the supposed circumstances," as the great Russian poet Alexander Pushkin put it. Nicolai Gogol, too, argued that the actor must so steep himself in the motivation of the character "that the thoughts and strivings of his character seem to become his own.... One should first grasp the soul of a part, not its trappings." The actor "must not present but transmit" the character's soul. Only in this way could playing a part "capture those features which are common to all mankind."[88] To do that, the actor and director Konstantin Stanislavski held, the actor should rely

85 Allan, *My Life and Dancing*, p. 36.

86 Duncan, *The Art of the Dance*, p. 121.

87 Claudia Thorun, *Sarah Bernhardt: Inszenierungen von Weiblichkeit im fin de siècle* (Hildesheim: Olms, 2006), p. 120; quotations from Elaine Aston, *Sarah Bernhardt: A French Actress on the English Stage* (New York: Berg, 1989), pp. 19–20, 24, 21.

88 Konstantin Stanislavski, *An Actor's Work* (New York: Routledge, 2008), p. 53; Jean Benedetti, *Stanislavski* (London: Methuen, 1988), p. 15.

on the "magical, creative *if*" – asking herself what it would be like if the play were her real life. How would she really perform the action required in the circumstances created by the script, and how would she genuinely feel about it? As early as 1848 the actor Mikhail Shchepkin explained that "an actor of feeling ... begins by wiping out his own self ... and becomes the character the author intended him to be." The aim, as the theater historian Jean Benedetti puts it, was "physical and vocal freedom, free-flowing emotion, clarity of expression, all apparently achieved without effort." In Stanislavski's words, the actor must "live the part." When he was really acting, truly in the "creative mood," Stanislavski reported, "I ceased to be afraid of the audience, and at times forgot that I was on the stage." In these moments, he could express "the truth of emotions ..., the truth that is within myself"; he was "truthful in his soul and body." When "my whole body and after it my soul, began to believe," he could express "spiritual and physical truth" through the "lies" of make-up, costumes, scenery, and performance.[89]

Similar theories were influential in Britain as well, where the theater critic George Henry Lewes, for example, described as "natural acting" the ability to *genuinely* fake a character, in the sense that one found deep within oneself the universal human feelings that motivated that character (at least a believably written one). This was the special talent of actors: to see through to the core of a person – including themselves. As the theater historian Lynn M. Voskuil puts it, in nineteenth-century English theater "theatricality" implied "masking and unmasking, multiple roles, double ... consciousness, flamboyance, spectacle, and self-display," while "authenticity" meant "interiority, nature, sincerity, truthfulness, empirical fact, verisimilitude, and coherent selfhood.... But ... the meanings of these clustered terms were not irretrievably opposed."[90] The actor could present a convincing fake only if she could genuinely find within her the person she was pretending to be.

These ideas had important counterparts in philosophy and in the arts more broadly at the time. Charles Baudelaire's essay on "The Painter of Modern Life," first published in 1863, had already given a rather precise definition of the connection between authenticity and theatricality. "Modernity," according to Baudelaire, is, on the one hand, the ability and need "to distil the eternal from the transitory" – to get at the essential

---

[89] Benedetti, *Stanislavski*, pp. 16–17; Constantin Stanislavsky, *My Life in Art*, trans. J. J. Robbins (Boston: Little, Brown, 1929), pp. 461, 464, 466–467.

[90] Lynn M. Voskuil, *Acting Naturally* (Charlottesville: University of Virginia Press, 2004), pp. 11–12.

truth of things. But, on the other hand, it is also "the burning need to create for oneself a personal originality" as a creative act, a performance – a work of fiction. "It matters but little that the artifice and trickery are known to all, so long as their success is assured and their effect ... irresistible."[91] Fourteen years later, in a massive tome on "The Philosophy of As If," the German philosopher Hans Vaihinger would develop the idea of "fictionalism," namely that "an idea whose theoretical untruth or ... falsity is admitted is not for that reason practically valueless; for such an idea ... may have great practical importance."[92] An example would be scientific hypotheses – provisional fictions that help us to achieve a closer approximation of truth, or at least practically useful results. Specifically identifying philosophical pragmatism as an influence on his thought, Vaihinger argued that every "purposeful activity is expressed in the identification of the means necessary and appropriate for the achievement of the established purpose"; and thinking, believing, is a purposeful activity – we do it not for its own sake but to accomplish things. So, a false belief or a made-up identity that leads us to achieve our goals serves the legitimate purpose of thinking, believing, or being.[93]

Modern dance built on all these ideas and programs. The qualities these theorists and actors aimed for were all qualities that modern dance aimed for as well: naturalness and freedom of expression, genuine feeling, universal emotional meaning, but also the achievement of practical ends – such as theatrical impact, and making a living – through make-believe, flamboyance, self-display, and double consciousness (chaste but wild, popular but elite, European but Oriental, etc.). In fact, the techniques used and taught by the modern dancers echo those of natural acting. Stanislavski, for example, argued that "everything that happens onstage must occur *for some reason or other*" – that is, the actor must know not only that the character did something, but why, what his or her motivation was. Isadora Duncan adopted precisely this position in her dance pedagogy: "We do not allow the child to make a single movement unless it knows why it makes it ... the motion must be of such a nature that the child feels the reason for it in every fiber."[94] And obviously this was precisely Loïe Fuller's argument regarding the "reconstruction" of ancient dances, too – if one

[91] Charles Baudelaire, *The Painter of Modern Life and Other Essays* (London: Phaidon, 1964 [1863]), pp. 12, 27, 33.
[92] Hans Vaihinger, *The Philosophy of As If* (London: Routledge and Kegan Paul, 1968 [1924]), p. viii.
[93] Hans Vaihinger, *Die Philosophie des Als-Ob* (Berlin: Reuther and Reichard, 1911), p. 7.
[94] Stanislavski, *An Actor's Work*, p. 39; Isadora Duncan, "A Child Dancing" (1906), in Sheldon Cheney, ed., *The Art of the Dance* (New York: Theatre Arts, 1928), p. 74.

could feel Greek, one would dance Greek. The biographers of some modern dancers have noted this tendency to get completely absorbed in their stage personas. Julie Wheelwright, for example, noted that "Mata Hari *became* whatever part she played. If she honestly believed she had been born in Java, had travelled throughout Asia and visited Russia ... she could convince an audience."[95] Iris Garland similarly wrote that "Tórtola Valencia became her invented self and seemingly did not exist outside it." In fact, she seems to have believed that she could transform her physical appearance at will: She remarked in an interview in Peru in 1916 that "when I look at myself, I see an Inca in the brow and the expression of the eyes.... My face is Gypsy when I want, but Hindu and Arab too."[96]

It is tempting to see all this as reflecting the willingness, in Ruth St. Denis's words, to be anything as long as it received attention. Perhaps it was also that; but again, it reflected an understanding that literal truth, factual accuracy, was not the decisive factor in human affairs or even in the pursuit of understanding. Some critics poked fun at what they saw as the essentially fraudulent character of much modern dance performance. But the theorists and performers of modern dance might instead have argued that their art was an exploration of ideas, feelings, human truths. As Vaihinger put it, where ideas were not *understood* to be false, they are merely "false hypotheses"; but they could "gain their real value ... through the consciousness that they are intentionally provisional imaginings."[97] Some critics, indeed, found this approach exciting, liberating, and even potentially necessary. Harry Graf Kessler remarked in his diary in 1903 that all of modern art seemed to be striving for "truth," but "the power of this concept 'truth' is beginning to wobble a bit. What is truth? And: What is truth for?"[98] As we have seen, Kessler soon "got" modern dance, becoming an important patron of both Ruth St. Denis and Grete Wiesenthal. And it is not coincidental that Havelock Ellis included in his 1923 book *The Dance of Life* an extended discussion of Vaihinger's "Philosophy of As If."[99]

The early dance critic J. E. Crawford Flitch captured the exploratory spirit inherent in the modern dancers' concept of truth, the soul, or

[95] Wheelwright, *Fatal Lover*, pp. 29–30.
[96] Garland, *Tortola Valencia*, p. 10; Valencia quoted in Murias Vila, "La magicienne aux yeux d'abîme," p. 24.
[97] Vaihinger, *Die Philosophie des Als-Ob*, p. 27.
[98] Carina Schäfer and Gabriele Biedermann, eds., *Harry Graf Kessler: Das Tagebuch Dritter Band 1897–1905* (Stuttgart: Cotta, 2004), p. 539.
[99] Havelock Ellis, *The Dance of Life* (Boston: Houghton Mifflin, 1923), pp. 87–103.

authenticity quite neatly on two pages of a history of the dance published in 1912. On one, he wrote that to become a Spanish dancer – that is, to dance in the style internationally recognized as Spanish dance – the performer "must first transform herself into a Spaniard." On the other, he wrote that St. Denis was not entirely successful as a dance artist because she was too "literal," she "attempts to interpret the East with both fidelity to the letter and the spirit, rather than to use its gestures freely, with the bold grasp of an artist, as elements of design." This is yet another example of the productivity of contradiction in dance: One must become what one is mimicking, but retain sufficient distance from it to be able merely to use it as a role to achieve one's own purposes.[100]

In many cases dance commentators used a rather paradoxical figure of speech to communicate the nature of the transformation that dance ideally involved: The dancer, in expressing herself through the medium of an assumed persona, did exactly what Shchepkin advocated – wiped her own self out. Ernst Schur, for example, wrote of Ruth St. Denis's ability to "strip away her own personality," to "dissolve" herself in the dance.[101] The Caffins too felt that in "saturating" herself with the "spirit" of the Orient, St. Denis "herself ceases to have a personality."[102] Hans Brandenburg believed that Gertrud Leistikow "forgot herself" in following the "call" of the dance.[103] The actress Mercedes de Acosta wrote that in the 1920s her lover Isadora Duncan often

> danced for me. She danced for me for three and four hours at a time. She would completely lose herself ... and became utterly unconscious of anything but the rhythm of her own body.... Often she danced until the first light of morning began to creep in, then suddenly she would stop and look about, bewildered, like someone returning from a long journey.[104]

And Niddy Impekoven, who became an important figure in German dance in the 1920s, reduced this feeling to a simple phrase: At her debut performance, something "completely new and unknown broke through that had nothing to do with my will or intention.... Something *was dancing me!*"[105]

The modern dancers, in short, were possessed by the dance; they became a vehicle for a foreign spirit or soul. Indeed one reviewer of Clotilde von

[100] Flitch, *Modern Dancing*, p. 196, 194.
[101] Schur, *Der moderne Tanz*, p. 90.
[102] Caffin and Caffin, *Dancing*, p. 92.
[103] Brandenburg, *München leuchtete*, p. 439.
[104] Mercedes de Acosta, *Here Lies the Heart* (New York: Reynal, 1960), pp. 178–179.
[105] Niddy Impekoven, *Die Geschichte eines Wunderkindes* (Zürich: Rotapfel, 1955), p. 82.

Derp reported that her performance was so lovely and joyful that he would have liked to join her, dancing "in happy self-forgetting."[106] The extreme case was that of Madeleine Guipet, who danced, allegedly, only when placed under hypnosis, and made a brief splash as a psychology exhibit in Munich in 1904 when she was taken up by the famed psychiatrist Albert von Schrenck-Notzing.[107] But the idea that dance induced a sort of trance state was commonplace in the discussion of modern dance. All of this was rather odd in light of the alleged centrality of personality, of the individual performer's soul, in modern dance. Obviously, this is a paradox very closely related to that noted in Chapter 2 – the paradox of the dancer performing for herself, rather than for an audience. A curious statement by Tórtola Valencia can help clarify what was going on here. She did have stage fright at the start of her performance, Valencia remarked; but then there came a moment "where I forget everything around me, the fear, the public, even myself. I would say that my soul has left me to make room for the person I am interpreting."[108] Valencia was activating Stanislawski's "magic if"; she was asking herself to dance as if she really were the person she was portraying. But the greatest American exponent of Delsarte movement techniques, Genevieve Stebbins, described the same process with respect to pantomime: The "perfect actor is he who becomes one with his part, and whose individuality is completely lost in the personality of the character he creates."[109]

The connections between the theory of acting and the theory of modern dance were not merely abstract or conceptual, however; there were direct links. The theory of acting developed by Stanislavski and others in Russia may have been directly influenced by the movement theory of François Delsarte, a crucial foundation for early modern dance, in which particular movements were believed to correspond to and awaken internal states of feeling and being.[110] Isadora Duncan's lover Edward Gordon Craig was the son of the actress Ellen Terry, one of the greatest English exponents of natural acting. When Duncan went to Russia for the second time in 1907 she met Stanislavski, who was swept away by her genius,

[106] "Tänze," *Dresdener Anzeiger*, February 7, 1912, clipping in DTAK Inventory no. 56, Clotilde und Alexander Sacharoff, II.2.7.
[107] See Kolb, *Performing Femininity*, pp. 127–142.
[108] Juan Carranza, "Los Reportajes sensacionales; Almorir un amor de Tórtola Valencia, su Arte Adquiere mayor excesitud," *El Escandalo* June/July 1926, clipping in MAE, Fonds Tórtola Valencia, L15.
[109] Genevieve Stebbins, *Delsarte System of Expression* (New York: Edgar S. Werner, 1902), p. 428.
[110] See George Taylor and Rose Whyman, "François Delsarte, Prince Sergei Volkonsky and Mikhail Chekhov," *Mime Journal* 23 (2005): 97–111.

helped to win over the Moscow audience in her favor (by rushing the footlights to applaud demonstratively), and remembered that "we understood each other almost before we had said a single word." Duncan was excited by Stanislavski's ideas, and summoned Craig to Russia to collaborate with the two of them. Stanislavski claimed to have begun to develop his concept of the "magic if" as early as 1906; but he may have reduced his ideas to a "system" of training only while working with Duncan and Craig in 1911. In any case, he recalled in 1929, "[W]e were looking for one and the same thing in different branches of art."[111]

The philosophical repositioning inherent in these methods made it possible to square the obvious make-believe and pretense central to modern dance with its claim to be serious art with a profound truth to tell. This reconciliation seems odd to us today; but it was not unusual at the turn of the twentieth century. Europeans at the time did not consider fiction to be "merely" fiction; instead, they regarded fiction as a legitimate way for educated people to communicate ideas, and to explore and express important human truths. In many disciplines in the human sciences, for example, fictional portrayals in novels or plays were considered to be legitimate evidence. In the early scholarly literature of sexology in just this period characters in modernist plays were believed to reveal something essential about people. One instance is the character of the nude dancer Lulu from Frank Wedekind's scandalous plays *Earth Spirit* and *Pandora's Box*. As one sexologist put it in 1913, " 'Lulu' might be pathological, but there's a bit of pathology in the feminine soul," and in real life there were "Lulu-characters wherever you look!"[112] Edward Said has shown that fictional portrayals of "the Orient" played a similar and important role in the discipline of Orientalism – the study of Middle Eastern cultures.[113]

It is not coincidental that this same period saw a sudden outpouring of interest in Europe and North America in the occult, in spiritualism, in reincarnation, in Buddhism and Hinduism, and in esoteric religions of more recent and Western origin. Such ideas, at the time, seemed to many to be potentially revolutionary discoveries. In many cases, they had an

---

[111] Benedetti, *Stanislavski*, pp. 16, 172, 179; Voskuil, *Acting*, p. 17; Duncan, *My Life*, p. 167; Stanislavski, *My Life*, pp. 461, 505–507. On Terry see Penny Farfan, *Women, Modernism and Performance* (New York: Cambridge University Press, 2004), pp. 41–43.

[112] J. Spier, "Lulucharaktere!," *Sexual-Probleme* 9 (1913): 687.

[113] Edward Said, *Orientalism* (London: Penguin, 1985 [1978]). On the "open traffic" between the human sciences and literature see Paul Peppis, *Sciences of Modernism: Ethnography, Sexology, and Psychology* (New York: Cambridge University Press, 2014), here p. 4; *A Concise Companion to Modernism*, ed. David Bradshaw (Malden, MA: Blackwell, 2003).

influence far beyond their reach in our own time. Ideas that seem from an early-twenty-first-century perspective to be certifiably loony had quite extraordinary social weight, and real consequences. An example is the great Mexican leader Francisco Madero, who helped start and lead the Mexican revolution in 1910 in part because he had become a devotee of Spiritualism during his years in exile in the United States and was directed by the spirits he contacted to become "a soldier of liberty and progress" and "carry out a great mission on earth" in the service of the Heavenly Father.[114] Similarly, an extraordinary number of important people in the period were influenced by the Theosophy movement, which was based on a bizarre mishmash of teachings allegedly discovered in ancient religious texts by Helena Blavatsky, a Russian emigrant living in New York – or perhaps revealed to her by a team of spiritual masters living in a hidden valley in the Himalaya but occasionally astral-projecting out to have a chat with her. On the basis of this goop, Blavatsky became legitimately a minor prophet in her own time. She established a worldwide organization, moved to India, studied with influential Buddhist and Hindu teachers, and played an important role in the development of Indian nationalism (about which more in Chapter 5) and the prehistory of New Age thought.[115]

Finally, the theater played an important role in some of the most far-reaching political upheavals of the period. Recent work on the women's movements of the turn of the century, for example, have shown that – as Susan A. Glenn has argued – "assertive self-spectacle by theater women was of crucial importance for changing concepts of womanhood at the turn of the century"; it was a forum for "elaborating new forms of female identity" that eroded the passivity, deference, and self-denial imposed by traditional gender roles."[116] As Lynn Voskuil puts it, people in the period "developed a sophisticated capacity to ... act authentically and be theatrical at the same time. In this way, they theatricalized the ideas ... they believed to be most authentic even as they authenticated the spectacles they made of themselves."[117]

[114] Thomas E. Skidmore and Peter H. Smith, *Modern Latin America* (New York: Oxford University Press, 1989), p. 224; Enrique Krauze, *Mexico: Biography of Power* (New York: HarperCollins, 1997), pp. 246, 250–251.
[115] Sylvia Cranston, *HPB* (New York: Putnam, 1993).
[116] Susan A. Glenn, *Female Spectacle: The Theatrical Roots of Modern Feminism* (Cambridge, MA: Harvard University Press, 2000), p. 3.
[117] Voskuil, *Acting*, p. 3; see also Lisa Tickner, *The Spectacle of Women: Imagery of the Suffrage Campaign, 1907–1914* (London: Chatto and Windus, 1987).

As the English sex reformer Edward Carpenter put it in his manifesto for erotic freedom in 1896, then, "We are what we make of ourselves."[118] This was not wishful thinking or New Age claptrap; it was an influential philosophical proposition, and one that both fiction and real life seemed to bear out. Dance, obviously, was part of this phenomenon.

3.4 Fake or Borrowed?

There is one further reason not to regard the modern dancers' use of Oriental themes or personas as fraudulent, however. For many of the modern dancers in fact did not make up their Oriental dances entirely from whole cloth, or from a few statues and knickknacks, or even from what they could pick up from dance troupes appearing in variety theaters or at international expositions. At least some of them did work with Asian artists.

The most striking case is that of Ruth St. Denis. Her interest in things Oriental was sparked first by the Orientalizing productions she encountered while working in variety theater, and her first model as an independent dancer (at least according to her autobiography) was an image of an Egyptian goddess in a cigarette advertisement. But she made her name as an "Indian" dancer after playing a goddess in a private theater group's production of the fifth-century Sanskrit playwright Kalidasa's work *Sakuntala*. In that production, she also met Edmund Russell, the "high priest" (so the dance historian Deborah Jowitt named him) of American Delsartism, who also had a fashionable interest in Eastern religion and gave public readings of the English teacher and journalist Sir Edwin Arnold's Buddhist-inspired poem "The Light of Asia." A key step, however, was her encounter with actual Indian performers (musicians, magicians, dancers, and so on) at the amusement park on Coney Island. Inspired, she did some research at the New York Public Library and hired several Indians as extras for the "Radha" dance that was the backbone of her early performances. Some of them were members of a global floating labor force of Indian or "Lascar" sailors and dock workers, in port between jobs; some were students at Columbia University; some were clerks at an Indian import store in Manhattan. She workshopped "Radha" with these Indian immigrants, picking up at least fragmentary elements of various Indian movement idioms. She also used some genuinely Indian props – for example, saris from

[118] Edward Carpenter, *Wenn die Menschen reif zur Liebe werden*, trans. Karl Federn (Leipzig: Hermann Seemann, 1902), p. 20.

the shop of an Indian family in New York.[119] The dance was a mishmash of authentic Indian dance idiom, waltz, skirt dancing, and poses copied from Indian statuary, and one Indian dance historian concludes that her dance "violates, exploits, and loves" genuine Indian dance traditions. But historically it was at least not 100 percent invented.[120]

Nor was this the end of St. Denis's efforts to include genuinely "exotic" elements in her performance. She appears to have practiced yoga with some seriousness. Later she would hire Indian extras in Europe as well, primarily sailors in London; hire a Ceylonese musical director; and engage the Indian musician and later (in 1913, in London) founder of the Universal Sufi Order Inayat Khan and his ensemble as accompaniment for her first major American tour. Khan was not particularly impressed with her, observing that it was "not satisfactory to combine real with imitation," and that it was "painful" to be treated as mere entertainers. But St. Denis was clearly not without genuine interest in Indian culture. Somewhat later, when she became interested in Japanese themes, she would add at least a veneer of authenticity to her performance by hiring a former geisha in Los Angeles to teach her some Japanese dance. Seeing the Japanese dancer and actress Sada Yacco perform in Paris too, had a lasting impact on her: "Her performance haunted me for years, and filled my soul with such a longing for the subtle and elusive in art that it became my chief ambition as an artist." Finally, while her religious beliefs appear to have been an evolving amalgam of Christian Science, Buddhism, Spiritualism, occultism, and Hinduism, she does appear to have engaged actively with these various faiths – for example, traveling in 1908 to meet a leader of the Ramakrishna Order of Vivekananda in England and eventually becoming active in the Vedanta movement.[121]

---

[119] St. Denis, *An Unfinished Life*, pp. 55–56, 58–59, 69; Meinzenbach, *"Tanz ist eine Sprache und eine Schrift des Göttlichen,"* p. 36. On Indian sailors see G. Balachandran, "Circulation through Seafaring Indian Seamen, 1890–1945," in Claude Markovits, Jacques Pouchepadass, and Sanja Subrhmanyam, eds., *Society and Circulation: Mobile People and Itinerant Cultures in South Asia 1750–1950* (Delhi: Permanent Black, 2003), pp. 89–130; Vivek Bald, *Bengali Harlem and the Lost Histories of South Asian America* (Cambridge, MA: Harvard University Press, 2013).

[120] Jowitt, *Time and the Dancing Image*, p. 131; Kendall, *Where She Danced*, pp. 50–51; Shelton, *Ruth St. Denis*, pp. 51–52, 56, 72; Uttara Asha Coorlawala, "Ruth St. Denis and India's Dance Renaissance," *DC* 15 (1992): 138–140.

[121] Meinzenbach, *"Tanz ist eine Sprache und eine Schrift des Göttlichen,"* p. 67; Kendall, *Where*, p. 89; Shelton, *Ruth St. Denis*, pp. 71, 94; St. Denis, *An Unfinished Life*, pp. 98, 56, 61, 112, 120, 127; Coorlawala, "Ruth St. Denis," p. 127; Khan, *Biography of Pir-o-Murshid Inayat Khan*, p. 124; Nancy Lee Chalfa Ruyter, *Reformers and Visionaries: The Americanization of the Art of Dance* (New York: Dance Horizons, 1979), p. 60.

In short, St. Denis was not just making stuff up. Her approach to Asian dance and religious traditions was certainly eclectic, amateurish, and informed by a good dose of show-business sensibility – as one might expect of an entertainer selling her work to the newly emerging mass culture market. But it would be unfair to characterize her use of "Oriental" elements as merely fraudulent. St. Denis was genuinely part of a very broad reception of Asian culture in the West – one that many Europeans and North Americans found enormously exciting. In an ecstatic appreciation of St. Denis published in 1906, for example, Hugo von Hofmannsthal saw her performances as embodying "the quite unique moment in which we live," in which the "imagination of Europe" was being "infused ... with Asiatic beauty" and "the sons of Brahmins wring confirmation of ancient wisdom from the material world in the laboratories of Cambridge and Harvard, [and] in which the English-language presses of Benares and Calcutta enrich our libraries with books written in masterfully composed, wonderfully focused books." Hofmannsthal was not exactly a discriminating observer of Asia, remarking for example that St. Denis's "Indian" dances were just like Javanese, Cambodian, and Annamese dances he had seen on other occasions ("Naturally it's the same thing that all Oriental dances seek"). But he certainly had an acute sense of the broadening of cultural horizons around 1900.[122]

Other modern dancers appear to have been far less immersed in this kind of excitement about cultural globalization than St. Denis; but they did take part in it. Cléo de Mérode, for example, hired genuine Cambodian musicians for her ersatz Cambodian dance in 1900.[123] Regina Woody/Nila Devi reported taking lessons in Indian dance from "some Indian person" (as her mother put it) in Paris, discovering that the Indian Kathakali dance tradition was not about "wiggles and undulations" at all. Mata Hari may have learned some Javanese dance while living in the Dutch East Indies as the wife of a Dutch colonial official; she at least tried taking a trip to Egypt; and she too later hired Inayat Khan and his ensemble on at least one occasion. Ida Rubinstein traveled to Egypt and Syria to try to learn some Middle Eastern dance for her own "Salomé" performance.[124] It is probably not coincidental that the performances of Stacia Napierkowska, who spent some time in Montenegro in her youth,

[122] Hofmannsthal, "Die unvergleichliche Tänzerin," pp. 257, 260.
[123] Ochaim and Balk, Varieté-Tänzerinnen, p. 92.
[124] Woody, Dancing, pp. 155–156; Keay, The Spy Who Never Was, pp. 57, 72; Wheelwright, Fatal Lover, p. 28; Vicki Woolf, Dancing in the Vortex, pp. 18–19.

appeared to at least one reviewer to owe a great deal to the "sacred delirium of the dancing dervishes."[125] None of this amounted to a serious and sustained interest in non-European dance; but equally clearly, these performers were incorporating some elements of Asian and Middle Eastern dance idioms into their work.

Even short of Asian or Middle Eastern influences, finally, it is worth focusing for a moment on just how cosmopolitan the world of modern dance was within Europe, as well. The role of Americans both as performers and as patrons of modern dance in Europe was decisive; and in some cases they were prominent in audiences as well – Ruth St. Denis even claimed that the Central German city of Dresden, at the time of her performances there in 1907, "was practically an American colony."[126] But even within Europe the dance world was characterized by a remarkable degree of mobility. Clotilde von Derp took dance lessons in Munich from both the Rice sisters (English) and Anna Ornelli (Italian); and the Falke sisters, in Hamburg, also had an English dance teacher.[127] Olga Sellin/Desmond was from Allenstein/Olsztyn in Prussian Poland, and managed to be called both the Venus of London and Prussia's Naked Venus. Gertrude Barrison had a career that stretched from Denmark to the United States and back to Vienna. Tórtola Valencia may or may not have been Spanish by birth, but in any case spoke five languages, spent time in England and in a boarding school in Paris, and eventually became a Catalan cultural icon.[128] Gertrud Leistikow, while German, is a good reminder of how tenuous nationality sometimes was in the first half of the twentieth century: She was born in Silesia, now in Poland; spent her youth in Metz, now in France; studied dance in Munich and Switzerland; and eventually settled permanently in Holland.[129]

At times, indeed, the web of international connections in the dance world became almost ludicrous. In her interpretation of the ubiquitous Salomé dance, for example, Adorée Villany (Hungarian-French) used

[125] Ochaim, *Varieté-Tänzerinnen*, 133 and Gomez-Carillo, "El teatro," 476.

[126] Denis, *An Unfinished Life*, p. 99.

[127] See Frank-Manuel Peter, "Die 'neie Minchener Derpsichore': Clotilde von Derp – die früheste Vertreterin des Ausdruckstanzes?," in Frank Manuel Peter and Rainer Stamm, eds., *Die Sacharoffs: Zwei Tänzer aus dem Umkreis des Blauen Reiters* (Cologne: Wienand, 2002), pp. 78, 86; Nils Jockel and Patricia Stockemann, *'Flugkraft in unendliche Ferne': Bühnentanz in Hamburg seit 1900* (Hamburg: Museum für Kunst und Gewerbe, 1989), p. 17.

[128] Runge, *Olga Desmond* and "Einladung zum zweiten öffentlichen Schönheit-Abend," LAB, APrBr 030-05. Tit. 74, Th. 1502, fol. 4–7; Ochaim, "Die Barfusstänzerin Olga Desmond," pp. 19–21; Garland, "Early Modern Dance," p. 5.

[129] Ehrich, "Im Sauseschritt," pp. 8–11.

a text written in French by an Irishman (Oscar Wilde) set to music by an Austrian (Richard Strauss). In another case, in Monte Carlo in 1910, Mata Hari (Dutch) danced Cleopatra (Egyptian) to music by Rimsky-Korsakov (Russian) in a play written by an Algerian and directed by a Frenchman.[130] In 1911, Harry Graf Kessler (German) persuaded both St. Denis (American) and Vaslav Nijinsky (Russian) to sit as models for the sculptor Aristide Maillol (Catalan-French) on a monument to Friedrich Nietzsche (German again). And for good measure, Kessler remarked in his journal that Nijinsky's face and manners seemed to him vaguely Japanese. That association may have owed something to his enthusiasm for Sada Yacco, whose performances during the 1900 world's fair in Paris had fascinated him.[131]

There was nothing particularly extraordinary in any of this; all the arts – painting, theater, music, opera, architecture – were very cosmopolitan in this period; and the ballet was no less so, even in the early nineteenth century. French, Italian, and German ballerinas danced all over Europe, and indeed all over the world; Italian and French ballet teachers were to be found in St. Petersburg, London, Berlin, New York, and farther afield as well.[132] Nevertheless, this internationalism is rather striking in modern dance, a performance genre in which the artist's "blood" was taken to define her identity. Obviously, the operative idea here was that mixing, cross-fertilization, was both fruitful and desirable. Here too, the modern dancers may be said to have played across an important tension in European culture at this time: that between the familiar and the foreign, "us" and "them."

That was a tension that was rising around 1900 due to two important but often mutually contradictory developments. One was the consolidation of national states in the nineteenth century, as exemplified in the unifications of Italy and Germany in 1860 and 1870; in expanding state bureaucracies and armies; in the imposition of national languages through expanding school systems, mass conscription, and the mass national press; in the growth of parliamentary government and national political parties;

---

[130] See Keay, *The Spy Who Never Was*, p. 60.
[131] Hildegard Burger, ed., *Hugo von Hofmannsthal/Harry Graf Kessler: Briefwechsel 1898–1929* (Frankfurt: Insel, 1968), pp. 132–133, 331; Jörg Schuster, ed., *Harry Graf Kessler: Das Tagebuch, Vierter Band 1906–1914* (Stuttgart: Cotta, 2004), pp. 689–690, 359; Fiedler, "Weimar contra Berlin," pp. 107, 119; Berg, "Sada Yacco in London and Paris, 1900," pp. 343–404. On Kessler see Laird McLeod Easton, *The Red Count: The Life and Times of Harry Kessler* (Berkeley: University of California Press, 2002).
[132] See, e.g., Ivor Guest, *The Romantic Ballet in Paris* (Middleton: Wesleyan University Press, 1966), p. 73.

and in the increasing density of national transportation and communications networks. The other was the early stages of modern globalization – the extensive imperial conquests in Africa, Asia, and the Pacific after about 1880, but also the increasing rapidity of travel and communication across national borders and even continental and hemispheric boundaries, and the growing economic importance of international trade and finance. Modern dance – like other forms of mass culture, such as the cinema, or social dancing (e.g., fox-trot, tango) – was nourished in part by, and indeed deliberately played on, the concern for identity *and* for exploration of alternatives that these contradictory but linked developments generated.

3.5 We Have Met the Other and He Is Us: The Ballets Russes

The phenomenon of the Ballets Russes neatly exemplifies this strategy of playing on the tension between self and other. Started in France in 1909 by the wealthy ballet enthusiast Serge Diaghilev, this dance company initially had support from the Russian imperial government, which was seeking to develop cultural as well as diplomatic ties with France in the lead-up to World War I. The imperial ballet "loaned" some key dancers to Diaghilev, and at first subsidized costumes and sets. But Diaghilev had never been able to make himself particularly well liked at court, and his company soon veered away from classical ballet, lost support from the Russian government, and never performed in Russia. Russian ballet was deeply indebted to the classical French ballet tradition; but after mounting a few ballets in that genre, the (so-called) Ballets Russes came increasingly to resemble modern dance both in its movement idiom and in its business strategy. Its choreography eschewed technical bravura in favor of fluid, "natural" movement and expressive power. That is not surprising, as Diaghilev and his choreographer Mikhail Fokine were deeply influenced by Isadora Duncan's first visit to Russia, in December 1904. Diaghilev later wrote that Fokine was "mad about" Duncan, and that her "influence on him was the initial basis of his entire creation"; another close associate wrote that Duncan's performance "inspired Fokine and shaped his creative life."[133] The influential designer Alexander Benois, who would later work with the Ballets Russes in France, observed in a review of Duncan's

---

[133] Quotations in Elizabeth Souritz, "Isadora Duncan and Prewar Russian Dancemakers," in Lynn Garafola and Nancy van Norman Baer, eds., *The Ballets Russes and Its World* (New Haven, CT: Yale University Press, 1999), pp. 97, 110. Fokine denied Duncan's influence (p. 109).

performances in Saint Petersburg in 1904 that the reforms she advocated could "re-animate the ballet, would make it more modern and indispensable, would rid it of the stain of acrobatism and of something not quite decent," and thereby "salvage this noble and even sacred art from total ruin."[134]

In fact, the company formed in 1909 borrowed a great deal from the strategy of modern dance. It adopted a physical profile like that of the modern dancers: Its female dancers were skinny, flexible, and lithe – though its star male dancer Vaslav Nijinsky combined slenderness with extreme strength in the legs. Cut loose from state funding, the company was dependent on the market, and aimed to reach "large masses," as Fokine put it; and in 1909 it presented its first season in a Parisian variety theater. But it was also dependent on the support of some of the very same people who were prominent as patrons of modern dance – including the Princess and Prince de Polignac, the Countess de Greffulhe, the Rothschilds, and through the Paris impresario Gabriel Astruc (who also acted for Mata Hari) various American zillionaires. The company built a comarketing agreement with Paris fashion, just as some of the modern dancers did: The fashion designer Paul Poiret took up some ideas from their costuming, and the designer Coco Chanel became a friend and collaborator of Diaghilev. And it attracted a coterie of avant-garde artists and intellectuals, such as the painters Salvador Dalí, Juan Miró, and Henri Matisse. Nijinsky, the company's star dancer and (after Fokine) choreographer, had even been abandoned by his father, and was briefly obsessed with ancient Greece.[135]

Diaghilev had made a name for himself as a conduit bringing authentic Russian culture to the West – for example, with a major exhibition of Russian art in Paris in 1906, a concert series of Russian music in 1907, and a season of Russian opera in 1908. But ballet dancers in Russia were trained and performed in the French tradition, and as Diaghilev put it, there really was no Russian ballet. So he set out to invent it. As he wrote to a composer in 1909, "I need a *ballet* and a *Russian* one – the *first* Russian ballet, since there is no such thing." Between 1910 and 1913 he produced a series of them, starting with *The Firebird* (which was, as one of his dancers observed, created "for export to the West") and including *Scheherezade,*

[134] Alexander Benois, "Music and Plastic Art," *Slovo*, December 23, 1904, translation in JRDD, Natalia Roslasleva files, folder 9.
[135] Homans, *Apollo's Angels*, pp. 313, 300, 292, 305, 294–295, 293 (quotation), 308; Kurth, *Isadora*, p. 73; Järvinen, *Dancing Genius*, pp. 33–38, 70; Karthas, *When Ballet Became French*, pp. 15–16; Lifar, *Serge Diaghilev*, pp. 122, 127.

Petrouchka, and *The Rite of Spring*. In the process, Diaghilev and his company engaged in a mounting frenzy of self-Orientalization. Increasingly through this series of ballets, "Russian" meant – as the ballet historian Jennifer Homans put it – "savage, rebellious, and Asiatic."[136] Diaghilev, Fokine, and Nijinsky invented a Russia that was primitive, elemental, ungoverned, passionate, sexual, inscrutable, and violent – one that fit all the European stereotypes about the Orient. Some critics responded enthusiastically, proclaiming that the Russian dancers gave expression to the "virile impulses of an untamed race, not yet sapped by civilization of its vigor," or that they were infused with a "Tartar element" and "brutally direct," but "too fresh, too zealous, and alive to be perverse." One close collaborator called them " 'barbarians' ... the Russian Savages, the Scythians."[137]

The Ballets Russes did differ from modern dance, of course, both in being a dance company under the control of men and in being explicitly rooted in and retaining more of the ballet tradition. Nevertheless, in most other respects the Ballets Russes can be fairly regarded as an offshoot or variant of modern dance; as the dance historian Hanna Järvinen puts it, the group offered "a fusion of ballet traditions and forms of new dance."[138] No lesser figure than Auguste Rodin even constructed a genealogy of dance innovation that ran from Loïe Fuller through Isadora Duncan to Vaslav Nijinsky.[139] What is more, the company had several performers who set out on their own with dance productions that combined some elements of ballet with a more modernist sensibility. Anna Pavlova in particular used ballet as her primary movement idiom, but built a career very similar to that of the modern dancers – with her own company (as one biographer puts it) as "a vehicle for a ballerina, herself" rather than for a choreographer; an emphasis on acting talent; a focus on variety-theater performance, supplemented with lucrative performances at private parties for the social elite; and skinny soulfulness – with contemporaries describing her as "delicate, svelte, and pliant," "graceful and fragile," "graceful, delicate and ethereal," and as having "conquered by ... some

[136] Homans, *Apollo's Angels*, pp. 300–301, 309. This was not unprecedented in Russian art; other Russians presented themselves in the West as "Eurasians." See Pericles Lewis, "Introduction," in *The Cambridge Companion to European Modernism* (New York: Cambridge University Press, 2011), p. 5.

[137] Järvinen, *Dancing Genius*, pp. 65, 74, 61, 63; Alexandre Benois, *Reminiscences of the Russian Ballet* (London: Putnam, 1947), p. 284. See Karthas, *When Ballet Became French*, pp. 77–85.

[138] Järvinen, *Dancing*, p. 33.

[139] Quoted in Lifar, *Serge Diaghilev*, p. 196.

indefinable faery quality, something spiritual and exclusive to herself."[140] Ida Rubinstein built on her roles in the Ballets Russes (and her enormous wealth and connections to the social and artistic elite) to build an independent career, producing a series of visually gorgeous and highly theatrical independent productions.[141]

There is something a bit bizarre about the story of a clique of very Europeanized Russians, some of them extremely wealthy, resident in France and starting from a highly Francophile art form, creating a vision of the "soul" of Russian culture as beyond the European pale, as "Oriental" and savage. And yet, this is precisely what Tórtola Valencia was doing for Spain (starting from variety theater rather than from ballet) in the same period. In both cases, these cultural entrepreneurs were simply exploiting a competitive advantage: The Orient was all the rage, and they came from places (or at least claimed to) that were half-Oriental in the minds of their audiences. Spain was on the border to the Muslim world, and had been partially conquered by the Moors; Russia was on the border between Europe and Asia, and had been partially conquered by the Mongols. In each case, the claim to have Oriental blood licensed these performers to pursue the themes of primitive or savage or ungoverned energy with greater freedom. And greater freedom was the path to expression of one's own soul, or selfhood. Here again, as in so many other respects, modern dance established not so much a contradiction as a productive tension. By producing the exotic, the other, the opposite, the modern dancers more authentically produced themselves ... and vice versa.

3.6 Good Dance, Bad Dance II: Race

As we have seen, historians of modern dance have been divided or ambivalent regarding what message it conveyed about gender. Again, Susan Glenn has argued that modern theater was a way for women to "act out" new forms of independent agency for themselves. But she also points out that the theater helped to create a new, commercialized femininity that was far from emancipatory – it "made a spectacle *of* women, positioning them as passive objects for audience consumption."[142] Again, modern dance did both things as well.

[140] Oleg Kerensky, *Anna Pavlova* (London: Hamilton, 1973), pp. 35 (quotation), 37, 40, 32, 40, 43; quotations in A. H. Franks, "A Biographical Sketch," in *Pavlova: A Biography*, ed. Franks (New York: Da Capo, 1979), pp. 15, 16, 32.
[141] Charles S. Mayer, "Ida Rubinstein: A Twentieth-Century Cleopatra," *DRJ* 20 (1988): 33–51; Fisher, "The Swan Brand," pp. 51–67.
[142] Glenn, *Female Spectacle*, p. 3.

There has been the same sort of ambivalence regarding the place of race in modern dance. The dance historian Amy Koritz, for example, suggests that the use of "Oriental" and ancient themes (and specifically the story of Salomé as told by Maud Allan) was meant to "enact the containment of female self-assertion" because it "raised the specter of the sexual woman" but "located her in a foreign time and place." It thereby made "the imagined aggressive sexuality of the Eastern woman safe for Western consumption," and at the same time "reaffirmed the Englishman's claims to racial superiority."[143] Jane Desmond has argued similarly that Ruth St. Denis's use of Oriental themes was part of the "commodification" and "appropriation" of non-European cultures – and of the female body – by the West. In that process, the "Orient" was conceived of as "incapable of speaking for itself," as "requiring explication, investigation, illustration, discipline, reconstruction, or redemption" by the West. And the "Orient" and femininity were associated – both were "mute"; both "spiritual" and sensual rather than rational; both targets of Western/male dominance, study, display, and use.[144] Hanna Järvinen made the same point with respect to the Ballets Russes: "The Orientals, including Russians, were perceived to be biologically more 'feminine' than the Western races, and thus 'naturally' inclined to dancing as well as to violent and unrestrained sexual behavior."[145] A similar argument can be made about Greek themes. "The fundamental strategy of [Isadora] Duncan's project to gain cultural legitimacy for dancing," the historian Ann Daly wrote, "was one of exclusion": By dancing Greek she was implicitly creating a distinction between Europeans and the savage, barbaric, or inferior peoples of the world. We might add that she explicitly held the Greeks to be not culturally particular, but universally human – making European art the measure of all things. At the same time, she appealed to "a growing upper-middle-class desire for social prestige" by insisting that what she was doing was art not entertainment, too elevated and pure for the mongrel variety-theater audience.[146]

There is doubtless a great deal of truth to such analyses, and indeed they are sometimes echoed rather precisely in the sources from the period – as when, for example, one London critic remarked (approvingly) in 1912 that

[143] Amy Koritz, *Gendering Bodies/Performing Art: Dance and Literature in Early Twentieth-Century British Culture* (Ann Arbor: University of Michigan Press, 1995), pp. 39, 38.
[144] Desmond, "Dancing out the Difference," pp. 28–49. Such perspectives draw implicitly or explicitly on Edward Saïd's analysis in *Orientalism*.
[145] Järvinen, "The Russian Dancing," p. 166.
[146] Daly, *Done into Dance*, pp. 16, 90.

Ruth St. Denis presented "the glamour of the East, but the East without its menace, without its material vice."[147] Yet it should give us pause that the modern dancers couldn't win, so to speak – they were racist if they danced as Greeks and racist if they danced as Orientals, they were patriarchalists whether they were male or female, wild or well behaved. Some historians of modernist art have argued that this kind of double-bind is an indication of an underlying failure to come to terms with complexity, ambivalence, and ambiguity. As the literary scholar Robert Harrison remarked in a comment on studies of the archaeological obsessions of modernism in the arts, the "countermodern tribunal does not acquit, it only condemns."[148]

One of the leading historians of imperialist culture in Europe, John MacKenzie, has offered a more detailed rebuttal, suggesting that in the European arts the enthusiasm for Oriental themes and subjects was intended not "to facilitate rule, but to encourage an invigorating contamination" of European thought and culture. Cultural radicals in particular used borrowings from other cultures to loosen the grip of European traditions and conventions, broaden horizons, increase degrees of freedom for self-expression within Europe. The overall result was a "dramatic liberation from existing conventions and constricting restraints" or even "a full-scale radical assault on Western conventions."[149] Some other historians have concurred. Lily Litvak, writing of Spanish modernists (like those who championed Tórtola Valencia), has argued that their Orientalism produced "a species of moral and cultural relativism" and "called European values into question."[150] And even Jane Desmond, whose more critical conclusions are cited earlier in this chapter, conceded that St. Denis and Duncan were "able to extend the bounds of propriety" by appealing to foreign or ancient cultures.[151] In this kind of analysis, obviously, the function of modern dance with respect to gender is also reversed: Rather than confirming gender stereotypes by "othering" or "Orientalizing" women who moved freely or passionately, modern dance was (as the historian

---

[147] Mark E. Perugini, "Sketches of the Dance and Ballet," *The Dancing Times* 3 (1912–1913): 76.

[148] Harrison, "Archaeology on Trial," p. 36.

[149] John MacKenzie, *Orientalism: History, Theory, and the Arts* (Manchester, UK: Manchester University Press, 1995), pp. 211, 209, 212. A similar point is made in Carole Sweeney, *From Fetish to Subject: Race, Modernism, and Primitivism, 1919–1935* (Westport, CT: Praeger, 2004), p. 7. For a thought-provoking discussion of the position of women with respect to Orientalism in the arts, see Reina Lewis, *Gendering Orientalism: Race, Femininity and Representation* (London: Routledge, 1996).

[150] Lily Litvak, *España 1900* (Barcelona: Anthropos, 1990), p. 203.

[151] Desmond, "Dancing Out," p. 37.

Gaylyn Studlar concluded) an instance of women's "desire to escape bourgeois domesticity's constraints and to create other, transformative identities that were convergent with those qualities of the New Woman that disturbed social conservatives."[152]

We do not need to decide whether modern dance was racist and imperialist, any more than we need to decide whether it was sexist and misogynistic. As the historian Reina Lewis has pointed out, women in particular (including most of the early modern dancers) approached the "Orient" from a more ambivalent position than men because "Orientalist" and gender stereotypes asserted that, although white Europeans, they shared important characteristics with "Orientals." Their use of Oriental themes was, therefore, "likely simultaneously to confirm and transgress social and textual codes" and stereotypes regarding non-Europeans (and women).[153] But male dance critics and commentators often picked up on this ambivalence, too. Here again, modern dance played on and drew energy from the tension set up between opposites. A 1913 article by Gordon Craig gives us a particularly distasteful but revealing instance. Craig recounted seeing a group of "dark niggers" dancing in the street in Genoa, Italy "like only a black man can dance ... Immoderate and yet masterly," and imagined how wonderful it would be if English dancers could "loosen" up and dance like that – "how all the senses of England would open and how the Imagination would call aloud for liberty.... If you want to dance you must take Life as your partner."[154] Here Europeanness is portrayed as a deficit when compared with a racist stereotype that portrayed non-European people as more natural, expressive, real, and alive. The aim was not to stigmatize those non-European "others," though that was certainly one effect; rather it was to "loosen up" and enrich European culture (which, obviously, was *also* stereotyped in this portrayal).

The example of Ruth St. Denis illustrates well the way this process could be made to work as part of the cult of the self that was at the heart of modern dance. St. Denis appears to have been guided all her adult life and throughout her career in dance by a vague and indiscriminate but powerful hunger for spiritual experience. As she put it in her memoirs (published in 1939), as a dancer she lived in "an atmosphere of unthinking reverence and blind devotion." Raised a Protestant, she "remained

[152] Gaylyn Studlar, *Visions of the East* (New Brunswick, NJ: Rutgers University Press, 1997), p. 114.
[153] Reina Lewis, *Gendering Orientalism: Race, Femininity and Representation* (New York: Routledge, 1996), p. 22.
[154] Craig, *Gordon Craig on Movement*, pp. 190–192.

devoted, with a daily and constant fidelity, to the Bible"; she was a convert to Christian Science; she was attracted to the Catholic Church and to Buddhism and Hinduism; and she remarked that she generally prepared for her performances by meditating for half an hour, and "by the time I had left to go on the stage I was truly the priestess in the temple." She admitted that the portrayal of Hinduism in her "Indian" dances was "theologically speaking ... inaccurate"; but that didn't matter because "at no time, then or in the future, have I been sufficiently the scholar or sufficiently interested to imitate or try to reproduce any Oriental ritual or actual dance – the mood to me is all." In fact, for her "Oriental" imagery merely "set into vibration an inward state that would inevitably express itself from a certain center and after a certain pattern, and it made no difference what the artistic environment or race or culture was that I transmitted through the dance."[155]

All this sounds somewhat confused and rather cavalier toward "exotic" religious traditions to our ear today; but at the time it made sense in light of the relationship between self and performance. Oriental themes were a way for St. Denis to explore her own *feeling* about spirituality rather than any particular tradition or theory of spiritual life. She was, as she put it, endlessly in search of "the immortal and essential Me."[156] She was using exotic imagery to set a mood that reflected and fed her own emotional experience of the sacred, free from any particular convention, institution, or system of thought. John MacKenzie has described this phenomenon with respect to musicians in the same period: "Time and again, composers discovered their most distinctive voice through the handling of the exotic."[157] St. Denis's approach was also characteristic of an important pattern in spiritual life in the modern world more broadly. As one historian of religion and globalization has put it, the modern world is increasingly "a global marketplace full of religious consumers who are looking for a wide variety of options out of which they can create their personal path to salvation."[158]

---

[155] St. Denis, *An Unfinished Life*, pp. 48–49, 57, 87, 56.
[156] Ibid., pp. 49, 57, 74, 87, 56, 55.
[157] MacKenzie, *Orientalism*, p. 210.
[158] Shandip Saha, "Hinduism, Gurus, and Globalization," in Peter Beyer and Lori Beaman, eds., *Religion, Globalization and Culture* (Leiden, The Netherlands: Brill, 2007), p. 498. For a good brief summary discussion see Olivier Tschannen, "La revaloración de la teoría de la secularizatión mediante la perspectiva comparada Europa Latina-América Latina," in Jean-Pierre Bastian, ed., *La Modernidad Religiosa: Europea Latina y América Latina en perspectiva comparada* (México: Fondo de Cultura Económica, 2004), esp. pp. 355–356.

Again, St. Denis was unusually omnivorous and unusually tenacious in her devotion to using the theme and props of "Oriental" spirituality. But her sense that the dance was fundamentally a sacred, spiritual experience was universal among the early modern dance stars. Also universal was the sense of connection between the erotic and the spiritual – the tendency to portray the nude female body and its potential for pleasure in sacred settings, as St. Denis did, for example, in her signature "Radha" dance. As she remembered of her young self, "I did not see clearly the dividing line between the territories of love, religion, and art."[159] This was true of most modern dancers before 1914. Chapter 4 explores this heady mix of eroticism, religion, and aesthetics.

---

[159] St. Denis, *An Unfinished Life*, p. 48.

CHAPTER 4

Embodied Revelation: Dance, Religion, and Knowledge

4.1 Dance as Spiritual Experience

As we have seen, the modern dance revolution before 1914 relied very heavily on a dense set of interrelated clichés or tropes, steadily and profusely repeated terms, statements, and images intended to communicate a particular set of ideas or meanings. The key terms *life, nature, soul, feeling,* and so on were among these; so was obsessive comment on the skinniness of the dancers; so was the idea that dance was an expression of joy. One more term, however, served to draw many of these others together: *revelation.* For at their most enthusiastic, commentators and performers alike believed that modern dance was an experience with religious significance.

The most extreme example of this belief was Isadora Duncan. Duncan's own writings and speeches were shot through with religious terminology. In 1903, for example, she declared that "dancing is the ritual of the religion of physical beauty"; that "the dance of the future will have to become again a high religious art, as it was with the Greeks"; that standing before the Parthenon in Athens she "had found my dance, and it was a Prayer" – an echo, perhaps, of François Delsarte's assertion that "art and prayer so confound themselves in one ineffable unity that I cannot separate the two things."[1] In her memoirs she remembered telling the Prince de Polignac in 1900 that she wanted to "compose religious dances inspired by your music"; shouting at a variety-theater manager in 1902 that "I had come to Europe to bring about a great renaissance of religion through the Dance," not "to dance for the amusement of the overfed Bourgeoisie after dinner"; and lecturing the German painter Franz von Stuck "for hours without stopping on the holiness of my mission." As late as 1920 Duncan

---

[1] "Address of François Delsarte before the Philotechnic Society of Paris," in Genevieve Stebbins, *Delsarte System of Expression* (New York: Edgar S. Werner, 1902), p. 28.

described true dancing as a kind of transfiguration: "[T]he dancer under-stands that the body, by force of the soul, can in fact be converted to a luminous fluid. The flesh becomes light and transparent ... his body is simply the luminous manifestation of his soul.... This is the truly creative dancer," who could speak "in movements out of himself and out of some-thing greater than all selves."[2]

Duncan's associates enthusiastically agreed. Karl Federn, who translated her speech on "The Dance of the Future" into German, announced in his foreword to the text that "her dance is a religious service." Her brother Raymond called her not "a dancer ... but a prophet"; her sister-in-law Margherita believed she was "in the true sense of the word, inspired.... We felt as if we had received the blessing of God, and looked upon her as one of His prophets, filled with the wine of His Spirit."[3] One Spanish sculptor who saw her dance in Paris recalled that "when she appeared we all had the feeling that God ... was present."[4] Paul Poiret called Duncan's performance (at a private party he organized) a "communion in the sac-rament of beauty," even a "miracle."[5] One German sex-reform journal reported of Duncan's early performances in 1902/1903 that she offered "redemption for all those who are capable of throwing off the weight of the past and striving higher in self-disciplined freedom," a "hymn to the beauty and purity of the human body; a laughing revelation of human joie de vivre," and the Christ-like "depth and strength of an intelligence that embraces the world with love."[6]

Such effusions were, again, at the extreme end of the spectrum; and for the most part modern dance enthusiasts used religious terminology less literally than this. And yet, the sheer mass of repetition of such language established a kind of semisacral atmosphere around modern dance, a sense that something sacred was going on, even if it was not named very pre-cisely. While none were as messianic as Duncan, many of the dancers were convinced that dance was religious in nature. Olga Desmond declared that "My dance is a religious service to beauty, a cult of art."[7] Later in life

---

[2] Duncan, "I Have a Will of My Own," *Isadora Speaks*, p. 33; Duncan, *Der Tanz der Zukunft*, p. 24; "The Parthenon," in Duncan, *The Art of the Dance*, p. 65; Duncan, *My Life*, pp. 81, 85, 110; "The Philosopher's Stone of Dancing," in Duncan, *The Art of the Dance*, pp. 51–52.

[3] Duncan, *Der Tanz*, p. 8; *The Art of the Dance*, pp. 13, 23.

[4] Quoted in Allan Ross Macdougall, *Isadora: A Revolutionary in Art and Love* (Edinburgh: Thomas Nelson, 1960), p. 76.

[5] Poiret, *My First Fifty Years*, p. 204.

[6] Maria Holgers, "Isadora Duncan – Eine Erlösung," *Die Schönheit: Erster Luxusband* (1902/1903): 486.

[7] Quoted in Runge, *Olga Desmond*, p. 93.

Figure 4.1 Ruth St. Denis's religious dance "Radha," 1906

Ruth St. Denis recalled as a child being inspired to "a motion of complete joy" by the "round silvery glory of the moon," the moment of the awakening of the "religious consciousness" that would "flower years afterward into the definite forms of religious dancing in which there is no sense of division between the spirit and the flesh, religion and art." Dance was for her the "language for communicating spiritual truths," and she dreamed of building a "Cathedral of the Future" in which she could "explore the limitless possibilities of religious dance" (see Figure 4.1).[8] Maud Allan believed that the dance in ancient times "was closely connected with religion and the drama," and that in "the East ... dancing was and is the language of religion."[9] Presumably her own Greek and Oriental dances, therefore, were religious as well. Tórtola Valencia was "convinced that the religious dance has been the foundation of all the others ... the dance was once a form of

---

[8] Ruth St. Denis, "Religious Manifestations in the Dance," in Walter Sorrell, ed., *The Dance Has Many Faces* (New York: Columbia University Press, 1966), pp. 12–14, 16.
[9] Allan, "Greek Art," *Maud Allan and Her Art*, p. 1.

worship" – and was so again, presumably, in her performance of ancient and Oriental dance.[10] One reviewer wrote even of the French author and actress Colette Willy (who included dance elements in her performances) that she "expressed herself by dancing. Exactly as David danced before the Ark ... she danced before Life." This echoed an earlier review of Mata Hari, who danced "like David before the Holy of Holies."[11] As these examples suggest, the modern dancers' use of "Oriental" themes referred specifically to the religious or spiritual as well as the erotic because of the close association in Western minds between the mystical and "Eastern" religion (see Figure 4.2).

The trance-like state of self-forgetting common among modern dancers was related to this sense that the dance was religious, or spiritual. Grete Wiesenthal's brother-in-law described it pithily as "sacred self-forgetting in the music."[12] In 1910 the London *Times* observed that the "true dancer is cut off from the world as if by a charm and moves in a kind of rapt isolation," and that authentic dance was performed "as if it were some kind of religious ritual."[13] One reviewer wrote of Maud Allan in the *San Francisco Chronicle* in 1910 that in "movement, she seems unconscious of all save her dancing."[14] Clotilde von Derp explained in her memoirs that before dancing she would "turn inwardly toward God" and then "let myself be carried away by the ecstasy" induced by the music.[15] And Havelock Ellis explicitly related trance-dancing to religion in his influential essay on "The Philosophy of Dancing" (1914): The "auto-intoxication of rapturous movement," he held, "brings the devotee ... into that self-forgetful self-forgetful union with the not-self which the mystic ever seeks."[16]

Dance commentators experienced modern dance in this way, as well. Again, the term *revelation* was the central one. One liberal German

---

[10] Quoted in Garland, "Early Modern Dancing," p. 10.

[11] Quoted in Claude Francis and Fernande Gontier, *Creating Colette*, vol. 1, *From Ingenue to Libertine, 1873–1913* (South Royalton, VT: Steerforth Press, 1998), p. 246, and in Waagenaar, *The Murder of Mata Hari*, p. 53.

[12] Huber-Wiesenthal, *Die Schwestern Wiesenthal*, p. 85.

[13] "Dancing," London *Times*, July 20, 1910. The reference here was actually to English folk dances, but the *Times* was advocating and celebrating the revival of dance in this spirit by the modern dancers.

[14] Ralph E. Renaud, "Maud Allan Wins Greener Laurels," *San Francisco Chronicle*, April 9, 1910, in Maud Allan clippings files, MPDSF.

[15] Clotilde Sacharoff, "La vie que nous avons dansée," in Frank-Manuel Peter and Rainer Stamm, *Die Sacharoffs–zwei Tänzer aus dem Umkreis des Blauen Reiters* (Cologne: Wienand, 2002), p. 157.

[16] Ellis, "The Philosophy of Dancing," p. 198, at https://www.unz.org/Pub/AtlanticMonthly-1914feb-00197.

Figure 4.2 Sent M'ahesa performs ancient Egyptian ritual dances, ca. 1913

newspaper, for example, found that a performance by Olga Desmond "had the effect of a revelation of a new and modern culture"; another found her the embodiment of the "cult of a free, inwardly entirely chaste" humanity; a third reported that "devout silence descended" on her audience in her performances.[17] A critic in Munich remembered more than three decades later that around the turn of the century Saharet's dancing "was like a revelation of a whole new spirit and a new physicality, it was so revolutionary."[18] Harry Graf Kessler described Ruth St. Denis as a "revelation" of "beauty, dignity and sincerity"; for Ernst Schur she was "an experience" and "a revelation."[19] The Austrian feminist Marie Lang too called Duncan a "revelation."[20]

Other religious terminology was freely used as well. The sex radical Johannes Guttzeit found that Isadora Duncan offered "an aesthetic-moral sermon through her body."[21] The playwright and sexual radical Max Halbe believed Adorée Villany's audience "left the theater with the feeling of having been uplifted by the divine nature of God's creation, by the beauty of the human body, and thankful to its Creator."[22] One enthusiastic sculptor in Munich told Villany that she was "the unattainable goddess"; a painter believed her to be "descended from the heavenly spheres" and a "revelation of a new world flooded with beauty."[23] Reviews of Gertrud Leistikow commented on the "visionary tendency" in her art, on her "affinity for the transcendental" or the "mystical," or on her gripping portrayal of "unconditional devotion to the divinity."[24] The Austrian painter and playwright Oskar Kokoschka told Grete Wiesenthal that "I would, if you wouldn't be too angry, truly pray to you."[25] Ida Rubinstein's colleague Serge Lifar wrote of "the religious fervor and ecstasy, which took possession of the audience" at her performance of Cleopatra.[26] And Gertrud Falke's father Gustav composed a poem that described her as Christ-like:

> Every line of her young body
> Reveals a divine idea

[17] Quoted in Desmond, *Mein Weg zur Schönheit*, pp. 5–6. The term used was *andächtig*, meaning rapt, devout, or pious; *Andacht* often means "prayer."
[18] Georg Fuchs, *Sturm und Drang in München um die Jahrhundertwende* (Munich: Georg D. W. Callwey, 1936), p. 236.
[19] Kessler quoted in St. Denis, *An Unfinished Life*, 93, 90; Hugo von Hofmannsthal, "Die unvergleichliche Tänzerin" (1906), in Herbert Steiner, ed., *Gesammelte Werke: Prosa II* (Frankfurt: S. Fischer Verlag, 1951), 262; Schur, *Der moderne Tanz*, 98.
[20] Lang, "Offenbarung," pp. 636–638.
[21] Guttzeit, *Schamgefühl*, p. 277.
[22] Halbe quoted in "Der Münchener Theaterskandal," *Berliner Tageblatt* no. 594 (November 21, 1911). On Halbe's sexual politics see Ruth Florack, "Liebe im Zeichen der Sittenrichter," in Helmut Scheuer and Michael Grisko, eds., *Liebe, Lust und Leid: Zur Gefühlskultur um 1900* (Kassel: Kassel University Press, 1999), pp. 217–236.
[23] Villany, *Tanz-Reform*, pp. 321, 323.
[24] Kleines Theater program, December 16–26, 1911, in STAM, Polizei-Direktion, 3806/4.
[25] Quoted in Fiedler and Lang, *Grete Wiesenthal*, p. 106.
[26] Quoted in Lifar, *Serge Diaghilev*, p. 158.

No mouth can ever capture it in words
The unity between the Creator and his creature. . . .
God himself leans forward on his throne
… Struck by wonder
The crowd bows, choked-up, in prayer.[27]

For all these people, modern dance was out of this world – it was part of a higher, better world of spiritual power and purity, expressing itself through the body of the dancer in a kind of self-induced spiritual ecstasy.

4.2 Dance and the Religion of Life, Love, Joy, and Sex

In some degree, we can account for the use of such language as simply part of a long tradition of gallantry among European men taken with the physical charms of young female dancers. No doubt ballet enthusiasts and patrons – the "ballet uncles," as the Austrian playwright Karl Kraus acidly called them – spoke of and to ballerinas this way, as well. In fact, Kraus considered the whole craze for modern dance (specifically Mata Hari) to be "the latest humbug," the product of the "gullibility" of parvenus who "at a pre-arranged signal declared the display of pretty legs to be a metaphysical revelation and who get their precious Buddhism at Wertheim's" (a major Berlin department store). It was all just about sex – soft-core porn dressed up as faux-religious art. The very different response of Peter Altenberg suggests there was an element of truth to this view: Altenberg found that Mata Hari's "absolutely ideal body" corresponded to "God's artistic plan" and pronounced "Mata Hari, blessed be thy physique!"[28]

At the same time, obviously a good deal of the spiritual atmosphere surrounding modern dance rested on straightforward ethnographic foundations – again, ancient dance and Oriental dance were thought to be (or have been) religious, so modern dances that emulated or sought to embody the spirit of dance in those times and places must be in some sense religious as well (see Figure 4.3). As one Vienna newspaper put it rather confusedly in 1906, "the Indian dances when he honors his gods," so it was natural that Mata Hari – as (at least in make-believe) the daughter of a Javanese prince – would honor her gods when she danced.[29]

[27] Gustav Falke, "Tanzphantasie," in DTAK, Inventory no. 10, Gertrud und Ursula Falke, I.
[28] Karl Kraus, "Der Schmock und die Bajadere" and Peter Altenberg, "Mata Hari im Apollotheater," both in Lüders, *Apropos Mata Hari*, pp. 87, 89, 91.
[29] "Brahmanentänze in Wien," in Lüders, *Apropos Mata Hari*, p. 83.

Figure 4.3 Tórtola Valencia, Buddhist dancer, at home, ca. 1911

Finally, however, the celebration of modern dance as a religious experience was clearly part of a broader understanding of *all* art as religious – one that was particularly influential among avant-garde artists and intellectuals. The Russian painter Marianne Werefkin, who was closely associated with Alexander Sacharoff and Clotilde von Derp, remarked, for example, in a comment on their performance that "art has been the expression of belief in all ages." Isadora Duncan's erstwhile lover Edward Gordon Craig wrote an essay in 1913 about "Art, the voice of Revelation."[30] Such ideas were part of a very widespread sense of the spiritual significance of art particularly among those for whom the established churches were no longer an attractive or acceptable framework for spiritual life – a common condition among "advanced" thinkers and intellectuals in the period.

The German historian Ulrich Linse has written a superb analysis of the cultural potentials of that situation, in an essay aptly titled "Secularization or New Religiosity?" Summarizing the work of many recent historians of religion, Linse argues that intellectuals, artists, and political radicals who were drifting out from under the influence of the traditional Christian confessions and Judaism were not for the most part simply becoming atheists. Instead they turned their spiritual sensibilities in other directions. Some looked toward cults and secret societies, occultism, Spiritualism, Theosophy, and various Eastern religions (or Western versions of Eastern religions). But many also turned to cultural forms or spheres of life that had until then not been regarded as sacred – what one German sociologist of religion called, in 1913, "religion without religion."[31] Nature enthusiasts celebrated the spiritual powers of landscape, the glory of the cosmos, and the creativity of biology, giving rise to a "religious apotheosis of 'life.'" Art enthusiasts and artists invested creativity with sacred importance, giving rise to "art-religions" of various colorations. Radical political movements created nascent modern political religions such as socialism or the various forms of fascism. Others sought to develop a new belief-system rooted in physics or Darwinian theory. All these new forms of religiosity, Linse points out, shared a common trait: the "subjectivization and individualization of religion." As one German theologian put it in 1905 in a study of "Modern Religion," the new religiosity was "drawn from one's own life, from the depths of one's own heart"; logically each individual

---

[30] Marianne Werefkin, "Über die Sacharoffs," in Peter and Stamm, *Die Sacharoffs*, p. 48; Craig, *Gordon Craig*, p. 96.
[31] Ludwig Heitmann, *Grossstadt und Religion* (Hamburg: C. Boysen, 1913), p. 4.

would develop "an individual religion" that would express the "religious experience of their soul."[32]

The vocabulary of the modern dance revolution was very closely related both to this underlying trend in modern religiosity and to many of its specific forms. Indeed, in the case of modern dance we could easily describe this form of religious life as modernist rather than merely modern because it shared so many characteristics with aesthetic modernism. The modern dancers sought to develop an individual aesthetic code, derived from their own inward experience; many were interested in Eastern religions; they appealed to nature and life as the arbiters of aesthetic quality; and by the 1920s many were – as we will see in Chapter 5 – attracted to the political religions of the early twentieth century. There is even a parallel between the aesthetic modernist approach to the past and this modernist religion, which often looked to ancient texts in its effort to develop/revive a purer doctrine. Theosophy is a good example: Helena Blavatsky actually claimed not to be the prophet of a new religion, but merely to have reconstructed an ancient wisdom about how the world really works (a "scientific" truth) that "is to be found scattered throughout thousands of volumes embodying the scriptures of the great Asiatic and early European religions."[33] The parallel to the modern dancers' researches in the museums of London, Paris, Berlin, and Rome should be obvious.

Most strikingly, however, in at least some cases the modern dancers belonged to that variety of modern/modernist religiosity that looked for revelation in science – especially in a particular understanding of the Darwinian theory of evolution.[34] Few of the modern dancers publicly subscribed to any of the various strands of modernist religiosity. But in several cases there were clear intellectual convergences and close personal connections between the world of modern dance and what some radical intellectuals at the time were seeking to define as a new religion of evolution.

One of the two greatest exponents of this pseudofaith was the German biologist Ernst Haeckel, perhaps the leading popularizer of Darwinian

---

[32] Ulrich Linse, "Säkularisierung oder Neue Religiösität? Zur religiösen Situation in Deutschland um 1900," *Recherches Germaniques* 27 (1997): 117–141 (quotations pp. 124, 130, 131). See also Saler, *As If*, esp. pp. 6–10, 14, and Fabio Ricci, *Ritter, Tod & Eros: Die Kunst Elisar von Kupffers (1872–1942)* (Cologne: Böhlau, 2007), esp. pp. 20–24, 61–72 for similar analyses.

[33] H. P. Blavatsky, *The Secret Doctrine: The Synthesis of Science, Religion and Philosophy* (Adyar: Theosophical Publishing House, 1962), p. 7.

[34] Dancers uniformly interpreted Darwinian theory to mean that mankind was evolving ever upward and onward; the idea that species merely adapted to their environment, much less that blind chance governed evolution, was almost nowhere appreciated outside the biological sciences (and often not even there).

theory in his day, whose 1899 work *The Riddle of the Universe* was translated into virtually every European language (and many non-European ones) in the early years of the twentieth century. In 1906 Haeckel became honorary president of the German Monist League, an organization dedicated to spreading the gospel of philosophical materialism – that is, the idea that body and soul are not separate, but are one substance (hence the Greek root "mono"). Haeckel explicitly conceived of Monism as a form of nature worship, and the upward evolution of the human species as our primary and final purpose.[35]

The other great prophet of Darwinist religion was the Swedish feminist Ellen Key, whose works were also translated into multiple languages and who exerted enormous influence on feminists, socialists, and particularly sex reformers across the European world. By 1905, Key was explicitly championing a new "religion of love" – sometimes she called it a "religion of life" or "evolutionism" – which took the endless upward evolution of life as the aim, purpose, and meaning of life. As she put it, "life itself" was "the meaning of life."[36] And evolution, she argued, was driven by sexuality, specifically by sexual selection. Sexual desire was therefore the "expression of the divine power at work in everything," driving all life toward greater perfection. In following our own desire, we follow the divine will of nature; hence, there is "no other freedom than the necessity of following our own nature." The new religion therefore resolved the antagonism between spirit and body that had been created by "dualist" religions like Christianity.[37] Key made procreative sexuality the heart of this new Monist religion: Sex was holy because it was "that power which carries the flame of life from generation to generation" through the upward steps of the evolutionary process, and "the more piously we honor it the more certainly each new generation will rise above the last."[38] Because satisfying the basic wants of the organism creates well-being, honoring and following our desire would make us happy. For this reason, Key sometimes also called her faith the "religion of joy" or of happiness.[39]

---

[35] See Alfred Kelly, *The Descent of Darwin: The Popularization of Darwinism in Germany, 1860–1914* (Chapel Hill: University of North Carolina Press, 1981), 39–51; Mike Hawkins, *Social Darwinism in European and American Thought, 1860–1945* (Cambridge: Cambridge University Press, 1997), 132–145; Ernst Haeckel, *Die Welträthsel: Gemeinverständliche Studien über Monistische Philosophie* (Bonn: Emil Strauss, 1903 [1899]).

[36] Ellen Key, *Über Liebe und Ehe* (Berlin: S. Fischer Verlag, 1911), 181.

[37] Ellen Key, *Der Lebensglaube: Betrachtungen über Gott, Welt, und Seele* (Berlin: Fischer, 1906), pp. 290–291, 302, 299.

[38] Ellen Key, *Liebe und Ethik* (Berlin: Pan, 1905), p. 18.

[39] Key, *Lebensglaube*, p. 294; Key, *Über Liebe und Ehe*, p. 59.

Obviously, this Monist or evolutionist faith was an enormously optimistic one. The inherent laws of life and of the universe were constantly operating to drive evolution ever forward to new heights. Ultimately, humanity would transcend itself, would become godlike. As the German feminist, sex reformer, and women's suffrage advocate Johanna Elberskirchen put it in 1903, we should be "honest and pure. Let's say 'yes' to our sexual desire, a joyful, cheerful, sacred 'yes.' God is in us. In us and in our desire. Let's be gods!"[40] The British scientist, science-fiction writer, free-love practitioner, world-government advocate, and social philosopher H. G. Wells delivered a similar message in a 1902 pamphlet titled "The Discovery of the Future." Based on current developments, Wells argued, we can predict "the greatest change humanity has ever undergone," characterized by "growing knowledge, growing order, and presently a deliberate improvement of the blood and character of the race" (i.e., the human species) through eugenics. "All this world is heavy with the promise of greater things, and a day will come, one day in the unending succession of days, when beings, beings who are now latent in our thoughts and hidden in our loins, shall stand upon this earth, as one stands upon a footstool, and shall laugh, and reach out their hands amid the stars."[41]

The parallels between this optimistic religion of joy – particularly as formulated by Ellen Key – and the theory of modern dance are obvious. Modern dancers freed themselves by obeying the imperative to follow their own nature, to express themselves; they experienced this liberation as joyful; that joy was a religious experience for them; and "nature" and "life" were central to that religion. And, in fact, the modern dancers were very much attracted to this new scientific faith. The most remarkable case is that of Isadora Duncan, who arrived in Central Europe at a critical moment in the emergence of Monism and of the sex-reform movement. Throughout the 1890s, German politics had been roiled by a bitter debate over a revision of the national criminal code that would have imposed stricter censorship and decency laws. That debate mobilized modernist artists en masse against what they saw as tyrannical conservative Christian efforts to muzzle their creativity. Just as that controversy died down (temporarily), in 1902 the editor of the feminist journal *Frauen-Rundschau*, Helene Stöcker, published an effusively positive review of the German translation of *Love's Coming of Age*, a paean to sexual individualism and

---

[40] Johanna Elberskirchen, *Die Sexualempfindung bei Weib und Mann, betrachtet vom physiologisch-soziologischen Standpunkte* (Leipzig: Jacques Hegner, 1903), pp. 55–56.
[41] H. G. Wells, *The Discovery of the Future* (New York: B. W. Huebsch, 1913), pp. 59–61.

sexual freedom by the English poet and philosopher Edward Carpenter (first published in English in 1896). Over the next two years she was subjected to intense attacks from more conservative fellow feminists who considered Christian morality to be women's best defense against men's sexual aggression and lack of conscience. By the end of 1904, she and like-minded radicals (men and women) formed the League for the Protection of Mothers (Bund für Mutterschutz), the aim of which was to help single mothers and advocate for a libertarian New Ethic in sexual life that would, for example, regard any relationship as moral if it were founded on genuine love, whether the couple in question got married or not. At that organization's first conference in Berlin in early 1905, Ellen Key was one of the keynote speakers.[42]

Duncan, who resided primarily in Germany in the years between 1902 and 1908, systematically aligned herself with this emerging sex-reform movement. In the second paragraph of her seminal address on "The Dance of the Future," given in Berlin in 1903, she announced that her "most revered teachers" were "Mr. Charles Darwin and Mr. Ernest Haeckel." A little later in her speech she adopted a deliberately evolutionary metaphor, arguing that the "fundamental movements of the new school of the dance must have within them the seeds from which shall evolve all other movements, each in turn to give birth to another in unending sequence of still higher and greater expressions." Further on she mused that the Greeks had understood "the laws of nature, wherein all is the expression of unending ever-increasing evolution." And toward the end of her address she announced that the new dancer would "help womankind to a new knowledge of the possible strength and beauty of their bodies and the relation of their bodies to the earth nature and to the children of the future" – a clear appeal to the ideas of the sex reformers, who were beginning to argue that women's sexual freedom to select healthy and admirable mates was the mechanism and guarantor of human evolution.[43] She corresponded with and later met Ernst Haeckel, telling him that "your works have brought me ... religion and understanding"; and she claimed in her autobiography that Haeckel likened her dance "to all the universal truths of nature, and said that it was an expression of monism."[44] Of Darwin she remarked in a letter to Gordon Craig that "if read aright his observations teach the living truth of universal life and Love."[45] "The Dance of the

---

[42] Helene Stöcker, *Bund für Mutterschutz* (Berlin: Pan, 1905).
[43] Duncan, *Der Tanz*, 11, 13, 17, 25; Duncan, *My Life*, p. 341; Kurth, *Isadora Duncan*, p. 18.
[44] Quoted in MacDougall, *Isadora*, p. 91; Duncan, *My Life*, 154; see Blair, *Isadora*, pp. 82–83.
[45] Quoted in Steegmuller, *Your Isadora*, p. 97.

Future" was translated by Karl Federn, who was also the translator – one year earlier – of Carpenter's *Love's Coming of Age*; and it was published by the firm of Eugen Diederichs, the publisher of choice for any number of reforming, new religious, and radical authors and movements. Not surprisingly, in his foreword to Carpenter's book Federn delivered a credo not dissimilar to H. G. Wells's view of the future of humanity, published in the same year. "Just as we have learned to turn the wildest forces of nature – fire and flood, electricity and steam – from enemies that threatened us into servants," he observed, "so too we must do with the forces of our own bodies and souls." In particular people must come to see their sexuality as "a priceless instrument for perfecting ourselves and the whole race."[46]

In short, Duncan got to Europe just in time for her art to be welcomed as a kind of liturgy of the new evolutionist/sex-reform faith. As one fan wrote in the nudist and sex-reform journal *Die Schönheit* (*Beauty*) in 1903, she gave people, and women in particular, "a little redemption from our 'sinful flesh' – this most disastrous of all false dogmas." One French art critic reported that "we wept when we saw her" because her performances "swept away from the corners of our soul all the filth which had been piled up there by those who for twenty centuries had bequeathed to us their critique, their ethics, their judgments" and recovered for her audience the "holy animality" of pre-Christian times.[47]

As one German observer argued in 1905, then, Duncan owed some of her success precisely to having "had more luck than is really coming to any respectable revolutionary" because she had arrived on the scene at such a fortuitous moment.[48] But Duncan was not simply an opportunist, and remained true to the principles of sex reform over the following years – for example, by not marrying the fathers of her children, or by arguing (in 1909) that "the beauty of woman is eternal. It is the guide of human evolution toward the goal of the human race, toward the ideal of the future which dreams of becoming God."[49] And, ultimately, the director of the dance academy opened by her sister Elizabeth in Darmstadt in 1911 set as one of its goals "the ennoblement of the race and the cultivation of the ethical and aesthetic expressions that it requires," remarking that

[46] Karl Federn, "Die Zeit und das Problem," in Carpenter, *Wenn die Menschen*, pp. 34, 32.
[47] Quoted in Allan Ross MacDougall, "Isadora Duncan and the Artists," in Paul Magriel, ed., *Nijinsky, Pavlova, Duncan: Three Lives in Dance* (New York: Da Capo, 1977), p. 53.
[48] Holgers, "Isadora Duncan," p. 486; Wilhelm Spohr, "Isadora Duncan," *Neue Magazin für Literatur, Kunst und soziales Leben* 74 (1905), clipping in DTAK, Inventory no. 69, Duncan-Archiv, II.2.6.1.
[49] Duncan, "Movement Is Life," *The Art of the Dance*, p. 79.

"we can dispense with long-winded proofs of the importance of eugenic questions ... for the education of the youth and the future of the nation" because that had long since been established.[50]

Duncan was not alone in her connections to "evolutionism" and sex reform. Another striking example is Olga Desmond. Her early performances in Berlin were produced by her lover and later husband Karl Vanselow, editor of the early nudist journal *Die Schönheit* as well as of *Geschlecht und Gesellschaft (Sex and Society)*, the first sex-reform journal in Germany. Her "beauty evenings" took place at first as private exhibitions for Vanselow's sex-reform organization, the League for Ideal Culture, which he had created primarily as a vehicle for *Die Schönheit* (which was ostensibly a kind of private newsletter for the membership, and might otherwise have fallen afoul of the censor). Reviewers praised these performances as a "celebration of individual beauty, the most noble transient embodiment of the eternal activity of Life," and reported that "she dances the new world-view" of modernism and Monism.[51] Later Desmond married a textile entrepreneur whose advertising journal carried, among other things, requests to help fund the Ernst Haeckel House in Jena, a scientific institute and headquarters for Monism.[52] The cover art for her memoirs was a precise graphic representation of the last sentence of H. G. Wells' "Discovery of the Future": a young woman, standing upon the earth as on a footstool, reaching out her hand amid the stars (see Figure 4.4).

Other cases suggest the relatively diffuse but dense intellectual, rhetorical, and personal connections that bound dance to the milieu of sex reform, evolutionism, and Monism. Clotilde von Derp's sometime surrogate father Rudolf von Delius formed a sex-reform group in Munich called World Garden: League for Realist Thinking and Reverence for Life. In the 1920s, Delius published works such as "The Philosophy of Love," in which he argued that Christian sexual morality was "harmful and stupid" and that "[t]here must be more love in the world! Otherwise humanity will not grow to perfection!"[53] Ernst Schur, author of one of the first book-length German studies on modern dance in 1910, also published articles

[50] Max Merz, "Die Ziele und die Organisation der Elizabeth Duncan-Schule," in *Elizabeth Duncan-Schule, Marienhöhe/Darmstadt* (Jena: Eugen Diederichs, 1912), p. 9.
[51] Quoted in Desmond, *Mein Weg*, p. 5, and Runge, *Olga Desmond*, p. 91; on Desmond's relationship with Vanselow see Karl Toepfer, *Empire of Ecstasy: Nudity and Movement in German Body Culture, 1910–1935* (Berkeley: University of California Press, 1997), p. 57.
[52] Runge, *Olga Desmond*, p. 121.
[53] Frank-Manuel Peter, "Die 'neie Minchener Derpsichore': Clotilde von Derp – die früheste Vertreterin des Ausdruckstanzes?," in Frank-Manuel Peter and Rainier Stamm, eds., *Die Sacharoffs*, 80; Rudolf von Delius, *Die Philosophie der Liebe* (Darmstadt: Reichl, 1922), 10–11, 86, 68.

Figure 4.4 Olga Desmond with her hand among the stars

in Germany's leading sex-reform journals, in which he anticipated, for example, the emergence of "a new generation of poets and artists" who would be able to portray "the erotic lives of mature, equal people."[54] The historian of the dance Marie Luise Becker published a discussion of dance in 1903 in Karl Vanselow's *Schönheit*.[55] The Falke sisters prided themselves on their North German sobriety; but they had close associations with the *Wandervogel*, a loose movement of young people who championed contact with nature (mostly through shared hiking and camping trips), communal spirit, and a more relaxed approach to sexuality. Many in the *Wandervogel* had close ties to various "life reform" movements, including sex reform and the homosexual rights movement. The Falkes and their dance pupils in Hamburg performed, for example, at the spring festival of the Hamburg branch of the *Wandervogel* in 1913. They danced, too, at a memorial festival for the painter, social reformer, nudist, pacifist, commune founder, atheist, and polygamist Karl Wilhelm Diefenbach in April 1914. Their collaborator at that memorial was the painter Fidus (Hugo Höppener), a colleague and apostle of Diefenbach who was the graphical voice, so to speak, of German life reform – not least because of the frequent use of his drawings in Karl Vanselow's *Die Schönheit*.[56]

These examples all pertain to Central Europe, where both sex reform and modern dance were particularly influential. But there were similar connections elsewhere. Ruth St. Denis, for example, regarded the great English sex reformer and sexologist Havelock Ellis as the "patron saint of the dance" – in part due to his 1914 essay on "The Philosophy of Dancing," which argued that dance was the first of all the arts, "the supreme symbol of spiritual life," the primitive expression of religion and love alike, and an important instrument of sexual selection because it was a way to "display all the force and energy, the skill and endurance, the beauty and grace" that were always "yearning" to be "poured into the vital stream of the race's life." St. Denis met Ellis in London in the early 1920s, and was particularly delighted when he gave her a letter of introduction to Edward Carpenter, "whose writings on the Yoga and whose beautiful and subtle analysis of love and desire [in *Love's Coming of Age* – ERD] I had long admired," and which "had given a focus to my thoughts." She shared with both men a rejection of Christianity's "contempt for the body," and

---

54 Ernst Schur, "Über das Erotische," *Die Neue Generation* 4 (1908): 50.
55 Marie Luise Becker, "Tanz," *Schönheit* 1 (1903): 277–290. See Becker, *Der Tanz* (Leipzig: Seemann, 1901).
56 "Frühlingsfest" of freistudentische Ortsgruppe Hamburg, December 1913 and "Diefenbach-Gedächtnisfeier," April 17, 1914, both in DTAK, Inventory no. 10, Gertud and Ursula Falke, II.2.2.

like them advocated "integration between soul and body." In the mid-1920s she would write that the dance would help make "our race ... finer and quicker to correct itself" because "the Dance reveals the soul. The Dance is motion, which is life, beauty, which is love, proportion, which is power."[57] Ellis asserted in 1923 that because primitive dance was a form of sexual selection, it was a kind of "unconscious eugenics" that "aided the higher development of the race" – and an "expression alike of religion and of love."[58] In 1926 he would write the introduction for St. Denis's husband Ted Shawn's study of *The American Ballet*; that work would include seven entire pages quoted directly from Ellis's *Studies in the Psychology of Sex* and a claim that nude dance would be eugenically beneficial – because it would "present ideals to the minds of the youth of this nation which would tend to make them select their mates nearer to this ideal, thus vastly improving the race in future generations." The English poet Arthur Symons – with whom Ellis had visited music halls to observe dance acts in the 1890s – regretted the fact that dance had been "cast out of religion when religion cast out nature" and the "gods of ecstasy" – a dual mistake he was happy to see being corrected in his own time.[59] And it is suggestive of the general tone in dance circles that by 1926 one dancer in Ruth St. Denis's touring company found a suitor unsatisfactory partly because he "doesn't even know who Havelock Ellis, Walt Whitman, or Bernard Shaw" were.[60] In 1938 another former member of the company, Martha Graham, wrote to her lover that the "reason people grow old is that they do not worship Sex as the great immortality – and because they do not know it is to be practiced deeply with concentration and simple delight." The prewar sex reformers would have been proud of their child.[61]

The notion that nude dance was "chaste" reflects this close connection between modern dance and sex reform. If sexual desire is just "divine" nature speaking through us, urging us together for the purpose of creating superior offspring and thus realizing its/our ultimate and transcendent purpose, then it could not be immoral, egoistic, or antisocial.

---

[57] St. Denis, "Religious Manifestations," p. 13; *An Unfinished Life*, pp. 228–229; Ruth St. Denis, "The Dance as Life Experience," in Jean Morrison Brown, ed., *The Vision of Modern Dance* (Princeton, NJ: Princeton Book Co., 1979), p. 22; Ellis, "The Philosophy of Dancing," pp. 197, 200, 201, at https://www.unz.org/Pub/AtlanticMonthly-1914feb-00197.

[58] Ellis, *The Dance of Life*, pp. 47, 35.

[59] Ted Shawn, *The American Ballet* (New York: Henry Holt, 1926), pp. 80, x; Arthur Symons, "The World as Ballet," in *Studies in the Seven Arts* (London: Archibald Constable, 1906), p. 387.

[60] Sherman, *Soaring*, p. 217.

[61] Quoted in Mark Franko, *Martha Graham in Love and War: The Life in the Work* (New York: Oxford University Press, 2012), p. 30.

Nor could it be dirty, furtive, and off-putting. No – it was lovely, and sacred. As Ellen Key put it, "[T]he erotic pleasure of the individual is of social value" because it serves evolution – as well, by making people happy, as "setting many of their best energies in motion and heightening them" and thereby benefiting human society more broadly. The "happiness of the individual is the essential precondition also for the vitalization [*Lebenssteigerung*] of humanity."[62] There was nothing crude or forbidden about the joy of sexual pleasure. Rudolf von Delius offered a pithier formulation in 1922: "[N]ecessity is innocent."[63] Obviously, this was as true of dance as it was of sex. The dancer was moved by an inner compulsion to express the joy of the healthy young human animal; in the religion of life, that literally could not be a bad thing. Neither could the desire felt by an audience that took pleasure in watching slender, vital young bodies on stage.

One further affinity between sex reform and dance is worth noting: Both celebrated the mixing of "blood." The sex reformers were, obviously, attracted to eugenics, as a method for accelerating evolution – a way for humankind to improve on nature by working consciously with nature, toward nature's ends. We are accustomed to thinking that eugenics enthusiasts were also likely to be attracted to the idea of racial purity. But this was not exclusively the case before the Nazis hijacked eugenics and imposed their own manias on it. Some eugenics advocates were also racists and racial purity freaks; but others believed that racial mixing was a good way to increase the vitality of the human race as a whole, by combining in individuals the various potentials developed over centuries and millennia within particular communities. Thus, for example, the influential sex-reform theorist Bruno Meyer believed in 1908 that if the Chinese were ever to conquer Europe (a favorite bogey of racists in the period) that would be a good thing because it would create "new blossoming of culture on the foundation of the new racial mixing."[64] Already in 1900 the socialist sociologist Ladislas Gumplowicz celebrated the fact that "the blood of a hundred races circulates in varied mixtures in our veins, the traditions of a hundred peoples are crossed in our literature, fertilizing each other." The result was that the "closed regional and national types" of the past were rapidly being eroded, with the happy result that "the individual is becoming ever more a unique person, undergoing his own particular nuanced

---

[62] Key, *Liebe und Ethik*, pp. 7, 33; Key, *Über Liebe und Ehe*, pp. 58–59.
[63] Delius, *Philosophie der Liebe*, p. 86.
[64] Bruno Meyer, "Etwas von positiver Sexualreform," *Sexual-Probleme* 4 (1908): 808.

development."[65] The parallel with the discussion of dance slightly later is obvious.

The sex-reform movement was the most ideologically explicit expression of the evolutionist understanding of the world, and the most closely related intellectually and personally to modern dance, but it was not the only one. There was a close connection, too, between modern dance and nudism – which was taking organizational form in Europe in precisely the same period in which modern dance was blossoming. In Germany in particular, four major nudist groups were formed between 1906 and 1909. The promise of the nudist movements was that a more natural, unconstrained relationship to the body would deprive it of the attraction of forbidden fruit, leading people back to a natural, chaste, and authentic reproductive love that genuinely served evolution – rather than prurient, overheated, and indiscriminate sensuality that often served only perverse and degenerate pleasure. "Noble nudity," as one spokesman put it, would give back to "the perverted civilized people of the present" that innocence that had characterized "natural man in paradise."[66] Like modern dance, the nudist movements across Europe took classical statuary as their model of physical perfection; indeed, reproductions of classical statues – in marble or even by bodybuilders – were regarded as an important means of fostering a healthy and chaste relationship to the body and sexuality. Such views were quite widespread in progressive political circles by 1913; one left-liberal deputy argued in the German parliament in that year, for example, that "young people can't be accustomed early enough to the sight of works of art depicted unclothed people; for keeping the naked secret works in the highest degree to irritate the fantasy of adolescents with the charm of the secret and the forbidden and is a cause of lasciviousness."[67] As one French apologist for nude dance put it in 1911, Europeans "have separated life and art, we have relegated art to the academies and the museums; that's why our life is ugly and vulgar, mean and dull." Another argued that "the Nike of Samothrace and the Venus de Milo have elevated more souls than the preachments of the evangelists," but unfortunately his society was still "imprisoned by the prejudices of Christianity."[68] In short, nudism like

---

[65] Ladislas Gumplowicz, "Ehe und freie Liebe," *Sozialistische Monatshefte* 6 (1900): 264.

[66] Waldemar Zude, "Nacktkultur und Vita sexualis," *Zeitschrift für Sexualwissenchaft* 3, no. 1 (1916): 80.

[67] Quoted in "Künstlerische Ausschreitungen und unzüchtige Schriften," *Volkswart* 7 (1914): 38. On nudism and classical art see Mahren Möhring, *Marmorleiber. Körperbildung in der deutschen Nacktkultur (1890–1930)* (Cologne: Böhlau, 2004).

[68] Both in Villany, *Phryné*, pp. 5, 8.

modern dance aimed at the desexualization of the body – the eradication of the erotic charge of secrecy, of the hidden and forbidden.[69]

Such arguments were advanced not only in favor of nudism, but also in favor of all kinds of activities designed to cultivate physical health and beauty. In a report to the Prussian Minister of the Interior on Karl Vanselow's League for Ideal Culture in 1908, for example, the Berlin police department reported that it regarded that organization as just one expression of a whole spectrum of more or less legitimate and at least legitimately popular fads, interests, and "movements" that were often referred to in Germany collectively as "life reform" (*Lebensreform*). These included club and professional sports; physical fitness, gymnastics, and bodybuilding; swimming in rivers, lakes, and pools; popular art education and appreciation; public parks and playgrounds; "youth cultivation" including particularly physical education; self-help regimes, rational living, temperance, and vegetarianism; and "sun and air baths" (or *Licht-Luft-Bäder*) where urban people could go to get sun, fresh air, and exercise in the nude or clad only in shorts or a one-piece. The department's report added that the membership of the League for Ideal Culture was indication enough that it did not aim to cultivate a low and lascivious tone because it included a large number of military men as well as jurists, professors, and members of the nobility, and a handful of respected artists, architects, and even members of the morality and temperance movements. The report's conclusion: The "legitimate kernel" of the movement should be respected, and one should "avoid throwing out the baby with the bathwater" even if there might occasionally be "isolated excesses" in the movement's activities.[70]

In short, as Bruno Meyer pointed out in 1911, modern dance was but one of "all those efforts ... that aim at a more rational and felicitous conception of sexual relations and of nature," and more broadly of a "generally felt need for greater freedom" and a more "natural" approach to health, fitness, and the body in European culture.[71] Conservative Christian critics of modern dance certainly saw it that way, as well, though they were far less sanguine about its implications – particularly in Germany, where

[69] See particularly Brandstetter, *Tanz-Lektüren*, pp. 120–123.
[70] Polizeipräsidium Berlin to Prussian Minister of the Interior, July 19, 1908 and Die Schönheit, Vereinigung für ideale Kultur to Polizeipräsident Freiherr von Ludringhausen, June 11, 1908, both in LAB, A.Pr.Br. 030-05, Tit 74, Th. 1502, fol. 41–46 and 38–40; Zude, "Nacktkultur," pp. 94, 93; Ulrike Traub, *Theater der Nacktheit: Zum Bedeutungswandel entblösster Körper auf der Bühne seit 1900* (Bielefeld: Transcript, 2010), p. 51. See Kai Buchholz et al., *Die Lebensreform* (Darmstadt: Häusser, 2001).
[71] Bruno Meyer, "Muss man nackt tanzen?," *Die Schönheit* 9, no. 11 (1911): 574.

sex reform and Monism were most organized and aggressive in their confrontation with Christianity. The leading German Catholic morality campaigner Ernst Lennartz, for example, published a pamphlet in 1908 in which he lumped together Duncan, Desmond, and other "nude" dancers with nudist organizations and variety-theater performances (such as women's wrestling matches) as constituting a single coherent movement determined to undermine morality, Christianity, the state, and social order.[72] During a struggle over Maud Allan's performances in Munich in 1907 a conservative journal with close ties to the morality movement in that city observed that "Monists stand at the forefront of the fight" for more permissive standards regarding nudity on stage.[73] During the scandal over Adorée Villany's performances (and arrest) in the same city in 1911 the same author argued that "it takes no great imagination to construct a relationship between" such performances and the "explicitly anti-Christian propaganda of the Monist League."[74] Modern dance, for these critics, was part of a generalized crisis of the old order – moral, political, social, and spiritual.

In other countries, the ideological lines were less clearly drawn, and the positions less extreme. Nevertheless, Christian activists in Spain, England, and even Paris did manage to create problems – and excellent advertising copy – for the modern dancers. And while the precise terms of the discussion of dance varied from country to country, the broad outlines were similar. In France, for example, the author, variety-theater actress, and dancer Colette Willy, among her many other enterprises, toured the country (as well as Belgium and Switzerland) for four years between 1908 and 1912 with the play *Le Chair* ("The Flesh"), with the alleged aim of convincing the public that nude performance was legitimate art, free of all salacious interest. The terms Colette and her supporters used to justify this venture were very like those used in Central Europe to defend similar undertakings, such as Olga Desmond's beauty evenings or Adorée Villany's nude dance. They celebrated the "chasteness" of the beautiful nude; played on the similarity between the nude performer's body and classical art; aimed to "unite body and soul as two halves of a whole being"; stressed the fact that Colette was active, capable, and had a will of her own and was "not an object that one needs merely reach out one's hand and possess"; praised

[72] Lennartz, *Duncan*, p. 3.
[73] Otto von Erlbach, "Das Nackte auf der Bühne," *Allgemeine Rundschau* 4, no. 5 (1907): 215.
[74] Otto von Erlbach, "Bühne und Neuheidentum," *Allgemeine Rundschau* 9, no. 12 (1912): 613.

Colette's "supple," "lithe," and slender body; and celebrated the exaltation of "the grace, strength, and nobility of the human race" through her performance. As the historian Patricia Tilburg writes, they championed "the nude in nature, a nude separated from debasing desire" as a force of moral and physical regeneration and liberation.[75] And in France, too, nude theater and dance was just one part of a much broader interest in the body, health, and fitness. Here too, for example, nudism and bodybuilding were being trumpeted in these same years as crucial instruments in the fight against the degeneration occasioned by urbanization, syphilis, unhealthy diet, the corset, a declining birth rate, and so on.[76]

Modern dance, then, was part of a whole complex of radical reform movements. These movements were founded at bottom on the rejection of Christian "dualism" and its alleged contempt for the merely physical. At its most explicit, this new vision of the importance of the body saw evolution – as one German sex reformer wrote in 1908 – as "a more valuable replacement" for Christianity and its belief in "heaven and hell"; for modern people, it held, the "need for redemption finds satisfaction in the idea of evolution." The "belief in the capacity of all life for evolutionary development" had become "our religion."[77] The connection between anti-Christianity and dance was particularly strong in Germany, and after the emergence of the organized sex-reform movement; but it was apparent elsewhere as well. To return to the origins of modern dance, for example, the same notion was apparent in the 1902 edition of Genevieve Stebbins's interpretation of the *Delsarte System of Expression*. Stebbins called on the authority of Darwin to substantiate her claim that beauty is "perfection of function," and hence "the expression of nature's highest truth in the law of evolution"; and she therefore demanded that we "must cast off from our souls the Chaldean incubus of original sin."[78]

[75] Patricia Tilburg, "'The Triumph of the Flesh': Women, Physical Culture, and the Nude in the French Music Hall, 1904–1914," *Radical History Review* 98 (2007): 64, 72, 73, 74. See Judith Thurman, *Secrets of the Flesh: A Life of Colette* (New York: Knopf, 1979); Francis and Gontier, *Creating Colette*.

[76] See Tamar Garb, "Modeling the Body: Photography, Physical Culture, and the Classical Ideal in Fin-de-Siecle France," in Geraldine A. Johnson, ed., *Sculpture and Photography: Envisioning the Third Dimension* (New York: Cambridge, 1998), pp. 86–99; Stewart, *For Health and Beauty*; Debora Silverman, "The 'New Woman,' Feminism, and the Decorative Arts in Fin-de-Siècle France," in Lynn Hunt, ed., *Eroticism and the Body Politic* (Baltimore: Johns Hopkins University Press, 1991), pp. 145–163; and Heather Dawkins, *The Nude in French Art and Culture 1870–1910* (New York: Cambridge University Press, 2002).

[77] Ernst Baars, *Sexuelle Ethik* (Berlin: Akademischer Bund Ethos, 1908), p. 7.

[78] Stebbins, *Delsarte System*, pp. 448, 453, 455. These references are absent in the 1887 edition.

Certainly, not everyone understood modern dance in this way. For some, it was simply light entertainment; for others – like Karl Kraus – it was "humbug," a mere commercial transaction dressed up in ethnographic-spiritual folderol; for others still it was "brothel art." Some dancers who did not appear nude (or relatively nude) agreed. Rita Sacchetto even accused Karl Vanselow of libel when he claimed that she would perform in a "beauty evening" organized by his League for Ideal Culture. It was, she claimed, "presumptuous" even to imagine that she would "appear in such circles and be seen as a kind of prostitute" because she was a "lady of position and honor" and even had friends at "princely courts."[79]

For those who did subscribe to the nascent faith of evolutionism, however, modern dance was a symbolic language of extraordinary power. For them modern dance occupied the strategic intersection between science and religion. It was an art form that acted out the tremendous, indeed transcendent optimism of the idea of inevitable and limitless progress built on Darwinist evolutionary theory. It was the liturgy of the new religion of evolutionary science. The modern dancer evoked on stage, through both the quality of her movements and the "chaste" sexual beauty of her body, the operation of those great benevolent laws of nature that had raised life from primordial slime to the beauty and nobility of the human form – "the most wonderful of nature's creations," as one reviewer put it in describing Adorée Villany; or in the words of another, "a statue-like vision of the master-work of Creation."[80] Those same laws would inevitably, in the fullness of time, raise humanity to godhood. As Margherita Duncan put it, her sister-in-law Isadora's dance recapitulated in miniature the whole history of evolution: "A gesture reaching toward the earth and then lifted upward recurred again and again, suggesting the love that nurtures children, that brings the whole race out of the bosom of the earth up into the arms of God."[81] And one Russian reviewer found in 1904 that Duncan's was a "prophetic art" because in it "outlines infinite prospects of human perfectibility ..., of man's future."[82] The beauty of the human form in movement was the embodied expression of that truth, that promise; in the dance, the sexual body of Woman (and sometimes Man) was transfigured, becoming the evolutionary body of Humankind on its way

[79] Rita Sacchetto to Polizeidirektion Berlin, October 28, 1908, in LAB, A.Pr.Br. 030-05, Tit. 74, Th. 1502, fol. 228.
[80] Clipping in Villany, *Tanz-Reform*, 287–288, 309–310; Felder, "Münchner Keuschheitsgelüste," p. 18.
[81] Raymond Duncan, "Isadora's Last Dance," *Art of the Dance*, p. 21.
[82] Excerpt from A. G. Hornfeld, "Books and People" (1908), translation in Natalia Roslasleva files, JRDD, folder 10.

to godhood. This was one reason nudity was so important: it asserted as a natural fact the identity between what we are now and what we will one day become. The beautiful, desirable, healthy, young, natural, chaste, joyful sexy female body was the sign of the ultimate perfection that we bear within ourselves even now, as the seed of our future divinity. It was, literally, a revelation. It made visible the God that humankind would, one day, become.

Few dance critics or reviewers explicitly used the terms of the religion of evolution as they were developed by its prophets, like Ellen Key. Yet the sense that modern dance had enormous symbolic importance, that it pointed toward a transcendent future, peeked through even much more pedestrian formulations. One German reviewer believed, for example, that Gertrud Falke's dance "shows us the way to a more free, more noble humanity."[83] In 1924 Ruth St. Denis would remark that the "Eternal Now of the Dance ... includes the knowledge and assurance that in the past bodily gesture was the first communication of the simple needs of primitive man, and it includes the vision of the future in which the Cosmic Consciousness, to which man gradually attains, will find expression in finer bodies and more beautiful and articulate gestures." The dance was an expression of the "divine urge to strength and beauty within ourselves!" Looking back from 1935, one English dance historian believed that Grete Wiesenthal was performing already before 1914 "the art ... of a future age."[84] In the same year the German dancer Elizabeth Selden, transplanted to the United States, described modern dance as embodying "the divine restlessness, the constant movement, of the human soul, on its way to larger horizons"; its ideal, its aspiration, was "the eternally unfinished dance of a future in which man becomes all that man can be."[85] Such remarks did not exactly reproduce the vocabulary of the new religion; but they echoed its emotional content.

4.3 Beyond Human Understanding: Words, Rhythms, Mountains

The power of religions lies not only in their ability to articulate explicit and highly abstract ideas; they also appeal on the nonrational level, at

[83] Unidentified clipping, Lübeck, October 2, 1913, in DTAK, Inventory no. 10, Gertrud und Ursula Falke, II.2.4.
[84] Perugini, *A Pageant of the Dance*, p. 264.
[85] St. Denis, "The Dance as Life Experience," pp. 23–24; Selden, *The Dancer's Quest*, p. 187.

the level of images, concepts, and metaphors that mobilize powerful emotions. Part of the power of those nonrational elements of religious experience is precisely that they are "mysterious" – that they cannot be explained or articulated.[86] It should not be surprising, therefore, that this was an important element of the cultural resonance of modern dance – the idea that one could not really explain its appeal, or what its "revelation" revealed, but simply had to experience it for oneself.

This too was something of a cliché or trope, scattered liberally throughout the discussion of modern dance in this period – the idea that its enormous emotional impact was indescribable, or that one could capture its power only through metaphor or poetry. Paul Poiret, for example, found the "majesty and gentleness" of Isadora Duncan's performance "beyond my power to express."[87] Edward Gordon Craig reported that in her dance Duncan "was speaking her own language," but

> what is it she is saying? No one would ever be able to report truly – or exactly – extraordinary, isn't it – yet no one present had a moment's doubt. Only this can we say – that she was telling the air the very things we longed to hear and until she came we had never dreamed we should hear, and now we heard them, and this sent us all into an unusual state of joy, and I... I sat still and speechless.[88]

Hugo von Hofmannsthal wrote of the "indescribable beauty" of Ruth St. Denis's dance, calling her "magnificent, indefinable, and elemental."[89] The bohemian journalist, playwright, and Catalan nationalist Pompeyo Gener found in 1912 that Tórtola Valencia's dance induced a kind of "sacred astonishment.... There are no words to describe how she dances." Eleven years later he repeated that "there are no words to describe how she dances. You have to see it."[90] The critic Carl Einstein wrote in an open letter to the dancer Stacia Napierkowska in 1912 that her performance "can never be described. Art and life met, like the sun gliding over a bough entwined with the wind" and "we understood – rare moment! – why human beings think themselves beautiful."[91] One Stuttgart newspaper wrote of Adorée Villany's performance that "one can't describe it, one can

---

[86] On this issue see Janet Lynn Roseman, *Dance Was Her Religion: The Sacred Choreography of Isadora Duncan, Ruth St. Denis, and Martha Graham* (Precott, AZ: Hohm, 2004), pp. 37–39.
[87] Poiret, *My First*, p. 205.
[88] Steegmuller, *Your Isadora*, p. 23.
[89] Hofmannsthal, "Die unvergleichliche Tänzerin," pp. 259, 262.
[90] Gener, "Tórtola Valencia," p. 527 and "Las danzas de Tórtola Valencia," *Diario de la Marina* 1923, Suplemento Literario, clipping in in MAE, Fonds Tortola Valencia, L14, fol. 1.
[91] Carl Einstein, "Lettre a la danseuse Napierkowska," *La Phalange* 12 (1912): 74–75.

only enjoy it in arrested devotion" (*ergriffener Andacht, ergriffen* meaning deeply moved or stirred and *Andacht* meaning literally prayer).[92] A newspaper in Lübeck found that it would be a "hopeless undertaking" to try to describe the charm of Gertrud Falke's performance; "some of its passages," he believed, simply "cannot be captured in words."[93] Of Gertrud Leistikow one reviewer wrote that it was pointless to give any description of her art; "one simply has to have seen and experienced it."[94] One reviewer wrote of Grete Wiesenthal that "one sees expressed in her movements that which one could never express in words, that for which language is too poor and too superficial, that which one can only feel."[95]

These statements may seem a little odd, given that many were penned by critics whose job it was to understand, assess, and describe the performances they reviewed. But such assurances served a clear purpose: They captured – or asserted – the mysterious, sacral, *religious* quality of modern dance. Like all transcendent truths, they implied, the truth of modern dance surpasses human understanding. We cannot see the face of God; but we feel His presence. H. G. Wells put it this way in "The Discovery of the Future": "We cannot see, there is no need for us to see, what this world will be like when the day has fully come"; but "what we can see and imagine gives us faith for what surpasses the imagination."[96]

There was an implicit claim to a special form of access to truth, to knowledge, in the idea that the dance expressed the inexpressible. Dance could discover and communicate deep, mysterious truths, knowledge that was not accessible to the rational mind. By the early 1920s and 1930s, this theory was being articulated with greater clarity. In 1924 Ruth St. Denis would write that the dance was "a means of communication between soul and soul" that could "express what is too deep, too fine for words."[97] The American dance critic (for the *New York Times*) John Martin remarked in a lecture at the New School for Social Research in 1931 or 1932 that the dance was "reaching farther and farther ahead into uncharted regions of thought, which, though not alarming to us as nature was to the savages, are just as far from being reducible to rational terms."[98] Doris Humphrey

[92] Clippings in Villany, *Tanz-Reform*, p. 271.
[93] "Gertrud Falke-Tanzabend," *Lübeckische Anzeiger*, undated clipping in DTAK, Inventory no. 10, Gertrud and Ursula Falke, II.2.4.
[94] Std., "Tanzabend Gertrud Leistikow," *Danziger Allgemeine Zeitung*, October 8, 1913, clipping in TBKUA, Archief Gertrud Leistikow, Map 4a.
[95] Gabriele Brandstetter, "Grete Wiesenthals Walzer," in Brandstetter and Oberzaucher-Schüller, eds., *Mundart der Wiener Moderne*, p. 32.
[96] Wells, *The Discovery*, p. 60.
[97] St. Denis, "The Dance as Life Experience," p. 22.
[98] John Martin, *The Modern Dance* (New York: Dance Horizons, 1965 [1933]), p. 10.

held in 1937 that the "dancer believes that his art has something to say which cannot be expressed in words or in any other way than by dancing."[99] And the great American dancer Martha Graham formulated this idea most strikingly in 1941: "Dance is an absolute. It is not knowledge about something, but it is knowledge itself."[100]

Modern dance enthusiasts and performers used one specific characteristic in particular to assert the homology or even identity between the dance and cosmic truths. Both the dance and the cosmos, they asserted, were governed by rhythm. In this, they shared an interest widespread among intellectuals working in many different fields at the time. It is difficult today to reconstruct why people at the turn of the century felt that rhythm had a cosmic significance; but the idea was widely influential – for example, from the thinking of the British sociologist and theorist of liberalism Herbert Spencer and the great theorist of evolution Charles Darwin to that of the French anthropologist Marcel Mauss and the German sociologist Georg Simmel, by way of various theorists of education, graphology (the interpretation of handwriting), psychology, the science of work, art criticism, and education.[101]

In some cases, the idea that rhythm was an underlying, universal reality could be explicitly combined with that of indescribability – as when, for example, one Paris reviewer wrote that "one would need special words, new words, to explain the tender and charming art of Mata Hari! Maybe one could simply say that this woman is rhythm."[102] But with or without such connections, the concept was scattered liberally throughout writings on dance in the period. Isadora Duncan once again set the tone in her 1903 address on "The Dance of the Future," calling the dancer "this human medium" through which "the movement of all nature runs.... It is a prayer, this dance, each movement reaches in long undulations to the heavens and becomes part of the eternal rhythm of the spheres." In an essay on "The Dancer and Nature" two years later, she asserted that a "great wave movement runs through all Nature ..., all movements in Nature seem to me to have as their ground-plan the law of wave movement ... all

[99] Doris Humphrey, "What a Dancer Thinks About," in Jean Morrison Brown, ed., *The Vision of Modern Dance* (Princeton, NJ: Princeton Book Co., 1979), p. 58.
[100] Cited in Amelie Soyka, *Tanzen und tanzen und nichts als tanzen* (Berlin: Aviva, 2004), p. 198. See also Kate Elswit, *Watching Weimar Dance* (New York: Oxford University Press, 2014), p. xxvii.
[101] See Michael Cowan, *Technology's Pulse: Essays on Rhythm in German Modernism* (London: Institute of Germanic and Romance Studies, 2011), esp. pp. 21, 28, 38–39; Christine Lubkoll, "Rhythmus: Zum Komplex von Lebensphilosophie und ästhetischer Moderne," in Lubkoll, ed., *Das Imaginäre des Fin de siècle* (Freiburg: Rombach, 2002), pp. 83–110.
[102] Waagenaar, *The Murder of Mata Hari*, p. 66.

energy expresses itself through this wave movement," whether sound, or light, or "the flight of birds ... or the bounding of animals" – or, of course, the movement of the dancer. In 1906 she held that a true dancer could "feel the rhythm of the dance throughout the whole of nature."[103]

Thereafter, this image was repeated incessantly. For the critic, theater director, and founder of Munich's Folk Festival, Georg Fuchs, who published a philosophico-political essay on "The Dance" in 1906, Duncan was too chaste and scholarly to be a truly powerful dancer – she had, he believed, about the same physical presence as a nun, and represented mere "abstract plaster-of-Paris culture." But he agreed with her that in modern dance the "body and the blood and the senses are demanding their rights, our race and the laws of the rhythm inborn in us are freeing themselves from the scholastic code of rules.... The dance can be nothing else for us other than an ecstatic experience ..., the bubbling up in us of the rhythmic forces bound up in our physical being."[104] Ruth St. Denis too recalled feeling, while looking up at the moon and stars as a child, "[M]y first dance urge to relate myself to cosmic rhythm ... I surrendered myself to the unseen pulsation of the Universe." Later she concluded that "rhythm was not only the basis of all art, but also of all religious worship."[105] Grete Wiesenthal's brother-in-law believed that "spiritual expression and rhythm" were "the two fundamental elements of every dance," and that modern dance was characterized by "living rhythm – in contrast to monotonous, soul-less beat" such as that used in ballet training.[106] The Caffins believed Grete Wiesenthal danced to "the rhythmic pulse of the core of the universe."[107] One Spanish reviewer claimed that to understand Tórtola Valencia's dances one had to become "attentive to the rhythms of eternity."[108] And Marianne Werefkin, writing about the Sacharoffs, asserted that "God manifests himself in art through ... rhythms of movement that accord with the cosmic rhythms and the rhythms of the movement of the soul."[109] This theme continued to be important in understandings of modern dance after World War I, and with growing emphasis on the universal significance of rhythm. The 1914 edition of Havelock Ellis's essay on "The Philosophy of Dancing," for example, referred only to "that general

[103] Duncan, Der Tanz, p. 16; "The Dancer in Nature" and "A Child Dancing," both in The Art of the Dance, pp. 68–69, 74. See also Steegmuller, Your Isadora, p. 91.
[104] Georg Fuchs, Der Tanz (Stuttgart: Strecker and Schröder, 1906), pp. 19–21.
[105] St. Denis, "Religious Manifestations," p. 12; An Unfinished Life, p. 116.
[106] Huber-Wiesenthal, Die Schwestern Wiesenthal, p. 85.
[107] Caffin and Caffin, Dancing, p. 249.
[108] Quoted in Garland, "The Eternal Return," p. 195.
[109] Werefkin, "Über die Sacharoffs," p. 48.

rhythm which marks all the physical and spiritual manifestations of life";
when he republished the same essay in revised form ten years later, he held
that it "marks, not only life, but the universe."[110] By 1935, Elizabeth Selden
was not untypical in referring to "that primal rhythmic pattern which
runs through all living, working, moving, pulsing, and acting things of
the universe."[111]

The message of all this rhythm talk was clear: There is that in us which
is cosmic, transcendent, eternal, and of deeper – or higher – meaning than
mere understanding can capture. The idea that rhythm was an essential characteristic of the entire universe made dance an embodiment of the alignment
of humankind with the cosmos. Obviously, that was the very same message
that was at the heart of the vision of human evolution into godhood.

That same message was at the root also of another association: that
between dance and mountains. This connection was more diffuse and tenuous than that between dance rhythms and cosmic rhythms; but it peeked
out again and again in indirect ways and in unexpected places in the discussion of modern dance. Rudolf von Delius, for example, found that in
performance Mary Wigman was "more akin to a mountain torrent or the
fearsome mountain peaks than to a human being." When she visited him
at his country house near the Bavarian Alps, she treated him to a display
of the familiar modern dance trance:

> [She] danced among the apple trees. She danced for hours in the spring-
> time sunshine. Behind her the snow-clad mountains. Around her bright
> blossoms.... She danced to the endless melody of the forces seething
> within her. She danced until dark.[112]

The early dance historian Hans Brandenburg discovered the dance in the
summer of 1908, at the same time he discovered his love for the landscape
at the foot of the Bavarian Alps; later, "overwhelmed" and "singed" from
laboring on a dance drama about incest, he hiked through the Alps from
Berchtesgaden to Salzburg "to escape from myself, or to find myself" – an
echo, of course, of what modern dancers did by dancing.[113] The English
sex reformer Edward Carpenter envisioned the future of man thus: "[O]n

[110] Ellis, "The Philosophy of Dancing," at https://www.unz.org/Pub/AtlanticMonthly-1914feb-00197,
and *The Dance of Life*, p. 37.
[111] Selden, *The Dancer's Quest*, p. 9. See also, for a particularly striking case, Rudolf Lämmel, *Der
modern Tanz* (Berlin: Oestergaard, 1928), p. 106. On rhythm more generally see Julia L. Foulkes,
Modern Bodies: Dance and American Modernism from Martha Graham to Alvin Ailey (Chapel
Hill: University of North Carolina Press, 2002), p. 21.
[112] Delius, *Mary Wigman*, pp. 7, 6.
[113] Betz, "Dichten und Trachten," p. 7; Brandenburg, *München leuchtete*, pp. 440–441.

the high tops once more gathering he will celebrate with naked dances the glory of the human form."[114] And some of the dancers shared the conviction that the mountains could heal their ills – or those of others. When Isadora Duncan's mother and sister flipped out over the fact that she had run away for some days to a hut in the country with her first lover, she took them to the Tirol to calm down.[115] Grete Wiesenthal retreated there to recover from the exertion of her first public performances "quite close to nature, to the earth," at the "gates of the Most Holy."[116]

This, too, was an association that persisted in the interwar years. The early dance theorist and teacher Rudolf Laban started a dance group in Munich in 1910 but taught in the summers of 1913 and 1914 at Monte Veritá, a nudist utopian arts community in the mountains near Locarno, in southern Switzerland. Later he would arrange semiritual dance-theater performances in the mountains above Zürich. In his autobiography he portrayed himself as a child of mountains and forests – as a boy swimming naked at a lake in the high Tatra mountains; as a young man battling the mountains, "jungles," vipers, wolves, bears, wild boars, and natives in Bosnia, where his father, a military officer, was stationed.[117] And the extreme case was Leni Riefenstahl, who in the 1920s starred as actress and dancer in the most celebrated of the "mountain movies" (*Bergfilme*) of the director Arnold Fanck, "The Sacred Mountain" (*Der heilige Berg*), and then made her own very successful *Bergfilm*, "The Blue Light" (*Das blaue Licht*).[118]

Perhaps it is not so surprising that people interested in dance were interested in mountains, or went there to recover from stress and trauma. Hiking in the mountains was an important part of the spectrum of "life-reform" and back-to-nature movements in Europe in this period, and in the two or three decades around 1900 the various national Alpine Clubs (Club Alpin Français, Club Alpino Italiano, Schweizer Alpenverein, and so on) expanded very rapidly. They were joined, too, by numerous regional clubs devoted to hiking in Europe's many smaller mountain

---

[114] Quoted in Alexandra Carter, "Constructing and Contesting the Natural in British Theatre Dance," in Alexandra Carter and Rachel Fensham, eds., *Dancing Naturally: Nature, Neo-Classicism and Modernity in Early Twentieth-Century Dance* (London: Palgrave-MacMillan, 2011), p. 17.

[115] Duncan, *My Life*, p. 105.

[116] Wiesenthal, *Der Aufstieg*, pp. 215–216.

[117] Alastair Bonnet, *White Identities: Historical and International Perspectives* (New York: Prentice Hall, 2000), p. 83; Martin Green, *Mountain of Truth* (Hanover, NH: University Press of New England, 1986); Rudolf Laban, *A Life for Dance: Reminiscences* (New York: Theater Arts, 1975), pp. 15–16, 23.

[118] Frank and Schneider, "Tanz und Tanzdebatte in der Moderne," pp. 4–10.

ranges – the Vosges, the Jura, the Pyrenees, the Hartz, the Black Forest, the Carpathians, and two or three dozen others. There was a long tradition in European Romanticism of seeing mountains (above all the Alps) as "sublime," as a spiritually significant experience. And there was a heavy concentration of spas and sanatoria in the Alps, in part because it was believed that the mountain air helped speed recovery from tuberculosis.

And yet, given the centrality of rhythm and waves in dance discourse, it is odd that it was not the sea that drew dancers – the North Sea, for example, where there was also a long tradition of seaside holidays, and a concentration of spas and sanatoria. But there was a specific message about dance in the association with mountains. The deeper logic of this juxtaposition of the human body and the mountains was that these were the two ends of the spectrum of beauty, of aesthetic value. Again, modern dance theory (following a long tradition in the European arts) held that the human body was the pinnacle of creation and thus the standard against which beauty should be measured. As Isadora Duncan put it in 1903, "Man's first conception of beauty is gained from the form and symmetry of the human body."[119] But European aesthetic theory around 1900 included another standard of beauty – not of human proportion and scale but of transcendent grandeur, of the sublime. Mountains and specifically the Alps were identified as the most important example of the sublime in nature in this period. To quote Kant's *Critique of Aesthetic Judgment* (1790) again, "[B]eauty in nature appertains to the form of the object, which is defined by limitations; the sublime, in contrast, can be found also in a formless object, insofar as it ... evokes limitlessness."[120] The Alps were the most important example in that period – vast, chaotic, frightful, beyond human scale. But that association persisted. The sociologist Georg Simmel made precisely this point in essay "On the Aesthetics of the Alps," published in 1911. Simmel argued in effect that the Alps were the aesthetic opposite of the human body. Where the latter (if it was beautiful) was ordered by clear rules of proportion and was literally human in scale, the Alps were "chaotic" and characterized by overwhelming size. But precisely these characteristics – the absence of order and the absence of relative scale – made the Alps a symbol of transcendence. The Alps "point constantly and limitlessly to the Transcendent, and belong to another order than that of the Earth." They were the Absolute, above and beyond

---

[119] Duncan, *Der Tanz*, p. 18.
[120] G. Hartenstein, ed., *Immanuel Kant's sämmtliche Werke*, vol. 5 (Leipzig: Leopold Voss, 1867), p. 251.

form or proportion. In the high Alps "the relationship to what is Above is established" because "we are no longer high relative to something else, but simply 'high' " in the absolute sense. Hiking or climbing in the high Alps therefore generated "the feeling of redemption."[121]

The thinking of the Czech-German philosophy professor and sex reformer Christian von Ehrenfels suggests the subconscious structure and appeal of this conceptual order. Ehrenfels was an early member of the League for the Protection of Mothers and of Karl Vanselow's League for Ideal Culture. He left the former shortly after it was formed when it became apparent that the feminists who ran it were not interested in his program of polygamous marriage – in which women would live in communal households and raise children while men lived on their own and paid child support to as many "wives" as they could afford to support. This system, he believed, corresponded to men's real desires, while monogamy was an artificial regime imposed by Christianity. Already in 1899 Ehrenfels had written a choral drama in which he imagined that the "high kingdom" (*Höhenreich*) of polygamous racial progress could be reached if one climbed to the top of snow-capped mountains, and then kept going.[122]

This image sums up the emotional content of the religion of evolutionism neatly: We will achieve transcendence through a "natural" sexual/ reproductive order, one in which our reason is no longer at war with our body. And that transcendence is symbolized by mountains. An odd metaphor used by the sociologist of religion Ludwig Heitmann in 1913 played on the same symbolism. If a new religion were to arise to counteract the secularization of modern society, he suggested, it would not come as an abstract doctrine, but as "a whole Alpine world, with the power and diversity of untrammeled nature, to enter into which makes people strong and healthy."[123]

The Alps, then, were not so much the opposite of the dancer as in a sense her apotheosis: The dancer was a symbol of the process of evolutionary progress, which was in principle and in its essence without limits. Mountains were a symbol of limitlessness – of the transcendental potential of that process, in a sense of its endpoint. The two represented different orders of beauty; but they were on the same spectrum, starting from

[121] Georg Simmel, "Zur Ästhetik der Alpen," *Gesamtausgabe* (Frankfurt: Suhrkamp, 1989), Bd. 12, pp. 163–164, 168.

[122] Die Schönheit, Vereinigung für ideale Kultur to Polizeipräsident Freiherr von Lüdringhausen, June 11, 1908, LAB, A.Pr.Br. 030-05, Tit 74, Th. 1502, fol. 38–40; Reinhard Fabian, *Christian von Ehrenfels: Leben und Werk* (Amsterdam: Rodopi, 1986), p. 29.

[123] Heitmann, *Grossstadt*, p. 157.

the beauty of human order and reaching to the grandeur of the cosmos. The promise of evolutionary theory, as it was interpreted at the time, was precisely that one day humanity too would be limitless, grand, and sublime.[124] Mountains symbolized the goal, dancers the means to reach it.

It might seem paradoxical that modern dancers combined so much religious imagery and earnestness with the business acumen analyzed in Chapter 1. And yet, this was not at the time an unusual combination. Vegetarians, fitness advocates, occultists, self-improvement experts, and even evangelists in the early twentieth century all used businesses – from restaurants and grocery stores to mail-order weight-lifting and séance equipment – as a vehicle for proselytization, and promises of spiritual or physical regeneration as the heart of marketing messages. They all sought to use the increasingly dominant institution of cultural life – the market – to democratize what they saw as the necessary spiritual revolution of modernity. In an early draft of her memoirs, written in the 1930s, and after passing through a Christian conversion experience, Ruth St. Denis developed a scheme that neatly summarized this connection between religion and business. She would bring together "a rhythmic choir of religious dancers," a group of clergy "liberal but enthusiastic," "well known artists," and businessmen from the motion picture industry to establish a "dynamic business of Christian conversion ... made for television." She believed that her coming to Christ had been a "rebirth, and the patterns of my life have been changed"; but clearly the fundamental pattern of her aspiration had not.[125] Into the 1930s, she was still seeking to use dance to communicate religious truth, spiritual knowledge.

---

[124] On this point see Edward Ross Dickinson, "Altitude and Whiteness: Germanizing the Alps and Alpinizing the Germans, 1875–1935," *German Studies Review* 33 (2010): 577–599; Stebbins, *Delsarte System of Expression*, pp. 422, 449, 453.

[125] "Our Travels in Japan," unpublished ms. in JRDD, Ruth St. Denis Papers, folder 226, p. 226.

CHAPTER 5

Legacies: Dance as Profession, Spectacle, Therapy, and Politics

5.1 Modern Dance in Interwar Context

The modern dance revolution did not have the transformative impact that some of its supporters thought it would. Most obviously, dance did not become the liturgy of a new evolutionary religion, in part because the bestial and apparently senseless violence of World War I suggested that human beings were not evolving toward godhood. References to cosmic rhythms, to mountains, to truths beyond language, to dance as a "revelation" or as "religious" (or even to "the great religion of reformed dance"), and to evolution remained commonplace in the speeches and publications of dancers, critics, and commentators. But they were of declining relative importance.[1]

The declining relative importance of those themes, however, reflected primarily the rapid expansion of the public discussion of dance more generally. In that broader discussion, many of the values central to the modern dance revolution did triumph in the decades after 1918. Darwinism, while it did not become a religion, did become firmly a part of popular consciousness. Changes in sexual behavior in the 1920s did not transform human biology, as sex reformers had hoped; but they did give rise to a more open regime of "dating" and serial monogamy, underpinned by piecemeal reforms in family law that significantly expanded the rights of women. An intensified general skepticism regarding tradition led to what the historian Cas Wouters has called a significant "informalization" of social life in favor of more open self-expression, including in bodily movement. Conventions regarding the relations between the sexes in particular loosened considerably; so too did standards of public decency regarding

---

[1] Oskar Bie, *Der Tanz* (Berlin: Julius Bard, 1919), p. 379. See also Elswit, *Watching Weimar Dance*, esp. pp. 5–6; Diana Brenscheidt, *Shiva Onstage: Uday Shankar's Company of hindu Dancers and Musicians in Europe and the United States, 1931–1938* (Zurich: Lit, 2011), pp. 201–216.

the display of bare skin.[2] Women's participation in employment, politics, and culture expanded significantly during and after the war. To give just one example, women secured the vote in Germany, Austria, Russia, the United States, Britain, and Spain between World War I and World War II.[3]

In European political life, too, some of the central assumptions, values, and ideas influential within modern dance clearly gained ground. The principle of democratic national self-determination – the right to self-expression of the national "soul" of people sharing one "blood" – was accorded a new legitimacy as empires collapsed under the impact of the war. Poland, Hungary, Czechoslovakia, the Baltic states, and Ireland all achieved independence. Germany and Austria became democratic republics; millions of speakers of French in Alsace and Lorraine rejoined the French Republic.

In this context, artistic modernism was further legitimated and radicalized, partly because the war appeared to suggest that many European traditions were bankrupt, dead-ended in death and destruction. The most striking example was the emergence of Dada, a movement started in Switzerland during the war that argued that the whole idea of art as something separate from life was a fraud. Creativity, self-expression, and above all the irrational must be acknowledged and allowed to reshape all of life, rather than being confined to the separate sphere of art. During the war years there were important connections between the Dada movement in its headquarters in Zurich and some of the dancers who would most shape German modern dance between the wars – including particularly Mary Wigman and Rudolf Laban (both discussed later in this chapter).[4] But Dada was just one of many movements that made the period between the wars an extraordinarily creative one in the European arts. At one end of the spectrum, Surrealism called the rationality of the world into question; at the other, the New Objectivity sought to dispense with convention and sentiment in favor of a sober assessment of life as it really is. The expanded importance and impact of modernism after the war also derived from the fact that the authoritarian imperial regimes of Central and

---

[2] See, e.g., Hannelore Palkow and André Marchand, *Liebeslexikon von A-Z* (Vienna: Verlag für Kulturforschung, 1932); Cas Wouters, "Etiquette Books and Emotional Management in the 20th Century: Part Two – The Integration of the Sexes," *Journal of Social History* 29 (1995): 325–339; Catherine Horwood, " 'Girls Who Arouse Dangerous Passions': Women and Bathing, 1900–1939," *Women's History Review* 9 (2000): 653–673.

[3] Kevin Passmore, "Politics," in Julian Jackson, ed., *Europe, 1900–1945* (Oxford: Oxford University Press, 2002), pp. 79, 83.

[4] Manning, *Ecstasy and the Demon*, pp. 68–69.

Eastern Europe collapsed and were replaced by democratic regimes that often actively supported modernism in the arts. A good example would be public commissions for modernist architects to build public housing in great cities like Berlin, Vienna, or Barcelona; another would be Mary Wigman's dance school in Dresden, which was partly supported by subsidies from city, state, and national governments.[5]

Modern dance flourished in this new environment; there was a veritable flood – or, as one recent study puts it, "legions" – of dancers offering performances and instruction across Europe in the 1920s.[6] In Germany, a second generation of influential dancers emerged numbering in the dozens and scores, consolidating that country's status as the world center of modern dance. In the United States, New York in particular was bubbling with dancers and dance schools by the early 1930s. In France, the dance scene was somewhat less vibrant; but dance in Paris in particular profited from the presence of performers from, for example, the United States, Russia, the Netherlands, Algeria, Indonesia, and India. By 1932 the Archives internationales de la Danse established a focal point for the dance, with a library, museum, lectures, exhibits, and an annual choreography competition.[7] In Britain, London played a similar role in bringing dancers together and to the public, including performers from Russia, India, Japan, and, after 1933, Germany.

In short, the enormous potentials built by the pioneering generation of modern dancers in the period before 1914 bore fruit in the 1920s and 1930s. By the late 1940s, one French observer believed that "Terpsichore [the muse of the dance – ERD] has never held such sway over humanity as she does at the present day."[8] This is not the place for a comprehensive history of modern dance after 1914; but six examples can help give a sense for the multifaceted contribution of modern dance to politics and culture in the interwar period. They suggest, too, the ways in which dance was entangled in this period with fundamental developments in the arts, politics, culture, and even individual psychology and identity.

---

[5] Ibid., p. 132.
[6] Susan Manning, "*Ausdruckstanz* across the Atlantic," in Susanne Franco and Marina Nordera, eds., *Dance Discourses* (New York: Routledge, 2007), p. 46.
[7] Lothar Fischer, *Tanz zwischen Rausch und Tod: Anita Berber 1918–1928 in Berlin* (Berlin: Haude and Spener, 1984), p. 19; Gabriele Postuwka, "Aufbruch in die Moderne: Konzeptionen von Tanzerziehung und Tanzausbildung in Europa und den USA," *Tanzdrama* 38 (1997): 9; Suquet, *L'Eveil des modernités*, pp. 289–290; Décoret-Ahiha, *Les danses exotiques*, pp. 138–139; Jacqueline Robinson, *Modern Dance in France* (London: Harwood, 1997), passim and pp. 117–126.
[8] Benois, *Reminiscences of the Russian Ballet*, p. 385.

5.2 Professionalizing Inspiration

As odd as it might seem given the emphasis in modern dance discourse on individuality and spontaneity, by about 1910 modern dance had become sufficiently well established as a performance form that the first signs of its professionalization began to appear. Increasingly modern dancers abandoned ethnographic posturing in favor of what Mary Wigman called "absolute" dance – dance that was justified purely by the inherent aesthetic and expressive qualities of movement, not by music, plot, ethnographic or exoticist themes, or elaborate costumes.[9] By 1912, for example, one reviewer in Hamburg praised Gertrud Falke because in her performances "the emphasis in these dances is on movement, not on portrayal" of a character or topic. In 1914 another reviewer praised her dances because they "do not tell stories . . ., do not present a thought or a picture or music – they are dances born out of the dance" alone, too "stylistically pure" to need any fanciful costuming.[10]

In the years just after the war, modern dance performers had mixed success with this stripped-down aesthetic. Reviewers found the performances of Gertrud Falke's sister Ursula, who developed dances of this sort, "cubistic," "deliberately stiff," "bizarre and grotesque," and "not accessible to all"; one reported simply that the audience was "left cold."[11] The Baltic German emigre Edith von Schrenck was more successful, and won praise for pursuing the "liberation of art dance from decorative and theatrical trimmings" and for her "ever clearer concentration on what is essential" to dance. But many found her performance style cold and overly technical. Her "movements are of extraordinary exactitude and rigor," one critic observed, but a little bit "cramped" and forced; another exclaimed "what a genius one must be to get along in the dance without any natural sensuality."[12] Of Gertrud Leistikow's performances already in 1913, one critic wrote

---

[9] Mary Wigman, "Stage Dance – Stage Dancer," in Jean Morrison Brown, eds., *The Vision of Modern Dance* (Princeton, NJ: Princeton Book Co., 1979), p. 35.

[10] "Frauenklub Hamburg," *Hamburger Fremdenblatt*, October 28, 1912; *Bremer Tageblatt*, February 27, 1914, clippings in DTAK, Inventory no. 10, Gertrud und Ursula Falke, no. II.2.4.

[11] "Tanzabend der Geschwister Falke," *Pädagogische Reform*, February 13, 1917, "Tanzabend," *München-Augsburger Zeitung*, April 24, 1922, "Tanzabend von Gertrud und Ursula Falke," *Leipziger Allgemeine Zeitung*, March 21, 1921, "Tanzabend Gertrud und Ursula Falke," *Leipziger Zeitung*, March 21, 1921, and "Tänze," *Münchener Zeitung*, January 28, 1921, all clippings in DTAK, Inventory no. 10, Gertrud and Ursula Falke, II.2.4.

[12] Brochure *Tanzschule Edith von Schrenck, Berlin* (no place, date, or publisher), pp. 10, 12; "Tanzabend Edith von Schrenck," *München-Augsburger Abendzeitung*, November 19, 1919; "Tanzabend Karin – von Schrenck," *Berliner Börsencourier*, November 4, 1919, in DTAK, Inventory no. 161 Edith von Schrenck, II.2.1 and II.2.4.

that she had a well-trained body and strong technique, but "what's missing is soul" – a criticism, of course, once reserved for ballet.[13] At her first public solo performances in Berlin in 1919, Mary Wigman garnered laughter and whistles from the audience. But by the middle of the 1920s this form began to gain much greater purchase on audiences. Wigman, for example, would make herself the most influential dancer in Germany, and indeed in Europe, precisely by pursuing the program of "absolute" dance. As one critic put it already in late 1920, "The Falkes present form, they give, they create enthusiasm; Mary Wigman *is* Form, she is the Gift, the enthusiasm."[14]

Such successes reflected broader trends in aesthetic sensibilities. Some dancers and critics at the time interpreted only this "absolute" movement idiom as really "modern" dance, and some dance historians have agreed. There is truth to this view in the sense that many modernist artists argued that art should address its audience through the medium (in this case movement; in poetry language; in painting paint and canvas) rather than presenting a narrative or an illusion of realism.[15] As the great American dancer Martha Graham put it in 1930, like "the modern painters and architects, we have stripped our medium of decorative unessentials. Just as fancy trimmings are no longer seen on buildings, so dancing is no longer padded. It is not 'pretty' but it is much more real."[16] Graham's approach to this "absolute" style was often angular, deliberately awkward, and intensely interior, even spiritual. In a collection of essays on Graham published in 1937 the composer Wallingford Riegger described her dance as "like a revelation"; the leading American dance critic John Martin characterized it as "essentially religious in its character"; the impresario and patron of modernist art Merle Armitage thought there was "something in her of the crusader and something of the saint." As Riegger pointed out, this religious force did not rely on any use of the movement idiom of sacred dance from other cultures; for her art was essentially "abstract," and she "is a true apostle of the 'modern' in doing away with the fripperies of a bygone age, stripping art down to its essentials."[17]

[13] "Gertrud Leistikow," *Hamburger Fremdenblatt*, November 29, 1913, clipping in TBCUA, Archief Gertrud Leistikow, Map 4a.

[14] "Tanzabend Gertrud und Ursula Falke," *Hamburger Echo*, November 30, 1920, clipping in ibid.; *Mary Wigman: Die Tänzerin, Die Schule, Die Tanzgruppe* (Überlingen: Seebote, 1927), p. 8.

[15] On this point see particularly Burt, *Alien Bodies*, pp. 11, 14–15, 136. For examples see Martha Graham, "A Modern Dancer's Primer for Action" (1941) and Mary Wigman, "The Philosophy of Modern Dance" (1933), both in Selma Jeanne Cohen, ed., *Dance as a Theater Art* (New York: Dodd, Mean, 1974), pp. 137, 152–153.

[16] Merle Armitage, ed., *Martha Graham* (New York: Dance Horizons, 1966 [original 1937]), p. 97.

[17] Ibid., pp. 36, 17, 5, 37–38.

In America as in Europe, some found this style "ugly and self-indulgent," "barbarian," and "dark"; and by 1935 Elizabeth Selden admitted that modern dance "has become a proverbially puzzling art." Merle Armitage conceded that "certain aspects of [Martha Graham's] work on first consideration are obscure"; some found her merely "'arty' and precious and solemn"; another critic found that she "baffles and perplexes almost as many as she inspires." Edwin Denby even found her "violent, distorted, oppressive and obscure." But like Wigman, Graham had enormous critical and audience success; indeed, as one dance historian comments, "[O]n stage [she] exerted a strange power over rapt and enraptured audiences." As Graham put it, "Ugliness may be actually beautiful if it cries out with the voice of power"; and at least some found her dance powerful enough, in Martin's words, to "strike like a blow."[18]

In this purified dance idiom, elements from exotic traditions (e.g., Indian or Spanish), Delsarte training, folk dance, social dance (such as the waltz or tango), or historical European forms (ballet, skirt dancing) were stripped of their specific historical and cultural references, becoming parts of a new synthesis.[19] The dance historian Gabriele Postuwka sees in this process a distinctive second "phase" in the development of modern dance, characterized by the increasingly precise and technical articulation of a coherent "new language of movement."[20]

Central to this shift was a new focus on technique – on intense training, exact knowledge of the body and its potentials, hard physical work, and relentless practice. The body had to be honed, refined, strengthened, stretched, pushed, and studied to become an effective instrument for expression. Expressive freedom was the product not of simple joyful dropping of convention and pretense, but of hard labor. As the influential American dancer Doris Humphrey put it, learning "to dance is primarily learning to mold the body into a fluid and transparent state, so as to express ideas or emotions in an art form." Real artistic creation required

---

[18] Robert Coe, *Dance in America* (New York: Dutton, 1985), pp. 141, 143; Selden, *The Dancer's Quest*, p. 1; quotation in Roseman, *Dance Was Her Religion*, p. 158; Edwin Denby quoted in Howard Gardner, "Martha Graham: Discovering the Dance of America," *Ballet Review* 22, no. 1 (1994), p. 74; Armitage, ed., *Martha Graham*, p. 9.

[19] This is a point made by Iris Garland in Mary Jo Fox, ed., *Tórtola Valencia*, p. 22. For a specific example (Gertrud Leistikow's appropriation of some Javanese dance idiom) see "Diligentia: Dansavand Gertrud Leistikow," *Haagsche Courant*, January 8, 1925; J. W. F. Weruments Bruning, "Afscheid Gertrud Leistikow," unidentified clipping (1927); U., "Dansavand Gertrud Leistikow," unidentified clipping, February 26, 1927, all in TBCUA, Archief Gertrud Leistikow, Map 4e and 4f.

[20] Postuwka, "Aufbruch," pp. 9–10.

equal parts of "inspiration" and the mastery of "technique."[21] Hanya Holm, an influential student of Wigman, argued that "to arrive at the essential fundamentals of conscious, controlled movement, I start with sheer, physical hard work" to create "a body that is alert and controlled." For Martha Graham training was important because "it frees the body to become its ultimate self." That was an arduous process. "It takes," she claimed, "ten years to build a dancer."[22]

As the demands of modern dance training ramped up the distinction between balletic discipline and modern-dance spontaneity steadily eroded. By 1937, the dance critic Edwin Denby wrote of Martha Graham that "she has trained herself to execute [her] extraordinary movements as accurately as a ballerina would her own most difficult feats."[23] Mary Wigman argued that the dancer must "struggle for years of hard work" to achieve the "transformation of his body"; "perseverance and tenacity, relentlessness and severity toward oneself, enthusiasm, fanaticism and patience, these are the qualities the dancer needs" for that process (see Figure 5.1).[24]

The emphasis on hard physical work brought with it a stress on the aesthetics of athleticism that could take on rather frightful forms. A disturbing example is the experience of Jane Sherman, a dancer in Ruth St. Denis's and Ted Shawn's Denishawn company on tour in Asia in 1925–1926. In December 1925 Sherman reported in a letter to her mother that "a Denishawn dancer would be forgiven almost any crime except that of gaining weight," but that she had done so, going from 121 to 125 pounds. The problem was that Sherman had a grueling performance schedule, and was putting on so much muscle mass that she no longer fit the sylph-like ideal – as she put it, the "true trouble is that I'm all muscle, hard as rocks." Terrified of being fired when the company got back to the United States, she starved herself into serious malnutrition, and by the summer of 1926 she wrote to her mother that "this 'fat' business is about killing me." That was almost literally true, and she had to start

---

[21] Doris Humphrey, "Interpreter or Creator?" (1929), in Selma Jeanne Cohen, ed., *Doris Humphrey: An Artist First* (Middletown, CT: Wesleyan University Press, 1972), p. 250.

[22] These quotations are taken from Michael Huxley, *The Dancer's World, 1920–1945: Modern Dancers and Their Practices Reconsidered* (New York: Palgrave-MacMillan, 2015), quotations pp. 75–77; Graham quotation from Merle Armitage, ed., *Martha Graham*, p. 106.

[23] Edwin Denby, "Graham's *Chronicle*; Uday Shankar" (1937), reprinted in Edwin Denby, *Dance Writings & Poetry*, ed. Robert Cornfield (New Haven, CT: Yale University Press, 1998), p. 37.

[24] Mary Wigman, "Die Schule," in Rudolf Bach, *Das Mary Wigman-Werk* (Dresden: Carl Reissner, 1933), p. 32.

Figure 5.1 Mary Wigman, athletic saint, 1936

eating again, on doctor's orders.[25] It took iron discipline – and near-starvation – to maintain a body like that of Mary Wigman, described by an American critic as "spare and smooth and finely muscled; of tissue

[25] Sherman, *Soaring*, pp. 72, 122, 148, 189.

and sinew refined; less strong than supple.... under a control as perfect as it is unflagging."[26]

The emotional tenor of modern dance also changed in the 1920s. The serene maidenly joyfulness that was a major feature of prewar dance gave way increasingly to darker emotions, the expression of an intense internal life, indeed often a pervasive sense of sadness and tragedy. Mary Wigman's or Martha Graham's most powerful dances addressed the topics of death, sacrifice, struggle, suffering, fate, obsession, despair, power, and – more traditionally – ecstatic self-forgetting, induced in Wigman's case, for example, by spinning around and around for eight minutes until she collapsed in a heap.[27] During the war Wigman developed a suite of dances with the titles "Death," "Torture," "Madness," and "The Scream"; and many of her dances addressed loss, grief, and loneliness. The religious intensity of her performances – she saw herself as a "priestess of the Dance" – was not joyful but somber and ascetic.[28] In many works, Wigman used masks, obliterating the "mimic" element so important before the war; and both she and Graham also often opted for baggy or heavy, floor-length robes that obscured the shape of the body. Wigman's own dance group, which performed from 1923 until 1928, was made up exclusively of women; so was Graham's company for most of the 1930s. In many pieces their movements, dress, and manner were austere, severe, and hieratic, not decorative or exuberantly expressive (see Figure 5.2). Some dance historians have seen in all this a profound feminist message – the denial of the commodification of women, of women's association with sensuality and lighthearted pleasure, and of their need to be "on show" *as women*.[29] Again, the body and the personal charisma of the performer were increasingly less important than technique and the new "language of movement" it taught.

The first efforts to develop formal systems of aesthetics, method, and training for modern dance were already taking shape in the years just before the war, particularly in two influential centers directed by men. One was Emile Jaques-Dalcroze's school of movement at Hellerau near Dresden, in Saxony. The other was Rudolf von Laban's school at Munich and at the nudist, vegetarian, alternative lifestyle commune at Monte Veritá, near Locarno in southern Switzerland. Laban was a Hungarian

---

[26] Henry Taylor Parker, "The Dancer in this Day without Peer" (1931), in *Arrested Motion: Dance Reviews of H. T. Parker*, ed. Olive Holmes (Middletown, CT: Wesleyan university Press, 1982), p. 187.

[27] See particularly Hedwig Müller, *Mary Wigman: Leben und Werk der grossen Tänzerin* (Weinheim: Quadriga, 1986), esp. pp. 186–196.

[28] Wigman quoted in Sabine Huschka, *Moderner Tanz: Konzepte – Stile – Utopien* (Reinbek: Rowohlt, 2002), pp. 179, 181–182.

[29] The best treatment is Manning, *Ecstasy and the Demon*.

Figure 5.2 Mary Wigman dances struggle and power, ca. 1930

from Bratislava/Pressburg who had moved to Paris to study art in 1900, then to Munich in 1907, where he started a dance school in 1912. In the summers of 1913 and 1914, he offered courses in movement and dance at Monte Veritá.[30] Dalcroze was an Austrian who grew up in Switzerland; he

[30] Valerie Preston-Dunlop, *Rudolf Laban: An Extraordinary Life* (London: Dance, 1998).

offered a form of musical and movement education variously referred to as rhythmic movement or "rhythmique," first in Geneva and then at the Hellerau school from 1910 until 1914. While he insisted that he was not a dance teacher, his understanding of the relationship between music and movement made his method productive for dancers.[31]

For many Central European dancers of the 1920s these centers were, above all, important sites of encounter. The school at Hellerau was part of an experimental garden city and center for the arts and various reform movements, one that attracted an extraordinary range of influential European intellectuals. Visitors or collaborators included the designer Mariano Fortuny (in his capacity as theater lighting expert), the Austrian writer Franz Kafka, the German poet Rainer Maria Rilke, the British playwright George Bernard Shaw, the American writer Upton Sinclair, the Russian actor and director Konstantin Stanislavski, and the German theater impresario Max Reinhardt, as well as Rudolf von Laban, the British choreographer Marie Rambert, the Indian dancer Uday Shankar, the German dancer and choreographer Kurt Jooss, Serge Diaghilev, and Vaslav Nijinsky. Among the six hundred students at Hellerau in 1913 were citizens of sixteen different countries, from the United States to Japan.[32] Monte Veritá constituted an equally important meeting ground for European reform movements and intellectuals. Visitors and temporary residents there included the Russian theorist of anarchy Peter Kropotkin, the psychoanalytic theorists Otto Gross and Karl Gustav Jung, the German novelist Hermann Hesse, the British writer D. H. Lawrence, and the German-Transylvanian poet, wandering philosopher, and countercultural hero Gustav "Gusto" Gräser.[33] Both places, then, were certainly stimulating environments for dancers, where they could refine and define their alignment with broader movements in modernist thought.

Insofar as they aimed to systematize modern movement generally, however, these schools faced an uphill battle. By the time they opened, the theory, vocabulary, and movement idiom of modern dance were already well established; and in practice modern dance was predisposed to reject any sort of homogeneity or external discipline. Not surprisingly, therefore,

---

[31] Irwin Spector, *Rhythm and Life: The Work of Emile Jaques-Dalcroze* (Stuyvesant, NY: Pendragon, 1990), pp. 115–116, 131, 164, 187–191.

[32] Spector, *Rhythm*, pp. 153, 161, 164, 168, 206; de Boer, *Dans voluit, dat is leven*, p. 36; Fritsch-Vivié, *Mary Wigman*, pp. 23–24; Anderson, *Art without Boundaries*, p. 47; Midori Takeishi, *Japanese Elements in Michio Ito's Early Period (1915–1924)*, ed. David Pacun (Los Angeles: California Institute of the Arts, 2006), p. 10.

[33] Green, *Mountain of Truth*, pp. 3, 7–9, 13; Ulrich Linse, *Barfüssige Propheten* (Berlin: Siedler, 1983), pp. 68–75.

many modern dancers were rather ambivalent about their experiences at each of these centers. Mary Wigman found Jaques-Dalcroze's method too rigid and disciplined. At one point, she admitted to Dalcroze's assistant Suzanne Perrottet that "I work alone in my room, Dalcroze doesn't want to know anything about me." In mid-1913 she left – following Perrottet, who had gone to Monte Verità to study the somewhat more free-form, spontaneous movement style cultivated there.[34] When Laban moved his school to Zürich at the outbreak of the war, Wigman and Perrottet went with it; there they experimented, among other things, with joint performances with the Dadaists headquartered in that city.[35] Wigman initially found that Laban "had the extraordinary quality of setting you free artistically, enabling you to find your own roots ... to discover your own potentialities, to develop your own technique." But Laban later moved toward greater system and discipline. In any case, he also appears to have slept with many of his students, and Wigman had no desire to be part of "his dancing harem," as she called it. She left his school in 1917, retreated for a time to the Alps to recover, and in 1920 established her own school in Dresden.[36] The Falke sisters appear to have had a somewhat similar experience. Gertrud Falke was at Hellerau for a short time in 1911, and both she and her sister Ursula went to Monte Verità in the summer of 1914. But they found instruction at both places boring, overly technical, and too focused on music and rhythm; and the alternative lifestyle and utopian atmosphere of Monte Verità seemed overly sentimental to two women who identified themselves as sober North Germans ("They're such South Germans, they feel too strongly and talk too loud").[37]

In practice, therefore, modern dance training flourished in an increasingly dense but autonomous network of small schools and studios run mostly by female dancers who, before the war, had been pioneers of purely individual dance. Rita Sacchetto opened a school in Berlin; prominent pupils included Anita Berber (discussed later in this chapter) and Valeska Gert, who pushed the movement vocabulary of modern dance by exploring grotesque, socially critical, and comic dance. Elizabeth Duncan reopened her school in Berlin in 1920 with support from the Prussian state, moving to near Salzburg in 1925. The Hellerau school reopened after

---

[34] Fritsch-Vivié, *Mary Wigman*, pp. 25 (quotation), 27.
[35] Ibid., p. 48.
[36] Karl Toepfer, *Empire of Ecstasy: Nudity and Movement in German Body Culture, 1910–1935* (Berkeley: University of California Press, 1997), pp. 100, 108–109; Manning, *Ecstasy*, pp. 56–58.
[37] Jöckel, "Aus dem Moment," p. 19; Ursula Falke to her parents, July 20, 1914, in DTAK, Inventory no. 10, Gertrud und Ursula Falke, II.2.4.

the war (without Dalcroze, who had alienated German nationalists by criticizing the conduct of the German army in Belgium), moving to near Vienna in 1925. The Falke sisters ran a dance school in Hamburg, and Grete Wiesenthal one in Vienna. Laban's student Kurt Jooss (who had also studied at Hellerau) opened an influential school in Essen, aiming at a synthesis of modern and ballet technique.[38]

Germany was clearly the epicenter of modern dance in the 1920s; but the modern dance scene in the United States was no less active, though concentrated heavily in New York. Ruth St. Denis and her husband Ted Shawn opened the extremely influential Denishawn School in Los Angeles in 1915, moving to New York in 1922; and branches opened in multiple other cities during the course of the 1920s.[39] Denishawn trained an entire generation of American dancers, who by the late 1920s and early 1930s were opening their own schools – for example, Martha Graham, Doris Humphrey, and Charles Weidman in New York in 1927 and 1928. But European currents were also influential in America: A Dalcroze school had already been in operation in New York since 1915, and in 1931 Wigman's student Hanya Holm opened a "Wigman" school there.[40]

Britain, in contrast, was never a very congenial home to modern dance in its "absolute" form, and Mary Wigman's style, for example, was seen by many there (in the words of one review) more as expressive gymnastics than as "dance in the accepted sense of the term." In the more conservative and traditionalist British cultural setting ballet (in its distinctive British variety-theater incarnation) continued to be the dominant dance idiom.[41] Yet here, too, there was a proliferation of modern dance schools. The London School of Dalcroze Eurhythmics had been formed already in 1913; in the same year Ruby Ginner formed a school of "Grecian" dance; Madge Atkinson started a School of Natural Movement in Manchester in

[38] Kurth, *Isadora*, p. 437; Gunhild Oberzaucher-Schüller, "Anmerkungen zur Wiesenthal-Rezeption," in Gabriele Brandstetter and Oberzaucher-Schüller, eds., *Mundart der Wiener Moderne: Der Tanz der Grete Wiesenthal* (Munich: Kieser, 2009), p. 261; Spector, *Rhythm*, p. 206; Fritz Böhme, *Der Tanz der Zukunft* (Dresden: Reissner, 1926), p. 13.

[39] Meinzenbach, *"Tanz ist eine Sprache und eine Schrift des Göttlichen,"* pp. 150–151; Baird Hastings, "The Denishawn Era," in Paul Magriel, ed., *Chronicles of the American Dance* (New York: Henry Holt, 1948), pp. 227–237.

[40] Postuwka, "Aufbruch," p. 9; Tresa Randall, "Hanya Holm and an American *Tanzgemeinschaft*," in Susan Manning and Lucia Ruprecht, eds., *New German Dance Studies* (Urbana: University of Illinois Press, 2012), pp. 79–98; Michael Stadlinger, "Beziehungen zwischen Modernem Tanz in Mitteleuropa und den USA in den 20er und 30er Jahren des zwanzigsten Jahrhunderts" (Ph.D. diss., Vienna, 1980), p. 76.

[41] See particularly Carole Kew, "Mary Wigman's London Performances: A New Dance in Search of a New Audience," *Dance Research* 30 (2012): 1–21 (quotation p. 11).

1918; Friderica Derra de Moroda opened a "School of Hellenic Dancing" in London in the same year; Margaret Morris and her students built up schools in seven cities in Scotland, England, and France before World War II; and in 1930 Maud Allan opened her own West Wing School of Movement.[42] In the 1930s the arts institute at Dartington Hall, in Devon, became a center for modern dance, strongly influenced by refugees from Nazi Germany (about which more later in this chapter).[43]

There was a similar proliferation of dance schools in France, though there a revival of ballet (discussed later in this chapter) limited the influence of modern dance. Here, many of these schools were founded in Paris by emigrants from around Europe and from the Asian colonies of France and other imperial nations. In the 1930s, Paris was home as well to numerous artists who had fled the communist regime in the Soviet Union and National Socialist Germany.[44]

Despite the increasing emphasis on technique and training, these widely scattered dance schools appear to have remained true to the original modern dance program of fostering their pupils' originality. Mary Wigman, as one (very critical) observer reported in 1929, "does not pretend to teach; she incites the pupil to create for herself.... As the high-priestess of her cult, she merely manipulates the flow of spontaneous inspiration."[45] Wigman wrote that the "task of the teacher is to find a way to the student, to recognize the nature of his gifts, to respect them as a world unto themselves" and not to impose "a universally valid and recognized norm" but rather to help him to a form of "expression particular to his nature."[46] One student of Rita Sacchetto was more laconic, recalling simply that "Sacchetto let us do whatever we wanted."[47] Isadora Duncan took a similar approach in her school in Moscow in the early 1920s (discussed later in this chapter): She sought to communicate the "great Spiritual treasure of my art, not ... paralyzed by theories and killed by systems – Dalcroze

---

[42] Dahms and Schroedter, eds., *Der Tanz*, pp. 23, 25; Alexandra Carter, "Constructing and Contesting," pp. 19, 21, 23 (quotation); Macintosh, "Dancing Maenads," pp. 198, 200; Hastie, "Margaret Morris," p. 171.

[43] Larraine Nicholas, *Dancing in Utopia: Dartington Hall and Its Dancers* (Alton, UK: Dance Books, 2007).

[44] Robinson, *Modern Dance in France*, pp. 82, 140, 148, 159; Thomas, *Dance, Modernity*.

[45] André Levinson, "The Modern Dance in Germany" (1929), in Joan Acocella and Lynn Garafola, eds., *Andre Levinson on Dance: Writings from Paris in the Twenties* (London: Wesleyan University Press/University Press of New England, 1991), p. 106.

[46] Mary Wigman, "Die Schule," in Rudolf Bach, ed., *Das Mary Wigman-Werk* (Dresden: Reissnerl 1933), pp. 33–34.

[47] Dinah Nelken quoted in Fischer, *Tanz zwischen Rausch*, p. 13.

and others – but this art spontaneous and true." Shortly before her death she wrote that

> I have no system. My only purpose and my only effort have been to lead the child each day to grow and to move according to an inner impulse ..., letting all the natural grace and loveliness come to expression.[48]

The Denishawn school, too, as the dance historian Helen Thomas puts it, "believed in cultivating their students' natural talents and powers of movement ... not subjugating their students to the demands of a single system" but fostering "diversity and individuality."[49]

The rapidly proliferating modern dance schools, then, increasingly emphasized technique and system; but as the German refugee critic Artur Michel put it in 1935, the

> skill which the dancer thus acquires is not mechanical movement-grammar, but the ability to transform each of his innumerable impulses into ... the form of dancing. Thus the dance is made a function of the dancer's desire for expression ..., producing movement of an unmistakably unique character.[50]

This, obviously, was precisely Isadora Duncan's prediction in 1903 – that the dance of no two dancers would be alike. Dance in the 1920s and 1930s became a serious matter of hard work and knowledge; but the new focus on technical excellence overlay precisely the same investment in individual expression.

The organization of modern dance did move forward rapidly particularly in Germany. Both Laban and Wigman built real dance-pedagogical empires. By the late 1920s, Mary Wigman's school in Dresden had 360 students, several dozen of them aiming to become dance professionals; and some of her pupils opened loosely associated schools in other cities. By the beginning of the 1930s there were eleven of them, with a total of between 1,500 and 2,000 students. Laban's dance imperium was even larger: By 1927 he oversaw more than two dozen schools, and by 1930 his student Dussia Bereska opened a Laban school in Paris.[51] A first

---

[48] Duncan, *The Art of the Dance*, pp. 110, 119. On the more authoritarian practice of her sister Elizabeth, however, see Irma Duncan, *Duncan Dancer: An Autobiography* (Middletown, CT: Wesleyan University Press, 1966), pp. 28–29.

[49] Thomas, *Dance, Modernity*, p. 85.

[50] Artur Michel, "The Development of the New German Dance," in Virginia Stewart, ed., *Modern Dance* (New York: Dance Horizons, 1970 [1935]), pp. 14–15.

[51] Manning, *Ecstasy*, pp. 90, 132–133; Randall, "Hanya Holm," p. 81; Claudia Jeschke and Gabi Vettermann, "Between Institutions and Aesthetics: Choreographing Germanness?," in André Grau and Stephanie Jordan, eds., *Dancing Europe: Perspectives on Theatre Dance and Cultural Identity*

German national dance congress was held in 1927, dominated by Rudolf von Laban and his followers; a second and third the following year and in 1930 were attended by up to 1,000 performers, critics, teachers, and theorists. At the 1928 conference Laban was able to get his dance notation system ("Labanotation") accepted as a standard tool for choreographers; and a national German Dancers' League (*Tänzerbund*) was formed at his instigation.[52]

But Germany was the extreme case. Elsewhere, centralization was far less extensive. In Britain, an Association of Operatic Dancing (for ballet) was formed in 1920, and an Association of Teachers of the Revived Greek Dance in 1923 (for modern dance).[53] But again, modern dance in particular did not have the influence it did in Germany. In France the Archives internationals de la danse was a center for the exchange of ideas, and, in the United States during the 1930s, regular summer conferences at Bennington College did offer a chance for dancers to compare notes and share ideas, while three organizations (the Concert Dancers' League, the Dancers' Club, and the Dance Repertory Theater) helped focus modern dance practices particularly in New York.[54] But in neither country was there an institutionalization of the profession comparable to that in Germany.

And yet, the sheer number and quality of modern dance schools and performance companies by the 1930s gave modern dance a cultural weight and an intellectual coherence that the individual pioneers of the prewar period could not have built, or perhaps even foreseen. There was a broad discussion of what modern dance was; there was an extensive international discussion of modern dance pedagogy; there were internationally aware and influential modern dance critics; there was a growing army of modern dance practitioners. By the early 1930s at the latest, modern dance was well established as a recognized art form with an institutional infrastructure. It was leaving behind its association both with cultural revolution and with the more protean world of popular entertainment, and becoming the professionalized and disciplined "high" art form it would be in the second half of the twentieth century.

(New York: Routledge, 2000), p. 69; Robinson, *Modern Dance in France*, pp. 61–63; Huschka, *Moderner Tanz*, p. 166.

[52] Peter Schelley, "Tänzerkongress 1928," reprinted in *Tanzdrama* 4 (1987): 16–17 (quotation p. 17); Guilbert, *Danser avec le IIIe Reich*, pp. 66, 68.

[53] Perugini, *A Pageant*, pp. 289–291.

[54] John Martin, "The Dance: Plans for the New Season," *New York Times*, September 21, 1930, p. 6.

Ironically, the establishment of dance as a respectable art form had a quite striking effect both on the gender balance in the dance world and on the relationship between ballet and modern dance. The pioneers of modern dance were almost exclusively women, and they largely scorned the ballet; and one thing they clearly did accomplish was to make dance a much more respectable profession for women.[55] But by the 1930s, male dancers and choreographers were increasingly important, and there was increasingly a rapprochement between modern and ballet traditions. In France, a self-conscious revival of ballet (discussed later in this chapter) was particularly important. In Britain, several important figures built bridges between ballet (whether "modern" along the lines of the Ballets Russes or more traditionalist and "neoclassical") and modern dance. They included in particular Marie Rambert and Ninette de Valois, both of whom had performed with the Ballets Russes in the 1920s.[56] In the United States, Ted Shawn and Ruth St. Denis drew on the traditions of ballet and theater dance, and were skeptical of the claims of "absolute" dance. And while modern dance flourished in New York, by 1934 ballet was making powerful comeback there was well, partly due to the influence of the Russian (and again, in the 1920s, Ballets Russes) dancer and choreographer George Balanchine.[57] From 1938 onward, Martha Graham collaborated with classically trained dancers (including men) on larger ensemble pieces that were thematic and narrative in ways familiar to ballet audiences.[58] In Germany, Rudolf von Laban actively worked to reconcile ballet, theatrical dance, and modern dance; and the Dancer's League he helped form in 1928 included German dancers in all genres. In his own choreographic and theatrical work, he aimed above all to explore the potentials of the disciplined and coordinated "movement choir," consisting of scores or even hundreds of performers. By 1930 he was ballet director at the Berlin State Opera.[59] His student Kurt Jooss was most famous for his ballet "The Green Table." Mary Wigman was very skeptical, continuing to champion "absolute" dance against a ballet tradition she saw as technically

---

[55] See, e.g., Ginner, *The Revived Greek Dance*, p. 12; Beth Genné, *The Making of a Choreographer: Ninette de Valois and Bar aux Folies-Bergère* (Pennington, NJ: Society of Dance History Scholars, 2012), p. 19.

[56] See, e.g., Ninette de Valois, "The Future of the Ballet" (1933), in *Ninette de Valois: Adventurous Traditionalist* (Alton, UK: Dance Books, 2012), esp. pp. 150–151; Marie Rambert, *Quicksilver* (London: Macmillan, 1972), esp. pp. 24, 32–39; Genné, *The Making*, esp. pp. 19–20, 30–32, 38–40.

[57] See Bernard Taper, *Balanchine: A Biography* (Berkeley: University of California Press, 1984).

[58] Franko, *Martha Graham in Love and War*, esp. pp. 26–37.

[59] Lillian Karina and Marion Kant, *Hitler's Dancers: German Modern Dance and the Third Reich*, trans. Jonathan Steinberg (Oxford: Berghahn, 2003), p. 36.

admirable but fundamentally irrelevant.[60] She and her supporters refused to join the Dancer's League until 1932, maintaining their own separate Dance Community (*Tanzgemeinschaft*) devoted to modern dance alone.[61] But her student Harald Kreutzberg, for example, developed a successful collaboration with the American ballerina Ruth Page.[62] Increasingly dance as a whole – modern, ballet, folk, theater – was understood as one common profession, and a very demanding and technical one in all genres.

In short, by the 1930s dance had established itself as a respectable art form, and as a profession. But as it did so, it became increasingly less revolutionary, and increasingly less woman-centered. Had she been able to see it in 1903, Isadora Duncan might have found much to dislike about the dance of the future.

5.3 Sex, Drugs, Death, and Dance: Celebrity and Self-Destruction

While some of the modern dance world was moving toward respectability and institutionalization, however, other performers veered in the early 1920s in the opposite direction – toward the scurrilous and obscene. This trend was most apparent in early Weimar Germany, where revolution, hyperinflation, financial and social chaos, and profound disorientation appear to have led a certain number of performers into outright meltdown.

The emblematic case was that of Anita Berber. Up to a certain point, Berber's career followed familiar patterns. Her parents were divorced soon after her birth; her father, a violinist and eventually professor of music, had virtually nothing to do with her thereafter. An unsteady character, he had five marriages and four divorces (he died two years after his last wedding). His daughter Anita had a slender, "boyish" figure, attended Dalcroze's school in Hellerau and then studied with Rita Sacchetto in Berlin, and took part late in the war in performances that garnered complaints to the police of immorality on stage. In fact, a colleague at Rita Sacchetto's school later recalled that "none of us could really dance ..., we were all just exceptionally pretty girls." As for Berber, "She wasn't really

[60] See Mary Wigman, "Tänzerisches Schaffen der Gegenwart," in Paul Stefan, ed., *Tanz in dieser Zeit* (Vienna: Universal-Edition, 1926), esp. p. 5.

[61] Evelyn Doerr, *Rudolf Laban: The Dancer of the Crystal* (Lanham, MD: Scarecrow, 2008), p. 129.

[62] See Joellen Meglin, "Blurring the Boundaries of Genre, Gender, and Geopolitics: Ruth Page and Harald Kreutzberg's Trans-Atlantic Collaboration in the 1930s," *Dance Research Journal* 41 (2009): 52–75.

interested in dancing, she just wanted attention."[63] In the years immediately after the war, she offered solo performances of familiar type – for example, a "Korean Dance" and a dance as a puppet, to music by Chopin, Debussy, Sibelius, and Saint-Saëns. With the collapse of censorship in Germany in the wake of the revolution of late 1918, various entrepreneurs and reformers took the opportunity to make a flood of "educational" films (*Aufklärungsfilme*) about sexual matters, including, for example, venereal disease, prostitution, and homosexuality. Berber took parts in some two dozen such films. Some were simply sensationalist kitsch, spiked here and there with sado-masochism and snakes; others were activist melodrama – such as the film *Unlike the Others* (Anders als die Anderen), a cinematic plea for the legalization of homosexual acts between men that was made with the collaboration of Magnus Hirschfeld, founder (in 1897) of the most important homosexual rights organization in Germany. Berber also stood model for various artists; did some fashion modeling; and continued her own career as a dancer – increasingly a nude dancer, in cabarets and nightclubs above all in Berlin (see Figure 5.3).[64]

By the early 1920s, Berber had fallen in with Sebastian Droste, a performer in the "Ballet Celly de Rheydt," a group formed under the leadership of Cäcilie Schmidt (from the town of Rheidt) that served up sensational cabaret and review shows involving a great deal of mass nudity.[65] In company with Droste, Berber came increasingly unstuck: Her performances became more and more obscene; her public behavior grew increasingly bizarre; and she became addicted to cocaine, morphine, and alcohol. She and Droste also repeatedly ran afoul of the law, not only for indecency but also for theft, fraud, breach of contract, and disturbing the public order – the last because Berber began to specialize in punch-ups with members of her audience who dared to make crude remarks about her performance. The couple's "Dances of Vice, Horror and Ecstasy" focused on the themes of drugs, madness, and death; their lives increasingly did so too.

With the imposition of a state of emergency in 1923 (which allowed the Berlin police to ban all nude performances) and the stabilization of the German currency and economy in early 1924, the frenetic urban

[63] Dinah Nelken quoted in Fischer, *Tanz*, p. 13.
[64] Mel Gordon, *The Seven Addictions and Five Professions of Anita Berber: Weimar Berlin's Priestess of Depravity* (Port Townsend, WA: Feral House, 2006), pp. 22, 55–57, 77; Ute Scheub, *Verrückt nach Leben:Berliner Szenen in den zwanziger Jahren* (Reinbek: Rowohlt, 2000), pp. 85–86. See also Traub, *Theater der Nacktheit*, pp. 127–138; Elswit, *Watching Weimar Dance*, pp. 21–24.
[65] See Jelavich, *Berlin Cabaret*, pp. 154–160 and Traub, *Theater der Nacktheit*, pp. 93–98.

Figure 5.3 Anita Berber, 1918

scene created during the inflation years began to disperse. Perversion, promiscuity, drugs, violence, and public craziness began to fall out of favor. It was too late for Droste and Berber. Berber developed an increasingly macabre repertoire, including dances titled "Suicide," "Madhouse," "The Nun and the Hanged Man," "The Corpse on the Autopsy Table," "Cocaine," "Morphine," and – going back to the roots – "Salomé." Droste wandered off to New York, returning home to Hamburg only to die of tuberculosis in 1926. Berber wandered off to the Middle East (with an American partner), and returned home to Berlin to die of tuberculosis in 1928.[66]

Berber and Droste were by no means unique. In inflation-era Germany enterprising young men and women like Celly de Rheydt and her company, or the owners and organizers of nightclubs, cabarets, and revues were busy producing semipornographic "dance" performances in some profusion. Three revue theaters in Berlin offered regular topless performances – for example, "Hot Dang, A Thousand Naked Women," with up to twenty-five half-clad women on the stage at once; "Get Undressed – An Amoral Evening in 30 Tableaux with 60 Prize-Winning Nude Models"; "Berlin Unclothed"; or "From Bed to Bed."[67] By November 1920 a long report by the Berlin police department listed forty locations in that city where nude "dances" – including on-stage sex acts – were performed. One Berlin newspaper developed a telling one-word (in German) characterization of such performances: "meat-inspections."[68]

The situation in other countries and cities was less colorful; but the early 1920s were a period of dislocation, demoralization, and disorientation across Europe. In fact, even some of the original modern dance pioneers appear to have lost their way – though less spectacularly. After returning from Soviet Russia (an episode addressed later in this chapter), Isadora Duncan became increasingly a public drunk, addicted to promiscuity, and dependent on the charity of friends and admirers

[66] Fischer, *Tanz*, pp. 32, 36, 47, 69, 81, 89; Soyka, *Tanzen und tanzen*, p. 96.

[67] Toepfer, *Empire of Ecstasy*, p. 75; Kolb, *Performing Femininity*, pp. 198–203; Katja Giazitzidis, "Eine goldene Zeit für den Tanz – die Zwanziger," in Petra Bock and Katja Koblitz, eds., *Neue Frauen zwischen den Zeiten* (Berlin: Hentrich, 1995), p. 214; Traub, *Theater der Nacktheit*, p. 138.

[68] Präsident der Genossenschaft deutscher Bühnenangehörigen Rickelt to Polizeipräsidium Berlin, April 1, 1920; Kriminal-Oberwachtmeister Vorwieger of the Zentralpolizeistelle zur Bekämpfung unzüchtiger Bilder und Schriften to Polizeipräsident Berlin, November 1, 1920, all in GSAPKB, Rep. 77, Ministerium des Innern, Tit. 425, no. 37, fols. 20, 103–105, 122–130; "Naturalismus und Ballett," *Berliner Zeitung am Mittag*, May 4, 1920, clipping in LAB, APr.Br 630-05, Tit. 74, Th. 1503, fol. 100. On early Weimar nude dance see Karl Toepfer, "One Hundred Years of Nakedness in German Performance," *Drama Review* 47 (2003): 161–163.

who understood her grief and remained, as one put it, "tolerant of her violence, her recklessness, of all her wild and uncontrolled love affairs."[69] She died in a bizarre automobile accident in 1927, having concluded by 1926 that "[t]here are only two things left: a drink, and a boy."[70] Maud Allan fell afoul of anti-Semitic and anti-German activists in Britain in 1918 – because she had lived in Berlin for many years before becoming an international dance star, and because popular theater was associated on the political Right with Jewish impresarios. She lost a scandalous libel suit in which her alleged lesbian affairs and the fact that her brother had been executed for murdering two schoolgirls – proof that her "blood" was tainted – played a central role. She spent much of the 1920s mired in depressive eccentricity.[71]

It is hard not to see in these individual destinies early examples of the culture of sex, drugs, neurosis, and celebrity that has plagued Western societies for a century or more. Anita Berber was, in a sense, the Sid Vicious of dance in the 1920s – chaotic, addicted, nihilist, violent, and self-destructive. But, of course, the broader development of low-brow nude dance was also part of the history of what came to be called, in English, "exotic" dance. Eventually, a legal framework would emerge in Europe that more or less (and increasingly) accommodated this form of entertainment as an alternative, accompaniment, or incitement to prostitution. Obviously, however, this strategy of containment and normalization has not entirely worked: For the spectacle of scandalous self-destruction – sex, drugs, and inescapable fate – has made for good "news" copy throughout the past century. We might say, then, that self-destruction was a form of "spectacular" success.

5.4 Totalitarian Temptations

But there are much worse things in the modern world than self-destruction and obscenity; and modern dance contributed to some of them, as well. In particular, several modern dancers were attracted to the totalitarian political "religions" that plunged Europe ever deeper into a sea of fire and death starting in the early 1930s. Most strikingly, a large proportion of the German dance world sought to align itself with Adolf Hitler's National Socialist regime.

[69] Acosta, *Here Lies the Heart*, p. 79.
[70] Kurth, *Isadora*, pp. 517, 554.
[71] Felix Cherniavsky, "Maud Allan, Part V: The Years of Decline, 1915–1956," *DC* 9 (1986): 184–185, 187, 189, 194.

This development was, of course, partly prefigured by the importance of "blood" in modern dance. While most in the dance world before 1914 believed that mixing "blood" would enhance creativity, others were already more concerned with the particular characteristics of their own "race" and its "blood." Already in 1906, for example, Georg Fuchs believed a new generation of Germans was coming forward to give a more vital "inner form" to the political structure created with the unification of the German Empire in 1870, an "all-encompassing culture of life" that could bring order to the "chaos of the modern machine age." After vain attempts to work in that direction through literature, painting, architecture, or fashion, German artists had at last found the proper medium for the development of such a culture: "our own bodies!" Fuchs was ecstatic about the potentials of modern dance. "The race, blood as bearer of rhythm …, has never expressed itself so directly," he believed; the true "rhythm of the race" was at last being discovered; a new and truly Germanic-racial "law of art … a new cultural principle" was being born.[72] In the 1920s and 1930s he would become involved in radical right-wing politics and eventually Nazism. Fuchs was an extreme case; but he was one instance of a very strong current of radical right-wing enthusiasm for the cultivation of healthy bodies – including through eugenics, mass gymnastics exercises, "natural" diets and health- or self-care regimes, and nudism. Some forms of modern dance could be drawn into the orbit of this nationalist physical culture. As they were, the language of blood came increasingly to be used in a new key, to denote and promote exclusion and hostility rather than cross-fertilization and sympathy.

An important case of the resulting sympathies between dance and Nazism is Mary Wigman. As Wigman's fame grew in the postwar years, she was frequently celebrated as a particularly "Germanic" dancer. In a 1922 study of "The Essence of the New Dance Art," for example, Ernst Blass even found that Wigman's performance was "a wilderness, barbaric and fruitful…. [Her] path leads to Nordic prehistory…. That is her spiritual home."[73] Wigman sought to establish "absolute" dance as the true German dance; in 1929 – adopting as her own a theory voiced in a highly critical comment by the Russo-French dance critic André Levinson – she characterized ballet as "Latin" (French and Italian) in origin and spirit, alien to the German racial soul. Ballet, she held, was light, pleasing, entertaining, insubstantial; German dance was

[72] Fuchs, *Der Tanz*, pp. 3–5, 27, 40–41; Fuchs, *Sturm und Drang*.
[73] Ernst Blass, *Das Wesen der neuen Tanzkunst* (Weimar: Lichtenstein, 1922), p. 48.

characterized by "intensity of expression," not mere "beauty of form."[74] In 1930 one of her followers cast her as the indispensable "community-forming leader" (*Führerin*) dance needed to inspire and guide the "holy struggle" to create a new culture. Her "relentless, iron energy and fiery autocratic nature [*Herrschertum*]," mixing "a little brutality and a little diplomacy," had created a new artistic community in which "individual destiny reclaims and finds meaning in communal destiny."[75] Wigman held that "*Führertum* and acknowledgement of *Führertum* is a precondition of community" and hence of successful ensemble dance.[76] All this echoed central themes in Nazi thought – leadership, community, the will, struggle, race.[77]

With the Nazi seizure of power, Wigman moved to establish herself as the central figure in German dance. Within months Wigman and her Dance Community joined the Fighting League for German Culture (*Kampfbund für Deutsche Kultur*) and then the National Socialist Teachers' Association, and she was able until 1936 to secure substantial government funding for her school. Among other things, Wigman and eighty of her students and associates performed as part of the artistic program associated with the Olympic Games in Berlin in 1936.[78] Her success owed something to her willingness to echo Nazi ideas. Already in 1933, for example, she held that the future of dance lay with ensembles welded together into a "community" in service to an "idea"; but "community requires leadership [*Führerschaft*] and acknowledgement of leadership."[79] In an essay on "German Dance Art" of 1935, Wigman argued that it was "only natural and logical that the German, deeply shaken up" by the defeat in 1918 "poses the question of true German-ness also in the arts," and that "we artists identify today more than ever with the fate of our people" and would answer the "call of the blood, which has gone out to all of us." The influence of the new German dance around the world was, she reported, a "victory," and "If we ask how this victory was won, we discover that precisely that which is German in the best sense of the word has

[74] Mary Wigman, "Das Land ohne Tanz," *Tanzgemeinschaft* 1 (1929): 12, on the compact disk *Die Akte Wigman*, ed. Heide Lazarus (Cologne: Olms/Deutsches Tanz-Archiv, 2006).

[75] Vera Skoronel, "Mary Wigmans Führertum," *Tanzgemeinschaft* 2 (1930): 4, on *Die Akte Wigman*.

[76] Mary Wigman, "Gruppentanz/Regie," in Bach, ed., *Das Mary Wigman-Werk*, p. 45.

[77] For a particularly scathing assessment see Marion Kant, "Death and the Maiden: Mary Wigman in the Weimar Republic," in Alexandra Kolb, ed., *Dance and Politics* (New York: Peter Lang, 2010), pp. 119–143.

[78] Manning, *Ecstasy*, p. 147; Guilbert, *Danser*, pp. 157, 188; Marion Kant, "Mary Wigman – Die Suche nach der verlorenen Welt," *Tanzdrama* 25 (1994), pp. 15–17.

[79] Wigman, "Gruppentanz/Regie," p. 45.

triumphed.... The tragic, the heroic ... gave the new dance its German face."[80]

Critics and commentators were enthusiastic. One critic believed already in 1932 that other Germans danced, but only she had "made dance *German*." Another wrote in 1935 that her "greatness is her universality. She is not alone a Nordic: she belongs to mankind" – though her inspiration was "at bottom ... the nature worship deeply ingrained in the Teuton soul, the romantic religion of all Germanic feeling people."[81] Hans Brandenburg, writing in 1936, saw her and Laban as pioneers of a dance form that was "the opposite of individualism ... German dance was from the very beginning community dance, an artistic prefiguring of the *Volksgemeinschaft*" (a term common on the political Right for the ideologically unified racial nation) and "an expression of heroism, of readiness for sacrifice, of submission to a Leader."[82]

After 1936, support from the regime ebbed – possibly because Wigman had dragged her feet a little in dismissing her Jewish students and collaborators, probably because Nazi political purposes were better served by mass choreography for lay groups rather than solo or ensemble performance, but also simply because Nazi figures with more traditionalist tastes (above all Hitler and Heinrich Himmler) increasingly steered public policy toward support for the ballet and light entertainment, and away from the more emotionally intense, individualistic, and woman-centered dance form championed by Wigman. As propaganda minister Joseph Goebbels put it, "Dance must be buoyant and show beautiful female bodies."[83] The National Socialist Labor Front's "Strength Through Joy" organization, for example, ultimately hired Friderica Derra de Moroda (caught in Central Europe at the outbreak of the war) to lead a Nazi ballet company. But Wigman stayed in Germany and remained thoroughly patriotic throughout the war and its aftermath. She did operate briefly (and very successfully) in the Soviet zone between 1945 and 1949, but then fled to the West after finding that she did not have enough "Eastern" (*ostisch*) blood to make her peace with the Russians.[84]

[80] Mary Wigman, *Deutsche Tanzkunst* (Dresden: Carl Reissner, 1935), pp. 11–12, 15–16.
[81] Rudolf Ibel, "Die deutsche Tänzerin," *Der Kreis* 9 (1932): 693; Selden, *The Dancer's Quest*, p. 74.
[82] Hans Brandenburg, "Von deutscher Tanzkunst: Rückblick und Ausblick," in *Die tänzerische Situation unserer Zeit: Ein Querschnitt* (Dresden: Reissner, 1936), pp. 55, 57.
[83] Quoted in Kolb, *Performing*, p. 279. See Mary Wigman, "The New German Dance," in Virginia Stewart, ed., *Modern Dance* (New York: Dance Horizons, 1970 [1935], esp. pp. 20–21; Reynolds, "Dancing as a Woman," pp. 297–310.
[84] Dahms and Schroedter, eds., *Der Tanz*, p. 88; Kant, "Mary Wigman," p. 16.

Rudolf von Laban, as an ethnic Hungarian, could not play on the same racial notions as Wigman. But he achieved even greater success and importance in the Nazi state by stressing other ideological connections, particularly ideas about leadership and mass, a new form of religiosity, and antimodernism. Laban had long been at work on his own idiosyncratic pseudoreligious dance-centered worldview, which combined elements of occultism, hermeticism, Freemasonry, Theosophy, theories about the cosmic significance of rhythm, eugenics, back-to-nature antimodernism, nudism and physical culture, and pantheistic "vital Darwinist" theories about the universal soul that organized all of nature according to "molecular-rhythmic organizing principles," as revealed by the structure of crystals.[85] As early as 1915, Laban had written scornfully in a private letter of "woman's emancipation, democracy, sentimentality," and the "half-education of the masses," and suggested that the state should be run by "educated men, doctors, really wise people" rather than "socialists and rogues."[86] In 1920, he had published an impenetrably turgid but very successful book on *The World of the Dancer*, in which he informed the reader that today "people are physically, spiritually and intellectually stunted and distorted in the service of the false needs of [our] civilization." Above all the "suggestive power of words, of concepts" had convinced them that "unhealthy temptations and abstractions are valuable," while "everywhere we see the chaotic-utilitarian railroad tracks, telegraph-poles, and even the trees of the forest stand in rank and file." It was this that explained the "unfathomable inner emptiness" of a society plagued by "abstract constructions," "exaggerated intellectualism," "ugly lust," a "mistaken, unharmonious and unrhythmic way of life, pessimistic self-examination, mistrust toward others," "pathological brutality," "mendacity," "sick sensuality," "arrogance," "nervous anxiety," "impotent rancor," and a few other things.[87]

The Nazis ate this kind of thing up; and they were eager to make use of Laban's concept of the mass movement choir and movement festivals. Late in 1934 the Nazi government appointed him head of a new German Dance Theater (*Deutsche Tanzbühne*) organization, with the goal of uniting – and instrumentalizing – all dancers in Germany under centralized

[85] Marion Kant, "Annäherung und Kollaboration: Tanz und Weltanschauung im 'Dritten Reich,'" *Tanzjournal* 3 (2003): 17; Marion Kant, "Mittel zur Transzendenz," *Tanz-Journal* 1, no. 6 (2003): 15–22; Doerr, *Rudolf Laban*, pp. 84, 86.

[86] Evelyn Dörr, *Also, die Damen voran! Rudolf Laban in Briefen an Tänzer, Choreographen und Tanzpädagogen*, vol. I, 1912–1918 (Norderstedt: Books on Demand, 2013), pp. 135, 146.

[87] Rudolf von Laban, *Die Welt des Tänzers* (Stuttgart: Walter Seifert, 1920), pp. 137–138, 141, 152.

direction. After presiding over two successful dance festivals and a Nazified dance summer camp, he was appointed director of a new Master Academy (*Meisterwerkstätten*) for dance, with the aim of setting up a centralized state system of dance training. In 1936 he published an essay declaring that the time had come for dancers to "place our expressive powers ... in the service of the great tasks that our people are fulfilling, and to which our *Führer* points with unerring clarity."[88] In short, Laban was on the verge of establishing himself as the Nazi empire's dance *Führer*.

At that point, however, the wheels came off. Assigned to create a mass dance performance for the opening ceremonies of the Olympics in Berlin in 1936, Laban failed to come up with what the Nazis demanded. The Nazi Minister of Propaganda, Joseph Goebbels, vetoed his first two proposals for getting the conceptual content wrong, before finally approving a third in which the message – "leader and mass" – seemed to be right. But at a rehearsal for the 1,000 lay performers involved, it became apparent that the choreography was all wrong – too thoughtful, too individualistic, not sufficiently monumental. As Goebbels put it, the piece "wears our robes but really has nothing to do with us." It did not help that Laban had been a Freemason (a group the Nazis outlawed); that he had been living with a Jewish girlfriend when Hitler came to power; that he was disastrously bad with money, in his public functions as in his private life; and that he was a pacifist – having written in 1920, for example, of "the profit-hungry terroristic methods of warfare of our time."[89] Ironically, Laban now found himself accused of intellectualism, abstraction, and homosexuality. Fired from his official positions, he was systematically prevented from working for his former students as well.[90] He lived for a time from the charity of friends; in early 1938, impoverished, ill, and miserable, he was rescued by his former student Kurt Jooss and taken in by the dance institute at Dartington Hall, in England. Jooss was a political leftist, pacifist, and winner of the first choreography contest at the Archives internationales de la Danse with the anticapitalist and antiwar ballet *The Green Table* in 1932. He had to flee Germany for Dartington already in 1933, bringing with him some two dozen students and teachers from his school.[91]

[88] Rudolf von Laban, "Die deutsche Tanzbühne: Vorgeschichte und Ausblick," in *Die tänzerische Situation unserer Zeit: Ein Querschnitt* (Dresden: Reissner, 1936), p. 7.
[89] Laban, *Die Welt*, p. 133.
[90] Doerr, *Rudolf Laban*, pp. 164, 173, 169.
[91] Quotation in Laban, *Die Welt*, p. 139. See Karina and Kant, *Hitler's Dancers*, p. 18; Nicholas, *Dancing in Utopia*, p. 86; Suzanne K. Walther, *The Dance of Death: Kurt Jooss and the Weimar Years* (Chur: Harwood Academic, 1994); Doerr, *Rudolf Laban*, p. 180.

As the case of Jooss suggests, it was not only the radical Right that attracted dancers; some were drawn to the Left, as well. The Communist parties around Europe created their own nonprofessional "movement choirs" in the late 1920s and early 1930s; and in the United States, a Workers' Dance League sought to unite some dozen lay dance groups in New York and others in Boston, Chicago, and Philadelphia. For the Communist parties, dance was primarily an element in mass demonstrations of working-class solidarity; Communist groups focused on broad participation, and on the themes of struggle, oppression, solidarity, and revolution.[92]

Isadora Duncan is a revealing individual case of the tensions between this kind of political program and some of the ideas central to modern dance – tensions similar to those Wigman and Laban encountered. Sick – as she wrote to Soviet officials – of "bourgeois, commercial art" and lured by the promise of a school with 1,000 students and by "cock-and-bull stories about the destruction of the monetary system in Soviet Russia" (as one Soviet supporter put it), Duncan decided already in 1921 that she could best realize her dream of the "dance of the future" by going to Soviet Russia and teaching the children of the proletarian masses to dance. Europe was, she observed, "too hopelessly bourgeois ever to understand what I am really after," while in the new world being born all "men will be brothers, carried away by the great wave of liberation that has just been born in Russia." Under the guidance of her students there, ultimately "the children of the whole world will become a joyous, beautiful and harmonious dancing mass." Anatoly Lunacharsky, the Bolshevik commissar for art and education, was somewhat nonplussed by her enthusiasm, remarking shortly after her arrival that "Comrade Duncan is going through a phase of rather militant communism that sometimes, involuntarily, makes us smile." But she did start a school, and briefly won the approval of the upper Bolshevik hierarchy, and some state support – including quarters in part of a house confiscated from a prominent ballerina and her "ex-millionaire" husband.[93]

---

[92] Guilbert, *Danser*, pp. 55–56; Ellen Graff, *Stepping Left: Dance and Politics in New York City, 1928–1942* (Durham, NC: Duke University Press, 1997), pp. 7–8, 10. See also Lynn Garafola, *Of, By, and For the People: Dancing on the Left in the 1930s* (New York: Journal of the Society of Dance History Scholars, vol. 5, 1994).

[93] Draft of a letter to Lunacharsky; Ilya Shneider, "Pages from the Past," trans from *Moskva* October 1960 by Peter Golden, JRDD-IDC, folder 170, pp. 3, 16; Kurth, *Isadora*, pp. 413, 417, 428, 437; quotation in Macdougall, *Isadora*, p. 194.

This odd alliance of totalitarian communism and bourgeois utopian "mysticism" (as some Communist critics called Duncan's theories) did not last long. Duncan became involved with a self-destructive alcoholic hooligan poet, and was soon objecting strenuously to Lunacharsky's directives that "everything you do should be kept within the limits of the strictest decorum."[94] More to the point, it gradually became apparent that the Soviet authorities saw dance as part of a broader program of physical training for revolutionary militants, rather than a vehicle for universal joy and brotherhood. As Lunacharsky put it, the "social life of the masses" had to be shaped by an "instinctive respect for higher order and rhythm"; otherwise it would never create anything more than "happy noise and the colorful running around of people in festive costume. The festival has to be strictly organized, like everything else in this world."[95] Duncan left the Soviet Union in 1922; her student and adopted daughter Irma Duncan led the school until she was shouldered aside by the Soviet authorities in 1929, as the Stalinist system consolidated – under people who, as Irma put it, "were out to kill the very root of our dance" as free individual expression and turn it into mere "gymnastics for women and children."[96] Duncan left before things got that bad; but she had been in the USSR long enough to discover the difference between an anarchistic, free-spirited, creative artistic revolution and a totalitarian political one.

Totalitarian connections were not the only political commitments formed by modern dancers, however. In the 1920s the German Social Democratic Party and its associated labor unions, youth groups, sports organizations, and theater groups organized numerous movement choirs, which performed mass spectacles at party or associational functions as part of a broader workers' culture movement. Often, they used methods drawn from Laban's pioneering efforts or even in collaboration with him or his students and schools. And there was a strong contingent of modern dancers who were attracted to Social Democracy. One of the more innovative German dancers of the 1920s was Valeska Gert, who developed a kind of social realist and socially critical dance closely aligned with the democratic Left. Even more influential was Kurt Jooss, whose leftist and

[94] Quotation in Ilya Ilyich Schneider, *Isadora Duncan: The Russian Years* (London: MacDonald, 1968), p. 40; Isadora Duncan, "Come, Children, Let's Dance," in Franklin Rosemont, ed., *Isadora Speaks* (San Francisco: City Lights, 1981), p. 83.
[95] Quoted in Natalia Stüdemann, *Dionysos in Sparta: Isadora Duncan in Russland* (Bielefeld: Transcript, 2008), esp. pp. 124–128.
[96] Lillian Loewenthal, *The Search for Isadora: The Legend & Legacy of Isadora Duncan* (Pennington, NJ: Dance Horizons, 1993), pp. 113–117; Duncan, *Duncan Dancer*), pp. 321–322.

pacifist leanings earned him harassment and ultimately a Gestapo arrest warrant.[97] As the historian Mark Roseman has remarked, by the late 1920s, "[N]o left-wing festival was complete without its dance group and theater presentations." Roseman has given us an account of one remarkable socialist group centered in part on a dance school formed in 1925, which helped hide fugitive Jews quite late into the Nazi period.[98] In the United States, too, some dance groups were supported by trade unions, and there was considerable overlap between Left dance groups and the leading modern dance studios, particularly in New York. In Britain, Ruby Ginner had been involved in the women's suffrage movement, and Margaret Morris was a Labour Party activist.[99]

Not all dance was associated with any political position at all, of course. Ruth St. Denis remained committed to a nonpolitical, universalist vision of the potential of the dance to become a spiritual force for reconciliation. In the "dance of the future," she wrote in 1934,

> national and racial dissonances will be forgotten in the universal rhythm of love. We shall sense our unity with all peoples who are moving to that exalted rhythm.... The divine rhythm of creative love will flow in effortless ecstasy and beauty, encircling the world and embracing all humanity in one harmonious pattern of divine awareness and transcendent joy.[100]

Some dancers were attracted to political religions; others, like St. Denis, to the Religion of Love.

As the fate of Wigman's, Laban's, and Duncan's alliances with totalitarian regimes demonstrate, the religion of love was a kinder master than that of the state; and it would be wrong to see modern dance as somehow totalitarian in its essence. Some dancers certainly contributed to the appeal of totalitarian regimes, lending them an aura of normalcy or of cultural depth. But like other forms of modernism in the arts, dance had divergent political potentials. Wigman and Laban were opportunists

[97] Peter, *Valeska Gert*; Gert, *Ich bin eine Hexe*; Manning, *Ecstasy*, pp. 163–165; Kolb, *Performing*, pp. 170–185; Yvonne Hardt, *Politische Körper: Ausdruckstanz, Choreographien des Protests und die Arbeiterkulturbewegung in der Weimarer Republik* (Münster: Lit, 2004), esp. pp. 58, 248, 300; Burt, *Alien Bodies*, pp. 450–453.

[98] Mark Roseman, "Ein Mensch in Bewegung: Dore Jacobs (1894–1978), in *Essener Beiträge*, no. 114 (Essen: Klartext, 2002), pp. 73–109, and *A Past in Hiding* (New York: Metropolitan, 2001), pp. 231–238 (quotation p. 233). For another case see Yvonne Hardt, "*Ausdruckstanz* on the Left and the Work of Jean Weidt," in Susanne Franco and Marina Nordera, eds., *Dance Discourses* (New York: Routledge, 2007), p. 46.

[99] Fiona Macintosh, "The Ancient Greeks and the 'Natural'" and "Dancing Maenads in Early 20th-Century Britain," both in Carter and Fensham, eds., *Dancing Naturally*, pp. 55, 200.

[100] Kamae A. Miller, ed., *Wisdom Comes Dancing: Selected Writings of Ruth St. Denis on Dance, Spirituality, and the Body* (Seattle: PeaceWorks, 1997), pp. 55–56.

rather than convinced Nazis; and the image of Isadora Duncan as a total-itarian sounds more like the lead-in to a joke than to a fruitful histori-cal insight. These artists were certainly guilty of careerism and/or gross naiveté; but most of them simply tried to make use of politics, rather than being genuinely committed to political ideologies or movements. Like so many others, they got caught up in the blender of early twentieth-century European politics and did not get out unscathed.

It is easy to understand what made totalitarian regimes attractive to some modern dancers, however. The conceptual vocabulary of modern dance and of totalitarianism of the Left and the Right did share important common elements. Many modern dancers shared with fascism the fasci-nation with "blood." Many shared the revolutionary aspiration to remake the world – to rebel against and demolish inherited political, moral, social, and artistic forms. Many shared the utopian goal of remaking humanity, of creating as Duncan put it "the new people of the new world," with the instinct, for example, to make "every little detail in life, in clothing, every label on every box" beautiful.[101] And they participated in the broad societal discussion that made these concerns and aspirations sound plau-sible, even necessary. In short, modern dance was not just caught up in the blender of totalitarian politics, it was an integral part of the cultural matrix in which that blender was created.

5.5 European Dance and Colonial Nationalism

Duncan's sojourn in Soviet Russia was part of a broader pattern in mod-ern dance in the two or three decades after the outbreak of World War I. The war, its lingering impact on the European economy in the 1920s, and then the Great Depression all posed a terrible problem for European artists. The art market in Europe collapsed during the war, and the arts continued to struggle with financial challenges well into the 1920s – only to be devastated again in the early 1930s. One obvious solution was to "export" one's art to other parts of the world; and many of the modern dancers did that starting in the 1910s, touring in the United States, Latin America, South and East Asia, and the Middle East.

In some important cases, this meant re-export to the United States: Four of Isadora Duncan's six tours of the United States took place during and after the war, and tours in the United States were important sources of

---

[101] Ilya Shneider, "Pages from the Past," trans. from *Moskva* October 1960 by Peter Golden, JRDD-IDC, folder 170, p. 7.

revenue for some European dancers in the 1920s and the Depression. Rather strikingly, however, in other cases it meant that modern dancers were exporting dance to the very societies or cultures they claimed to have been representing when they performed "Oriental" or ethnographic dance. This seems like a rather awkward moment, because they had largely invented the non-European dances they performed. But in practice it turned out that it *wasn't* awkward. Modern dance, including in its faux-ethnic mode, was very successful as a cultural export. More than that, in some cases modern dancers were welcomed with open arms by cultural nationalists in non-European societies because their performances seemed to legitimize the artistic traditions of peoples striving to assert their cultural autonomy against the very North Atlantic societies from which these dancers came. In short, in the two decades between the wars modern dancers became contributors to the culture of resistance to European hegemony.

An early example is Tórtola Valencia. Again, we know nothing certain about Valencia's provenance, but she claimed to be Spanish – in fact, to have Castilian "blood" from her father and Andalusian blood from her mother. In other accounts, her mother was a Gypsy from Seville and her father Catalán. In any case, she "returned" to Spain to perform in 1911. This was in a sense an early example of the export of modern dance, because Spain at that time was regarded as being – in both cultural and socioeconomic terms – on the margin of Europe. Audiences in Madrid were relatively unfamiliar with the movement idiom of modern dance, and newspaper reviewers reported initial skepticism; audiences found her performance "absurd" and too closely related to "circus acrobatics," and they "protested noisily." But Valencia was picked up and lionized by Spanish modernist intellectuals – what one called "an intelligent minority, a group of artists and literati" who "immediately saw in the dancer a unique, exceptional artist." They secured the triumph of art over "barbarism," and Valencia became a great critical and commercial success.[102]

This success was surprising because there was at the time a well-established international dance idiom called "Spanish" dance – which included, for example, flamenco, fandango, bolero, and corrido. Some internationally influential and successful modern dancers worked in this

---

[102] "Las Grandes Bailarinas Españolas," *Mundo Gráfico*, December 13, 1911; Tomas Borrás, "El arte de la danza: Tórtola de Valencia," *España Nueva*, December 14, 1911; Frederico García Sanchiz, "Tórtola ... de Triana," *España Libre*, December 6, 1911; Kurro Kastañares, "'Tórtola' triunfante," *España Libre*, December 12, 1911, all clippings in MAE, Fonds Tortola Valencia, L3.

genre. Valencia did *not* perform in that style; on her first arrival in Spain, in fact, she performed primarily "Indian" dances. Within about a year, however, she announced that real Andalusian and Gypsy dancers didn't stamp and stomp and click castanets, as was done in mere commercial café dance. She was studying "the noble primitive dance of Andalucía, which is all grace and rhythm." Real Spanish dancers, it turned out, danced like Orientals – or at least like Tórtola Valencia pretending to be Oriental. These dances, she claimed, expressed "the soul of Spain."[103]

An important part of the background to this story was that there was at the time an intellectual movement of pan-Latinism in Spain, Italy, France, and Latin America. Particularly in the wake of the defeat of Spain by the United States in 1898, the extraordinary expansion of British power (including in the Mediterranean, for example with the occupation of Cyprus in 1878 and Egypt in 1882), and of growing British, American, and German economic penetration of Latin America, the pan-Latinists argued that all the Latin peoples shared certain ethnic or civilizational qualities and gifts, and that they had to find a way to bring those gifts to fruition in the modern world or end up being dominated by these "Teutonic" peoples. As an exponent of the very latest in cultural modernism, but in a distinctively Spanish-Latin key, Valencia offered an attractive recipe for people interested in these ideas. They celebrated, for example, her extraordinary fire, passion, and energy – a raw physicality quite distinct from the more ethereal characteristics of Northern European dancers. Thus, for example, the theater correspondent in Paris for the Madrid arts journal *Mundial* compared her earthy, passionate style favorably to Adorée Villany's "Protestant beauty, rigid and prudish."[104]

With the outbreak of the war Valencia went on tour in Latin America – first in 1916, then for a period of five years between 1921 and 1925, and again in 1930. For the most part, the story of those tours recapitulated that of her success in Spain – initial skepticism, complaints that she wasn't really a "Spanish" dancer, the rallying of the intellectuals, and eventual commercial success. There was, however, one extraordinary episode during Valencia's visits to Peru in the 1920s. While there, Valencia decided that she would develop an "Ancient Inca War Dance of Peru." In the 1920s there was a very important "indigenist" movement among Latin American nationalists. *Indigenismo* argued that the cultures and peoples of Latin

---

[103] Solrac, *Tortola Valencia*, p. 16; XXX, "Tórtola Valencia," *La Publicidad*, January 22, 1912, clipping in in MAE, Fonds Tortola Valencia, L3.
[104] "El Teatro in Paris," *Mundial* 2 (1913): 475.

America formed a new *raza* or race that combined elements of Hispanic and Amerindian culture and tradition. Acknowledging, understanding, celebrating, and cultivating this fusion was the key to developing a vital, dynamic, autonomous, and united culture and society – one that could withstand the cultural imperialism of Europeans and Americans. The Peruvian poet and socialist José Mariátegui, for example, celebrated indigenous Peruvian culture as the "foundation of our nationality ... without the Indian, Peruvianness is not possible."[105]

Valencia set out to appeal to this *indigenista* sentiment. She studied Inca art in the museums of Lima, particularly the private collection of the extremely wealthy landowner, politician, and cosmopolitan patron of the arts Rafael Larco-Herrera; she discussed the Inca heritage with various *indigenista* intellectuals; and she first performed her dance at the annual "Fiesta de la Raza" in Lima in 1925, alongside a Spanish guitarist and two Peruvian poets. The president of the republic, the city council, the diplomatic corps, the military leadership, and much of the social elite of the city attended.[106] For this dance, Valencia broke with the convention of using European classical music, dancing instead to "authentic Incan folkloric music, played on Andean flutes" by two local musicians. The dance was a great success. The nationalist novelist of the Inca past Augusto Aguirre Morales wrote that it was "heroic, conquering like the hosts of Huayna Capac," and possessed a "truth greater than mere exactitude, the truth of deep feeling.... She resurrects in ... her barbaric poses, generous and sensual, the truth of this race." Another report held that she had achieved a "choreographic poem" of the "whole soul of a race."[107] She was urged to perform it abroad as a representation of Peruvian culture; intellectuals published essays encouraging Peruvians to recover their own "ancient civilization" with "acceptance and love" rather than imitating "poor collapsing Europe"; and a publicity photograph for the performance was used in 1929 as a centerpiece for Peru's exhibition at the 1929 Pan-American Exhibition in Seville (see Figure 5.4).[108]

---

[105] Jesús Chavarría, *José Carlos Mariátegui and the Rise of Modern Peru, 1890–1930* (Albuquerque: University of New Mexico Press, 1979), p. 91.

[106] "En el Teatro del Forero: La Fiesta de la Raza," *La Prensa* (Lima), October 11, 1925 and "De Teatros," *El Tiempo*, October 13, 1925, clippings in MAE, Fonds Tortola Valencia, L14, fols. 335, 337.

[107] Augusto Aguirre Morales, "Tórtola Valencia y la musica Incaica," *Mundial* (Lima), June 19, 1925; "La beneficio de Tórtola Valencia en el Forero," *El Tiempo* (Lima), September 19, 1925, both clippings in MAE, Fonds Tortola Valencia, L14, fol. 284, 325.

[108] "Tórtola Valencia Triunfa en Lima," *La Raza*, October 15, 1925 and Antonio de Hoyos y Vincent, "America: Rutas Ideales de la Bailarina de los Pies Desnudas, *La Esfera13*, February 6, 1926, clippings in MAE, Fonds Tortola Valencia, L15; Clayton, "Touring History," p. 46.

Figure 5.4 Tórtola Valencia, ancient Inca princess, 1925

The Peruvian political, social and cultural elite were overwhelmingly people of predominantly Spanish descent; and the spectacle of a European artist recovering "their" Inca past for them seemed a little odd even at the time. But explanations of her achievement echoed the theory of dance and acting familiar from the period before 1914. One reviewer conceded, for example, that "her creation does not reconstruct Inca history ... [instead] she expresses the concept that the artist has of the soul of our ancestors." Another claimed more hopefully that "her penetrating spirit, after long study and after her own intelligent observations, has penetrated our past and brought it to life." Valencia offered a more mystical interpretation. A local collector had given her, she claimed, an authentic Inca war costume to use for her performance; when she put it on she "felt the spirit of the ancient owner"; and during the performance the "spirit of the Inca guided my steps."[109] This meant that Valencia was, by her own reckoning, a South Asian reincarnated as a (perhaps half-Gypsy) Spaniard and raised in London, possessed by a five-hundred-year-old Inca spirit. Extraordinarily, that worked for her audience.

The example of Ruth St. Denis's tour of India in 1926 is no less remarkable. As we have seen, St. Denis first rose to stardom performing primarily faux-Indian dances. She did hire Indian extras and musicians, and may have learned from them some genuine Indian dance idiom; but her dances were a mishmash of various Indian and Western elements. She did not actually travel to India until 1926, when she went on an extended tour of Asia. St. Denis's autobiography, which for the period of this trip was cast in the form of diary entries, is a remarkable testament to the power and contradictions of make-believe. Upon seeing Mount Fuji rise above the sea as her ship approached Japan, she wrote "I am as one returned to a home from which I have been exiled." But after three months of touring there, she reported that "Japan has filled my aesthetic sense with a curiously complete beauty, but my soul is untouched. I am waiting for India." In China, she discovered "the core and meaning of the spiritual life of China" and developed some dances on that basis; but neither there nor in Burma did she feel inspiration or enthusiasm. When she finally got to India, though, she was horrified by the poverty and suffering she saw – for example when, on the way to a popular festival at the Ganges, she encountered long lines of beggars, "the most horrible array of human beings we had ever witnessed ... I was so depressed ... I sat

---

[109] "Tórtola Valencia nos habla de su excursion por América y de sus projectos," *El Dia Grafica*, March 31, 1926, clipping in MAE, Fonds Tortola Valencia, L15.

for an hour without moving [in her hotel room]; for it seemed to me ... that God had forsaken this world.... If twenty years before I had seen any such sight there would have been no Radha, and perhaps no career."[110] Watching the wives of the Nizam of Hyderabad being "herded" into a purdah box on her stage and behaving "like ill-mannered servant girls on a holiday" made her exclaim "Alas, our dreams! Alas our illusions of oriental beauty and splendor."[111]

Indian dance traditions – both popular and religious – had been under attack for decades by Western and Westernizing reformers who regarded them as degraded and often as a form of prostitution; and traditional Indian dance was virtually invisible in urban India by the 1920s. St. Denis did eventually manage to track down a genuine nautch (dancer) in her sixties, "one of the few survivors of a great dance tradition." She was a little disappointed, however, to find her ensconced in her French salon with crystal chandeliers, a sari imported from Paris, and "at the least, fifty thousand dollars' worth of jewelry." It wasn't until she got to Java that she at last found "all that I had hoped for for so many years from the East" – rather tellingly in an experience that gave her "that feeling of unreality, of the *Arabian Nights* come true, of being in another world!" This at last, she believed, "was the Other-Other Land" she had sought. Her conclusion, aboard ship back across the Pacific, was this:

> I do not know what I expected to find in the Orient, in India.... Perhaps the outward manifestation of secret things in my own nature.... [But] I am beginning to see that I already possessed the soul of India right here in America ... that the India I had adored ... existed now for me much more intensely in the depth of my own spirit than in the poor huddled beggars lining the roadsides, or in the politicians shouting in the assemblies, or in mobs silently resisting the government.[112]

Having seen the real thing, she preferred the fake. The historian Timothy Mitchell – writing not about dance but about European perceptions of the "Orient" in general – has given us a rather precise description of St. Denis's experience: To Europeans, he found, the real Orient "appeared to suffer from an essential lack" when compared to their preconceived notions, derived from representations of "the Orient" in Western culture. Specifically, the real Orient "lacked those effects they knew as order and meaning"; instead, it was messy, chaotic, diverse, unintelligible, human.

---

[110] St. Denis, *An Unfinished Life*, pp. 263, 274, 277, 285–286.
[111] "India," unpublished ms. in JRDD, Ruth St. Denis Papers, folder 228, p. 24.
[112] St. Denis, *An Unfinished Life*, pp. 286, 294–295, 299, 301–302, 292.

In one typical response "the Orient ... became a place the European felt he 'already knew by heart'" – and the real "Orient" did not need to be consulted for its own sense and meaning.[113]

What is extraordinary though is that St. Denis and her company got a very warm reception in India, including for her "Indian" dances. Ticket sales were good, and at least English-language reviews were very positive. One English-language Indian paper in Rangoon (in Burma) reported that a "more faithful representation of Indian dancing has probably seldom, if ever been seen here." A Calcutta paper reported that "[h]er rendering of the Indian dances is of a very high order.... She has not only caught the Indian spirit, she is experiencing the joy of that spirit; and she is imparting that joy to her spectators."[114] Doris Humphrey, who toured with the company, reported of St. Denis's first performance of her "Indian" dances that the "balcony and gallery, full of East Indians, went wild with excitement ... Miss Ruth was the darling of the people." Jane Sherman, another dancer in the company, wrote to her mother that "I will never forget the roar of approval" – though she was disturbed by her later realization that it might have been "tinged by the nationalism that was burgeoning among the oppressed Indians."[115] The great nationalist poet, educator, and advocate for the revival of Indian dance traditions, Rabindranath Tagore, visited the company backstage, and even urged St. Denis to stay in India and teach dance in Calcutta (and would later appear with her in a joint dance-poetry recital in New York, in 1930). The leading Indian nationalists Motilal Nehru (father of Jawaharlal, later first prime minister of independent India) and Sarojini Naidu were enthusiastic backstage visitors as well.[116]

In fact, St. Denis's appearances and those of other Western dancers, such as Maud Allan already in 1914, Roshanara in 1915, or Anna Pavlova in 1928, helped to spark a renaissance of Indian traditional dance – or a flourishing of invented dance traditions – among Indian cultural nationalists, particularly those close to the Theosophical Society. By the mid-1930s, Rukmini Devi Arundale, wife of the president of the Theosophical Society, was performing Indian dance and was president of a new

---

[113] Timothy Mitchell, "Orientalism and the Exhibitionary Order," in Nicholas B. Dirks, ed., *Colonialism and Culture* (Ann Arbor: University of Michigan Press, 1992), pp. 310–311.

[114] St. Denis, *An Unfinished Life*, pp. 283, 285.

[115] Humphrey, *Doris Humphrey*, p. 52; Sherman, *Soaring*, p. 91.

[116] Sherman, *Soaring*, p. 92; Coorlawala, "Ruth St. Denis," p. 142; Shawn, *One Thousand*, p. 188. See also Pallabi Chakravorty, *Bells of Change: Kathak Dance, Women and Modernity in India* (Calcutta: Seagull, 2008), pp. 42–55; "Tagore in Recital," *New York Times*, December 15, 1930, p. 5.

International Academy of the Arts in Madras, funded by the Theosophical Society. There South Indian dance was codified and taught as Bharata Natyam.[117] Many Indian cultural nationalists would ultimately reject the conventions of Westernized "Oriental" dance as practiced, for example, by Uday Shankar, an Indian performer who spent ten years in Britain, enjoyed a successful collaboration with Anna Pavlova, and opened a competing (and eventually failed) dance school in North India in 1934, funded by the same British American philanthropic family that owned the dance center at Dartington Hall.[118] Yet the program of the Indian dance renaissance was strikingly similar to that of modern dance in Europe; in particular, it sought to recover authentic traditions allegedly derived from deep antiquity, in order – as one historian of nationalism puts it – to "suggest the nation's antiquity and continuity, its noble heritage and the drama of its ancient glory and regeneration."[119] Its champions studied ancient Indian sculpture and Sanskrit texts to recreate a putative classical dance tradition and reclaim it from the degeneracy of modern times. They sought to free dance traditions from disreputable sexual connotations, making it an art that could be appreciated (and practiced) by middle-class urban progressives. And at least in some cases the independent female dancer emerged as a respectable artist in her own right, not merely a practitioner of an art controlled by male patrons, priests, and directors.

In the process they created a dance form that, ultimately, the newly independent Indian state would support aggressively in the 1940s and 1950s as the living legacy of India's "classical" and ancient greatness, the "gold standard of India's heritage and future identity," as one dance historian has put it.[120] This development illustrates a process described by the historian of religion Tomoko Masuzawa: Indians "came to articulate their own identity by using concepts and ideas initially forged by others"; that process aimed to make them "irreversibly modern" but "also entailed a fresh assessment and selective recuperation and revivification of the past."[121] In fact, in the same period the institutional arrangements

[117] Joan L. Erdman, "Dance Discourses: Rethinking the History of the 'Oriental Dance,'" in Gay Morris, ed., *Moving Words: Re-Writing Dance* (New York: Routledge, 1996), pp. 288–303; "Minute Visits in the Wings," *New York Times*, September 12, 1915, p. X3; Ram Gopal, "Pavlova and the Indian Dance," in *Pavlova: A Biography*, ed. A. H. Franks (New York: Da Capo, 1979), pp. 98–110.

[118] Prathana Purkayastha, "Dancing Otherness: Nationalism, Transnationalism, and the Work of Uday Shankar," *DRJ* 44, no. 1 (2012): 69–92.

[119] Anthony D. Smith, *National Identity* (Reno: University of Nevada Press, 1991), p. 92.

[120] Nicholas, *Dancing in Utopia*, p. 124.

[121] Tomoko Masuzawa, *The Invention of World Religions* (Chicago: University of Chicago Press, 2005), pp. 282–283. See also Janet O'Shea, "Dancing through History and Ethnography: Indian

and rituals that had actually supported and constituted the art form, historically, were demolished. Historically Indian dance traditions had been cultivated as part of a system of patronage of temples by the political and social elite, who had been able to claim entertainment, ceremonial, and sometimes also sexual services from the dancers. This was regarded by nationalists as a degenerate form of true Indian classical dance, and was abolished by law in 1947.[122] Having seen the real thing, Indian cultural nationalists too preferred to reinvent it.

In the cases of both Valencia and St. Denis, cultural nationalists welcomed the effort of foreign performers to express the "soul" of their culture. We could read this as an instance of the involuntary subservient mentality of colonial (or neocolonial) nationalists – happy to have their own national past recognized and validated by someone from the imperial metropole. But one review of Tórtola Valencia's Inca dance suggests a different reading. "Since no one has understood the whole soul of the Orient as she has, is there anything extraordinary about the fact that she has also brought to life in her own soul that of our glorious Inca race?" Others had tried, but had created only "ridiculous parodies.... It took a woman of the mentality and spirit of Tórtola Valencia to give them" (the "moving and virile dances" of the Incas) "the stamp of nobility and force that is theirs." In the form she had given them, they "have what it will take to cause a sensation among the European public" – thus proving the worth and dignity of the Inca past and the Peruvian nation.[123] Another argued that "she possesses, as no one else, the secret of taking on ... the whole spirit" of another people.[124] These reviewers cast Valencia as a kind of spiritual antenna, as a sensitive soul with the ability to grasp and represent alien and ancient cultures *generally*. And in fact, ultimately Valencia's repertoire included dozens of faux-ethnic dances – Greek, Mexican, Chilean, Peruvian, Spanish, Arab, Indian, African, Hawai'ian, and so on (see Figure 5.5).[125] Similarly, Ruth St. Denis danced primarily faux-Indian but also Greek,

Classical Dance and the Performance of the Past," in Theresa Jill Buckland, ed., *Dancing from Past to Present: Nation, Culture, Identities* (Madison: University of Wisconsin Press, 2006), esp. p. 131.
[122] Amrit Srinivasan, "Reform and Revival: The Devadasi and Her Dance," *Economic and Political Weekly* 20, no. 44 (1985): 1869–1876. On official policy toward dance see Pallabi Chakravorty, "Dancing into Modernity: Multiple Narratives of India's Kathak Dance," *DRJ* 38 (2006): 115–136.
[123] "Teatros y artistas," *El Comercio* (Lima), September 19, 1925, clipping in MAE, Fonds Tórtola Valencia, L15.
[124] Antonio de Hoyos y Vinent, "America: Rutas Ideales de la Bailarina des los Pies Desnudos," *La Esfera*, February 6, 1926, clipping in MAE, Fonds Tórtola Valencia, L15.
[125] Clayton, "Touring History," p. 37.

LA TÓRTOLA VALENCIA EN ESPAÑA

Figure 5.5 The many ethnic identities of Tórtola Valencia, 1911

Cambodian, Japanese, Chinese, Ceylonese, and Javanese dances.[126] One Indian commentator on St. Denis's performances in India remarked that it was "a pity that the soul of the East in its spiritual expression

---

[126] Denis, *Unfinished*, pp. 301–302.

should be left for the artists of another land to reveal"; but the point is that he believed that she *did* reveal it.[127]

These performers' success in this role tells us something important about the idea of identity in this period. Everyone in the modern world seems to have been certain that they had an identity, something essential about them and their nation that was vital, noble, legitimate, and authentic. If you didn't have an identity, you were nobody. But it was difficult to know what that identity was – it took hard work. Much of the historical scholarship on the modern concept of identity relies on terms like "the invention of tradition," or the "construction" of identities; and invention or construction – making things up – requires imaginative labor.[128] Having built a language of identity (of "blood" and "soul") and a technique for portraying it (the technique of the "magic if") in the earliest phase of modern dance in Europe, a number of modern dancers were able to cast themselves in effect as foreign consultants in this work of invention. They could market themselves as, so to speak, identity experts. As Ruth St. Denis put it, there "is no mode of study more thorough or effective than the effort to impersonate an alien humanity," than the "sympathetic relationship ... that inevitably grows out of an artistic ability to change one's skin." This was a technique, she believed, that often yielded more insight than living among those "alien" people because it established genuine "depth of spiritual understanding" unclouded by merely quotidian experience. The modern dancers were adept at this form of study.[129]

In all this, the modern dancers were adopting a posture a bit like that of psychoanalysts, though for a whole culture rather than for individual patients. They were not telling people what to be and do. They were just listening to them – to their past, their artifacts, their unconscious or forgotten feelings and traditions – and helping them to discover who they already were. Their posture, implicitly, was of allies making themselves useful in the self-liberation of non-European peoples from the cultural blackmail implicit in colonialism: You are only civilized if you are like us. Instead, their message was: You are only free if you are like yourself.

---

[127] Sherman, *Soaring*, p. 92.
[128] E. J. Hobsbawm and Terence O. Ranger, *The Invention of Tradition* (Cambridge: Cambridge University Press, 1983); Benedict Anderson, *Imagined Communities: Reflections on the Origins and Spread of Nationalism* (London: Verso, 1991).
[129] "India," unpublished ms. in JRDD, Ruth St. Denis Papers, folder 228, p. 27.

5.6 Dance and Therapy: Psychoanalysis, Occupational Therapy, PTSD

It may well be that some modern dancers understood dance in this way because they had experienced something quite similar in their own internal lives – the discovery of who they were through dance. As they described it, after all, dance was a search for liberation and expression of the innermost self. Perhaps the most telling case was that of Rudolf von Laban, who experienced precisely this kind of liberation at the outset of his extraordinary career as a dance teacher, and as the psychological precondition and foundation for his success. In his younger years, Laban struggled to find his feet financially and professionally. After enjoying a rather dissolute period as a student funded by his family, he fell on hard times and worked for some years as a graphic artist, a magazine salesman, and a bookkeeper, perennially broke and itinerant. Ultimately, tortured and paralyzed by depressive states, in 1912 he checked himself into a sanatorium. Guided by a sympathetic psychiatrist, he discovered that he was not a "sickly being" and a failure, but a man of "especially refined artistic nature" who had been sabotaged by the authoritarian methods and conventional expectations of his father, a military man who expected his son to follow in his footsteps. After some months of treatment including particularly carefully dosed physical exercise, Laban emerged as (in his own words) a "strong, self-confident and ambitious artist." His letters reveal him to have been something of a Nietzschean amoralist and megalomaniac; but his newfound sense of identity and self-assurance did make him an extraordinarily effective cultural entrepreneur. Curiously, he characterized this transformation as the product of a "complete regeneration of the blood."[130]

This potential of modern dance became clearer after the war. In his book of 1923 on *The Dance of Life*, Havelock Ellis would summarize the purpose of Hans Vaihinger's philosophy of "As If" in terms rather similar to that of psychotherapy, remarking that Vaihinger's message was that we "make our own world" through useful fictions, and "when we make it awry, we can remake it, approximately truer … to the facts."[131] By 1941, the great American dancer and choreographer Martha Graham had reduced the message to a pithy formula: "Power means to become what one is."[132]

---

[130] Dörr, *Also, die Damen voran!*, pp. 41, 25, 44.
[131] Ellis, *The Dance of Life*, p. 103.
[132] Martha Graham, "A Modern Dancer's Primer for Action" (1941), in Selma Jeanne Cohen, ed., *Dance as a Theater Art* (New York: Dodd, Mead 1974), p. 140.

Some of Graham's students experienced the training they received from her in precisely this way. Dorothy Bird, for example, recalled that while preparing to perform a Graham composition about grief the "most amazing transformation took place in me ... I was releasing my own agonizing suppressed emotions. I could at last express feelings I had never allowed to surface before." This psychological process exactly echoed both Vaihinger's conception of the usefulness of fiction and the theory of theatrical training that grew (at least partially) from it: The "movement was strictly choreographed," Bird remarked, but because its effect depended on accessing genuine feelings and potentials in the performers, "it retained the appearance of total spontaneity."[133]

In fact, in the 1920s dance or ideas derived from dance were built into therapeutic programs as a means of helping various categories of troubled people recover their balance. That connection grew out of one of the most important postulates of modern dance: That in dance, one found one's essential self.

A good example is Gertrud Falke. Married to a Jewish professor of international law, she emigrated with him to Spain in 1933, where he soon died of heart failure. With three half-Jewish children, she could not make a life back in Germany; so she moved on to England, where the Dartington Hall institute took her in and eventually paid for her training in occupational therapy. She wound up teaching relaxation techniques to schizophrenics, shell-shock victims, neurotics, and asthmatics; her techniques eventually returned to Germany as one element of a form of movement therapy used in psychotherapy. With that, she had come full circle from her days as a dance teacher in Hamburg, where "the aim for me was the release of creativity and spontaneity" and to encourage her students to do "something really worth-while – to find oneself."[134] Margaret Morris is another case. She eventually moved on from teaching dance to work in postnatal and postoperative exercise rehabilitation, a collaboration with the National Council for Physical Fitness, and eventually fitness programs for the British army, before ultimately forming the National Ballet of Scotland after World War II.[135] Sent M'ahesa/Elsa von Carlberg settled in Sweden in the 1930s and ran a convalescent home for the mentally ill

[133] Dorothy Bird, "Martha," in Robert Gottlieb, ed., *Reading Dance: A Gathering of Memoirs, Reportage, Criticism, Profiles, Interviews, and Some Uncategorizable Extras* (New York: Pantheon, 2008), p. 736.
[134] Gertrud Falke Heller, "From Dance to Psychotherapy," from Charlotte Selver Foundation *Bulletin*, no. 11 (1983), clipping in DTAK, Inventory no. 10, Gertrud and Ursula Falke, II.2.7.
[135] Hastie, "Margaret Morris," pp. 170–171.

in the countryside near Stockholm.[136] In the United States, by 1942 the dancer Marian Chace – a graduate of the Denishawn school – was using dance therapy to help in the treatment of soldiers suffering from posttraumatic stress disorder ("shell shock") in a hospital in Washington, D.C.[137]

Dance could become therapy not only for individuals, however, but also for whole societies. A good case is Ruby Ginner, founder of the school of Revived Greek Dance in Britain. Ginner argued that dance training could be a therapeutic antidote to certain pervasive negative aspects of modern life. People in industrial society, she believed, faced unrelenting "nerve-tension" in the workplace, where individually paced autonomous labor had given way to mechanization; they dealt with a relentlessly hectic "pace of living" in daily affairs; they had to master the "clamor and complexity" of the media sphere and public life; and the "natural physical rhythms of mankind are being slowly crushed out of existence" as people took trains rather than walked, worked to the clock rather than the sun or the seasons, and abandoned the "free, glorious, and rhythmic movement of the body" for the "Speed and Noise" of machine civilization. The Revived Greek Dance could help compensate for all that, by offering a "system of normal, sanely-balanced movement," one that could foster "harmony between mind and body ... serenity of the spirit through the beauty" of the body, rest to tired eyes, and better sleep. It would also foster "control of action, restraint of passions, the renunciation of the self" and "desire to serve the community" through the experience of collaborative performance.[138]

There was a similar development in France, where Irène Popard's "harmonic gymnastics" (among other similar systems) offered a balanced movement training "synonymous," as the dance historian Jacqueline Robinson writes, "with health and grace, a physical education from which the brutality and competitiveness of sport were excluded, a proper, well-mannered artistic activity." Popard claimed her system was not a form of dance at all because "its sole aim is a healthy mind in a healthy body."

[136] Brygida Ochaim, "Biographien," in Brygida Ochaim and Claudia Balk, *Varieté-Tänzerinnen um 1900: Vom Sinnenrausch zur Tanzmoderne* (Frankfurt: Stroemfeld/Roter Stern, 1998), p. 141.

[137] See Laurice D. Nemetz, "Moving with Meaning: The Historical Progression of Dance/Movement Therapy," in Stephanie L. Brooke, ed., *Creative Arts Therapies Manual* (Springfield, IL: Charles C. Thomas, 2006), p. 103; Martha Schwieters, "Marian Chace: The Early Years in Life and Art," in Susan L. Sandel, Sharon Chaiklin, and Ann Lohn, eds., *Foundations of Dance/Movement Therapy: The Life and Work of Marian Chace* (Columbia, MD: Marian Chace Memorial Fund, 1993), pp. 3–11. For an early example of a belief in the therapeutic benefits of dance see Lady Constance Stewart Richardson, *Dancing, Beauty and Games* (London: Arthur L. Humphreys, 1913).

[138] Ginner, *The Revived Greek Dance*, pp. 14, 17–21, 67.

Nevertheless, it was clearly influenced by Delsartean tradition, Dalcroze's eurhythmics, and Isadora Duncan. And as Robinson remarks, its aim was to help restore and strengthen "the moral and physical health of a community ravaged by war."[139] Meanwhile Renée Kintzel offered training in "redemptory dance" as "one of the most complete, reliable, and effective means of achieving the purification, regeneration and betterment of humanity," and published books urging parents to teach their children to move gracefully and maintain good posture to cultivate self-awareness, self-discipline, and "spiritual culture."[140]

It was not only modern dance that played this kind of role in France, however. As the dance historian Ilyana Karthas has shown, in the 1920s and 1930s ballet became the focus for a very self-conscious and deliberate "recovery" of French national tradition and identity. Challenged by the success of the Ballets Russes just before the war and into the 1920s, the French ballet community was revitalized by a return to what were regarded as "classical" ballet traditions – the very traditions that, so it was argued, the Russians had preserved since the early nineteenth century and then re-exported to France starting in 1909.[141] Ironically, two Russians – the critic André Levinson and the ballet director Serge Lifar – were critical to this effort to "revive" the explicitly "French" ballet. Levinson, for example, argued in a 1923 article titled "For the French Ballet" that it was necessary to "recreate an art of French dance," to "express with clarity the essential matters of the soul," and to "recover the complete and normal expression of the national spirit in its plastic form."[142]

These Russians played for France a role similar to that played by Ruth St. Denis for India. As Karthas points out, this development reveals "the potential for ballet to serve as a vehicle for any national identity and spirit" – just as modern dance did. That potential was enhanced by ballet's own discovery in the 1920s of "absolute" dance, free of any specific folkloric or narrative content – what Levinson called "the intrinsic beauty of the dance step, its innate quality, its aesthetic reason for being."[143] In fact, the former Ballets Russes star Anna Pavlova was at least as important in the "revival" of Indian dance in this period as was Ruth St. Denis,

---

[139] Robinson, *Modern Dance in France*, pp. 30–31.
[140] Ibid., pp. 82–83.
[141] See, e.g., Lifar, *Serge Diaghilev*, p. 177.
[142] Karthas, *When Ballet Became French*, passim and particularly pp. 91, 115–116, 123, 125–126, 129–130 (quotation), 180.
[143] Andrei Lewinson, "Technik und Geist: Bemerkungen zum 'klassischen' Tanz," in Paul Stefan, ed., *Tanz in dieser Zeit* (Vienna: Universal-Edition, 1926), p. 36.

particularly through her influence on Rukmini Devi Arundale and on Uday Shankar. By the 1920s and 1930s, then, increasingly it was dance as a whole, and not just "modern" dance, that was coming to be seen as a means of finding oneself – as an individual, but also as part of a national community of "blood."[144]

5.7 Dancing Democracy

The revaluation of ballet in France may have been influenced by the fact that Germany was the epicenter of modern dance in the 1920s. In fact, André Levinson offered a blistering critique of German modern dance in 1929, observing that too many of Mary Wigman's dances were just ugly and overwrought. The "dancer's eyes exclaim, her fingers flare; her body writhes with terror; she squirms on the ground, stamps furiously, collapses exhausted." As for Laban and other "gymnasiarchs," they seemed to want to "obliterate individuality ... imitating the monstrous rhythms of machinery by their rectilinear alignments and the automatism of their 'Robot'-like gestures." In either case, the "unsmiling and unremitting conviction" of it all was just too much. It made one want to see something pretty and graceful.[145] There may have been a similar political implication to Ruby Ginner's advocacy of a moderate variety of "Greek" dance that stressed grace and harmony. In her manifesto for this style, published in 1933, Ginner argued explicitly for using the "moral reflex" of movement to teach children to "restrain evil desires" and encourage "beautiful and sane" ones. But her rejection of "Spartan" methods on the grounds that "the constant repression of natural desires eventually made this race hard, narrow, and arrogant" was probably – in 1933 – a deliberate implicit reference to Hitler's Germany.[146] And within Germany, too, the left-wing dancer Valeska Gert largely agreed. The problem with Wigman, she wrote already in 1926, was that she was self-absorbed, mired in mystical and spiritual angst, and seemed to think that "dance performances must smell like sour sweat, [and] be ethical, confusing, and boring." Wigman was so successful only because "the average German has no self-confidence, he thinks art great only if it bores him." Instead, she argued, art should be a form of political expression and of social criticism, it should speak

[144] Erdman, "Dance Discourses," pp. 288–303.
[145] Levinson, "The Modern Dance," pp. 102–103.
[146] Ginner, *The Revived Greek*, p. 70.

to people about their real concerns – not indulge in pseudospiritual tragic-heroic posturing.[147]

The development of modern dance in the United States, however, is a more striking – and paradoxical – example of this ideological divergence. For in the 1930s and 1940s, modern dance came to be identified in the United States with "Americanism" or cultural nationalism, and increasingly played on distinctively American themes. Ted Shawn, writing in 1926, developed an argument rooted in the language of blood and ethnicity – here, as in Germany in the same period, veering in the direction of purity and exclusiveness rather than creative hybridization. He found that Native American dance was "more worthy of our study than the art forms of ancient Egypt, India or Persia." In contrast, New York was "un-American" and therefore could not be the source of a modern American dance because "New York is cosmopolitan, it is a city of the world and not of America ... the ideas and ideals of New York are not American in spirit" because its "huge foreign population" was not "Anglo-Saxon." The "principles upon which our constitutions are built," he wrote, "are the principles of Anglo-Saxon men – high-souled, religious, spiritual-minded men who wanted to found a nation on a higher moral basis." The real power of American dance came from this "center of our being," not from "imitating ... the dying systems of the older nations."[148] Writing in 1930, Martha Graham deplored the fact that America had been "fettered ... to things European ... imitative of a culture foreign to us ... fatuous in our adulation of all things European" rather than striving to create "an art which was the fruit of a people's soul." America was also flooded with immigrants, so that "waves" of foreign "influence almost engulfed us." In 1935, she wrote that "America must develop its own dance," rooted in the "essential spirit of the country" and particularly in people's experience of the wide-open spaces of American landscapes and not, for example, in "the cosmopolitan seaport" – presumably New York (Graham, like Isadora Duncan and Maud Allan, had spent part of her childhood in California).[149]

This nationalist and even chauvinist Americanism in dance was explicitly linked to democratic politics. Anglo-Saxonism (as it was called at the time)

---

[147] Kolb, *Performing*, pp. 171, 176. On the animosity between Wigman and Gert see Susanne Foellmer, *Valeska Gert: Fragmente einer Avantgardistin in Tanz un Schauspiel der 1920er Jahre* (Bielefeld: Transcript, 2006), pp. 171–200.

[148] Shawn, *The American Ballet*, pp. 20, 8, 10.

[149] Martha Graham, "Seeking an American Art of the Dance," in Oliver M. Sayler, ed., *Revolt in the Arts: A Survey of the Creation, Distribution, and Appreciation of Art in America* (New York: Brentano, 1930), pp. 249–250; "The American Dance," in Stewart, ed., *Modern Dance*, pp. 54, 57.

identified self-government as the unique achievement of the English-speaking peoples. But as the global confrontation with totalitarianism loomed, a more universalist and democratic position began to supersede explicitly ethnic nationalism in talk about dance in America. Emphasis shifted from blood to institutions and history as the focus of pride and loyalty. American modern dance advocates enthusiastically adopted the program of developing dances on explicitly American themes: the frontier, the pioneers, the Shakers, the cultures of the Southwest, spirituals, the poetry of Emily Dickinson and Walt Whitman. But they also developed an explicitly and increasingly important democratic political content. Martha Graham is the most striking case. Though preserving a largely apolitical stance, Graham was sympathetic to labor, African Americans, Native Americans, and the traditions of American radical reformism, and in the later 1930s increasingly was drawn into explicit support for international anti-Fascism (see Figure 5.6).

Graham's *Frontier* of 1935 became her "signature work," a piece one critic described as "pure America: forthright, free, the very spirit of an indomitable westward moving people."[150] In 1936, while German dancers (Mary Wigman, Rudolf von Laban, Gret Palucca, Harald Kreutzberg, Leni Riefenstahl) were being willingly mobilized by the Nazis to take part in the festivities surrounding the Olympic Games in Berlin, Graham refused an invitation from the German government to take part, on the grounds that the regime was persecuting many dancers or forcing them into emigration. In 1936 and 1937 she choreographed two pieces highly critical of Francisco Franco and Spanish fascism, at that moment engaged in a civil war against the Spanish Republic. By 1938 her company was performing "American Document," with a spoken element that asked "The United States of America – what is it?" and answered with the words *courage, justice, power, freedom, faith*, and above all and as the embodiment of them all "*Democracy!*" The piece made her effectively a spokeswoman for militant American progressive democratic culture and won her a national audience.[151] Not coincidentally, Graham's teaching methods conformed to her political program. Extremely demanding, she also made her students her active collaborators. As one recalled later, "She'd do something, then get you to do it. If you made her movement look alive, made something

---

[150]   Quotation in Gardner, "Martha Graham," p. 78.
[151]   On Graham's politics see in particular Franko, *Martha Graham in Love and War*, esp. pp. 14–44 (quotations pp. 32–33).

Figure 5.6 Martha Graham in "Strike," 1927

out of it, it had value for her. We could contribute to Martha's work in that way."[152]

Doris Humphrey followed a similar trajectory. She turned her back on the more overtly theatrical tradition of Denishawn in the late 1920s in part because, as she recalled in 1956, after performing dances based on Euro-American folk tradition and Native American, African American, and various Asian dance idioms

> I felt as if I were dancing everyone but myself. I knew something about how the Japanese moved, how the Chinese or Spanish moved, but I didn't know how I moved.... [I]t was imperative to find out what we were as Americans and as contemporary dancers.

But by the 1930s, in addition to the urge to "work indigenously," as she put it, Humphrey clearly felt that the highly theatrical Denishawn style did not capture the spirit, dignity, and pragmatism of American political traditions.[153] Dance was about movement, not "static ideas"; it should illustrate how something worked in practice, how it moved, not the abstract idea of it. "Four abstract themes," she held in 1932, "all moving equally and harmoniously together ... would convey the significance of democracy far better than would one woman dressed in red, white, and blue, with stars in her hair." And indeed, Elizabeth Selden wrote of Humphrey's choreography and teaching methods in 1935 that they "seemed to express so fully the American idea of education – the free individual as self-acting agent within the group" (see Figure 5.7).[154]

There was in all this unmistakably an echo of anticolonial cultural nationalism elsewhere in the world during the same period. As the leading American dance critic John Martin put it in 1936, these dancers were trying to shake off the "xenophilia" and awed respect for European aesthetic traditions (and innovations) that was "the last survival of our colonial-mindedness."[155] At the same time, though, the aesthetic developed by the American theorists and practitioners of modern dance in the 1930s very clearly echoed that of German dance in the 1920s, favoring the stripped-down, simplified form that Mary Wigman called "absolute" dance. Contemporaries were very aware of

[152] May O'Donnell, in Marian Horosko, *Martha Graham: The Evolution of Her Dance Theory and Training* (Gainesville: University of Florida Press, 2002), pp. 37–38.

[153] "Doris Humphrey Speaks" (1956), reprinted in Humphrey, *Doris Humphrey*, pp. 266, 265.

[154] Doris Humphrey, "What Shall We Dance About?," *Trend: A Quarterly of the Seven Arts* 1 (1932): 46; Selden, *The Dancer's Quest*, p. 76. See Coe, *Dance in America*, pp. 131–133, 142.

[155] John Martin, *America Dancing: The Background and Personalities of the Modern Dance* (New York: Dodge, 1936), p. 33.

Figure 5.7 Modern dance athleticism: Doris Humphrey and Charles Weidman, 1938

this parallel. John Martin even identified Graham and Humphrey (for example) as "Central-European or sometimes frankly German" in their aesthetic agenda. Ruth St. Denis explicitly saw Graham, Humphrey, and their colleagues as shaped by the "power of the new influences that were then coming from Germany."[156] And Ted Shawn observed that many of the American modern dancers had "been greatly influenced by the personal style of Mary Wigman and other Germans of her school," and "although this American group are at great pains to disclaim any such influence ..., they can, for all practical purposes, be discussed as one."[157] Others even remarked on how similar Wigman and Graham, in particular, looked.[158]

---

[156] Martin, *America Dancing*, p. 37; St. Denis, *An Unfinished* Life, p. 321. On this point see Thomas, *Dance, Modernity*, p. 86. These similarities are apparent, e.g., in Martha Graham's "A Modern Dancer's Primer for Action" (1941) and Mary Wigman's "The Philosophy of Modern Dance" (1933), both in Selma Jeanne Cohen, ed., *Dance as a Theater Art* (New York: Dodd, Mean, 1974), pp. 136–141 and 149–153.

[157] Ted Shawn, *Fundamentals of a Dance Education* (Girard, KS: Haldeman-Julius, 1937), p. 25.

[158] John Martin, "The Dance: Mary Wigman's Art," *New York Times*, August 3, 1930, p. 101.

What is paradoxical here is that American dancers and critics in the 1930s and 1940s came to understand modern dance specifically in this "absolute" form – most explicitly articulated in Germany and by artists sympathetic to fascism – as fundamentally and distinctively American in character, and as antiauthoritarian, individualistic, and democratic. In the case of Martha Graham, critics and commentators returned to this theme almost obsessively. Graham was, as various authors put it in a collection of essays on her published in 1937, an "authentic American manifestation"; she "has crystallized something in her dance which could only have happened in this country"; she "has a specifically American quality which cannot be ignored ..., a kind of candid, sweeping and wind-worn liberty"; to understand her "one needs to understand America"; she was "the very essence of America."[159] "American Document" in 1938 cemented this connection in the minds of the broader public; "Appalachian Spring" (1944) consolidated it; her role as a cultural ambassador for the United States in the 1950s and 1960s crowned it. By the 1970s, Graham had been turned into an icon of American democratic identity – a development that culminated in her receiving the Presidential Medal of Freedom in 1976 (see Figure 5.8).[160]

Strikingly, the blood-and-soil Americanism evident in Shawn's or Graham's earlier theorizations of "American" dance persisted even as this explicitly democratic aesthetic was articulated; and it sometimes closely echoed Mary Wigman's understanding of what made modern dance in Germany so German. Doris Humphrey, for example, argued in 1932 that American dancers had a particularly difficult task because while dance must express "the meaning of one's personal experience," one could only really understand that meaning when one understood "what part it takes in the organic progression of his [sic] race" – and Americans had a "conglomerate racial heritage without a common folk-lore or mythology." She was also deeply concerned with the function of leadership, which (in her piece "New Dance" of 1936) she believed "compelled and molded ... the whole group into an integrated whole." Humphrey "wished to insist that there is also an individual life within that group," and was thoroughly committed to democracy; but there are eerie parallels here, obviously,

[159] Merle Armitage, Lincoln Kirstein, Evangeline Stokowski, George Antheil, all in Armitage, ed., *Martha Graham*, pp. 2, 5–6, 32, 71–72.

[160] Coe, *Dance*, p. 152. It did not hurt that First Lady Betty Ford was a former student and friend; see Betty Bloomer Ford in Horosko, *Martha Graham*, p. 47.

Figure 5.8 Martha Graham dances American freedom, 1944

to the language – race, leadership, community – of Nazified dance in Germany.[161] Martha Graham, too, thought in 1937 that art "finds its roots

---

[161] Doris Humphrey, ""What Shall We Dance About?," *Trend: A Quarterly of the Seven Arts* 1 (1932): 46–47; and "New Dance" (1936), in Selma Jeanne Cohen, ed., *Doris Humphrey: An Artist First – An Autobiography* (Middletown, CT: Wesleyan University Press, 1972), pp. 252–253, 238, 240.

in man's unconscious – race memory" and that in it "the history and psyche of race" is "brought into focus." Wrestling with the problem of America's polyglot ethnic makeup, she concluded that American dance "will contain a heritage from all other nations, but it will be transfigured by the rhythm, and dominated by the psyche of this new land ... a certain quality of movement will come to be recognized as American."[162] Even as late as 1941, Graham remarked that one purpose of dance training was to "awaken the memory of the race through muscular memory."[163]

These parallels are not entirely surprising because contacts between German and American dance were intensive. As the dance historian Susan Manning in particular has shown, students of the Wigman school were active in the United States at least as early as 1925; Wigman's students Harald Kreutzberg and Yvonne Georgi had triumphal American tours in 1928 and 1929; and Wigman toured the United States three times between 1930 and 1933, achieving enormous critical and audience success and meeting, among others, Martha Graham, Doris Humphrey, and Humphrey's close collaborator Charles Weidman. The director of the Wigman school in Berlin taught at Denishawn in 1930; another Wigman student taught at the Cornish School in Seattle; a third, Hanya Holm, opened a Wigman school in New York in the same year; and in 1931 half the students at the summer session of Wigman's school in Dresden were Americans.[164]

A particularly important bridging figure was Louis Horst, a German American from St. Louis who grew up (from the age of nine) in San Francisco, and became accompanist and musical director for the Denishawn company in 1915. In 1925 he left Denishawn to study in Vienna for five months; when he returned, he became accompanist for Martha Graham, with whom he had started a romantic and mentoring relationship while she was a member of Denishawn. The two were close artistic and professional collaborators for more than two decades. Horst lectured his American colleagues on the ideas of Nietzsche, Schopenhauer, Wagner, and free love; but he also translated for them German-language media coverage of German dance. When European modern dancers

[162] Graham in Armitage, *Martha Graham*, pp. 84, 100.
[163] Martha Graham, "A Modern Dancer's Primer for Action" (1941), in Selma Jeanne Cohen, ed., *Dance as a Theatre Art* (New York: Dodd, Mead, 1974), p. 136.
[164] Susan Manning, "Mary Wigman's Erbe in Amerika," *Tanzdrama* 3 (1987): 7; Manning, "*Ausdruckstanz* across the Atlantic," esp. pp. 48–49; Walter Sorell, *Mary Wigman: Ein Vermächtnis* (Wilhelmshaven: Noetzel, 1986), pp. 117–120; Claudia Gitelman, ed., *Liebe Hanya: Mary Wigman's Letters to Hanya Holm* (Madison: University of Wisconsin Press, 2003), pp. 12–13. See also Michael Stadlinger, "Beziehungen zwischen Modernem Tanz in Mitteleuropa und den USA in den 20er und 30er Jahren des zwanzigsten Jahrhunderts" (Ph.D. diss., Vienna, 1980), esp. pp. 54–83.

began touring in the United States in the late 1920s, he played accompaniment for them as well – in particular Harald Kreutzberg during his American tour in 1928, and again in 1929 when Kreutzberg toured with Yvonne Georgi. During the 1928 tour Kreutzberg used Martha Graham's studio for rehearsal, with Graham looking on; during the 1929 tour Horst (according to his biographer Janet Soares) gave Graham "detailed descriptions after each session." But he played too for Hans Wiener/Jan Veen, Adolf Bolm (ethnic German Russian), Ronny Johansson (ethnic Swedish Russian), and Michio Ito (Japanese), again apparently passing tips on to Graham.[165] Graham insisted that the "American dance today is in no sense German"; but Horst was more realistic in assessing her work, and that of many of her colleagues, as part of a broad international development "exemplified by the German school and, more recently, here in America."[166] Ruth St. Denis, writing in 1963 (to protest Ford Foundation funding for the "European art" of ballet), struck a middle path, arguing that "whatever ... returns to us from Europe in the person of Laban, Mary Wigman, came as the result of the work and influence" of the originators of "the American Dance" – Isadora Duncan and herself.[167]

Soon after Hitler's rise to power these connections began to fray. Most American dancers were, as Horst put it, "a little 'pink' " (attracted to the Left); there was an important contingent of Jewish dancers in New York, the center of American dance; and the Depression made foreign competition particularly unwelcome. Hanya Holm's school, for example, had to be renamed due to Wigman's relationship with the Nazis. And yet, the rhetorical and theoretical similarities persisted. In a volume of essays on modern dance in Germany and America published in 1935, for example, Graham argued that "[o]f things American the American dance must be made"; that "the pallid hot-house sentimentalities of interpretive dancing, the traditional ballet, the involved philosophy of the Orient" were "not of us"; and that America should "bring forth an art as powerful as this country." To do that, the dancer had to do "an amazing amount of hard work. Learning how to dance is not a parlor game.... The dance is no ... light entertainment." In the same collection, Wigman argued that "[s]trong and convincing art has never arisen from theories. It has always grown

---

[165] Janet Mansfield Soares, *Louis Horst: Musician in A Dancer's World* (Durham, NC: Duke University Press, 1992), pp. 34, 42, 62, 66, 73, 77 (quotation). For Horst as Graham's "mentor" see Marie Marchowsky in Horosko, *Martha Graham*, p. 42.

[166] Quoted in ibid., p. 81.

[167] "A Manifesto for the American Dance," December 22, 1963, in JRDD, Ruth St. Denis papers, folder 273.

organically," championed by those "few creative natures" whose "destiny"
it was, by their "relentless efforts," to fight the "battle" of creativity. She
had won this battle, making way for the triumph in German dance (as in
"any true German art") of "the tragic, the heroic," and the "laws of existence" – the "essence of life," which had until then been "crowded out by
too much playfulness" and Latin superficiality in dance.[168]

By now, we should not be surprised by such contradictory similarities.
Wigman and Graham were telling Germans and Americans who they
already knew themselves to be, no less than Tórtola Valencia was telling
Peruvians. "Absolute" dance was a quintessentially German dance form,
the dance of Teutonic soulfulness and interiority and heroic leadership
and community; but it was also a quintessentially American dance form,
the art of open spaces, of individuals finding themselves, of democracy.
In all this, modern dance was, truly, modern. This is what the twentieth
century was like.

---

[168] Martha Graham, "The American Dance"; Mary Wigman, "The New German Dance," both in
Stewart, ed., *Modern Dance*, pp. 56, 54, 55, 58, 17, 16, 20–21. On German American dance contacts, see Burt, *Alien Bodies*, pp. 122–131.

Conclusion: Coherent Contradictions in Modernism and Modernity

In a marvelous critical comment published in 2001, the feminist literary theorist Susan Stanford Friedman observed that historians and art historians have used the term *modernism* in very contradictory ways. Modernism for some has meant elitism: high culture retreating into complexity and obscurity in the face of cultural democracy; master narratives and grand theories that seek to explain everything; state planning, centralized systems, and the power of experts; Enlightenment rationality, progress, science, the idea of objective truth as against subjective individual experience and feeling; and imperialism, both cultural and political. For others, modernism meant just the opposite: a revolt against tradition and authority, and resistance to the centralizing rational schemes of powerful people and institutions; discontinuity, rupture, indeterminacy, and creative chaos; individualism and radical subjectivity; multiplicity, "contamination" and openness to experimentation. "Just what **IS** modernism," Friedman asked, "where the word means not just different things, but precisely opposite things?"[1] Friedman was not alone: A sense of the contradictory character of our understandings and definitions of modernism and of modernity is everywhere in the historical literature. The historical sociologist Perry Anderson even wrote some thirty years ago that modernism was "the emptiest of all cultural categories ... it designates no describable object in its own right at all; it is completely lacking in positive content ... what is concealed beneath the label is a wide variety of very diverse – indeed incompatible – aesthetic practices."[2] Other students of modernism have concluded variously that "few ages have been more multiple, more promiscuous in artistic style"; that "on the question of what Modernism is,

[1] Susan Stanford Friedman, "Definitional Excursions: The Meanings of *Modern/Modernity/Modernism*," *Modernism/Modernity* 8 (2001): 495. See also Tim Cresswell, *On the Move: Mobility in the Modern Western World* (New York: Routledge, 2006), pp. 15–21.
[2] Quoted in Anthony Wohl, "Heart of Darkness: Modernism and its Historians," *Journal of Modern History* 74 (2002): 574.

no two critics agree"; that modernism was characterized by "fabulous diversity." One recent history finds that modernism was composed of nine different responses to modern social development, ranging from nihilism and antimodernism to "modernolatry" (worship of modernness).[3] In fact, one common approach to the study of modernism in the past two decades has been not to try to define it, but simply to present a representative sampling of "modernist" ideas or works of art – with or sometimes even without a convincing assertion that the sample reveals underlying commonalities. As the eminent cultural historian Peter Gay has put it, "Modernism is far easier to exemplify than to define."[4]

It is quite common to see ambiguity and contradiction as a weakness. Historians often see a generalization or an ideal type that must be maintained in the face of contradictions between the different phenomena it is attempting to encompass as a weak generalization – one that is too broad to be useful. If the generalization that there was a discrete and (in some way) coherent cultural phenomenon we can call "modernism" can be maintained only at the cost of ignoring fundamental differences, radical contradictions, and even outright conflicts, then perhaps it is too broad to be accurate or fruitful.

The same skepticism is commonly applied to historical phenomena, not just to the way we organize our thinking about them. If a cultural phenomenon in the past sent mixed messages, was ambivalent, or was internally contradictory it must be because it was not yet mature; had not yet fully freed itself from a dominant tradition or the influence of powerful institutions and the ideas and values they championed; had not yet fully articulated its own principles sufficiently to be clear, consistent, and monovalent. Or it is because it was self-subverting, falling victim to and/or secretly a vehicle for the wiles of power and the ideas power propagates – such as racism, sexism, or authoritarianism. For example, if we see scientific matters discussed in terms derived from religious traditions, it must be because new and genuinely scientific ways of thinking had not yet replaced or demolished old religious patterns of thought. If we see people from one society celebrating the alleged "racial" characteristics of people in another society, it must be because they have not yet escaped from racist patterns of thinking.

[3] Richard Sheppard, "The Problematics of European Modernism," in Steve Giles, ed., *Theorizing Modernism* (New York: Routledge, 1993), pp. 1–2, 38; Tobias Boes, "Germany," in Pericles Lewis, ed., *The Cambridge Companion to European Modernism* (Cambridge: Cambridge University Press, 2011), p. 33.
[4] Peter Gay, *Modernism* (New York: Norton, 2007), p. 1.

This study has discovered something quite different. Modern dance "worked" *because* it was contradictory. Contradiction made it powerful; its paradoxes were productive. Modern dance was chaste because it was so sexy, and it was sexy because it was so chaste. Modern dance was a religious rite because it expressed or symbolized a truly grandiose scientific theory; and that scientific theory was powerful and important because it justified a faith in (evolutionary) transcendence. It deployed religious and spiritual terminology as a marketing tool; but it spread its spiritual or religious message to the extent that it was a successful commercial undertaking. It liberated women by commodifying their bodies as a spectacle for consumption by the entertainment-industry audience; it was commercially successful partly because it commodified the image of the liberated woman. It played on and thus reinforced racial stereotypes, but undermined the ideology of racial and cultural superiority by offering a positive appreciation of the alleged innate characteristics and gifts of various peoples and cultures. It claimed not to be an art, but to be rather simply the direct bodily expression of emotional states, or of the rhythm of the cosmos; and this was why it was deemed truly artistic. It valued individuality above all else, but it operated through the tireless repetition of clichés or tropes; and among those tropes were precisely the ones that "guaranteed" originality – for example, life, soul, or feeling. By the 1920s it sought to develop discipline, technique, and instructional systems that would enable the individual to express herself with complete freedom. Modern dancers could express universal human truths because they were expressing their true, real, and unique individual selves. They could express that true, deeper, essential human self because they could obliterate their own individual personalities in performance. They were so good at being themselves, at tuning in to their own souls, that they could tune in to other people's souls too, and "be" them. Modern dancers were openly, playfully mendacious, but absolutely authentic and truthful – to the point even of forgetting that they had an audience. Modern dancers thought that "blood" was so important and so powerful and so freighted with psychological and cultural and even spiritual meaning that (particularly before World War I) they advocated mixing different bloods to create something spectacular. Modern dance was popular in part because it was known to be a fad among the political, social, and cultural elites; it was a fad among the political, social, and cultural elites partly because it was known to be a popular performance form. It was revolutionary, new, modern, and iconoclastic because it ransacked archaeological museums for costumes, postures, and aesthetic conventions. It was obsessed with the dances of the past; it was obsessed with the dance of the future; it was modern and American; it was ancient and Greek/"Oriental."[5]

In each case, modern dance was *more* the one thing *because* it was the other thing – more than it could ever have been if it had been purely the one thing or the other. It worked as a performance both on and off stage not despite its contradictions, but because of and through them. Contradiction, ambivalence, and ambiguity were not its weaknesses but its strengths – in fact, its strategy. Indeed, we might even read the personal lives of the modern dancers this way: They experienced such self-abandoned joy in the creative process because they were so unhappy; they were unhappy in part because they would not give up the joy of creativity.

Can we read this pattern from modern dance into modernism in the arts more broadly? That is, can we treat modern dance as a "case study" of modernism generally, and find this same strategy at work in the other arts? Not entirely. Modernism was, again, characterized by profound internal contradictions; but in very few cases did individual artists or works embody and work with or through those contradictions as effectively as modern dance did.

A good example is the ability of modern dance to be both a popular performance form (particularly in variety theater) and a "high" art form. As Walter L. Adamson has pointed out, some historians have asserted that in modernism "popular and elite culture came together again" after some centuries of separation, while others suggest that modernism represented "a sharpening and stiffening of cultural hierarchies, as the upper and middle bourgeoisie sought safe or 'sacralized' cultural forms that would differentiate them from the surging masses." Adamson believes "modernism aimed at a democratic audience modeled on a universalizing of an aesthetically informed elite" – that is, an audience that was democratic in size but aristocratic in refinement. But almost none of those we think of today as great modernists, in any discipline of the arts, did achieve much popular success (particularly in their own time, but usually never).[6]

Or take another example: Modernist painting as a whole was characterized by a radical divergence between the hyperrationalism of, say, French Cubism, or the Italian Futurist's worship of the potentials of technology (for speed, for violence, for creating a totally new aesthetic) and the

[5] For a brief discussion of contradiction and complementarity as a broader pattern in modernism and modernity, see Michael Saler, "Introduction," in Michael Saler, ed., *The fin-de-siècle World* (New York: Routledge, 2015), pp. 1–8.
[6] Walter L. Adamson, *Embattled Avant-Gardes: Modernism's Resistance to Commodity Culture in Europe* (Berkeley: University of California Press, 2007), pp. 6, 21.

fascination with emotional states that we see in Edvard Münch's painting *The Scream*, or in Henri Rousseau's paintings of dream-states. But very few artists combined the two in the way that the modern dancers' nascent religion of Darwinian science did. The potential power of doing so is evidenced by the iconic status of Pablo Picasso's painting *Les Demoiselles d'Avignon* (1907), in which nude women's bodies are depicted using smooth, almost abstract geometrical shapes, but their heads are African tribal masks.

Modernist literature yields a similar picture. Again, some works did aim for the kind of synergistic contradictions or tensions that we have seen in dance – or at least addressed them thematically. Bram Stoker's Count Dracula (1897) is a wonderful example: Dracula was immortal and hence godlike, but driven by the most primitive of urges, the thirst for blood. In Robert Louis Stevenson's *Dr. Jekyll and Mr. Hyde* (1886) the main character is both a highly educated, civilized, and decent man and a primitive bloodthirsty murderer. But, for the most part, what we identify today as great modernist literature wallowed straightforwardly in the themes of irrationalism, violence (particularly murder and rape), adultery, divorce, bad sex, drugs, moral cowardice and/or turpitude, madness, loneliness, and misery. It also prided itself on being stylistically difficult and demanding. The great English modernist author T. S. Eliot famously observed (in 1921) that this difficulty was a necessary product of the age: "[I]t appears likely that poets in our civilization ... must be *difficult*. Our civilization comprehends great variety and complexity, and this variety and complexity, playing upon a refined sensibility, must produce various and complex results."[7] Modern dance was quite good at complexity of meaning; but complexity of meaning is not the same as formal complexity – complexity of language or expression. Modern dance was seldom formally complex or obscure. As we have seen in Chapter 5, that changed some after World War I, as modern dance became a more established and accepted art form. Some placed Martha Graham, for example, among the "morbid moderns," creating "obscure" and "austere" dances that "do not make an easy diet"; and John Martin criticized the "hectic writhings," "Teutonic" heaviness, and "philosophical contortions" of much of German dance, while others found Mary Wigman "abstruse."[8] But for the most part, and

[7] Quoted in Leonard Diepeveen, *The Difficulties of Modernism* (New York: Routledge, 2003), p. xi. There is an excellent discussion of the central themes of modernist art in Sheppard, "The Problematics," pp. 7–32.
[8] Armitage, ed., *Martha Graham*, p. 8; John Martin, "The Dance: A Futile Congress," *New York Times*, July 20, 1920, p. X6; Martin, "Martha Graham, Dancer, Is Cheered," *New York Times*,

particularly at the outset, modern dance was unfamiliar, but rarely "difficult" in this sense.

Dance was, then, in this particularly important way rather unique as
a modernist art form. That was certainly not because it addressed themes
that modernists in other arts did not. The modern dance pioneers shared
with many modernists in every artistic discipline an interest in the irrational, in spontaneity, emotion, intuition, and imagination; a fascination
with and emulation of the so-called primitive; a sense of the sacral character of art; a sense of the plurality and contingency and invented quality
of selfhood; a sense for the limitations of language and the burning desire
to capture or experience "life" in its immediacy and urgency. The Salomé
dance in particular explored the favorite modernist themes of sex, madness, murder, and misery; and several of the Ballets Russes' productions
(particularly "Rite of Spring" or "Scheherezade") did so as well. Like most
modernists, further, the modern dance pioneers were deeply influenced by
Friedrich Nietzsche, one of the key authors of the modernist concept of
"life" as primary, irrational, powerful, and natural, and hence superior to
artifacts of civilization like morality, science, philosophy, or metaphysics.
The ideas of Ellen Key and other sex reformers on this subject, too, were
partly derived from Nietzsche's *Birth of Tragedy* (1872) and *The Twilight
of the Idols* (1888). It is not clear how directly reading Nietzsche's unsys-
tematic references to dance in these works may have influenced the modern dancers. Isadora Duncan, for example, appears to have tackled him
systematically only in 1905, well after she had developed her distinctive
performance style, and even then with some ambivalence. She remarked
in a letter to Gordon Craig that "after perusing him for 7 hours I feel a
profound gloom mingled with a sensation that my brain will go pop."
But in broad terms modern dance could make use of Nietzsche's concept
of the "Dionysian" aspects of creativity – unconstrained, ecstatic, intoxicating, consuming – as a point of reference familiar to many of the better
educated in their audience.[9]

Nor was modern dance exceptional because it was not well integrated
into the larger field of modernism in the arts. Several leading (and controversial) modernist figures appear to have been inspired particularly by

December 7, 1931, p. 23; Martin, "The Dance: Artist and Audience," *New York Times*, December 27,
1931, p. 94.
[9] See Michael Bell, "The Metaphysics of Modernism," in Michael Levenson, ed., *The Cambridge
Companion to Modernism* (Cambridge: Cambridge University Press, 1999), pp. 26–28; Kimerer
LaMothe, *Nietzsche's Dancers* (New York: Palgrave MacMillan, 2006); quotation in Steegmuller,
Your Isadora, pp. 78–79.

variety-theater dancers, especially in Paris. Frank Wedekind's "Lulu" character may have been modeled on performers he saw in Paris in the 1870s.
Oscar Wilde was apparently inspired to write his *Salomé* in part by dancers he saw there in the early 1890s – establishing the kind of circularity
already familiar from the trope of dancers' resemblance to statuary.[10] As
we have seen, modernists in all sorts of fields (drama, literature, painting,
sculpture, music) were enthusiastic promoters of modern dance, in not a
few cases even collaborating directly with leading dancers. In the years just
before World War I, some of the great modernist authors and playwrights
were incorporating dance into their latest works. William Butler Yeats,
influenced by the Japanese dancer Michio Ito (a student at Hellerau and
later influential dancer in the United States), made use of some of the
movement vocabulary of modern dance and Japanese Noh dance in his
late "plays for dancers"; Oskar Kokoschka did the same in his singularly
distasteful play *Murder, Hope of Women* (1909).[11] Why, then, did dance
have this unique capacity to embody and make use of the contradictions
of modernism? Modernism was so diverse, its boundaries (stylistic, thematic, chronological, sociological) so indistinct, that any answer must
be speculative and general. But it may be worth thinking about some
suggestions.

The first is that modern dancers did not struggle as desperately as did
painters or writers with what art historians commonly refer to as the
modernist "crisis of representation" and turn toward formal "difficulty"
because it was, in one sense, self-evident what they were representing. For
literature, theories such as those of Ferdinand de Saussure and Ludwig
Wittgenstein that suggested that the relationship between words and
things was purely arbitrary were profoundly unsettling. But dance did
not have to worry so much about words. For painters, the abandonment
of pictorial realism and the evolution of abstraction were revolutionary,
and opened a whole new world of aesthetic possibilities. It is not possible
to make an abstraction of one's own body – though by the 1920s some
would use masks and unconventional costuming to make gestures in that

[10] Jane R. Goodall, *Performance and Evolution in the Age of Darwin* (New York: Routledge, 2002), pp. 199, 206.
[11] Christopher Innes, "Modernism in Drama," in Lewis, *The Cambridge Companion*, pp. 133, 137; Susan Jones, *Literature, Modernism, and Dance* (Oxford: Oxford University Press, 2013); Terri A. Mester, *Movement and Modernism: Yeats, Eliot, Lawrence, Williams, and Early Twentieth-Century Dance* (Fayetteville: University of Arkansas Press, 1997); Takeishi, *Japanese Elements*, pp. 20–36; Helen Caldwell, *Michio Ito: The Dancer and His Times* (Berkeley: University of California Press, 1977), pp. 37–54; Les Hammer, "Michio Ito," *Ballet Review* 28, no. 1 (2001): 69–74; Mary Fleischer, *Embodied Texts: Symbolist Playwright-Dancer Collaborations* (Amsterdam: Rodopi, 2007).

direction.[12] Modern dance, therefore, was left (free?) to explore complexities and dichotomies of meaning, not of its medium. In modern dance
the crisis of representation took the form, most importantly, of implicit
or explicit play with/across the boundaries between self and other, fact
and fiction, performance and "naturalness" – something dancers could
do with great immediacy and transparency because they were physically
present in their art form. In literature, painting, or music, in contrast,
modernists were increasingly fascinated by the potentials of exploring the
medium – paint, canvas, words, grammar, tone, sound – rather than the
"story" or "picture" that it was used to create. Of course, the emphasis
on nudity in early modern dance was in part an insistence on the importance of the dancer's medium (the body). In the context of the religion of
evolution, further, the modern dancers' fascination with the unadorned,
naked female might also be seen as an instance of the modernist principle that form follows function, and of the stripped down, minimalist,
anti-decorative aesthetic that came to characterize, for example, modern
architecture. And again, by the 1920s some dancers would move in the
direction of exploring the potentials of pure movement in space, rather
than narrative or representation. But the possibilities for them were more
limited and far less obvious than in, for example, painting. At least before
World War I, this kind of pure formalism was relatively rare; and even in
the 1930s or 1950s it was often theorized but seldom really attempted –
most dance (like Martha Graham's) remained at least thematic, and usually narrative.

It may be, too, that modern dance benefitted from the breadth of its
expressive potentials, which included not only the moving body but also
music, narrative, sets and costumes, and acting ("mimic" expression). This
could give dance a multivocality that painting or literature or music could
not really achieve – and that could be used to layer contradictory meanings or associations over each other. An example would be the ability of
dancers to appeal to multiple aesthetic registers by combining "Oriental"
themes, sets, and movement (sexy) with European orchestral or chamber
music (chaste).

Third, dancers may have felt less pressure to explore formal and difficult styles and themes because dance was already partly beyond the pale,
at least before World War I. Modernist literature, painting, and music
had to go to great lengths to shock the bourgeoisie by eschewing com-
prehensibility in favor of convoluted arcane references in literature, or

---

[12] See Lewis, *The Cambridge Introduction*, pp. 3–10.

"wild" and "savage" slashing at canvas with brush (such as the so-called Fauves advocated), or the clashing of cymbals and plonking of strings. Modernist drama had to establish itself as radical and unconventional by compulsively addressing themes like immorality, violence, and self-destruction, or through unconventional staging. Again, some of modern dance did address such themes; and in some cases it did deliberately seek to be ugly or grotesque. But it pursued such strategies much less commonly than did the other arts. A great deal of modern dance strove straightforwardly to be beautiful, meaningful, and even joyful. That may be because dance was already edgy, already considered sexy and unrespectable. Its "unconventionality" credentials were less in doubt.

What is more, the modern dancers particularly before 1914 were overwhelmingly female. This too made dance less respectable, simply because women were generally accorded less respect in European societies than men, and so-called effeminate men less than anyone. That meant modern dance was less tortured by the relentless machismo that underlay much of the modernist effort to be stylistically difficult or demanding – or by the accompanying misogyny among male artists, which plagued literary modernism in particular.[13] Because the "masses" were often coded as feminine, this may have meant modern dance was less ambivalent about seeking to appeal to a broader public, as well.

In fact, modern dance appears to have been different from modern literature and drama in one further important respect: It was not so miserable. Again, most of the modern dancers were not very happy people, and they did address topics like grief, murder, and madness in their performances – for example, in Salomé dances, or the "Rite of Spring," or the many dances to Chopin's "Funeral March." This tendency became much more marked in the 1920s and 1930s, when Martha Graham or Mary Wigman – much less Anita Berber or left-wing dance activists – emphasized spiritual or social struggle as the subject matter for modern dance. But certainly before the war both performers and reviewers more commonly used a very different lexicon, one that included grace, charm, beauty, and, above all, joy. Further, while art historians frequently comment on how tortured and despairing and pessimistic modernism in general was, to the extent that the modern dancers were committed to the religion of evolution it was a profoundly optimistic art. This may suggest that art historians have been a little too obsessed with the grim side of modernism. And yet, it is

---

[13] See particularly Marianne Dekoven, "Modernism and Gender," in Lewis, ed., *The Cambridge Companion to Modernism*, esp. pp. 213–317.

striking that the concept of joy was so central to the vocabulary of modern dance, and so apparently peripheral to modernism more broadly.

These last two features – the fact that most dancers were female, and that joy was central to the conceptual vocabulary of modern dance – may well be related. Men of the middle classes, and particularly the cultural elite, had very good reasons to be troubled by modern social developments. Women were increasingly emancipated, increasingly questioning the extraordinary privileges and predatory behavior of men, and increasingly invading areas of life once reserved to men – including politics, the teaching profession, clerical work, and the arts. Technical and managerial skills were increasingly well rewarded relative to older forms of cultural capital, like classical education. Some historians have written of a "crisis of masculinity" in this period. It might be more accurate to speak of a transformation of masculinity; but many men heavily invested in older forms of masculine cultural, sexual, and social privilege experienced transformation as crisis. Strikingly, for example, precisely the same pattern can be discerned in the debate over sexuality in this period. Most female sex reformers were excited about the possibility of creating a new sexual culture, and were profoundly optimistic, even ecstatic, about the future of gender relations. Many male sexologists were deeply hostile to the women's movements, fearful about the future of gender relations, and haunted by the fear that the liberation of women would lead to demographic collapse in Europe and geo-political defeat by allegedly inferior races.[14] Again, by the 1920s modern dancers were less blithe than they had been in the 1910s – perhaps reflecting some of the complexities and ambivalences of the very limited forms of emancipation that women achieved in the interwar years. But dance was still generally a happier art than, say, literature.

One way to interpret this constellation would be to suggest that modern dance was a peculiar, in some ways atypical, offshoot or instance of modernism. I would like to suggest instead that modern dance embodied – more successfully and extensively than any other art form – the multifarious potentials and therefore the enormous revolutionary power of modernism. Because of its peculiar aesthetic characteristics modern dance could combine, in one form, divergent potentials that were characteristic of modernism as a whole but of few of its individual expressions.[15]

[14] Edward Ross Dickinson, *Sex, Freedom and Power in Imperial Germany* (New York: Cambridge University Press, 2014), p. 280; Burt, *Alien Bodies*, p. 24.
[15] On this point see particularly Silvia Carandini, "Il laboratorio del nuovo. L'arte della danza e la rivoluzione teatrale del primo Novecento" and Elisa Vaccarino, "Le arti del Novecento e la avanguardie

Conclusion

In particular, dance confronted the questions modernity posed with unusual insistence. The political, social, technological, and intellectual conditions of modernity posed the question of the self with particular urgency. Is the self authentic? Is it irreducible either in its individual uniqueness or in its inescapable ethnic foundations? Is it constructed? Is it a performance? Is it an illusion – a mere "mobile army of metaphors, metonyms, and anthropomorphisms," as Friedrich Nietzsche put it?[16] Modernity posed the question of the relationship between this self and the other with a new poignancy, as well. Imperial conquest particularly after 1880 posed the question of the relationship between savagery and civilization in profoundly unsettling ways – particularly when allegedly civilized imperialists engaged in savage wars of extermination against indigenous populations, as happened repeatedly between the 1860s and World War I. But the rapid integration of the world economy and the building out of the global communications and transportation infrastructure also increasingly brought non-Europeans and non-European ideas to Europe. One example would be the Indian sailors Ruth St. Denis hired in New York and London; another would be Inayat Khan, whom she hired to accompany some of her dances; a third would be Yoga, or the Vedanta movement, both of which she studied. Modernity posed the question of the relationship between science and religion, too, as rapid scientific and technological development expanded the reach and prestige of science. It posed the question of relationships between male and female, as rapid social change transformed women's roles. The growth of great cities in Europe and North America and the emergence of modern metropolitan cultural forms (such as the variety theater, or the cinema) posed the problem of the relationship between elite and mass culture in new and more urgent ways.

This was the great power of modernism, understood as the culture of modernity, if we take it as a whole: not that it answered these questions, but that it posed them, and left them open. Questions come first and are open-ended; they are much more powerful than answers, which merely respond to questions already posed and which in any case are always only partial or provisional. More than any other art form, modern dance embodied those questions – performed them, in fact.

As the final chapter of this study suggests, some other important and powerful modern phenomena conform to a similar pattern, in which

di danza," both in Silvia Carandini and Elisa Vaccarino, eds., *La Generazione Danzante: L'Arte del movimento in Europa nel primo Novecento* (Rome: Di Giacomo, 1997), esp. pp. 18, 24.
[16] Quoted in Lewis, *The Cambridge Introduction*, p. 21.

what should in theory be contradictory was in fact synergistic. Most obviously, modern dance appears to have thrived in the 1920s in part by drawing on the enormous political energies generated by the clash of radically divergent ideological programs in the interwar period. Communism, fascism, and liberal democracy were competing ways of organizing modern societies – competing visions of what modernity could, should, or must be like. Martha Graham or Doris Humphrey in the United States, Laban or Wigman in Germany, Duncan (briefly) in the USSR, or the Workers' Dance League in New York all sought to align their aesthetic projects with one another of these ideological projects, and – crucially – against the others. In a sense, they played across the tension that boiled up in the space where the question of what modernity is stood, unanswered, debated, and charged with enormous potential.

But beyond that, all three of these political answers to the questions posed by modernity/modernism shared with modern dance precisely the characteristic that they mobilized the energy of the tensions between contradictory elements, thereby generating greater power than could regimes that sought simpler answers. National Socialism, Fascism, and Communism all claimed to be both authoritarian and democratic – each the more so because of the other. They were so effective at imposing tyranny because, unlike more traditional (and less effective) authoritarian regimes, they tapped the energies of mass movements and mass participation. But they claimed to be more democratic than liberal democracies because dictatorial power gave them the ability to ignore the agendas of special interests and defeat alleged hidden conspiracies – for example, of capitalists, or of Jews, or trade unions, or employers' associations. Thus Adolf Hitler referred to his projected dictatorship in *Mein Kampf* as "Germanic Democracy"; Benito Mussolini called Fascism "an organized, centralized, authoritarian democracy"; Vladimir Lenin called Communism and the dictatorship of the proletariat democracy for the vast majority, in contrast to the liberal-democratic tyranny of money – it was "democracy for the people, and not democracy for the money-bags."[17]

Democratic states mobilized contradictions that were, at the time, no less striking. By the 1920s and 1930s liberal democracy in Western Europe and North America had begun to give way to the nascent welfare state,

[17] Adolf Hitler, *Mein Kampf* (Boston: Houghton Mifflin, 1943), p. 91; Benito Mussolini, *Fascism: Doctrine and Institutions* (Rome: Ardita, 1935), p. 23; Vladimir Lenin, "The State and Revolution," excerpt in Albert Fried and Ronald Sanders, eds., *Socialist Thought: A Documentary History* (Garden City, NY: Anchor, 1964), p. 472.

as even the champions of the free market came to recognize that markets only function freely where they are regulated, and where the ability of individuals to negotiate is underpinned by noneconomic interventions that give them the concrete wherewithal (knowledge, skills, health) to pursue their interests and exercise their rights effectively, and often collectively. For that reason, the rights of labor and public funding for education, health, and welfare were all expanded. It was these stabilizing policy interventions that made market capitalism work as it was supposed to, to generate rising affluence and greater social and political stability. But of course – as the Depression of the 1930s was tragically to show – it was also the economic success of market capitalism that made such stabilizing interventions affordable. Nor was it coincidence that democracy was most stable and effective in the United States and Britain, where executive power was most established and where simple majority electoral systems made parliaments less representative than they were in, for example, Germany, Italy, or France, which all had systems of proportional representation.

As we have seen in Chapter 5, moreover, by the 1920s modern dance inhabited not just the Euro-American region, but other parts of the world as well. And here too it played successfully across acute tensions within major political and cultural-political currents. There was a deep tension within many nationalist projects in the colonial world between often explicitly anti-European cultural commitments and ideas of explicitly European origin, such as nationalism and socialism. Modern dance fit this model perfectly. A cultural import from the Euro-American world, it provided a template or method for the "discovery" of the power and the modern relevance of precolonial, non-European aesthetic traditions.[18]

Those familiar with the scholarly literature on the history of modern sexuality will see a familiar pattern here, too. The modern European concept of sexuality as it developed in the late nineteenth and early twentieth century encouraged people to explore their own individual erotic desires, tastes, and needs. It gave people a growing list of sexual identities to choose from (heterosexual, homosexual, bisexual, polygamous, fetishist, and so on). Sexual subcultures emerged in European cities that created new opportunities to explore or live out those sexual identities. And yet, those identities were also targeted by new regimes of discipline, policing, and therapy; in fact, they were defined in a process of (willing

---

[18] For an example of a similar pattern in religious life, see Masuzawa, *The Invention*, esp. pp. 121–146.

or unwilling) collaboration between psychiatric, psychoanalytic, spiritual, sexological, and forensic experts and the targets of their study or intervention. There was increasing cultural pressure to identify with, and to act out, one or another of these sexual identities; that pressure probably generated as much confusion as clarity; that confusion moved growing numbers of people to seek help from the experts and specialists who claimed that they understood people's sexuality better than people understood it themselves. One result was a growing mass of talk about sex – in the print media, in films (such as *Anders als die Anderen*), in specialist medical journals, in reform pamphlets and conferences, in parliaments and courts and social service agencies. Sex loomed larger and larger in the public consciousness, it became ever more powerful as a set of references, concerns, and policy issues. The more people talked about sex, then, the more it needed to be repressed, contained, controlled, defined; but the more it needed to be repressed, contained, controlled, and defined, the more people were compelled to talk about it. As one historian has put it recently, the twentieth century was "the century of sex" – more and more so over time.[19] Some historians argue that the century of sex was a century of expanding intervention and discipline in sexual matters; others argue that it was a century of advancing sexual liberation and self-discovery.[20] But it was precisely because *both* statements are true that sex was more and more important in political, cultural, and social life over the course of the century.

Another powerful cultural phenomenon in modern European and Euro-American societies that was riddled with such synergistic contradictions was psychoanalysis. According to Freudian theory, we achieve a high level of civilization by sublimating our sexual energies, redirecting them into other endeavors like art, or technology, or politics and thereby achieving greater comfort, security, opportunity, wealth, refinement, and enjoyment of life. But that makes us unhappy because we would rather be having sex. So the happier we are, the more miserable we become. In the psychotherapeutic process, we free ourselves from the past by dredging it up and wallowing in it. That is because it is what we have forgotten that

---

[19] Dagmar Herzog, *Sexuality in Europe: A Twentieth Century History* (New York: Cambridge University Press, 2011), p. 1.

[20] See, e.g., Anna Clark, *Desire: A History of European Sexuality* (New York: Routledge, 2012); Harry Oosterhuis, *Stepchildren of Nature: Krafft-Ebing, Psychiatry, and the Making of Sexual Identity* (Chicago: University of Chicago Press, 2000); Lawrence Birken, *Consuming Desire: Sexual Science and the Emergence of a Culture of Abundance, 1871–1914* (Ithaca, NY: Cornell University Press, 1988); Jeffrey Weeks, *The World We Have Won: The Remaking of Erotic and Intimate Life* (New York: Routledge, 2007).

is the thing that is most on our minds, and we must remember it to forget it. In that dredging-up process, the therapist remains strictly emotionally neutral and uninvolved; but therapy works because the patient comes to see the therapist as a wise and loving parent (transference). And yet, according to the theory of the Oedipus and Electra complexes, we hate and fear our parents, because we want to be them – or at least to kill them and have sex with their spouse. We find that most disgusting which we are most attracted to; we say what we most don't want to say; we bring into our lives that which we most want to avoid. It is these contradictions that make psychoanalytic thought so powerful, so revealing, so attractive – for at bottom, really, what's *not* to like in a system of thought like this? It scratches one of the most fundamental human itches of all: our sense of irony.[21]

Modern dance was paradoxical in character; it was effective in communicating each of its messages because it also communicated the opposite message. In this it appears to exemplify an underlying quality characteristic of the world of/in modernity more generally. As Carrie J. Preston has observed, "[T]he purported crisis of modernity has happened consistently since the Enlightenment."[22] That is because "crisis" and contradiction are the way modernity works. In the modern world, driving more energy into any system just makes that system more energetic; so what is repressed returns, stronger than ever. An effective structure, therefore, draws on the energies of elements that are in tension, in mutual contradiction. Self-contradiction is more powerful than consistency. In the modern world, any structure (political, intellectual, institutional, aesthetic) is more effective, more powerful, more dynamic, and more purely what it is if it is also the opposite. Modern dance was in some ways a unique expression of modernism and modernness, then. But it was also one that was uniquely revealing of the deeper structure – and the deeper power – of modernism and of modernity.

---

[21] See Sigmund Freud, "Civilization and Its Discontents" (1930), in James Strachey, ed., *The Standard Edition of the Complete Psychological Works of Sigmund Freud*, vol. 21 (London: Hogarth, 1961), pp. 64–148 and "An Outline of Psychoanalysis" (1940), in ibid, vol. 23, pp. 144–208..

[22] Preston, *Modernism's Mythic Pose*, p. 7.

Bibliography

Scholarly Publications

Adamson, Walter L. *Embattled Avant-Gardes: Modernism's Resistance to Commodity Culture in Europe* (Berkeley: University of California Press, 2007).

Adelsbach, Karin, and Andrea Firmenich, eds. *Tanz in der Moderne. Von Matisse bis Schlemmer* (Cologne: Wienand, 1996).

Anderson, Benedict. *Imagined Communities: Reflections on the Origins and Spread of Nationalism* (London: Verso, 1991).

Anderson, Jack. *Art without Boundaries* (Iowa City: University of Iowa Press, 1997).

Aston, Elaine. *Sarah Bernhardt: A French Actress on the English Stage* (New York: Berg, 1989).

Balachandran, G. "Circulation through Seafaring Indian Seamen, 1890–1945," in Claude Markovits, Jacques Pouchepadass, Sanja Subrhmanyam, eds., *Society and Circulation: Mobile People and Itinerant Cultures in South Asia 1750–1950* (Delhi: Permanent Black, 2003), pp. 89–130.

Bald, Vivek. *Bengali Harlem and the Lost Histories of South Asian America* (Cambridge, MA: Harvard University Press, 2013).

Balk, Claudia, "Vom Sinnenrausch zur Tanzmoderne," in Brygida Ochaim and Claudia Balk, eds., *Varieté-Tänzerinnen um 1900* (Frankfurt: Stroemfeld/Roter Stern, 1998), pp. 7–68.

Barche, Gisela, and Jeschke, Claudia. "Bewegungsrausch und Formbestreben," in Gunhild Oberzaucher-Schüller, Alfred Oberzaucher, and Thomas Steiert, eds., *Ausdruckstanz* (Wilhelmshaven: Florian Noetzel, 1986), pp. 317–346.

Bardsley, Kay. "Isadora Duncan's First School," *Dance Research Annual* 10 (1979): 219–249.

Baril, Jacques. *La danse modern (Isadora Duncan a Twyla Tharp)* (Paris: Vigot, 1977).

Batson, Charles R. *Dance, Desire and Anxiety in Early Twentieth-Century French Theater: Playing Identities* (Aldershot, UK: Ashgate, 2005).

Bayertz, Kurt. "Biology and Beauty: Science and Aesthetics in *Fin-de-siècle* Germany," in Mikulas Teich and Roy Porter, eds., *Fin de Siecle and Its Legacy* (Cambridge: Cambridge University Press, 1991), pp. 278–295.

Bell, Michael. "The Metaphysics of Modernism," in Michael Levenson, ed., *The Cambridge Companion to Modernism* (Cambridge: Cambridge University Press, 1999), pp. 9–32.

Bellver, Catherine G. *Bodies in Motion* (Lewisburg, PA: Bucknell University Press, 2010).

Benedetti, Jean. *Stanislavski* (London: Methuen, 1988).

Bentivoglio, Leonetta. *La danza moderna* (Milan: Longanesi, 1977).

Bentley, Toni. *Sisters of Salome* (New Haven, CT: Yale University Press, 2002).

Berg, Shelley C. "Sada Yacco: The American Tour, 1899–1900," *DC* 16 (1993): 147–196.

"Sada Yacco in London and Paris, 1900: Le Rêve Réalisé," *DC* 18 (1995): 343–404.

Betz, Thomas. "Dichten und Trachten: Hans Brandenburg und der Tanz," *Tanzdrama* 55 (2000).

"Der Russe und die Münchnerin," *Tanz-Journal* 1, no. 1 (2003).

"Die Duncan dichtet, die Sacchetto malt," *Tanz-Journal* 1, no. 5 (2003).

Birken, Lawrence. *Consuming Desire: Sexual Science and the Emergence of a Culture of Abundance, 1871–1914* (Ithaca, NY: Cornell University Press, 1988).

Blair, Fredrika. *Isadora: Portrait of the Artist as a Woman* (New York: McGraw-Hill, 1986).

Boes, Tobias. "Germany," in Pericles Lewis, ed., *The Cambridge Companion to European Modernism* (Cambridge: Cambridge University Press, 2011), pp. 33–51

Bonnet, Alastair. *White Identities: Historical and International Perspectives* (New York: Prentice Hall, 2000).

Bradshaw, David, ed. *A Concise Companion to Modernism* (Malden, MA: Blackwell, 2003).

Brandon, Ruth. *The Dollar Princesses: Sagas of Upward Nobility, 1870–1914* (New York: Alfred A. Knopf, 1980).

Brandstetter, Gabriele. "Tanzreform und Reformkleid: Zur Textilkunst von Mariano Fortuny," *Tanzdrama* 14 (1991): 4–7.

Tanz-Lektüren: Körperbilder und Raumfiguren der Avantgarde (Ph.D. diss., Frankfurt, 1995).

"Grete Wiesenthals Walzer," in Gabriele Brandstetter and Gunhild Oberzaucher-Schüller, eds., *Mundart der Wiener Moderne: Der Tanz der Grete Wiesenthal* (Munich: Kieser, 2009), pp. 15–39.

Brandstetter, Gabriele and Gunhild Oberzaucher-Schüler, eds., *Mundart der Wiener Moderne: Der Tanz der Grete Wiesenthal* (Munich: Kieser, 2009).

Brandstetter, Gabriele, and Brygida Maria Ochaim. *Loïe Fuller: Tanz–Licht-Spiel–Art Nouveau* (Freiburg: Rombach, 1989).

Brenscheidt, Diana, *Shiva Onstage: Uday Shankar's Company of hindu Dancers and Musicians in Europe and the United States, 1931-1938* (Zurich: Lit, 2011).

Buchholz, Kai, et al. *Die Lebensreform* (Darmstadt: Häusser, 2001).

Burger, Hildegard, ed. *Hugo von Hofmannsthal/Harry Graf Kessler: Briefwechsel 1898–1929* (Frankfurt: Insel, 1968).

Burt, Ramsay. *Alien Bodies: Representations of Modernity, 'Race' and Nation in Early Modern Dance* (New York: Routledge, 1998).

Butler, Christopher. *Early Modernism: Literature, Music, and Painting in Europe, 1900–1916* (Oxford: Oxford University Press, 1994).

Butler, Eliza Marion. *The Tyranny of Greece over Germany* (Cambridge: Cambridge University Press, 1935).

Caldwell, Helen. *Michio Ito: The Dancer and His Times* (Berkeley: University of California Press, 1977).

Cameron, Theresa. "The Tannhäuser Bacchanale in Bayreuth," in Gunhild Oberzaucher-Schüller, Alfred Oberzaucher, and Thomas Steiert, eds., *Ausdruckstanz* (Wilhelmshaven: Florian Noetzel, 1986), pp. 278–293.

Carandini, Silvia and Elisa Vaccarino, eds. *La Generazione Danzante: L'Arte del movimento in Europa nel primo Novecento* (Rome: Di Giacomo, 1997).

Carter, Alexandra. "London, 1908: A Synchronic View of Dance History," *DRJ* 23 (2005): 36–50.

"Constructing and Contesting the Natural in British Theatre Dance," in Alexandra Carter and Rachel Fensham, eds., *Dancing Naturally: Nature, Neo-Classicism and Modernity in Early Twentieth-Century Dance* (London: Palgrave-MacMillan, 2011), pp. 16–30.

Chakravorty, Pallabi. "Dancing into Modernity: Multiple Narratives of India's Kathak Dance," *DRJ* 38 (2006): 115–136.

Bells of Change: Kathak Dance, Women and Modernity in India (Calcutta: Seagull, 2008).

Chavarría, Jesús. *José Carlos Mariátegui and the Rise of Modern Peru, 1890–1930* (Albuquerque: University of New Mexico Press, 1979).

Cheng, Anne Anlin. *Second Skin: Josephine Baker & the Modern Surface* (New York: Oxford University Press, 2011).

Cherniavsky, Felix. "Maud Allan, Part I: The Early Years, 1873–1903," *DC* 6 (1983): 1–36.

"Maud Allan, Part II: First Steps to a Dancing Career, 1904–1907," *DC* 6 (1983): 189–227.

"Maud Allan, Part III: Two Years of Triumph, 1908–1909," *DC* 7 (1984): 119–158.

"Maud Allan, Part IV: The Years of Touring, 1910–1915," *DC* 8 (1985): 1–50.

"Maud Allan, Part V: The Years of Decline, 1915–1956," *DC* 9 (1986): 177–236.

Clark, Anna. *Desire: A History of European Sexuality* (New York: Routledge, 2012).

Clayton, Michelle. "Touring History: Tórtola Valencia between Europe and the Americas," *DRJ* 44 (2012): 29–49.

Coe, Robert. *Dance in America* (New York: Dutton, 1985).

Cohen, Barbara Naomi. *The Borrowed Art of Gertrude Hoffman* (New York: Dance Horizons, 1977).

Conyers, Claude. "Courtesans in Dance History: *Les Belles de la Belle Époque*," *DC* 26 (2003): 219–243.

Cook, James W. *The Arts of Deception: Playing with Fraud in the Age of Barnum* (Cambridge, MA: Harvard University Press, 2001).

Coorlawla, Uttara Asha. "Ruth St. Denis and India's Dance Renaissance," *DC* 15 (1992): 123–152.

Cowan, Michael. *Technology's Pulse: Essays on Rhythm in German Modernism* (London: Institute of Germanic and Romance Studies, 2011).

Cranston, Sylvia. *HPB* (New York: Putnam, 1993).

Cresswell, Tim. *On the Move: Mobility in the Modern Western World* (New York: Routledge, 2006).

Current, Richard Nelson, and Marcia Ewing Current. *Loie Fuller: Goddess of Light* (Boston: Northeastern University Press, 1997).

Dahms, Sibylle and Stephanie Schroedter, eds. *Der Tanz – Ein Leben: In Memoriam Friderica Derra de Moroda* (Salzburg: Selke Verlag, 1997).

Daly, Ann. "Isadora Duncan's Dance Theory," *DRJ* 26 (1994): 24–31.
Done into Dance: Isadora Duncan in America (Bloomington: Indiana University Press, 1995).

Dawkins, Heather. *The Nude in French Art and Culture 1870–1910* (New York: Cambridge University Press, 2002).

De Boer, Jacobien. *Dans voluit, dat is leven: Gertrud Leistikow (1885–1948)* (Wezep: Uitgeverij de Kunst, 2014).

De Cossart, Michael. *Ida Rubinstein (1885–1960): A Theatrical Life* (Liverpool, UK: Liverpool University Press, 1987).

Décoret-Ahiha, Anne. *Les danses exotiques en France, 1880–1940* (Paris: Centre Nationale de la Danse, 2004).

Dekoven, Marianne. "Modernism and Gender," in Michael Levenson, ed., *The Cambridge Companion to Modernism* (New York: Cambridge University Press, 2011), pp. 174–193.

Desmond, Jane. "Dancing Out the Difference: Cultural Imperialism and Ruth St. Denis's 'Radha' of 1906," *Signs* 17 (1991): 28–49.

Dickinson, Edward Ross. "Citizenship, Reaction, and Technical Education: Vocational Schooling and the Prussian 'Youth Cultivation' Decree of 1911," *European History Quarterly* 29 (1999): 109–147.
"Altitude and Whiteness: Germanizing the Alps and Alpinizing the Germans, 1875–1935," *German Studies Review* 33 (2010): 577–599.
"'Must We Dance Naked?': Art, Beauty and Politics in Munich and Paris, 1911 and 1913," *Journal of the History of Sexuality* 20 (2011): 95–131.
Sex, Freedom and Power in Imperial Germany (New York: Cambridge University Press, 2014).

Diepveen, Leonard. *The Difficulties of Modernism* (New York: Routledge, 2003).

Doerr, Evelyn. *Rudolf Laban: The Dancer of the Crystal* (Lanham, MD: Scarecrow, 2008).

Dorf, Samuel N. "Dancing Greek Antiquity in Private and Public: Isadora Duncan's Early Patronage in Paris," *DRJ* 44 (2012): 5–27.

Dörr, Evelyn. "'Wie ein Meteor tauchte sie in Europa auf . . .': Die philosophische Tänzerin Isadora Duncan im Spiegel der deutschen Kritik," in Frank-Manuel Peter, ed., *Isadora & Elizabeth Duncan in Deutschland/in Germany* (Cologne: Wienand, 2000), pp. 31–48.

Drehsen, Volker. "Körper Religion: Ausdruckstanz um 1900," in Volker Drehsen, Wilhelm Gräb, and Dietrich Korsch, eds., *Protestantismus und Ästhetik* (Gütersloh: Chr. Kaiser, 2001), pp. 197–232.

Easton, Laird McLeod. *The Red Count: The Life and Times of Harry Kessler* (Berkeley: University of California Press, 2002).

Ehrich, Karin. "Im Sauseschritt: Über das Leben von Gertrud Leistikow," *Tanzdrama* 58 (2001): 8–11.

Elswit, Kate. *Watching Weimar Dance* (New York: Oxford University Press, 2014).

Erdman, Joan L. "Dance Discourses: Rethinking the History of the 'Oriental Dance,'" in Gay Morris, ed., *Moving Words: Re-Writing Dance* (New York: Routledge, 1996), pp. 288–305.

Fabian, Reinhard. *Christian von Ehrenfels: Leben und Werk* (Amsterdam, The Netherlands: Rodopi 1986)

Facos, Michelle, and Sharon L. Hirsch, eds., *Art, Culture, and Identity in Fin-de-Siecle Europe* (New York: Cambridge University Press, 2003).

Farfan, Penny. *Women, Modernism and Performance* (New York: Cambridge University Press, 2004).

Faulk, Barry J. *Music Hall and Modernity: The Late-Victorian Discovery of Popular Culture* (Athens: Ohio University Press, 2004).

Fiedler, Leonhard M., and Martin Lang, eds. *Grete Wiesenthal: Die Schönheit der Sprache des Körpers in Bewegung* (Salzburg: Residenz, 1985).
   "'nicht Wort – aber mehr als Wort …': Zwischen Sprache und Tanz – Grete Wiesenthal und Hugo von Hofmannsthal," in Gabriele Brandstetter and Gunhild Oberzaucher-Schüller, eds., *Mundart der Wiener Moderne: Der Tanz der Grete Wiesenthal* (Munich: Kieser, 2009), pp. 127–150.

Fiedler, Theodor. "Weimar contra Berlin: Harry Graf Kessler and the Politics of Modernism," in Françoise Forster-Hahn, ed., *Imagining Modern German Culture: 1889–1910* (Hanover: National Gallery of Art, Washington, 1996), pp. 107–125.

Finney, Gail. *Women in Modern Drama* (Ithaca, NY: Cornell University Press, 1989).

Fischer, Lothar. *Tanz zwischen Rausch und Tod: Anita Berber 1918–1928 in Berlin* (Berlin: Haude and Spener, 1984).
   "Getanzte Körperbefreiung," in *"Wir sind nackt und nennen us Du": Von Lichtfreunden und Sonnenkämpfern – Eine Geschichte der Freikörperkultur* (Giessen: Anabas, 1989), pp. 106–123.

Fisher, Jennifer. "The Swan Brand: Reframing the Legacy of Anna Pavlova," *DRJ* 44 (2012): 50–67.

Fleischer, Mary. *Embodied Texts: Symbolist Playwright-Dancer Collaborations* (Amsterdam: Rodopi, 2007).

Florack, Ruth. "Liebe im Zeichen der Sittenrichter," in Helmut Scheuer and Michael Grisko, eds., *Liebe, Lust und Leid: Zur Gefühlskultur um 1900* (Kassel: Kassel University Press, 1999) pp. 215–236.

Foellmer, Susanne. *Valeska Gert: Fragmente einer Avantgardistin in Tanz un Schauspiel der 1920er Jahre* (Bielefeld: Transcript, 2006).

Foulkes, Julia L. *Modern Bodies: Dance and American Modernism from Martha Graham to Alvin Ailey* (Chapel Hill: University of North Carolina Press, 2002).

Francis, Claude, and Fernande Gontier. *Creating Colette*, vol. 1, *From Ingenue to Libertine, 1873–1913* (South Royalton, VT: Steerforth Press, 1998).

Frank, Gustav, and Katja Schneider. "Tanz-Technik: Körperdispositive in der Massenkommunikation der Moderne," *Tanzdrama* 54 (2000): 6–15.

Frank, Gustav, and Katja Schneider. "Tanz und Tanzdebatte in der Moderne: Voraussetzungen von Leni Riefenstahls Film *Das blaue Licht*," *Tanzdrama* 63 (2002): 4–10.

Franko, Mark. *Martha Graham in Love and War: The Life in the Work* (New York: Oxford University Press, 2012).

Franks, A. H. "A Biographical Sketch," in *Pavlova: A Biography*, ed. Franks (New York: Da Capo, 1979), pp. 11–52.

Fraser, Mariam, and Monica Greco, eds. "Marcel Mauss: Techniques of the Body," in *The Body: A Reader* (London: Routledge, 2005), pp. 73–77.

Freydank, Ruth, ed. *Theater als Geschäft: Berlin und seine Privattheater um die Jahrhundertwende* (Berlin: Hentrich, 1995).

Friedman, Susan Stanford. "Definitional Excursions: The Meanings of *Modern/Modernity/Modernism*," *Modernism/Modernity* 8 (2001): 493–513.

Fritsch-Vivié, Gabriele. *Mary Wigman* (Reinbek: Rowohlt, 1999).

Fritzsche, Peter. *Reading Berlin 1900* (Cambridge, MA: Harvard University Press, 1996).

Funkenstein, Susan Laikin. "There's Something About Mary Wigman: The Woman Dancer as Subject in German Expressionist Art," *Gender & History* 17, no. 3 (2005): 826–859.

Garafola, Lynn. "The Travesty Dancer in Nineteenth-Century Ballet," *DRJ* 18 (1985): 35–40.

ed. *Of, By, and For the People: Dancing on the Left in the 1930s* (New York: Journal of the Society of Dance History Scholars, vol. 5, 1994).

Garb, Tamar. "Modeling the Body: Photography, Physical Culture, and the Classical Ideal in *Fin-de-Siecle* France," in Geraldine A. Johnson, ed., *Sculpture and Photography: Envisioning the Third Dimension* (New York: Cambridge, 1998), pp. 86–99.

Gardner, Howard. "Martha Graham: Discovering the Dance of America," *Ballet Review* 22, no. 1 (1994): 67–93.

Garland, Iris. "Early Modern Dance in Spain: Tórtola Valencia, Dancer of the Historical Intuition," *DRJ* 29 (1997): 1–22.

"The Eternal Return: Oriental Dance (1900–1914) and Multicultural Dance (1990–2000)," *Dancing in the Millennium: An International Conference: Proceedings* (Washington, DC: n.p., 2000), pp. 193–198.

Tortola Valencia: Modernism and Exoticism in Early Twentieth Century Dance, ed. Mary Fox (Vancouver, BC: Five/Cinq, 2013).

Gay, Peter. *Modernism* (New York: Norton, 2007).

Genné, Beth. *The Making of a Choreographer: Ninette de Valois and Bar aux Folies-Bergère* (Pennington, NJ: Society of Dance History Scholars, 2012).

Georgen, Jeanpaul. "Der pikante Film: Ein vergessenes Genre der Kaiserzeit," in Thomas Elsaesser and Michael Wedel, eds., *Kino der Kaiserzeit: Zwischen Tradition und Moderne* (Munich: text + kritik, 2002), pp. 45–62.

Giazitzidis, Katja. "Eine goldene Zeit für den Tanz – die Zwanziger," in Petra Bock and Katja Koblitz, eds., *Neue Frauen zwischen den Zeiten* (Berlin: Hentrich, 1995), pp. 194–219.

Glenn, Susan A. *Female Spectacle: The Theatrical Roots of Modern Feminism* (Cambridge, MA: Harvard University Press, 2000).

Goodall, Jane R. *Performance and Evolution in the Age of Darwin* (New York: Routledge, 2002).

Gopal, Ram. "Pavlova and the Indian Dance," in *Pavlova: A Biography*, ed. A. H. Franks (New York: Da Capo, 1979), pp. 98–110.

Gordon, Mel. *The Seven Addictions and Five Professions of Anita Berber: Weimar Berlin's Priestess of Depravity* (Port Townsend, WA: Feral House, 2006).

Graff, Ellen. *Stepping Left: Dance and Politics in New York City, 1928–1942* (Durham, NC: Duke University Press, 1997).

Green, Martin. *Mountain of Truth* (Hanover, NH: University Press of New England, 1986).

Guest, Ivor. *The Romantic Ballet in Paris* (Middleton: Wesleyan University Press, 1966).

The Dancer's Heritage: A Short History of Ballet (London: Dancing Times, 1977).

Guilbert, Laure. *Danser avec le IIIe Reich* (Paris: Editions Complexe, 2000).

Hammer, Les. "Michio Ito," *Ballet Review* 28, no. 1 (2001): 69–74.

Haney, Lynn. *Naked at the Feast: A Biography of Josephine Baker* (London: Robson, 1981).

Hardt, Yvonne. *Politische Körper: Ausdruckstanz, Choreographien des Protests und die Arbeiterkulturbewegung in der Weimarer Republik* (Münster: Lit, 2004).

"*Ausdruckstanz* on the left and the work of Jean Weidt," in Susanne Franco and Marina Nordera, eds., *Dance Discourses* (New York: Routledge, 2007), pp. 61–79.

Harrison, Robert. "Archaeology on Trial," *Modernism/Modernity* 11 (2004): 35–36.

Hastie, Jim. "Margaret Morris (1891–1980)," in Jean-Yves Pidoux, ed., *La danse: Art du XXe siècle?* (Lausanne: Editions Payot, 1990), pp. 167–171.

Hastings, Baird. "The Denishawn Era," in Paul Magriel, ed., *Chronicles of the American Dance* (New York: Henry Holt, 1948), pp. 227–237.

Hause, Steven C. "Social Control in Late Nineteenth-Century France: Protestant Campaigns for Strict Public Morality," in Christopher E. Forth and Elinor Accampo, eds., *Confronting Modernity in Fin-de-Siècle France* (New York: Palgrave-MacMillan, 2010), pp. 135–150.

Hawkins, Mike. *Social Darwinism in European and American Thought, 1860–1945* (New York: Cambridge University Press, 1997).

Heath, Deana. *Purifying Empire: Obscenity and the Politics of Moral Regulation in Britain, India and Australia* (New York: Cambridge University Press, 2010).

Herzog, Dagmar. "Hubris and Hypocrisy, Incitement and Disavowal: Sexuality and German Fascism" in Dagmar Herzog, ed., *Sexuality and German Fascism* (New York: Berghahn Books, 2005), pp. 3–21.

Sexuality in Europe: A Twentieth Century History (New York: Cambridge University Press, 2011).

Hindson, Catherine. *Female Performance Practice on the Fin-de-Siècle Popular Stages of London and Paris* (Manchester, UK: Manchester University Press, 2007).

Hoare, Philip. *Wilde's Last Stand* (London: Duckworth, 1997).

Hobsbawm, E. J., and Terence O. Ranger. *The Invention of Tradition* (Cambridge: Cambridge University Press, 1983).

Homans, Jennifer. *Apollo's Angels: A History of Ballet* (New York: Random House, 2010).

Horosko, Marian. *Martha Graham: The Evolution of Her Dance Theory and Training* (Gainesville: University of Florida Press, 2002).

Horwood, Catherine. "'Girls Who Arouse Dangerous Passions': Women and Bathing, 1900–1939," *Women's History Review* 9 (2000): 653–673.

Howe, Dianne S. *Individuality and Expression: The Aesthetics of the New German Dance, 1908–1936* (New York: Peter Lang, 1996).

Hughes, Russell Meriwether (La Meri). *Dance Out the Answer* (New York: Marcel Dekker, 1977).

Huschka, Sabine. *Moderner Tanz: Konzepte – Stile – Utopien* (Reinbek: Rowohlt, 2002).

"Bildgebungen tanzender Körper: Choreographierte Blickfänge 1880 bis 1920," *Fotogeschichte* 101 (2006): 41–50.

Huxley, Michael. *The Dancer's World, 1920–1945: Modern Dancers and Their Practices Reconsidered* (New York: Palgrave-MacMillan, 2015).

Innes, Christopher. "Modernism in Drama," in Michael Levenson, ed., *The Cambridge Companion to Modernism* (New York: Cambridge University Press, 2011), pp. 130–156.

Järvinen, Hanna. "The Russian Dancing – Vaslav Nijinsky in Western Imagination," *Conference Proceedings, Congress on Research in Dance, October 26–28, 2001* (New York: New York University, 2001), pp. 165–166.

Dancing Genius: The Stardom of Vaslav Nijinsky (New York: Palgrave MacMillan, 2014).

Jelavich, Peter. *Berlin Cabaret* (Cambridge, MA: Harvard University Press, 1993).

Jeschke, Claudia, and Gabi Vettermann. "Isadora Duncan, Berlin and Munich in 1906: Just an Ordinary Year in a Dancer's Career," *DC* 18 (1995): 217–229.

"Between Institutions and Aesthetics: Choreographing Germanness?," in Andrée Grau and Stephanie Jordan, eds., *Dancing Europe: Perspectives on Theatre Dance and Cultural Identity* (New York: Routledge, 2000), pp. 55–72.

Jockel, Nils. "Aus dem Moment des Empfindens," *Tanzdrama* 7 (1989): 18–23.

Jockel, Nils, and Patricia Stöckemann. *"Flugkraft in goldene Ferne": Bühnentanz in Hamburg seit 1900* (Hamburg: Museum für Kunst und Gewerbe, 1989).

Jones, Susan. *Literature, Modernism, and Dance* (Oxford: Oxford University Press, 2013).

Jowitt, Deborah. "Images of Isadora : The Search for Motion," *DRJ* 17 (1985): 21–29.

"The Impact of Greek Art on the Style and Persona of Isadora Duncan," *Proceedings, Tenth Annual Conference of the Society of Dance History Scholars* (Irvine, CA, 1987).

Time and the Dancing Image (New York: Morrow, 1988).

Kahan, Sylvia. *Music's Modern Muse: A Life of Winaretta Singer, Princesse de Polignac* (Rochester, NY: University of Rochester Press, 2003).

Kant, Marion. "Mary Wigman – Die Suche nach der verlorenen Welt," *Tanzdrama* 25 (1994): 16–21.

"Annäherung und Kollaboration: Tanz und Weltanschauung im 'Dritten Reich,'" *Tanzjournal* 3 (2003): 13–23.

"Mittel zur Transzendenz," *Tanz-Journal* 1, no. 6 (2003): 15–22.

"Death and the Maiden: Mary Wigman in the Weimar Republic," in Alexandra Kolb, ed., *Dance and Politics* (New York: Peter Lang, 2010), pp. 119–143.

Karina, Lillian, and Marion Kant. *Hitler's Dancers: German Modern Dance and the Third Reich*, trans. Jonathan Steinberg (Oxford: Berghahn, 2003).

Karthas, Ilyana. *When Ballet Became French: Modern Ballet and the Cultural Politics of France, 1909–1939* (Montreal: McGill-Queen's University Press, 2015).

Keay, Julia. *The Spy Who Never Was: The Life and Loves of Mata Hari* (London: Joseph, 1987).

Kelly, Alfred. *The Descent of Darwin: The Popularization of Darwinism in Germany, 1860–1914* (Chapel Hill: University of North Carolina Press, 1981).

Kendall, Elizabeth. *Where She Danced* (New York: Knopf, 1979).

Kerensky, Oleg. *Anna Pavlova* (London: Hamilton, 1973).

Kermode, Frank. "Poet and Dancer before Diaghilev," in Roger Copeland and Marshall Cohen, eds., *What Is Dance? Readings in Theory and Criticism* (Oxford: Oxford University Press, 1983), pp. 145–160.

Kew, Carole. "Mary Wigman's London Performances: A New Dance in Search of a New Audience," *Dance Research* 30 (2012): 1–21.

Khan, Inayat. *Biography of Pir-o-Murshid Inayat Khan* (London: East-West, 1979).

Kischke, Roland. "'Die Berauschendste Verkettung von Gebärden': Faszination des Tanzes um 1900," in Gernot Frankhäuser, Roland Krischke, and Sigrun Paas, eds., *Tänzerinnen um Slevogt* (Munich: Deutscher Kunstverlag, 2007), pp. 23–40.

Koegler, Horst. "A Single Being and a Single Soul with Two Bodies," *DC* 26, no. 2 (2003): 253–259.

Kolb, Alexandra. *Performing Femininity: Dance and Literature in German Modernism* (New York: Peter Lang, 2009).

Koritz, Amy. *Gendering Bodies/Performing Art: Dance and Literature in Early Twentieth-Century British Culture* (Ann Arbor: University of Michigan Press, 1995).

"Dancing the Orient for England: Maud Allan's *The Vision of Salomé*," in Jane C. Desmond, ed., *Meaning in Motion: New Cultural Studies of Dance*

(Durham, NC: Duke University Press, 1997), pp. 133-152; also in *Theater Journal* 46 (1994): 63–78

Krauze, Enrique. *Mexico: Biography of Power* (New York: HarperCollins, 1997).

Kurth, Peter. *Isadora: A Sensational Life* (Boston: Little, Brown 2001).

LaMothe, Kimerer. *Nietzsche's Dancers* (New York: Palgrave MacMillan, 2006).

Lewis, Pericles. "Introduction," in *The Cambridge Companion to European Modernism* (New York: Cambridge University Press, 2011), pp. 1–11.

Lewis, Reina. *Gendering Orientalism: Race, Femininity and Representation* (London: Routledge, 1996).

Linse, Ulrich. "Säkularisierung oder Neue Religiösität? Zur religiösen Situation in Deutschland um 1900," *Recherches Germaniques* 27 (1997): 117–141.

Barfüssige Propheten (Berlin: Siedler, 1983).

Lista, Giovani. *Loïe Fuller: Danseuse de la Belle Époque* (Paris: Somogy-Stock, 1995).

Litvak, Lily. *España 1900* (Barcelona: Anthropos, 1990).

Lloyd, Jill. *German Expressionism: Primitivism and Modernity* (New Haven, CT: Yale University Press, 1991).

Loewenthal, Lillian. *The Search for Isadora: The Legend & Legacy of Isadora Duncan* (Pennington, NJ: Dance Horizons, 1993).

Lubkoll, Christine. "Rhythmus: Zum Komplex von Lebensphilosophie und ästhetischer Moderne," in Christine Lubkoll, ed., *Das Imaginäre des Fin de siècle* (Freiburg: Rombach, 2002), pp. 83–110.

Lüders, Christine. *Apropos Mata Hari* (Frankfurt: Verlag Neue Kritik, 1997).

Macdougall, Allan Ross. *Isadora: A Revolutionary in Art and Love* (Edinburgh: Thomas Nelson, 1960).

"Isadora Duncan and the Artists," in Paul Magriel, ed., *Nijinsky, Pavlova, Duncan: Three Lives in Dance* (New York: Da Capo, 1977), pp. 35–51.

Macintosh, Fiona. "Dancing Maenads in Early 20th-Century Britain," in Fiona Macintosh, ed., *The Ancient Dancer in the Modern World: Responses to Greek and Roman Dance* (Oxford: Oxford University Press, 2010), pp. 188–209.

MacKenzie, John. *Orientalism: History, Theory, and the Arts* (Manchester, UK: Manchester University Press, 1995).

Manning, Susan. "Feminism, Utopianism, and the Incompleted Dialogue of Modernism," in Gunhild Oberzaucher-Schüller, Alfred Oberzaucher, and Thomas Steiert, eds., *Ausdruckstanz* (Wilhelmshaven: Florian Noetzel, 1986), pp. 105–115.

"Mary Wigmans Erbe in Amerika," *Tanzdrama* 3 (1987): 6–8.

"Isadora Duncan, Martha Graham und die lesbische Rezeption," *Tanzdrama* 44/45 (1999): 18–25.

"The Female Dancer and the Male Gaze: Feminist Critiques of Early Modern Dance," in Jane Desmond, ed., *Meaning in Motion* (Durham, NC: Duke University Press, 1997), pp. 153–166.

"*Ausdruckstanz* across the Atlantic," in Susanne Franco and Marina Nordera, eds., *Dance Discourses* (New York: Routledge, 2007), pp. 46–60.

Ecstasy and the Demon: Feminism and Nationalism in the Dances of Mary Wigman (Berkeley: University of California Press, 1993).

Mansfield, Janet. *Louis Horst: Musician in a Dancer's World* (Durham, NC: Duke University Press, 1992).

Marcovitch, Heather. "Dance, Ritual, and Arthur Symons's London Nights," *English Literature in Transition, 1880–1920* 56 (2013), pp. 462–482.

Marwick, Arthur. *IT: A History of Human Beauty* (London: Hambledon Press, 2004).

Masuzawa, Tomoko. *The Invention of World Religions* (Chicago: University of Chicago Press, 2005).

Mayer, Charles S. "Ida Rubinstein: A Twentieth-Century Cleopatra," *DRJ* 20 (1988): 33–51.

Meglin, Joellen. "Blurring the Boundaries of Genre, Gender, and Geopolitics: Ruth Page and Harald Kreutzberg's Trans-Atlantic Collaboration in the 1930s," *DRJ* 41 (2009): 52–75.

Meinzenbach, Sandra. *Neue alte Weiblichkeit: Frauenbilder und Kunstkonzepte im Freien Tanz* (Marburg: Tectum, 2010).

"Tanz ist eine Sprache und eine Schrift des Göttlichen": Kunst und Leben der Ruth St. Denis (Wilhelmshaven: Florian Noetzel, 2013).

Mester, Terri A. *Movement and Modernism: Yeats, Eliot, Lawrence, Williams, and Early Twentieth-Century Dance* (Fayetteville: University of Arkansas Press, 1997).

Miller, Kamae A., ed. *Wisdom Comes Dancing: Selected Writings of Ruth St. Denis on Dance, Spirituality, and the Body* (Seattle: PeaceWorks, 1997).

Mitchell, Timothy. "Orientalism and the Exhibitionary Order," in Nicholas B. Dirks, ed., *Colonialism and Culture* (Ann Arbor: University of Michigan Press, 1992), pp. 289–317.

Möhring, Mahren. *Marmorleiber. Körperbildung in der deutschen Nacktkultur (1890–1930)* (Cologne: Böhlau, 2004).

Money, Keith. *Anna Pavlova: Her Life and Art* (London: Collins, 1982).

Mosse, George L. *Toward the Final Solution: A History of European Racism* (New York: Fertig, 1978).

Müller, Hedwig. *Mary Wigman: Leben und Werk der grossen Tänzerin* (Weinheim: Quadriga, 1986).

"Von der äusseren zur inneren Bewegung: Klassische Ballerina – moderne Tänzerin," in Renate Möhrmann, ed., *Die Schauspielerin: Zur Kulturgeschichte der weiblichen Bühnenkunst* (Frankfurt: Insel, 1989), pp. 283–299.

Nead, Lynda. *The Female Nude: Art, Obscenity and Sexuality* (New York: Routledge, 1992).

Nemetz, Laurice D. "Moving with Meaning: The Historical Progression of Dance/Movement Therapy," in Stephanie L. Brooke, ed., *Creative Arts Therapies Manual* (Springfield, IL: Charles C. Thomas, 2006).

Nicholas, Larraine. *Dancing in Utopia: Dartington Hall and its Dancers* (Alton, UK: Dance Books, 2007).

Oberzaucher, Alfred, and Gunhild Oberzaucher. "Wer waren die Lehrer von Gertrud Bodenwieser," *Tanzdrama* 33 (1996): 15–22.

Oberzaucher-Schüller, Gunhild. "Das bislang verschattete Leben der Miss Gertrude," *Tanzdrama* 50 (2000): 6–11.

"Anmerkungen zur Wiesenthal-Rezeption," in Gabriele Brandstetter and Oberzaucher-Schüller, eds., *Mundart der Wiener Moderne: Der Tanz der Grete Wiesenthal* (Munich: Kieser, 2009), pp. 261–263.

Ochaim, Brygida Maria. "Die getanzten Bilder der Rita Sacchetto," *Tanzdrama* 14 (1991): 22–25.

"Miss Saharet," *Tanzdrama* 16 (1991): 34–36.

"Die Barfusstänzerin Olga Desmond," *Tanzdrama* 39 (1997): 19–21.

"Biographien," in Brygida Ochaim and Claudia Balk, eds., *Varieté-Tänzerinnen um 1900* (Frankfurt: Stroemfeld/Roter Stern, 1998), pp. 117–143.

"Varieté-Tänzerinnen um 1900," in Brygida Ochaim and Claudia Balk, eds., *Varieté-Tänzerinnen um 1900* (Frankfurt: Stroemfeld/Roter Stern, 1998), pp. 69–116.

Ochaim, Brygida and Claudia Balk, eds., *Varieté-Tänzerinnen um 1900* (Frankfurt: Stroemfeld/Roter Stern, 1998).

Oosterhuis, Harry. *Stepchildren of Nature: Krafft-Ebing, Psychiatry, and the Making of Sexual Identity* (Chicago: University of Chicago Press, 2000).

O'Shea, Janet. "Dancing through History and Ethnography: Indian Classical Dance and the Performance of the Past," in Theresa Jill Buckland, ed., *Dancing from Past to Present: Nation, Culture, Identities* (Madison: University of Wisconsin Press, 2006), pp. 123–152.

Paret, Peter. *The Berlin Secession* (Cambridge, MA: Harvard University Press, 1980).

"The Tschudi Affair," *Journal of Modern History* 53 (1981): 589–618.

Parker, Henry Taylor. *Motion Arrested: Dance Reviews of H. T. Parker*, ed. Olive Holmes (Middletown, CT: Wesleyan University Press, 1982).

Passmore, Kevin. "Politics," in Julian Jackson, ed., *Europe, 1900–1945* (Oxford: Oxford University Press, 2002), pp. 77–115.

Pastori, Jean-Pierre. *A corps perdu: La dance nue au XXe siècle* (Lausanne: Favre, 1983).

Peppis, Paul. *Sciences of Modernism: Ethnography, Sexology, and Psychology* (New York: Cambridge University Press, 2014).

Peri, Paolo. "La trama della sua vita," in Leonardo Fumi, ed., *Fortuny nella belle époque* (Milan: Electa, 1984), pp. 62–64.

Peter, Frank-Manuel. *Valeska Gert: Tänzerin, Schauspielerin, Kabarettistin* (Berlin: Frölich and Kaufmann, 1985).

"Die 'neie Minchener Derpsichore': Clotilde von Derp – die früheste Vertreterin des Ausdruckstanzes?," in Frank-Manuel Peter and Rainer Stamm, eds., *Die Sacharoffs–zwei Tänzer aus dem Umkreis des Blauen Reiters* (Cologne: Wienand, 2002), pp. 75–136.

Peter, Frank-Manuel, and Rainer Stamm, eds. *Die Sacharoffs – zwei Tänzer aus dem Umkreis des Blauen Reiters* (Cologne: Wienand, 2002).

Peypach, Irene. *Tórtola Valencia* (Barcelona: Edicions de Nou Art Thor, no year).

Postuwka, Gabriele. "Aufbruch in die Moderne: Konzeptionen von Tanzerziehung und Tanzausbildung in Europa und den USA," *Tanzdrama* 38 (1997): 8–11.

Preston, Carrie J. "The Motor in the Soul: Isadora Duncan and Modernist Performance," *Modernism/Modernity* 12 (2005): 273–289.

Modernism's Mythic Pose: Gender, Genre, Solo Performance (New York: Oxford University Press, 2011).

Preston-Dunlop, Valerie. *Rudolf Laban: An Extraordinary Life* (London: Dance, 1998).

Purkayastha, Prathana. "Dancing Otherness: Nationalism, Transnationalism, and the Work of Uday Shankar," *DRJ* 44, no. 1 (2012): 69–92.

Queralt, Maria Pilar. *Tórtola Valencia* (Barcelona: Lumen, 2005).

Randall, Tresa. "Hanya Holm and an American *Tanzgemeinschaft*," in Susan Manning and Lucia Ruprecht, eds., *New German Dance Studies* (Urbana: University of Illinois Press, 2012).

Reynolds, Dee. "Dancing as a Woman: Mary Wigman and 'Absolute Dance,'" *Forum for Modern Language Studies* 35 (1999): 297–310.

Reynolds, Nancy, and Malcolm McCormick. *No Fixed Points: Dance in the Twentieth Century* (New Haven, CT: Yale University Press, 2003).

Ricci, Fabio. *Ritter, Tod & Eros: Die Kunst Elisàr von Kupffers (1872–1942)* (Cologne: Böhlau, 2007).

Roberts, Mary Louis. "Rethinking Female Celebrity: The Eccentric Star of Nineteenth-Century France," in Edward Berenson and Eva Giloi, eds., *Constructing Charisma* (New York: Berghahn, 2010), pp. 103–116.

Robinson, Jacqueline. *Modern Dance in France* (London: Harwood, 1997).

Rodriguez, Suzanne. *Wild Heart* (New York: HarperCollins, 2002).

Roseman, Janet Lynn. *Dance Was Her Religion: The Sacred Choreography of Isadora Duncan, Ruth St. Denis, and Martha Graham* (Prescott, AZ: Hohm, 2004).

Roseman, Mark. *A Past in Hiding* (New York: Metropolitan, 2001).

"Ein Mensch in Bewegung: Dore Jacobs (1894–1978)," *Essener Beiträge* 114 (Essen: Klartext, 2002): 73–108.

Runge, Jörn. *Olga Desmond: Preussens nackte Venus* (Friedland/Mecklenburg: Steffen, 2009).

Ruyter, Nancy Chalfa. "American Delsartism: Precursor of an American Dance Art," *Educational Theater Journal* 25, no. 4 (1973): 421–435.

Reformers and Visionaries: The Americanization of the Art of Dance (New York: Dance Horizons, 1979).

Saha, Shandip. "Hinduism, Gurus, and Globalization," in Peter Beyer and Lori Beaman, eds., *Religion, Globalization and Culture* (Leiden, The Netherlands: Brill, 2007), pp. 485–502.

Said, Edward. *Orientalism* (London: Penguin, 1985 [1978]).

Saler, Michael. *As If: Modern Enchantment and the Literary Prehistory of Virtual Reality* (Oxford: Oxford University Press, 2013).

"Introduction," in Michael Saler, ed., *The Fin-de-siècle World* (New York: Routledge, 2015), pp. 1–8.

Samuels, Maurice. "France," in Pericles Lewis, ed., *The Cambridge Companion to European Modernism* (New York: Cambridge, 2011), pp. 13–32.

Scheub, Ute. *Verrückt nach Leben: Berliner Szenen in den zwanziger Jahren* (Reinbek: Rowohlt, 2000).

Schmidt, Jochen. *Tanzgeschichte des 20. Jahrhunderts in einem Band* (Berlin: Henschel, 2002).

Schnapp, Jeffrey, Shanks, Michael, and Tiews, Matthew. "Archaeology, Modernism, Modernity," *Modernism/Modernity* 11 (2004): 1–16.

Schneider, Ilya Ilyich. *Isadora Duncan: The Russian Years* (London: MacDonald, 1968).

Schneider, Katja. "Schlank, biegsam, grazil: Das Körperbild im klassischen Tanz des 20. Jahrhunderts," *Tanzdrama* 36 (1997): 11–15.

Schwieters, Martha. "Marian Chace: The Early Years in Life and Art," in Susan L. Sandel, Sharon Chaiklin, and Ann Lohn, eds., *Foundations of Dance/Movement Therapy: The Life and Work of Marian Chace* (Columbia, MD: Marian Chace Memorial Fund, 1993), pp. 3–11.

Shedel, James. "Aesthetics and Modernity: Art and the Amelioration of Change in *Fin de Siècle* Austria," *Austrian History Yearbook* 19, no. 1 (1983): 135–142.

Shelton, Suzanne. *Ruth St. Denis: A Biography of the Divine Dancer* (Austin: University of Texas, 1981).

Sheppard, Richard. "The Problematics of European Modernism," in Steve Giles, ed., *Theorizing Modernism* (New York: Routledge, 1993), pp. 1–50.

Silverman, Debora. "The 'New Woman,' Feminism, and the Decorative Arts in Fin-de-Siècle France," in Lynn Hunt, ed., *Eroticism and the Body Politic* (Baltimore, MD: Johns Hopkins University Press, 1991), pp. 144–163.

Simonson, Mary. *Body Knowledge* (New York: Oxford University Press, 2013).

Skidmore, Thomas E. and Peter H. Smith. *Modern Latin America* (New York: Oxford University Press, 1989).

Smith, Anthony D. *National Identity* (Reno: University of Nevada Press, 1991).

Soares, Janet Mansfield. *Louis Horst: Musician in A Dancer's World* (Durham, NC: Duke University Press, 1992).

Solrac, Odelotte. *Tórtola Valencia and Her Legacy* (New York: Vintage, 1982).

Sorell, Walter. *Mary Wigman: Ein Vermächtnis* (Wilhelmshaven: Noetzel, 1986).

Souritz, Elizabeth. "Isadora Duncan and Prewar Russian Dancemakers," in Lynn Garafola and Nancy van Norman Baer, eds., *The Ballets Russes and Its World* (New Haven, CT: Yale University Press, 1999), pp. 97–116.

Soyka, Amelie. *Tanzen und tanzen und nichts als tanzen* (Berlin: Aviva, 2004).

Spector, Irwin. *Rhythm and Life: The Work of Emile Jaques-Dalcroze* (Stuyvesant, NY: Pendragon, 1990).

Srinivasan, Amrit. "Reform and Revival: The Devadasi and Her Dance," *Economic and Political Weekly* 20, no. 44 (1985): 1869–1876.

Stadlinger, Michael. "Beziehungen zwischen Modernem Tanz in Mitteleuropa und den USA in den 20er und 30er Jahren des zwanzigsten Jahrhunderts" (Ph.D. diss., Vienna, 1980).

Stamm, Rainer. "Alexander Sacharoff – Bildende Kunst und Tanz," in Frank-Manuel Peter and Rainer Stamm, eds., *Die Sacharoffs–zwei Tänzer aus dem Umkreis des Blauen Reiters* (Cologne: Wienand, 2002), pp. 11–45.

Stearns, Peter N. *Fat History: Bodies and Beauty in the Modern West* (New York: New York University Press, 2002).

Steegmuller, Francis. *Your Isadora: The Love Story of Isadora Duncan & Gordon Craig* (New York: Random House, 1974).

Stewart, Mary Lynn. *For Health and Beauty: Physical Culture for Frenchwomen, 1880s–1930s* (Baltimore, MD: Johns Hopkins University Press, 2001).

Stüdemann, Natalia. *Dionysos in Sparta: Isadora Duncan in Russland* (Bielefeld: Transcript, 2008).

Studlar, Gaylyn. *Visions of the East: Orientalism in Film* (New Brunswick, NJ: Rutgers University Press, 1997).

Suquet, Annie. *L'Eveil des modernités: Une histoire culturelle de la danse (1870–1945)* (Paris: Pantin/Centre national de la danse, 2012).

Sweeney, Carole. *From Fetish to Subject: Race, Modernism, and Primitivism, 1919–1935* (Westport, CT: Praeger, 2004).

Takeishi, Midori. *Japanese Elements in Michio Ito's Early Period (1915–1924)*, ed. David Pacun (Los Angeles: California Institute of the Arts, 2006).

Taper, Bernard. *Balanchine: A Biography* (Berkeley: University of California Press, 1984).

Taylor, George and Rose Whyman, "François Delsarte, Prince Sergei Volkonsky and Mikhail Chekhov," *Mime Journal* 23 (2005): 97–111.

Terry, Walter. *Miss Ruth: The "More Living Life" of Ruth St. Denis* (New York: Dodd, Mead, 1969).

Thomas, Helen. *Dance, Modernity and Culture: Explorations in the Sociology of Dance* (London: Routledge, 1995).

Thomas, Julian. "Archaeology's Place in Modernity," *Modernism/Modernity* 11 (2004): 17–34.

Thoms, Ulrike. "Dünn und dick, schön und hässlich: Schönheitsideal und Körpersilhouette in der Werbung 1850–1950," in Peter Borscheid, ed., *Bilderwelt des Alltags: Werbung in der Konsumgesellschaft des 19. und 20. Jahrhunderts* (Stuttgart: Steiner, 1995), pp. 242–281.

Thorun, Claudia. *Sarah Bernhardt: Inszenierungen von Weiblichkeit im fin de siècle* (Hildesheim: Olms, 2006).

Thurman, Judith. *Secrets of the Flesh: A Life of Colette* (New York: Alfred A. Knopf, 1979).

Tickner, Lisa. *The Spectacle of Women: Imagery of the Suffrage Campaign, 1907–1914* (London: Chatto and Windus, 1987).

Tilburg, Patricia. "'The Triumph of the Flesh': Women, Physical Culture, and the Nude in the French Music Hall, 1904–1914," *Radical History Review* 98 (2007): 63–80.

Toepfer, Karl. *Empire of Ecstasy: Nudity and Movement in German Body Culture, 1910–1935* (Berkeley: University of California Press, 1997).

"One Hundred Years of Nakedness in German Performance," *Drama Review* 47 (2003): 144–188.

Tomko, Linda J. *Dancing Class: Gender, Ethnicity, and Social Divides in American Dance, 1890–1920* (Bloomington: Indiana University Press, 1999).

Traub, Ulrike. *Theater der Nacktheit: Zum Bedeutungswandel entblösster Körper auf der Bühne seit 1900* (Bielefeld: Transcript, 2010).

Tschannen, Olivier. "La revaloración de la teoría de la secularizatión mediante la perspectiva comparada Europa Latina-América Latina," in Jean-Pierre Bastien, ed., *La Modernidad Religiosa: Europea Latina y América Latina en perspectiva comparada* (México: Fondo de Cultura Económica, 2004), pp. 353–366.

Van Os, Henk, et al., *Femmes Fatales, 1860–1910* (Antwerp: Groninger Museum, 2002).

Veroli, Patrizia. "Auf der Suche nach der Ekstase," *Tanzdrama* 20 (1992): 20–27.

   Baccante e dive dell'aria: Donne danza e società in Italia, 1900–1945 (Castello: Edimond, 2001).

   "Der Spiegel und die Hieroglyphe: Alexander Sacharoff und die Moderne im Tanz," in Frank-Manuel Peter and Rainer Stamm, eds., *Die Sacharoffs* (Cologne: Wienand, 2002).

Voskuil, Lynn M. *Acting Naturally* (Charlottesville: University of Virginia Press, 2004).

Waagenaar, Sam. *The Murder of Mata Hari* (London: Arthur Barker, 1964).

Wagner, Ann. *Adversaries of Dance: From the Puritans to the Present* (Urbana: University of Illinois Press, 1997).

Walkowitz, Judith R. *City of Dreadful Delight* (Chicago: University of Chicago Press, 1992).

   "The 'Vision of Salomé: Cosmopolitanism and Erotic Dancing in Central London, 1908–1918," *American Historical Review* 108 (2003): 337–376.

   Nights Out: Life in Cosmopolitan London (New Haven, CT: Yale University Press, 2012).

Walther, Suzanne K. *The Dance of Death: Kurt Jooss and the Weimar Years* (Chur: Harwood Academic, 1994).

Weeks, Jeffrey. *The World We Have Won: The Remaking of Erotic and Intimate Life* (New York: Routledge, 2007).

Wheelwright, Julie. *The Fatal Lover: Mata Hari and the Myth of Women in Espionage* (London: Collins and Brown, 1992).

Wilhelm, Hermann. *Die Münchener Bohème* (Munich: Buchendorfer, 1993).

Wohl, Anthony. "Heart of Darkness: Modernism and Its Historians," *Journal of Modern History* 74 (2002): 573–621.

Wohler, Ulrike. "Tanz zwischen Avantgarde und klassischer Moderne: Anita Berber und Mary Wigman," in Lutz Hieber and Stephan Moebius, eds., *Avantgarden und Politik: Künstlerischer Aktivismus von Dada bis zur Postmoderne* (Bielefeld: transcript, 2009).

Wollen, Peter. "Fashion/Orientalism/The Body," *New Formations* 1 (1987): 5–33.

Woolf, Vicki. *Dancing in the Vortex: The Story of Ida Rubinstein* (Amsterdam, The Netherlands: Harwood, 2000).

Wouters, Cas. "Etiquette Books and Emotional Management in the 20th Century: Part Two – The Integration of the Sexes," *Journal of Social History* 29 (1995): 325–339.
Informalization: Manners and Emotions Since 1890 (Los Angeles: SAGE, 2007).

Primary Sources

Archival Sources

Deutsches Tanzarchiv Köln/SK Stiftung Kultur, Cologne
Inventory no. 0118, La Argentina/Antonia Mercé
Inventory no. 69, Duncan-Archiv
Inventory no. 56, Clotilde und Alexander Sacharoff
Inventory no. 10, Gertrud und Ursula Falke
Inventory no. 161, Edith von Schrenck
Inventory no. 193, Schwestern Wiesenthal

Jerome Robbins Dance Division, New York Public Library of the Performing Arts
Ruth St. Denis Papers
Natalia Roslasleva files
Sent M'ahesa Clippings
Irma Duncan Collection of Isadora Duncan Materials

Museo de les Arts Escèniques (MAE), Institut del Teatre, Barcelona
Fonds Tórtola Valencia

Theatercollectie, Bijzondere Collecties, Universiteit Amsterdam
Archief Gertrud Leistikow

Museum of Performance and Design, San Francisco
Maud Allan clippings files

Staatsarchiv Munich
Polizei-Direktion, no. 3806/4
Polizei-Direktion, no. 1010/4

Landesarchiv Berlin
APrBr, Repositur 030-05, Tit. 74, Th. 1502

Geheimes Staatsarchiv Preussischer Kulturbesitz, Berlin
Rep. 77, Ministerium des Innern, Tit. 425, no. 37

Institut für Zeitungsforschung, Dortmund
Newspaper article in *Münchner Post, Berliner Tageblatt, Münchner Neueste Nachrichten, Germania*

Books and Articles

Acosta, Mercedes de. *Here Lies the Heart* (New York: Reynal, 1960).
Allan, Maud. *My Life and Dancing* (London: Everett, 1908).
  "Greek Art," in *Maud Allan and Her Art* (London: n.p., n.d.), p. 1.
  "My Aims and Ideals," *Maud Allan and Her Art* (London: n.p., n.d.), pp. 2–3.
Altenberg, Peter. *Das grosse Peter Altenberg Buch*, ed. Werner J. Schweiger (Vienna: Paul Zsolnay, 1977).
  "Mata Hari im Apollotheater," in Christine Lüders, ed., *Apropos Mata Hari* (Frankfurt: Neue Kritik, 1997), p. 91.
Armitage, Merle, ed. *Martha Graham* (New York: Dance Horizons, 1966 [original 1937]).
Aubel, Hermann and Marianne. *Der künstlerische Tanz unserer Zeit* (Königstein/ Ts: Langewiesche, 1930).
Baars, Ernst. *Sexuelle Ethik* (Berlin: Akademischer Bund Ethos, 1908).
Bach, Rudolf, ed. *Das Mary Wigman-Werk* (Dresden: Reissnerl 1933).
Baudelaire, Charles. *The Painter of Modern Life and Other Essays* (London: Phaidon, 1964 [1863]).
Becker, Marie Luise. *Der Tanz* (Leipzig: Seemann, 1901).
  "Tanz," *Schönheit* 1 (1903): 277–290.
  "Die Sezession in der Tanzkunst," *Bühne und Welt* 12 (1910): 27–43.
Belasco, David. *The Theatre through Its Stage Door* (New York: Harper and Brothers, 1919).
Benois, Alexandre. *Reminiscences of the Russian Ballet* (London: Putnam, 1947).
Bie, Oskar. *Der Tanz* (Berlin: Julius Bard, 1919).
Bird, Dorothy. "Martha," in Robert Gottlieb, ed., *Reading Dance: A Gathering of Memoirs, Reportage, Criticism, Profiles, Interviews, and Some Uncategorizable Extras* (New York: Pantheon, 2008), pp. 735–740.
Blass, Ernst. *Das Wesen der neuen Tanzkunst* (Weimar: Lichtenstein, 1922).
Blavatsky, H. P. *The Secret Doctrine: The Synthesis of Science, Religion and Philosophy* (Adyar: Theosophical Publishing House, 1962).
Bloch, Iwan. *Beiträge zur Aetiologie der Psychopathia sexualis* (Dresden: Dohrn, 1902).
Boehn, Max von. *Der Tanz* (Berlin: Wegweiser, 1925).
Böhme, Fritz. *Der Tanz der Zukunft* (Dresden: Reissner, 1926).
  Tanzkunst (Dessau: Dünnhaupt, 1926).

Brandenburg, Hans. *Der modern Tanz* (Munich: Georg Müller, 1921).

"Von deutscher Tanzkunst: Rückblick und Ausblick," in *Die tänzerische Situation unserer Zeit: Ein Querschnitt* (Dresden: Reissner, 1936), pp. 50–58.

München leuchtete: Jugenderinnerungen (Munich: Herbert Neuner, 1953).

"Drei Walzer und die Schwestern Wiesenthal," in Leonhard M. Fiedler and Martin Lang, eds., *Gertrude Wiesenthal* (Salzburg: Residenz, 1985).

Browne, Junius H. "The Ballet as a Social Evil," *The Northern Review* 2 (1868): 522–538.

Caffin, Caroline and Charles H. *Dancing and Dancers of Today* (New York: Dodd, Mead and Company, 1912).

Carpenter, Edward. *Wenn die Menschen reif zur Liebe werden*, trans. Karl Federn (Leipzig: Hermann Seemann, 1902).

Cohen, Selma Jeanne, ed. *Dance as a Theater Art* (New York: Dodd, Mean, 1974).

Cooper, Diana. *The Rainbow Comes and Goes* (Boston: Houghton Mifflin, 1958).

Coote, William Alexander, ed. *A Romance of Philanthropy* (London: National Vigilance Association, 1916).

Craig, Gordon. *Gordon Craig on Movement and Dance*, ed. Arnold Rood (New York: Dance Horizons, 1977).

Croce, Benedetto. *Aesthetik als Wissenschaft des Ausdrucks und allgemeine Linguistik*, trans. Karl Federn (Leipzig: E. A. Seemann, 1905).

Delius, Rudolf von. *Die Philosophie der Liebe* (Darmstadt: Reichl, 1922).

Mary Wigman (Dresden: Carl Reissner, 1925).

"Clotilde von Derp (1910)," in Frank-Manuel Peter and Rainer Stamm, eds., *Die Sacharoffs* (Cologne: Wienand, 2000).

dell'Era, Antonietta. "Muss man nackt tanzen?," *Berliner Tageblatt* 628, December 3, 1911.

Delsarte, François. "Address of François Delsarte before the Philotechnic Society of Paris," in Genevieve Stebbins, *Delsarte System of Expression* (New York: Edgar S. Werner, 1902), pp. 21–68.

Denby, Edwin. *Dance Writings & Poetry*, ed. Robert Cornfield (New Haven, CT: Yale University Press, 1998).

Desmond, Olga. *Mein Weg zur Schönheit* (Berlin: Bücherzentrale, n.d.).

Döblin, Alfred. "Tänzerinnen," *Alfred Döblin, Kleine Schriften*, vol. I (Freiburg: Walter, 1985), pp. 128–130.

Dörr, Evelyn. *Also, die Damen voran! Rudolf Laban in Briefen an Tänzer, Choreographen und Tanzpädagogen*, vol. 1, 1912–1918 (Norderstedt: Books on Demand, 2013).

Dransfeld, Hedwig. "Die Teilnahme des katholischen Frauenbundes an der Bekämpfung gefährlicher und unsittlicher Bestrebungen," *Die christliche Frau* 12 (1914): 109–114.

Duncan, Irma. *Duncan Dancer: An Autobiography* (Middletown, CT: Wesleyan University Press, 1965).

Duncan, Isadora. *Der Tanz der Zukunft (The Dance of the Future): Eine Vorlesung*, trans. Karl Federn (Leipzig: Diederichs, 1903).

The Art of the Dance (New York: Theatre Arts, 1928).

"A Child Dancing" (1906), in Sheldon Cheney, ed., *The Art of the Dance* (New York: Theatre Arts, 1928), pp. 74–76.

"The Dancer and Nature," in Sheldon Cheney, ed., *The Art of the Dance* (New York: Theater Arts, 1928), pp. 66–70.

"Depth," in Sheldon Cheney, ed., *The Art of the Dance* (New York: Theater Arts, 1928), pp. 99–100.

"Movement Is Life," in Sheldon Cheney, ed., *The Art of the Dance* (New York: Theater Arts, 1928), pp. 77–79.

"The Parthenon," in Duncan, *The Art of the Dance*, ed. Sheldon Cheney (New York: Theatre Arts, 1928), pp. 64–65.

My Life (New York: Liveright, 1955 [1927]).

"Come, Children, Let's Dance," in Franklin Rosemont, ed., *Isadora Speaks* (San Francisco: City Lights, 1981), pp. 81–84.

"I Have a Will of My Own," *Isadora Speaks*, ed. Franklin Rosemont (San Francisco: City Lights, 1981), p. 33.

Isadora Speaks, ed. Franklin Rosemont (San Francisco: City Lights, 1981).

Duncan, Margherita. "Isadora," in Sheldon Cheney, ed., *The Art of the Dance* (New York: Theatre Arts, 1928), pp. 16–23.

Duncan, Raymond. "Isadora's Last Dance," in Sheldon Cheney, ed., *The Art of the Dance* (New York: Theater Arts, 1928), pp. 13–15.

Einstein, Carl. "Lettre a la danseuse Napierkowska," *La Phalange* 12 (1912): 73–76.

Elberskirchen, Johanna. *Die Sexualempfindung bei Weib und Mann, betrachtet vom physiologisch-soziologischen Standpunkte* (Leipzig: Jacques Hegner, 1903).

Ellis, Havelock. "The Philosophy of Dancing," *Atlantic Monthly*, February 1914, at https://www.unz.org/Pub/AtlanticMonthly-1914feb-00197.

The Dance of Life (Boston: Houghton Mifflin, 1923).

Erlbach, Otto von (Armin Kausen). "Das Nackte auf der Bühne," *Allgemeine Rundschau* 4, no. 5 (1907): 215.

"Bühne und Neuheidentum," *Allegemeine Rundschau* 9, no. 12 (1912): 613.

Ernst, Clara. *Der feine Ton im gesellschaftlichen und öffentlichen Leben* (Mülheim: Bagel, 1885).

Was sich schickt—Was sich nicht schickt (Mülheim: Bagel, 1900).

Ettlinger, Karl. "Sent M'ahesa," *Tanzdrama* 14 (1991): 32–34.

Federn, Karl. "Die Zeit und das Problem," in Edward Carpenter, ed., *Wenn die Menschen reif zur Liebe werden*, trans. Karl Federn (Leipzig: Seemann, 1902), pp. 7–36.

"Einleitung," in Isadora Duncan, *Der Tanz der Zukunft* (Leipzig: Eugen Diederichs, 1903), pp. 5–10.

Felder, Erich. "Münchner Keuschheitsgelüste," *Der Turm* 1, no. 1 (December 1911): 18.

Flitch, J. E. Crawford. *Modern Dancing and Dancers* (Philadelphia: Lippincott, 1912).

Foerster, Friedrich Wilhelm. *Sexualethik und Sexualpädagogik* (Kempten: Josef Kösel, 1907).

Fokine, Vitale. *Fokine: Memoirs of a Ballet Master* (Toronto: Little, Brown, 1961).

Freud, Sigmund. "Civilization and its Discontents" (1930), in James Strachey, ed., *The Standard Edition of the Complete Psychological Works of Sigmund Freud*, vol. 21 (London: Hogarth, 1961), pp. 64–148.

"An Outline of Psychoanalysis" (1940), in James Strachey, ed., *The Standard Edition of the Complete Psychological Works of Sigmund Freud*, vol. 23 (London: Hogarth, 1961), pp. 144–208.

Fuchs, Georg. *Der Tanz* (Stuttgart: Strecker and Schöder, 1906).

Sturm und Drang in München um die Jahrhundertwende (Munich: Georg D. W. Callwey, 1936).

Fuller, Loïe. *Fifteen Years of a Dancer's Life* (Boston: Small, Maynard, 1913).

Gautier, Theophile. "Fanny Elssler in 'La Tempête,'" in Roger Copeland and Marshall Cohen, eds., *What Is Dance?: Readings in Theory and Criticism* (Oxford: Oxford University Press, 1983), pp. 431–438.

Gener, Pompeyo. "Tortola Valencia," *Mundial* 2 (1912): 527–531.

Gert, Valeska. *Mein Weg* (Leipzig: A. F. Devrient, 1931).

Ich bin eine Hexe: Kaleidoskop meines Lebens (Munich: Schneekluth, 1968).

Giese, Fritz. *Girlkultur: Vergleiche zwischen amerikanischem und europäischem Rythmus und Lebensgefühl* (Munich: Delphin, 1925).

Ginner, Ruby. *The Revived Greek Dance: Its Art and Technique* (London: Methuen, 1933).

Gitelman, Claudia. *Liebe Hanya: Mary Wigman's Letters to Hanya Holm* (Madison: University of Wisconsin Press, 2003).

Gomez-Carrillo, Enrique. "El teatro en Paris," *Mundial* 3 (1913): 384-388, 474–477.

El misterio de la vida y de la muerte de Mata Hari (Madrid: Renaciemento, 1923).

Graham, Martha. "Seeking an American Art of the Dance," in Oliver M. Sayler, ed., *Revolt in the Arts: A Survey of the Creation, Distribution, and Appreciation of Art in America* (New York: Brentano, 1930), pp. 249–255.

"The American Dance," in Virginia Stewart, ed., *Modern Dance* (New York: Dance Horizons, 1970 [1935]), pp. 53–58.

"A Modern Dancer's Primer for Action" (1941), in Selma Jeanne Cohen, ed., *Dance as a Theater Art* (New York: Dodd, Mean, 1974), pp. 136–141.

Grete Wiesenthal in Amor und Psyche und Das Fremde Mädchen: Szenen von Hugo von Hofmannsthal (Berlin: S. Fischer, 1911).

Gumplowicz, Ladislas. "Ehe und freie Liebe," *Sozialistische Monatshefte* 6 (1900): 255–267.

Guttzeit, Johannes. *Schamgefühl, Sittlichkeit und Anstand* (Dresden: Berthold Sturm, 1908).

The Habits of Good Society: A Handbook for Ladies and Gentlemen (New York: Carleton, 1872).

Haeckel, Ernst. *Die Welträthsel: Gemeinverständliche Studien über Monistische Philosophie* (Bonn: Emil Strauss, 1903 [1899]).

Halbe, Max. *Jahrhundertwende: Geschichte meines Lebens 1893–1914* (Danzig: Kasemann, 1935).

Heitmann, Ludwig. *Grosstadt und Religion* (Hamburg: C. Boysen, 1913).

Heppenstall, Rayner. "Apology for Dancing" (1936), in Roger Copeland and Marshall Cohen, eds., *What Is Dance?* (Oxford: Oxford University Press, 1983), pp. 267–288.

Hitler, Adolf. *Mein Kampf* (Boston: Houghton Mifflin, 1943).

Hofmannsthal, Hugo von. "Die unvergleichliche Tänzerin," *Gesammelte Werke: Prosa*, vol. 2 (Frankfurt: S. Fischer, 1951), pp. 256–263.

Hugo von Hofmannsthal/Harry Graf Kessler: Briefwechsel 1898–1929, ed. Hilde Burger (Frankfurt: Insel, 1968).

Hugo von Hofmannsthal, Briefwechsel mit Alfred Walter Heymel, ed. Werner Vole (Freiburg: Rombach, 1998).

Holgers, Maria. "Isadora Duncan – Eine Erlösung," *Die Schönheit: Erster Luxusband* (1902/1903): 536–538.

Holley, Horace. "To Maud Allan," *Maud Allan and Her Art* (London: n.p., n.d.).

Huber-Wiesenthal, Rudolf. *Die Schwestern Wiesenthal: Ein Buch eigenen Erlebens* (Vienna: Saturn, 1934).

Humphrey, Doris. "What Shall We Dance About?," *Trend: A Quarterly of the Seven Arts* 1 (1932): 46–48.

Doris Humphrey: An Artist First – An Autobiography, ed. Selma Jeanne Cohen (Middletown, CT: Wesleyan University Press, 1972).

"What a Dancer Thinks About," in Jean Morrison Brown, ed., *The Vision of Modern Dance* (Princeton, NJ: Princeton Book Co., 1979), pp. 55–64.

Ibel, Rudolf. "Die deutsche Tänzerin," *Der Kreis* 9 (1932): 692–696.

Impekoven, Niddy. *Die Geschichte eines Wunderkindes* (Zürich: Rotapfel, 1955).

Kant, Immanuel. *Immanuel Kant's sämmtliche Werke*, vol. 5, ed. G. Hartenstein (Leipzig: Leopold Voss, 1867).

Critik der Urtheilskraft (London: Routledge, 1994 [1790]).

Kessler, Harry Graf. *Harry Graf Kessler: Das Tagebuch, Dritter Band 1897–1905*, eds. Carina Schäfer and Gabriele Biedermann (Stuttgart: Cotta, 2004).

Harry Graf Kessler: Das Tagebuch, Vierter Band 1906-1914, ed. Jörg Schuster (Stuttgart: Cotta, 2004).

Key, Ellen. *Liebe und Ethik* (Berlin: Pan, 1905).

Der Lebensglaube: Betrachtungen über Gott, Welt, und Seele (Berlin: Fischer, 1906).

Über Liebe und Ehe (Berlin: S. Fischer Verlag, 1911).

Kraus, Karl. "Der Schmock und die Bajadere," in Christine Lüders, ed., *Apropos Mata Hari* (Frankfurt: Neue Kritik, 1997), pp. 85–90.

Laban, Rudolf von. *Die Welt des Tänzers* (Stuttgart: Walter Seifert, 1920).

"Die deutsche Tanzbühne: Vorgeschichte und Ausblick," in *Die tänzerische Situation unserer Zeit: Ein Querschnitt* (Dresden: Reissner, 1936), pp. 3–7.

A Life for Dance: Reminiscences (New York: Theater Arts, 1975).

Lämmel, Rudolf. *Der Moderne Tanz: Eine allgemeinverständliche Einführung in das Gebiet der Rhythmischen Gymnastik und des Neuen Tanzes* (Berlin: Oestergaard, 1928).

Lang, Marie. "Offenbarung," *Dokumente der Frauen* 6 (1902): 637.

Lenin, Vladimir. The State and Revolution, excerpt in *Socialist Thought: A Documentary History*, eds. Albert Fried and Ronald Sanders (Garden City, NY: Anchor, 1964).

Lennartz, Ernst. *Duncan – She – Desmond: Beiträge zur Beurteilung und Geschichte der Nackt-Kultur* (Cologne: Benziger, 1908).

Levinson, André. "Technik und Geist: Bemerkungen zum 'klassischen' Tanz," in Paul Stefan, ed., *Tanz in dieser Zeit* (Vienna: Universal-Edition, 1926), pp. 36–39.

"The Modern Dance in Germany" (1929), in Joan Acocella and Lynn Garafola, eds., *Andre Levinson on Dance: Writings from Paris in the Twenties* (London: Wesleyan University Press/University Press of New England, 1991), pp. 100–109.

Lifar, Serge. *Serge Diaghilev: His Life, His Work, His Legend – An Intimate Biography* (New York: Putnam, 1940).

Marinetti, Filippo. "The Futurist Manifesto," in Adrian Lyttleton, ed., *Italian Fascism* (New York: Harper, 1973), pp. 209–215.

Martin, John. "The Dance: A Futile Congress," *New York Times*, July 20, 1930, p. X6.

"The Dance: Mary Wigman's Art," *New York Times*, August 3, 1930, p. 101.

"The Dance: Plans for the New Season," *New York Times*, September 21, 1930, P. 6.

"Martha Graham, Dancer, Is Cheered," *New York Times*, December 7, 1931, p. 23

"The Dance: Artist and Audience," *New York Times*, December 27, 1931, p. 94.

The Modern Dance (New York: Dance Horizons, 1965 [1933]).

"The Dance: On Bringing Back Yesterday's Beauty," *New York Times*, February 19, 1933, p. X2.

America Dancing: The Background and Personalities of the Modern Dance (New York: Dodge, 1936).

Mary Wigman: Die Tänzerin, die Schule, die Tanzgruppe (Überlingen: Seebote, 1927).

Mausbach, Joseph. "Der Kampf gegen die moderne Sittenlosigkeit–eine Kulturaufgabe des deutschen Volkes," *Volkswart* 5 (1912): 129–136.

Mérode, Cléo de. *Le ballet de ma vie* (Paris: Horay, 1985 [1955]).

Merz, Max. "Die Ziele und die Organisation der Elizabeth Duncan-Schule," in *Elizabeth Duncan-Schule, Marienhöhe/Darmstadt* (Jena: Eugen Diederichs, 1912), pp. 9–17.

Meyer, Bruno. "Etwas von positiver Sexualreform," *Sexual-Probleme* 4 (1908): 703–722, 790–811.

"Muss man nackt tanzen?" *Die Schönheit* 9, no 11 (1911): 564–574.

Michel, Artur. "The Development of the New German Dance," in Virginia Stewart, ed., *Modern Dance* (New York: Dance Horizons, 1970 [1935]), pp. 3–18.

Möckel, Gustav. "Isadora Duncan," *Kraft und Schönheit* 1 (1902/1903): 137–138.

Moeller-Bruck, Arthur. *Das Varieté* (Berlin: Julius Bard, 1942).

Murias Vila, Carlos. "La magicienne aux yeux d'abîme," *Danser* 103 (1992): 24–27.

Mussolini, Benito. *Fascism: Doctrine and Institutions* (Rome: Ardita, 1935).

Oertzen, Dietrich von. "Sittlichkeit und Standesehre," in *Verhandlungen der Halle'schen Konferenz der deutschen Sittlichkeits-Vereine vom 8. und 9. Mai 1890* (Berlin: Berliner Stadtmission, 1890).

Osborn, Max. *Der bunte Spiegel; Erinnerungen aus dem Kunst-, Kultur-, und Geistesleben der Jahre 1890 bis 1933* (New York: F. Krause, 1945).

"Grete Wiesenthal," in Leonhard M. Fiedler and Martin Lang, eds., *Grete Wiesenthal: Die Schönheit der Sprache des Körpers in Bewegung* (Salzburg: Residenz, 1985), pp. 72–74.

O'Sheel, Shaemas. "To Maud Allan," *Maud Allan and Her Art* (London: n.p., n.d.).

Otero, La Belle/Caroline Otero. *My Story* (London: Philpot, 1927).

Palkow, Hannelore, and André Marchand, *Liebeslexikon von A-Z* (Vienna: Verlag für Kulturforschung, 1932).

Perugini, Mark E. "Sketches of the Dance and Ballet," *The Dancing Times* 3 (1912–1913): 74–78.

Perugini, Mark Edward. *A Pageant of the Dance and Ballet* (London: Jarrolds, 1935).

Poiret, Paul. *My First Fifty Years*, trans. Stephen Haden Guest (London: Gollancz, 1931).

Rambert, Marie. *Quicksilver* (London: Macmillan, 1972).

Richardson, Lady Constance Stewart. *Dancing, Beauty and Games* (London: Arthur L. Humphreys, 1913).

Sacharoff, Alexander. "Clotilde," in Frank-Manuel Peter and Rainer Stamm, eds., *Die Sacharoffs: Zwei Tänzer aus dem Umkreis des Blauen Reiters* (Cologne: Wienand, 2005), pp. 153–156.

Sacharoff, Clotilde. "La vie que nous avons dansée," in Frank-Manuel Peter and Rainer Stamm, eds., *Die Sacharoffs* (Cologne: Wienand, 2002), pp. 156-165.

Schelley, Peter. "Tänzerkongress 1928," reprinted in *Tanzdrama* 4 (1987): 16–17.

Schikowski, John. *Geschichte des Tanzes* (Berlin: Büchergilde Gutenberg, 1926).

Schur, Ernst. "Über das Erotische," *Die Neue Generation* 4 (1908): 47–50.

Der moderne Tanz (Munich: Gustav Lammers, 1910).

Selden, Elizabeth. *The Dancer's Quest: Essays on the Aesthetic of the Contemporary Dance* (Berkeley: University of California Press, 1935).

Shawn, Ted. *The American Ballet* (New York: Henry Holt, 1926).

Fundamentals of a Dance Education (Girard, KS: Haldeman-Julius, 1937).

One Thousand and One Night Stands (Garden City, NY: Doubleday, 1960).

Sherman, Jane. *Soaring: The Diary and Letters of a Denishawn Dancer in the Far East, 1925–1926* (Middletown, CT: Wesleyan University Press, 1976).

Simmel, Georg. "Zur Ästhetik der Alpen," *Gesamtausgabe* (Frankfurt: Suhrkamp, 1989), pp. 162–169.

Skoronel, Vera. "Mary Wigman's Führertum," *Tanzgemeinschaft* 2 (1930): 4, on the compact disk *Die Akte Wigman*, ed. Heide Lazarus (Cologne: Olms/Deutsches Tanz-Archiv, 2006).

Sokolova, Lydia. *Dancing for Diaghilev: The Memoirs of Lydia Sokolova*, ed. Richard Buckle (New York: Macmillan, 1961).

Spier, J. "Lulucharaktere!," *Sexual-Probleme* 9 (1913): 676–688.

St. Denis, Ruth. *An Unfinished Life* (New York: Harper and Brothers, 1939).

"Religious Manifestations in the Dance," in Walter Sorrell, ed., *The Dance Has Many Faces* (New York: Columbia University Press, 1966), pp. 12–18.

"The Dance as Life Experience," in Jean Morrison Brown, ed., *The Vision of Modern Dance* (Princeton, NJ: Princeton Book Co., 1979), pp. 21–25.

Wisdom Comes Dancing: Selected Writings of Ruth St. Denis on Dance, Spirituality, and the Body, ed. Kamae A. Miller (Seattle: PeaceWorks, 1997).

Stanislavski, Konstantin. *My Life in Art*, trans. J. J. Robbins (Boston: Little, Brown, 1929).

An Actor's Work (New York: Routledge, 2008).

Stebbins, Genevieve. *Delsarte System of Expression* (New York: Edgar S. Werner, 1902).

Stenographische Berichte über die Verhandlungen des preussischen Hauses der Abgeordneten, 13. session, January 13, 1909, columns 937–968.

Stöcker, Helene. *Bund für Mutterschutz* (Berlin: Pan, 1905).

Storck, Karl. "Ganz ohne Cancan," *Tanzdrama* 1 (1987): 24.

Symons, Arthur. "The World as Ballet," in *Studies in Seven Arts* (London: Archibald Constable, 1906), pp. 387–391.

Török, Alphons. *Tanzabende: Kritische Monographien* (Vienna: Merker, 1918).

Urlin, Ethel. *Dancing Ancient and Modern* (London: Simkin, Marshall, Hamilton, Kent & Co., 1912).

Vaihinger, Hans. *The Philosophy of As If* (London: Routledge & Kegan Paul, 1968 [1924]).

Die Philosophie des Als-Ob (Berlin: Reuther and Reichard, 1911).

Valencia, Tórtola. "Mis danzas," *Nuevo Mundo*, January 16, 1913.

Valois, Ninette de. "The Future of the Ballet" (1933), in *Ninette de Valois: Adventurous Traditionalist* (Alton, UK: Dance Books, 2012), pp. 149–152.

Vechten, Carl van. *The Dance Writings of Carl van Vechten*, ed. Paul Padgette (New York: Dance Horizons, 1974).

"Duncan Concerts in New York," in Paul Magriel, ed., *Nijinsky, Pavlova, Duncan: Three Lives in Dance* (New York: Da Capo, 1977).

"The New Isadora," in Paul Padgette, ed., *The Dance Writings of Carl van Vechten* (New York: Dance Horizons, 1977), pp. 22–27.

Villany, Adorée-Via. "Muss man nackt tanzen? Eine Antwort," *Berliner Tageblatt* 628, December 10, 1911, p. 1.

Tanz-Reform und Pseudo-Moral: Kritisch-satyrische Gedanken aus meinem Bühnen- und Privatleben, trans. Mirjam David (Paris: Villany, 1912).

Phryné moderne devant l'Areopage (Munich: Bruckmann, 1913).

Vischer, Friedrich Theodor. *Aesthetik, oder die Wissenschaft des Schönen*, part 3, section 2 (Stuttgart: Mäcken, 1857).

Weigl, F. "Das gegenwärtige Hervordringen des Nackten in die Öffentlichkeit," *Volkswart* 1 (1908): 18–22.

Wells, H. G. *The Discovery of the Future* (New York: B. W. Huebsch, 1913).

Wells, H. G., and Julian Huxley, *The Science of Life* (London: London Amalgamated Press, 1929).

Werefkin, Marianne. "Über die Sacharoffs," in Frank-ManuelPeter and Rainer Stamm, *Die Sacharoffs*(Cologne: Wienand, 2000), p. 48.

Wiesenthal, Grete. *Der Aufstieg* (Berlin: Rowohlt, 1919).

"Unsere Tänze," in Leonhard M. Fiedler and Martin Lang, eds., *Grete Wiesenthal* (Salzburg: Residenz, 1985), pp. 55–57.

Wigman, Mary. "Tänzerisches Schaffen der Gegenwart," in Paul Stefan, ed., *Tanz in dieser Zeit* (Vienna: Universal-Edition, 1926), pp. 5–7.

"Die Schule," in Rudolf Bach, ed., *Das Mary Wigman-Werk* (Dresden: Reissnerl 1933), pp. 32–34.

"Gruppentanz/Regie," in Rudolph Bach, ed., *Das Mary Wigman-Werk* (Dresden: Reissner, 1933), pp. 45–47.

Deutsche Tanzkunst (Dresden: Reissner, 1935).

Die tänzerische Situation unserer Zeit: Ein Querschnitt (Dresden: Reissner, 1936).

"The New German Dance," in Virginia Stewart, eds., *Modern Dance* (New York: Dance Horizons, 1970 [1935]), pp. 19–23.

"The Philosophy of Modern Dance" (1933), in Selma Jeanne Cohen, ed., *Dance as a Theater Art* (New York: Dodd, Mean, 1974), pp. 149–153.

"Stage Dance – Stage Dancer," in Jean Morrison Brown, ed., *The Vision of Modern Dance* (Princeton, NJ: Princeton Book Co., 1979), pp. 33–40.

"Das Land ohne Tanz," *Tanzgemeinschaft* 1 (1929): 12, on the compact disk *Die Akte Wigman*, ed. Heide Lazarus (Cologne: Olms/Deutsches Tanz-Archiv, 2006).

Wilde, Oscar. "Phrases and Philosophies for the Use of the Young" (1894), in *The First Collected Edition of the Works of Oscar Wilde, 1908–1922*, ed. Robert Ross (London: Dawsons, 1969), pp. 176–178.

Wilhelm II, "Die Wahre Kunst. 18. Dezember 1901," in Johannes Penzler, ed., *Die Reden Kaiser Wilhelms II* (Leipzig: Philipp Reclam, 1913), pp. 57–63.

Wilson, Margery. *The New Etiquette: The Modern Code of Social Behavior* (New York: Frederick Stokes, 1937).

Woody, Regina. *Dancing for Joy* (New York: Dutton, 1959).

Zepler, Margarete. "Der Tanz und seine neueste Priesterin Isadora Duncan," *Frauen-Rundschau* 1 (1902): 189–190.

Zude, Waldemar. "Nacktkultur und Vita sexualis," *Zeitschrift für Sexualwissenchaft* 3, no. 1 (1916): 37–45, 80–89.

Index